ADVANCE PRAISE FO

Until six or seven years ago, the borders of European brewing were tidy, well-understood, and well-documented—or so we English-speakers thought. That was when Lars Marius Garshol started publishing incredible stories about farmhouse brewing traditions in Eastern Europe and Scandinavia. Suddenly the brewing world seemed a lot bigger than anyone imagined. It's not an exaggeration to say that *Historical Brewing Techniques* is the most important book on brewing in at least twenty years.

—JEFF ALWORTH, Author of *The Beer Bible*

Imagine brewing as a mansion of known knowledge, ingredients, recipes, and equipment living beneath a single shared roof. With *Historical Brewing Techniques*, Lars Marius Garshol has rediscovered a secret garden, revealing hidden-in-plain-sight farmhouse yeast strains and revolutionary brewing and fermentation approaches that will require brewers and drinkers to rethink beer's very foundation.

—JOSHUA M. BERNSTEIN, author of *The Complete Beer Course* and *Drink Better Beer*

Brilliantly written! Lars provides a wealth of technical and historical knowledge to his readers in *Historical Brewing Techniques*. His writing is fascinating and evocative—the reader can't help but feel they are traveling through Scandinavia and eastern Europe alongside him. This book is a must read for anyone passionate about the histories and techniques of true farmhouse beer making.

—AVERIE SWANSON, Founder and Beermaker, Keeping Together

"Farmhouse ale" is a term used by many yet understood by few. Lars Marius Garshol is one who gets it, and he shares his wealth of knowledge in this book. It's not a beer style guide, but rather a fascinating look into the myriad ways beer was made prior to industrialization. Compelling read for brewers and beer aficionados alike.

—STEPHEN BEAUMONT, co-author of *The World Atlas of Beer* and author of *Will Travel for Beer*

It's rare that a new book on beer catches my attention. *Historical Brewing Techniques* reveals valuable knowledge, perspectives, techniques, and beer culture from a time and place almost forgotten. It's as though these isolated farms have incubated their brewing heritage and now Garshol reveals their secrets to us in an entertaining, exciting, and enlightening fashion. The fun part is exploring these unique techniques and considering how they fit into your brewing world. There's enough to engage any brewer who loves to explore unheard of possibilities.

—CHARLIE PAPAZIAN, author of *The Complete Joy of Homebrewing*

Lars Marius Garshol has brought our prehistoric "Nordic grog" to life in his new book, which is bubbling up and brimming over with close observation and practical advice about wild yeasts, herbs, household brewing, and much, much more. It's a delightful and informative paean to historic Scandinavian and Baltic brews, benefitting the serious homebrewer and enthusiastic beer connoisseur alike.

—PATRICK E. MCGOVERN, author of *Ancient Brews Rediscovered and Re-created* and *Uncorking the Past: The Quest for Wine, Beer, and Other Alcoholic Beverages*

Lars Marius Garshol has written the definitive work on kveik and traditional eastern European farmhouse brewing. He has witnessed and laboriously documented yeasts and traditions to help preserve and spread this wondrous art. Whether discussing ingredients, malting techniques, the practical nature of brewing on a working farm, or the rituals and superstitions of farmhouse brewers, this book gives a detailed explanation of all aspects of this unique and ancient practice. I cannot recommend this book enough.

—MATTHEW HUMBARD, Head Brewer/Lead Scientist, Patent Brewing Company and Patent Laboratories

An eye-opening excursion into beer's European roots, and an astonishing work of historical and cultural research. Thanks to Lars Marius Garshol, I'll never see beer, farmhouse or otherwise, the same way again.

—MAUREEN OGLE, author of *Ambitious Brew: A History of American Beer*

People have brewed since the dawn of civilization, largely with techniques that never survived into archeological findings or historical documents. Instead, these techniques have been stored in the folk wisdom of farmhouse brewers, and *Historical Brewing Techniques* is an outstanding documentation of this forgotten craft. Lars Marius Garshol has filled an enormous gap of brewing knowledge with years of extensive data collection in the Nordic and Baltic countries, and Russia.

—**MIKA LAITINEN,** author of *Viking Age Brew: The Craft of Brewing Sahti Farmhouse Ale*

Before reading *Historical Brewing Techniques*, Lars had already inspired my brewing through his blog. Initially I brewed beers with the traditional Norwegian trio of smoked malt, juniper infusion, and kviek. Lars' detailed and perceptive accounts have since led me to apply the ingredients and techniques to New World styles. It is invaluable to have his years of research and interviews distilled into this insightful and encyclopedic tome.

—**MICHAEL TONSMEIRE** Co-Founder of Sapwood Cellars and author of *American Sour Beers*

Wow! This book shows us how much we have forgotten and reminds us there is so much still to discover. Many of these old brewing methods were on the brink of extinction, but now I find I am super excited to try to make a *keptinis*! The brewing methods preserved in northern and eastern Europe provide insight into other countries' beer making origins as well. As a Belgian, I think this book sheds light on how Waghebaert, Cuyte, zwert bier, and roetbier were made. I'm inspired now to dig out the documents for those beers and try again. What a gift! Thank you, Lars.

—**PETER BOUCKAERT,** Founder of Purpose Brewing and Cellars and co-author of *Wood & Beer: A Brewer's Guide*

Lars Marius Garshol has done his homework. This book opens an illuminating window into an ancient and mostly hidden world of brewing little touched by the modern world. I believe this book will do what history and research do best: change the future.

—**RANDY MOSHER,** author of *Tasting Beer* and *Radical Brewing*

HISTORICAL BREWING TECHNIQUES

The Lost Art of Farmhouse Brewing

BY LARS MARIUS GARSHOL

Brewers Publications®
A Division of the Brewers Association
PO Box 1679, Boulder, Colorado 80306-1679
BrewersAssociation.org
BrewersPublications.com

Proudly Printed in the United States of America.
10 9 8 7 6 5 4 3 2 1
ISBN-13: 978-1-938469-55-8
ISBN-10: 1-938469-55-0

Library of Congress Cataloging-in-Publication Data

Names: Garshol, Lars Marius, 1973- author.
Title: Historical brewing techniques : the lost art of farmhouse brewing /
  by Lars Marius Garshol.
Description: First. | Boulder : Brewers Publications, 2020. | Includes
  bibliographical references and index. | Summary: "Equal parts history,
  cultural anthropology, social science, and travelogue, Historical
  Brewing Techniques explores brewing and fermentation methods passed down
  for generations on farms throughout northern Europe. Learn about kveik,
  which ferments a batch of beer in just 36 hours. Brew recipes gleaned
  from years of travel and research"-Provided by publisher.
Identifiers: LCCN 2019048123 (print) | LCCN 2019048124 (ebook) | ISBN
  9781938469558 (trade paperback) | ISBN 9781938469619 (ebook)
Subjects: LCSH: Breweries--Europe, Northern--History. | Brewing--Amateurs'
  manuals.
Classification: LCC TP573.E853 G37 2020 (print) | LCC TP573.E853 (ebook)
  | DDC 663/.30948--dc23
LC record available at https://lccn.loc.gov/2019048123
LC ebook record available at https://lccn.loc.gov/2019048124

Publisher: Kristi Switzer
Copyediting: Iain Cox
Proofreading: Kristina Wagner Moore
Technical Editor: Christopher and Nancy McGreger
Indexing: Doug Easton
Art Direction: Jason Smith
Interior Design & Production: Justin Petersen
Interior Photos and Translations: Lars Garshol unless otherwise noted
Maps generated by Lars Garshol using Mapnik (https://mapnik.org/) and geographic data from Natural Earth (http://naturalearthdata.com/). Regions hand-drawn by the author.

To Stine, for giving me the freedom to explore all this,
and Oda, who likes screaming at the *kveik*.

TABLE OF
CONTENTS

Foreword .... **xv**
Acknowledgments .... **xix**
Introduction **1**
1. Understanding Farmhouse Ale **7**
The World of Yesterday 8
Kaupanger: First Meeting with the Tradition 15
2. History **29**
3. Malt **41**
Stjørdal: Malt-Making Hotspot 42
Grain Types in Farmhouse Brewing 45
Barley Varieties 49
How the Grain Was Grown 54
Steeping and Sprouting 57
Malt Drying Methods 59
Low Heat, Not Smoked 61

    Lightly Smoked, High Heat 64

    Heavily Smoked 70

    Caramel 75

    Strong, Uneven Heat 76

  Undried Malt 78

4. Yeast **81**

  Voss: Discovering Kveik 81

  First Laboratory Analysis 90

  Yeast, Wild and Domesticated 91

  The Yeast Revolution 92

  Yeast on the Farm 94

  Origins of the Yeast 99

  Yeast Species 103

  The Yeast Family Tree 105

  European Farmhouse Yeast: What We Know 107

    Kveik 110

    Non-Kveik Farmhouse Yeasts 116

    Bread Yeast 118

  Dying Out 120

  Kveik Renaissance 123

  The Word "Kveik" 123

5. Farmhouse Brewing Processes **127**

  Hornindal, Norway 128

  Stone Beer 134

  Raw Ale 140

  Boiled Ale 142

  The Mash Boiled 143

  Complex Mashes 149

  Keptinis 151

  The Great Stove 157

    Vsekhsvyatskoye, Russia 159

    Understanding Oven Beers 162

  The Mash Fermented 164

  The Evolution of Brewing Processes 165

6. Beer as Part of Farm Life **173**

  Harvest Ale 176

  Ritual Beer 177

  Superstition 182

  Brewers or Brewsters? 187

  Equipment 190

  Preparations 194

  Milling 196

  Water 199

Carbonation 201
Oppskåke 202
Cellaring 205
Drinking Vessels 207
Serving Beer 213
Beer Flaws 214

7. Herbs, Spices, and Adjuncts **219**
    Herbs, Spices, and Other Flavorings 221
        Hops 221
        Juniper 227
        Sweet Gale 233
        Wormwood 235
        Caraway 236
        St. John's Wort 236
        Bitter Orange Peel 237
        Yarrow 237
        Tansy 237
        Bay Laurel 238
        Marsh Tea 238
        Heather 239
        Other Flavorings 239
    Adjuncts 241
        Potatoes 241
        Bran 242
        Carrots 242
        Peas 243
        Honey 243
        Other Adjuncts 243
    Filter Materials 243
        Straw 244
        Alder Sticks 244
        Other Materials 244

8. The Drink Problem: Making It Safe **247**
    Flour-Based Beverages 251
    Blande 251
    Small Beer 251
    Rostdrikke 253
    Kvass 254
    Birch Sap Beer 258
    Juniper Berry Beer 259
    Mead 262
    Sugar Beer 264

9. Styles and How to Brew Them **267**

Brewing Like a Farmer 267
Carbonation 268
Working with Kveik 268
Working with Non-Kveik Farmhouse Yeast 272
Brewing with Juniper 273
Making Your Own Malt 275
What is Farmhouse Ale? 276
   Styles in Farmhouse Brewing 276
   Defining Farmhouse Ale 279
A Note About the Recipes 279
Raw Ales 280
   Brewing Raw Ales 280
   Kornøl 281
      Terje Raftevold's Kornøl 283
      Reidar Hovelsen's Kornøl 284
   Sahti 285
      Olavi Viehroja's Sahti 288
      Eila Tuominen's Sahti 289
   Island Koduõlu 290
      Paavo Pruul's Koduõlu 292
   Kaimiškas 293
      Julius Simonaitis's Kaimiškas 294
      Šimonys-Style Kaimiškas 295
   Danish Landøl 296
   Gammeltøl 296
      Jensgård i Tiufkjær 297
      Landøl from North Jutland 298
Dark, Smoky Ales 299
   Stjørdalsøl 299
      Jørund Geving's Stjørdalsøl 300
      Roar Sandodden's Christmas Beer 302
   Gotlandsdricke 303
      Anders Mattson's Gotlandsdricke 305
      Gotlandsdricke from Fide 306
      Landøl from South Funen 307
Brown Boiled Beers 308
   Heimabrygg: Western Norwegian Beers 308
      Hardangerøl 310
      Sigmund Gjernes's Vossaøl 311
      Vossaøl à la Vossestrand 312
      Dyrvedal-Style Vossaøl 313
      Sogneøl 314
   Eastern Norway 315
      Telemark 315

Hallingdal 317
Swedish Farmhouse Ale: Öxabäck 318
Öxabäck Ale 319
Oven Beers 320
Seto Koduõlu 320
Seto Koduõlu "Bread" 320
Oven-Mashed Russian Farmhouse Ale 321
Dmitriy Zhezlov's Farmhouse Ale 321
Chuvashian Farmhouse Ale 322
Marina Fyodorovna's Farmhouse Ale 324
Sur 325
Marina Ivanovna's Sur 326
Keptinis 326
Vytautas Jančys's Keptinis 329
Žiobiškis-Style Keptinis 330
Mainland Estonian Oven-Based Beer 331
Fermented Mash 332
Luumäki-Style 332
Vanylven-Style 333
Stone Beer 334
Nössemark Stone Beer 334
Rågö Stone Beer 335
Solvychegodsk Stone Beer 336
Farmhouse Beer from Other Regions 337
Corn Ale 337
English Farmhouse Ale 337
Suffolk Farmhouse Ale 338
Welsh Farmhouse Ale 339
Welsh Farmhouse Ale 339
Westphalian Farmhouse Ale 340
Aludi 340
Oat Beer 341
Oat Beer 342

10. Today and Tomorrow **345**
Baltic Time Capsule 346
The Baltic States Today 347
Status in the West 351
Farmhouse Ale in the Twenty-First Century 352
Into the Future 355

Notes **357**
Bibliography **371**
Index **389**

FOREWORD

On the first Sunday of September 2018, Lars Marius Garshol settled into a seat on a train bound for Bergen, Norway's second largest city. He pulled out a notebook and began to write about what he had learned during a particularly a good day in the Dyrvedalen Valley.

"I'm glad I got to meet Svein. That was a big hole in my portfolio," he said. Svein Rivenes became the best known farmhouse brewer in Norway after beer writer Michael Jackson visited in 1991, later describing the experience in *The Independent*, a London newspaper. Jackson pulled back to the curtain to reveal practices that barely changed for centuries, but in the years since a broad family of beers continued to hide in plain sight.

Heading out in the morning, Garshol talked about taking a similar path into the Voss region north of Bergen in May of 2014. "It's amazing all that has happened in four years," he said. He's dug through records from Norway, Sweden, Denmark, Finland, Estonia, Latvia, Lithuania, Russia, the United Kingdom, Germany, and Austria to help make sense of what amounts to an alternative brewing world. As important, he visited many of those countries to witness farmers making stone beers, raw ales, oven beers and others so far outside the experience of modern day brewers that it seems as if they must have come from both another time and another world.

I've written four books for Brewers Publications. History, including words about beers that may or may not have once been notable and now are footnotes, is central to each one. However, I consider outlining process, which need not be confined to the brewhouse, the most essential ingredient. Want to learn how to brew like a monk? Start with the first prayers of the day at Mount Angel Abbey in Oregon, watch Brother Jos mash in at abbey Saint Sixtus at Westvleteren, or listen to Brother Joris talk about checking the status of fermentation in the middle of the night.

Digging through history is joy, except when the results introduce questions that don't have answers. American colonial era immigrant brewers sometimes used native ingredients, but there are few descriptions about *how* they used them. For instance, *The William and Mary Quarterly* offered only three sentences about using persimmon: "Persimmon is treated very much as a 'wine brick.' The fruit, seeds and all, are crushed, mixed with wheat bran, then baked in cakes. As occasion arises, the cakes are soaked in water and the beer brewed." Likewise, when Ben Franklin shared a recipe for spruce beer that would produce 80 bottles, but did not specify *how big* the bottles were.

Within the book you are holding in your hands, Lars Marius Garshol provides far more information about an astonishing range of farmhouse beers. A software engineer by trade, he lives outside of Oslo. He began blogging in 2005 about both beer and technology, writing about the beer scene on Latvia one week and big data and the semantic web the next. Some of us have been ready for him to write this book since the focus of his posts shifted in 2014, documenting first a trip to farmhouse breweries in western Norway.

His blog posts the last six years established his expertise, but they only hint of both the breadth and depth of what is here. History, culture and process are all served by the same meticulous detail.

I spent one day with him in late summer of 2018, visiting two farm breweries in Dyrvedalen Valley, along with my wife and Joe Stange, another beer writer. It was not exactly a typical day, because Garshol was playing host as well as researcher. Nonetheless, a conversation turned with Bjørne Røthe turned intense as he sought details about the juniper piled in a trailer outside a large eighteenth century shed that serves as a brewery and smokehouse on Røthe's farm. Røthe's grandfather made beer, but his father did not and the brewing equipment sat idle for 20 years. He learned to brew from his uncle. "They say it tastes like my grandfather's beer," he said.

This, of course, is how farmhouse brewers learned for centuries. In the pages that follow, Garshol writes about the man who could have become last traditional brewer in Balestrand, Norway. When he was diagnosed with cancer he said he would teach anybody in the village who wanted to learn the tradition how to brew, but reneged when the only volunteer was a woman. In western Norway, superstition held than allowing a woman to step inside the brewhouse resulted in sour beer. After the man changed his mind, the woman brewed two batches with him. He died not long after the second. The woman continues to brew in the traditional way today. "Which is fortunate, because once the tradition dies it cannot really come back. A tradition that is documented can be recreated, but it will never be the same as the living tradition," Garshol writes.

Not to spoil the ending, but in the final chapter he writes, "In most of the places in Europe where farmhouse ale is brewed today, the tradition seems likely to go extinct within one or two generations. Only in a few places, like Finland, Saaremaa in Estonia, and Stjørdal in Norway, does farmhouse brewing seem quite safely established." His wish is that if modern brewers embrace these traditions perhaps local brewers will as well.

Our first stop in the Dyrvedalen Valley was to see Svein Rivenes, who is a wonderful storyteller as well as farm brewer. He went into detail about how his grandfather would dip a ring of straw into the slurry of kveik left after brewing, then hang it high in the rafters of the barn to let it dry. This preserved the yeast for use in future brews. That birds nested in the rafters and left dung on the kveik did not bother him. His grandfather would simply knock off the crap before tossing the ring in waiting wort. Rivenes was laughing by the time Garshol finished translating.

Jackson had taken kveik from Rivenes back to England to be used in a beer that would be called Norvig Viking Ale. Rivenes had also provided details instructions about how to make a beer like he did. He later tasted a sample of the beer. Garshol asked him if it tasted like his own.

He quickly shook his head from side to side, reminding us that re-creations are not simple.

In 1981, well before he had achieved international fame, Jackson wrote about what he would like to see in his own obituary. "I wouldn't mind being remembered . . . like an archeologist (or perhaps an anthropologist, since the culture I uncovered was still functioning, and by no means dead)," he wrote. "My sorrow, of course, is that some die nonetheless – in that case a better comparison might be Alan Lomax recording country blues singers before they were lost to the world."

British journalist Martyn Cornell, a colleague of Jackson's and a highly regarded beer historian in his one right, has already made the case that Garshol's "writings have made him the Michael Jackson of *gårdsøl* ('farm ale')."

He has done more than capture history before it becomes history. His name will likely always be linked to kveik, the family of yeast strains that many brewers outside of Scandinavia now use. But the beers he writes about, and the processes he describes, will inform many new ones that present and future brewers fashion.

Working without equipment that a novice homebrewer would consider essential and employing methods that make no sense to a modern day brewer – such as baking the mash for three hours – farmhouse brewers are producing flavors not found in other beers. Garshol provides basically step-by-step instructions on how to replicate those flavors, and then more. The idea of thinking outside the box has become cliché, so consider this a book about beers that were first brewed before there was a box.

Stan Hieronymus
Author of *Brew Like a Monk*, *Brewing with Wheat*,
Brewing Local, and *For the Love of Hops*

ACKNOWLEDGMENTS

So many people have been helpful to me in this work that to thank them all as they really deserve would require a second volume. Obviously, that cannot be done, so I must do as best I can in the space I have. If I have forgotten anyone, I beg your forgiveness.

First of all, I want to thank the brewers for keeping the tradition and the yeast alive. Without them there would be little to write about except old documents describing strange brewing methods that probably produced bad beer. To you brewers—the entire world of beer in general owes you endless thanks.

Thank you so much to all the brewers who let me visit them, interview them, observe their brewing methods, and gave me their yeast. Those who are referred to in the text I will not repeat here.

The chapters describing my travels make it sound like I did everything on my own, but that is not true at all. I have left out a large number of people who traveled with me and, in some cases, did things that the text claims I did. I apologize deeply, but it was considered necessary to in order to make the text more readable. More thanks than I ever could express in print to my friends, fellow travelers, and brothers in farmhouse ale: Martin Thibault, Amund Polden Arnesen, Martynas Savickis, Mika Laitinen, Ilkka Miettinen, Aleksandr Gromov, Morten Rønningen, Timo Alanen, Francis Simard, and Vidmantas Laurinavičius.

In Norway, my thanks to: Sjur Rørlien and Roar Sandodden for information, hospitality, discussions, and samples of real farmhouse ale; Morten Rønningen for help with the text and many, many discussions; Geir Ove Grønmo and Hans Christian Alsos for discussions and brewing tests; Anders Christensen for discussions yielding valuable insights; and Per Bruland and Bjørn Roth for work on yeast and discussions. For sources and information, my thanks to: Ivar Geithung, Lars Olav Muren, Geir Ove Grønmo, Unni Irmelin Kvam, Roger Bruland, Halvor Bjåland, Anders Volle, and Atle Råsberg. Also thanks to Eirik Storesund for help on Old Norse background information and translations. I am also grateful to Thor Humberset for helping me conduct interviews in Ørsta; to Knut Albert Solem for useful feedback on the manuscript; and to Jørund Geving for much information, many discussions, feedback on the text, and making me laugh. Thank you to Svein Ølnes for the invitation to Kaupanger, and Andreas Rübner Johnsen for transporting the beer.

In Sweden, thank you to Lucy Clarke and Marcus Brand for brewing tests.

In Finland, my thanks to: Ilkka Miettinen for all his amazing work in finding sources, tracking down information, and his help on the Finnish expedition. I am very grateful to Mika Laitinen for many useful discussions, much help, and useful feedback on the manuscript. I also want to thank Timo Alanen for driving and help, including setting up the brewing session with Olavi Viheroja.

In Denmark, thank you to Asgerd Gudiksen and Anne-Mette Marchen Andersen for all their help accessing the archive collections at Afdeling for Dialektforskning and Nationalmuseets Etnologiske Undersøgelser.

In Estonia, warm thanks to Andrus Viil for acting as a guide and providing many translations, and Virgo Vjugin for translations. Thanks to Helgi Põllo for sources and information. A huge thanks to Margo Samorokov for all his translations of the Estonian National Museum (ERM) material. Thank you also to Hans Üürike, Rene Kostrokin, Lauri Saluveer, and Anneli Andersen for ERM translations. Thank you to Semmo Horn for information on Seto brewing. Huge thanks to Paavo Pruul for showing us how to brew koduõlu and answering many questions.

In Latvia, my thanks to Signe Pucena for sources, Ugis Pucens for information and a brewing demonstration, Reinis Plavinš for information and yeast, and Juris Cinitis for information.

In Lithuania, above all, many many thanks to Remigijus Tranas for all his translation work. I am also grateful to: Simonas Gutautas and Vykintas Motuza for much information, yeasts, and the invitation to Vikonys; Ričardas Počius for sources; Martynas Savicikis for sources and many discussions; and Vytautas Laurinavičius for sources, acting as a guide, translation, and much help.

In Russia, many thanks to: Aleksandr Gromov for being a great travel companion, help on planning the expedition, background information, and help with sources; Ivan Kamarinskiy for many key sources; Dake Aachen for help in finding Yasna; and Eugene Tolstov for sources. Also thank you to Ivan and Elias of Sabotage Brewing in Perm, who arranged the visit to Kudymkar.

In Belarus, my thanks to Jury Pleskačeŭski for all his work in gathering information.

In the UK, I am grateful to Merryn and Graham Dineley for much help, many valuable sources, many discussions, and feedback on the text. Also thanks to Aled Murphy and *Boak & Bailey* for valuable sources. Many, many thanks to the support and help from Chris Bond and Adrian Turner at the National Collection of Yeast Cultures.

Many thanks to Stan Hieronymus for encouragement, connecting me with Brewers Publications, and useful feedback on the manuscript. Warm thanks to Martin Thibault for many useful discussions, much information, and useful feedback on the text. Thank you to Susan Verberg for discussions and useful sources. Thanks to Sam Fleet for useful feedback on the manuscript. Thanks to Dan Pixley for his work on the Milk the Funk wiki, which has been very useful to me. Many thanks to Ian Crane for sending me a sample of his raw ale made with kveik and *Juniperus virginiana*.

For microbiology work and helpful discussions, many thanks above all to Richard Preiss, but also to Jan Steensels, Kristoffer Krogerus, Freek Spitaels, Kara Taylor, and Martin Zarnkow. Thank you also to Richard Preiss and Kristoffer Krogerus for feedback on the yeast chapter.

This book would not have been possible if it were not for the tireless work of countless ethnographers in many countries over many decades. Also, innumerable archivists, librarians, and museum curators went far beyond what anyone could expect to help me collect information. I do not know your names, but you wonderful, wonderful people at the Adomas Mickevičius Public Library in Vilnius; Gotlands Fornsal, Norsk Folkemuseum, and Mølstertunet Museum in Voss; Nordfjord Folkemuseum at Sandane; the Russian Ethnographic Museum in St Petersburg; the Asikkala Folk Museum in Finland; and more institutions than I could possibly name have done invaluable work, and I thank you all.

Last, but not least, warm thanks to William Holden for information, yeast gathering, arranging the farmhouse ale festival, and just being William.

INTRODUCTION

I can still remember the moment of discovery, when I realized there were important things in the world of beer not mentioned in any beer book. At that point, I had been a dedicated beer enthusiast for nearly a decade, traveling all over the world to try different beers. This was the first time I tasted a kind of beer I had never heard of before.

It all began when my wife gave me a book for Christmas. Danish brewer Per Kølster had written about his visit to a traditional farmhouse brewer in Lithuania.[1] This Lithuanian brewer grew his own barley and malted it himself; he also grew his own hops and kept his yeast in the well. His methods were unlike anything I had ever heard of. "Hmmm," I thought, "Lithuania sounds like an interesting place to visit."

I tasted my first Lithuanian beer in an ancient vaulted brick cellar underneath the Street of the Glass Blowers in Vilnius old town. The beer had been recommended to me by the bartender, and I knew nothing at all about it, except that the label said "Salaus alus." It looked like a normal pale ale, but the flavor was totally different. The aroma was very complex, mainly earthy and floral, but with fruity honey-like notes. The flavor was intense, with powerful earthy, straw-like notes emerging from a peppery, oily background. It felt like the beery equivalent of being dropped face first from a crane into a bale of straw that had been baking in the sun all day. I was really excited and asked the bartender how on earth the brewers had come up with this extremely unusual flavor. Was it the hops, perhaps? The bartender just looked at me blankly. "What ees hops?" she asked. With a sinking feeling I realized I was not going to get any answers out of her. This beer would be on my mind for days and days afterward. I spent that weekend trying more beers with incomprehensible names and learned that the beer scene in Lithuania was a world unto itself, a world that resisted all my efforts to understand *why* these beers were so different.

Eventually, I found a local beer guide and went on a tour with him, which opened the door to discovery and gave me some real insight. That was how I came to find myself in a barn in Dusetos, northern Lithuania, listening to farmhouse brewer Ramūnas Čižas explaining how he did a step mash by judging the temperature of each step using a separate finger. He formed the wet malt into bread-like shapes and baked them in an oven, which meant his beer was an example of *keptinis*, an extremely obscure style.

His yeast is a carefully guarded family heirloom of which he refused to speak. The only person in the family who was allowed to even go near it was his eldest daughter, because she was the one chosen to carry on the family farmhouse brewing tradition. The beer tasted like nothing I had even heard of, as is so often is the case in Lithuania. Microbiological analysis indicated that the yeast consisted of two closely related strains of *Nakazawaea holstii*. It was not normal beer yeast at all. In fact, this species of yeast is so obscure that microbiologists are not sure exactly where it belongs in the taxonomy of yeast.

The next morning in my hotel room in Panevėžys, tossing and turning in bed while recovering from a roaring hangover,[*] I began to understand. The unique thing about Lithuania was that they were selling real farmhouse ales, that is, beers brewed according to an ancient tradition that had somehow survived in the fertile farm country of northern Lithuania. These beers tasted different because they were brewed in a completely different way, by brewers who had virtually no contact with modern brewing.

Coming home to Norway, I started thinking about the old Norwegian farmhouse brewing tradition. The previous summer I had tasted one Norwegian farmhouse beer, a smoke bomb that had utterly blown me away. I had heard rumors that the tradition was still alive in several places in Norway, but I knew almost nothing about it. So, I thought, why not take a closer look? It took nine months of careful research and planning, but eventually two friends and I set out in 2014 for a week-long trip to explore Norwegian farmhouse brewing.[2]

What followed was a week of jaw-dropping discoveries that so shook us, that by the end of the week we were barely able to absorb any new information at all. This tradition of farmhouse brewing was so obscure that, despite my intense interest in beer, I had completely failed to realize it existed in my own country. And nothing had prepared me for how rich and how far removed from modern beer this brewing culture was.

Coming home, I realized I needed to know more, and started collecting all the documentary sources I could find. I quickly discovered that Nordic and Baltic ethnological institutes have vast amounts of information on farmhouse brewing. Several books and many articles have been written on farmhouse ale, but the work has all been done by ethnographers who had no real

---

[*] The tale of that night is told in my blog, http://www.garshol.priv.no/blog/247.html.

understanding of beer. They never approached the beer in terms of flavor or compared farm-house methods with modern brewing techniques. It became clear to me that this gigantic field of study was overdue for a fresh look.

Farmhouse brewing has existed all over the world where people have grown grain: in Europe, Asia, Africa, and the Americas. But I soon saw that even if I restricted myself to just Europe alone, coming to grips with all the material might be beyond me. I decided to limit myself to Europe, and so that is the scope of this book.

Norwegian Ethnological Research in Oslo sent me the responses to their 1952 questionnaire on farmhouse brewing. As it turned out, there were 182 separate responses from all over Norway, each describing how people brewed in a specific location.* In many cases, the respondents were describing their own brewing methods, or that of their mothers or grandmothers. That makes this type of source unique, because these people are describing brewing as it was where they lived.

Working with these accounts was not easy. They arrived as 1392 JPEG files on a CD-ROM, most of them handwritten. It took me two years to digest these intensely detailed descriptions of malting, brew-ing, and hop growing. Later on, I added more material from ethnographic collections in Denmark, Sweden, Finland, Germany, Lithuania, and Estonia, amounting to 22,468 pages so far. On top of that came a large collection of books and articles from Norway, Sweden, Denmark, Finland, Estonia, Latvia, Lithuania, Russia, the UK, Germany, and Austria. Many of these are written in languages I cannot read, so I have relied on help from both paid translators and volunteers to translate them into English.

Unfortunately, farmhouse brewers did not do much in the way of measurement, so precise ratios of ingredients and temperatures tend to be missing. Measurements of original gravity (OG) and final gravity (FG) are almost never found. And, in some cases, if you try following the descriptions of brewing in older documents you find that they do not turn out right. The result is not even beer, because some important piece of information is missing. So, to understand the brewers and how they brewed, I traveled to meet, brew with, and taste the beers produced by farmhouse brewers in Norway, Sweden, Estonia, Latvia, Lithuania, Russia, Denmark, and Finland.

What I found has turned my view of beer upside down. Traditional farmhouse brewers make beer that is totally unlike any modern beer, using techniques and ingredients that have been com-pletely forgotten by modern brewers. The reason is that these brewers have been working in a tradi-tion that is completely separate from modern brewing science. But, as you will see, their techniques have been honed by centuries of trial and error. True farmhouse brewers usually learn to brew when young from their parents, then brew the same beer for the rest of their lives. They know exactly what they are doing, even if they cannot explain it in scientific terms. This is one reason why so many of these beers are of outstanding quality.

By reading older documents, studying biochemistry, and watching brewers in action, I have been able to learn many of the secrets of farmhouse brewing. Many of the brewing processes and methods should, according to modern brewing theory, not work at all. I have tried to figure out why these brewers brew the way they do, and why it works even when modern brewing textbooks in many cases say it should not. As Arthur C. Clarke put it: "If an elderly but distinguished scientist says that something is possible, he is almost certainly right; but if he says that it is impossible, he is very probably wrong." The same turns out to be the case for modern brewers.

---

* This is the set of sources cited as "NEG" throughout the book. See "Archival Sources" in the bibliography.

This book is my attempt to teach you what I have learned, and to show that modern brewers can learn many exciting techniques and methods from farmhouse brewers. The beers are ancient, yet they are new and inspiring for people outside of the farmhouse brewing regions. In fact, the farmhouse brewing tradition is so rich in previously untapped knowledge that it has potential to launch a second brewing revolution to follow the craft brewing revolution.

Lars Marius Garshol
Rælingen, Norway
May 2019

1

UNDERSTANDING FARMHOUSE ALE

Our prehistoric fathers may have been savages, but they were clever and observant ones . . . The brewer learnt from long experience the conditions, not the reasons for success.

—John Tyndall
Fermentation and Its Bearings on the Phenomena of Disease, 5–6

Beer is, above all, an agricultural product. Both grain and hops are grown by farmers, leaving only yeast and water to be sourced. People tend to think of beer as something that comes from breweries, but once the harvest is gathered the farmer has everything needed to make beer. All that remains is a bit of work. And since work was a low price to pay, every farmer who grew grain also brewed beer.

From the late Stone age until about 1970, more than half the people on earth were farmers.[1] A very large proportion of humanity has been brewing farmhouse ale for millennia. Commercial brewing is a mere footnote by comparison.

It is only in the last century or two that farmhouse brewing has become something unusual. Before that it was like baking bread, something every household in the countryside did. Until recently, commercial breweries only existed in towns, and because of poor transportation their products were not available in the countryside. Out in the country nobody needed to buy beer anyway, since they had their own grain. So, for most of history, farmhouse brewing has been much more common than commercial brewing, and yet somehow this enormous branch of the beer world has been almost totally ignored.

Modern brewers have dramatically changed brewing over the last few centuries by drawing on advances in biology and chemistry. These new approaches have replaced older methods that were based on the slow evolution of traditions over millennia. The new methods are more economical, more consistent, and reduce the risk of accidentally spoiling the end product. But they also change the flavor, so that beer tastes different than it used to.

The world of brewing used to have an enormous variety of brewing processes, but the methods taught in brewing schools and brewing textbooks have gradually displaced most of the older methods. Today, craft brewing is a monoculture where everyone brews in more or less the same way. The old methods and their unusual flavors have been forgotten.

What people did long ago may not seem important today, since recreating old brewing techniques is extremely difficult, and in any case the beer may not have been any good. There is no way to know what flavors the old methods were supposed to produce, so attempts at recreating them will always be a shot in the dark.

Except that, as it turns out, there is no need to recreate the old methods, because they are still with us. In the early twentieth century farmhouse brewing was still alive and well across most of northern Europe. Although farmhouse brewing has been dying off ever since, the process has been slow enough that it still survives, surprisingly unchanged, in far more places than anyone would expect.

These brewers are still following ancient brewing practices, producing beers that are totally unlike modern beers, whether craft or industrial. And, what is more, many of these beers are truly outstanding. Since it is the remains of an ancient tradition that slowly developed across most of northern Europe, this type of farmhouse brewing is hugely diverse, differing dramatically from place to place.

Farmhouse brewing offers enormous potential for modern brewers who want to brew beer that is different from what you can buy today. It offers surprising opportunities for creating interesting flavors throughout the entire process, from the field to the glass. Farmhouse brewers make malt in different ways, use a variety of brewing processes and ingredients, and even serve the beer in ways we are not familiar with.

To see why farmhouse brewing is so different from modern brewing, it is necessary to understand where it comes from.

The World of Yesterday

Imagine living out in the country in a world with no cars, no trains, and where horses are rare and expensive. Visiting even a nearby town is going to take a long time and transporting goods will be expensive and slow. It follows that you will have to make nearly everything you need yourself, and, indeed, that is exactly what people did.

Figure 1.1. The main road between eastern and western Norway, not far from Kaupanger in western Norway, in 1890. Parts of this road remained challenging, and even dangerous, until 1872. Photo taken by Nils Olsson Reppen, County Archives in Sogn og Fjordane..

The farmers of a century or two ago made their own clothes, bread, cheese, butter, soap, malt, beer, sausages, houses, brewing equipment, rope, farming implements, and so on. To grow up in the country was to become the jack of a dozen trades or more. The farmers only bought things they could not make themselves: large metal items, salt, and a few luxuries.

In the Nordic Museum in Stockholm hangs a woman's shirt where the top half is made from linen, but the linen harvest must have failed, because the bottom half is made of hop fibers. The stems of hop vines have coarse "hairs" that they use to climb, so the shirt must have been very uncomfortable to wear. The museum's description says the first few times you wore such a shirt it would "chafe you bloody."[2] In Lithuania, the peasants had a ritual in which they prayed, "Dear god Waizganthos, please let the linen grow to my height, don't let us go naked."[3] A shirt made of hop bines was better than no shirt at all.

Beer was central to the old peasant society to an extent that is difficult to fathom today. Where there was enough grain beer was the everyday drink, a key source of safe liquid and nutrition. But more than that, beer was the focus of every social and religious ritual of any importance. To celebrate childbirth, weddings, religious feasts, and burials, beer had to be supplied by the farm itself. In even older times beer was seen as sacred, as a drug that put the drinkers in contact with the divine. This association was weakened by the advent of Christianity, but aspects of it hung on into modern times. Therefore, all celebrations of importance required the farmers to host their neighbors and serve them beer. Thus, in rural areas, brewing was in effect a necessity, at times even required by law.

In farmhouse brewing before the twentieth century, geography determined everything. What grain grew on the farm depended on the soil and the climate, which again depended on where the farm was. Barley was by far the most commonly used grain for beer, but not everyone grew enough barley to be able to use it for beer, so malt might also be made from rye or oats.

Soil and climate also determined how much grain could be grown on the farm, which determined how it would be used. In a rich farming country like Denmark, the farmers used beer as an everyday drink against thirst. Danish farmers brewed strong beer for celebrations, but they also had weaker beer for farm work and to drink with meals. Further north the farmers simply did not have enough grain for this, so they were forced to choose between brewing strong beer a few times a year or weak beer for everyday drinking.

The people on the farms lived by what they could make, so farmhouse brewing was shaped by the prevailing economic conditions. People back then were poor in a way that is hard to understand today, so even the most basic things might have been out of reach. If the farmers could not grow grain they could not brew beer. If there was not enough barley, the malt would have to be augmented with other grains. Perhaps a farmer didn't have a metal kettle or a large oven. If a specific herb did not grow in the area, it would not be used in the beer at all. And so on.

Since the beer was brewed from the farm's own grain, malting was a key part of making beer. Larger farms usually had a dedicated building for drying malt, and often this building was also used to dry grain, linen, and even meat. In some places, the kiln was shared among the people of the village. The building or other equipment used to make the malt determined what the product would be like: pale or dark, smoky or not.

Brewers really had no choice about what kind of malt to use because they only had one way to make malt. The same was true for the brewing process. Brewers knew one brewing process, learned in their youth, and that was it. The farmers were making the same beer each time,

Figure 1.2. Man from Setesdal, southern Norway, in his work clothes.

because they had no choice. Of course, depending on what the beer was brewed for, it might be weaker or stronger.

Usually, people used the same brewing process throughout the local region, because it was the only process they knew. However, people in different places would have developed different processes as time passed. If you crossed any major body of water, a mountain range, or a large forest, you would find people on the other side who brewed in a different way.

Nearly everyone could, and did, grow their own hops. Growing enough to supply the household was not much work. One resident explained, "Once the hops were planted there wasn't much more to do except add fertilizer. Well-fermented horse manure was the best. Also, we had to set up hop poles."[4] Many farmers say the hops grew "like weeds." Once planted, hops could grow for decades without help.

The only work involved was picking the hops and drying them. For most farmers, this did not require much effort, as the annual consumption of hops was limited to a couple of kilograms, maybe even less.

Herbs seem to have been used much less frequently than people like to imagine, with one major exception: juniper. However, juniper was only used in places where it grew quite well, which means that no juniper was used in Denmark and the UK. Other herbs too were only used in the areas where they actually grew, which means that wild rosemary was not an ingredient in Norwegian beer, for example. The brewers seem to have mostly used the same herbs every time, if they used any at all. Fruit in the beer seems to have been completely unknown.

The brewing equipment was very basic. Usually the main items were a copper kettle over a wood fire, and one or two wooden vessels closely resembling a very large bucket. Such vessels, with a hole in or near the bottom, were used as mash tuns. The most common vessel had a hole in the bottom through which a vertical pole was inserted. The pole was tapered at the end so that lifting it allowed wort to run out through the opening. In the bottom of the vessel was a rough filter, usually made of juniper branches or straw.

All liquid was moved with a ladle or a bucket, which, together with the wood firing, meant that brewing involved a lot of physical labor. Water had to be carried from the well, the mash transferred by bucket, and so on. The use of slow brewing processes like step mashing or decoction could make brewing even more laborious, but farmers in the old days were used to back-breaking work, so brewing was almost a holiday by comparison.

Once the beer was finished fermenting the yeast was collected and set aside for the next batch. Before the mid-nineteenth century, every farm had to have their own yeast because there was no alternative. You could not buy yeast in the countryside before that time and some places had to wait another century or more for it to become available.

The farmer's children watched their parents at work and that way learned how to do the job themselves. Of course, an illiterate farmer did not know the scientific theory behind the things he did, but he still knew what to do. And so, the children learned to repeat what their parents did in order to get the same result. Exactly why it worked was not clear, but that did not really matter, as long as it actually worked.

Since the ingredients were grown and prepared on the farm there was no knowing how much could be extracted from the malt. It would depend on the weather that summer, as well as the details of malting, which the farmer was not in full control of. In the same way, the strength of the hops depended on the weather. This is one reason farmhouse brewers did not rely on recipes:

a kilo of malt from one year would not yield the same result as a kilo of malt made the next year. Instead, the brewers used only very rough measures, relying on taste and smell to make adjustments during brewing.

The thermometer and the hydrometer were both invented in the eighteenth century, but the thermometer did not become common in farmhouse brewing until the last half of the twentieth century, and the hydrometer is still very rare. The farmers were not brewing on a large scale, so precise control over the result was not necessary. They were brewing the same beer over and over, and simply using their fingers and taste buds got them close enough to the result they wanted. And if the beer turned out to be 6.7% ABV instead of 7.4% nobody would know, or even notice.

The only way to judge the strength of the beer was by its effect, as the following story shows. Ivar at the Frøyne farm, in Hardanger, western Norway, served his beer to a guest, watching intently as he drank, looking for signs of intoxication. Drinking the beer to test its effect was the only way to tell how strong it was. So, when his guest happily drank and talked for a long time without showing any effects, Ivar was annoyed and decided to follow him when he left. But the guest walked straight and fast, seemingly none the worse for wear. After a few kilometers, Ivar gave up and turned back. He never saw his guest collapse in the ditch just a little further on. Thinking his beer had come out far too weak, Ivar was so angry that he went straight home and started a new brew right away.[5]

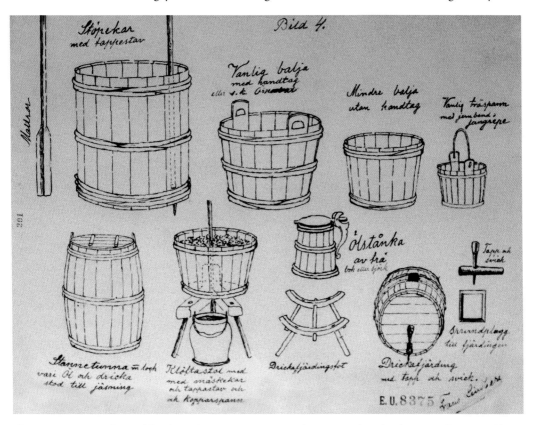

Figure 1.3. Drawing of typical farmhouse brewing equipment in the nineteenth and early twentieth century. The equipment probably looked the same many centuries earlier, as well. By Frans Lindberg, Sweden, 1935. EU 8375.

Even today, if you ask a farmhouse brewer what the original gravity of their beer is, the answer is likely to be, "I don't know, I'm not a scientist." Most of the brewers do not know how strong their beer is and have never even tried to measure it. They do not really need to know either, having grown up with the beer. As one of them put it when asked how strong his beer was, "Well, I know I can't drive after having one."[6] Of course, beers made like this do not taste the same from batch to batch, but, in any case, that is not necessary because it is not a commercial product.

Figure 1.4. Tver Karelians brewing stone beer outdoors (note the tongs with the stone). Tver oblast, Russia, northwest of Moscow, roughly 1912. Photo by Joh. Kujola. Reproduced by permission from the Finnish Heritage Agency.

This worked well for the brewers, who brewed the same beer over and over again and knew from experience exactly how to get it right. It does mean, however, that anyone wanting to learn to brew the same beer without physically being present to see, smell, and taste the beer has a problem. To be able to write recipes that can be shared in a book, I have made measurements where I could by visiting the brewers and participating in the brewing process, but no exact recipes exist for most of these historical beers.

But could beer brewed in wood, with no proper measurements, with homemade malt, and yeast reused for centuries, be any good? I know it sounds unlikely to modern brewers, but some of the best beers I have ever had were brewed by farmhouse brewers using these traditional methods. Traditional malt, yeast, and brewing methods yield a depth and complexity of flavor beyond what you get with modern alternatives, so that even a very simple recipe for a balanced and drinkable beer can still yield amazing depth of flavor. And that is something that has not changed over the centuries.

In 1812, Hans Birch Dahlerup, a Danish naval officer, was travelling overland across western Norway. When he reached Vik in Sogn, he spent the night at the house of an elderly colonel, who naturally served his farmhouse ale. Dahlerup later became a Danish baron and the commander-in-chief of the Austro-Hungarian navy, so by the time he wrote his memoirs he had tasted many fine beverages. Still, in his memoirs he wrote:

> After dinner a large silver mug of Christmas beer was brought in. It
> was so excellent a drink as none of us had ever tasted the like of. I don't
> know what to compare it to: it was thick and sweetish, like Malaga [a
> Spanish sweet fortified wine], but had a vinous spirit and lightness, and
> a power that penetrated bone and marrow. I had heard of the strong
> home-brewed beer in Norway, but this was beyond anything I'd ever
> heard of, and beyond any Porter, "doublebrownstout" or treble X I've
> ever had. The colonel seemed to be a moderate drinker, and assumed
> that so were we, because the mug disappeared the moment we'd drunk
> from it. (Dahlerup, quoted by Råsberg [2015, 17].)

It should not have come as a surprise that the beer was good, because their beer was a source of pride. The beer reflected the wealth of the farm, the quality of the soil, the skill of the farmer, maltster, and brewer, and also their generosity. In many villages certain farms had a reputation for brewing good beer. Speaking of Voss in the 1970s, Sjur Rørlien told me that "a man was judged on two things: how good he was as a farmer, and how good his beer was."

Not every farmer was a good brewer. "Some brew all their lives, and never make good beer," as Hans Saakvitne put it.[7] One farmhouse brewer told me that one local farmer had made really good beer, but after his son took over that family never had good beer again. "When we had a bad beer, we used to joke that 'this one has a <name of farm>-flavor,'" he said. When brewing poor beer gives you this kind of reputation locally, the incentive to do your best must have been powerful indeed.

So, of course, not all farmhouse ale was good. Some must have been infected, or made from low-quality or poorly malted grain, which in some cases was adulterated with carrots, potatoes, and even weeds. There must have been some truly horrible examples.

Farmhouse brewing really is a completely different world from that of modern brewing, so this book will describe many things that seem unlikely or even impossible to a modern brewer. Many years of studying farmhouse ale has taught me that many things modern brewers believe about brewing are wrong. Just because it seems impossible to you does not mean it is impossible.

You know the things you have tried do indeed work. You do not know that something you have not tried does not work, even if your knowledge of theory makes it seem very, very unlikely. The world of beer is a lot bigger than you think. When people report that everyone in their village has brewed a certain way for centuries, obviously the method they use has to work, otherwise they would have given it up long ago. So, as you read on, it is important to keep an open mind.

But enough generalities. The only way to really understand farmhouse brewing is to visit the brewers, see what they do, and taste their beer. With that in mind, let us go visit one.

Kaupanger: First Meeting with the Tradition

The name Kaupanger literally means "trading fjord," because in Viking times Kaupanger was one of the main trading points on the west coast of Norway. The local stave church still stands, and some of the timber in it has been dated to the twelfth century. Today, Kaupanger is a small village deep in the fjord country of western Norway, about 80 kilometers into the Sognefjord from the sea. The region is called Sogn, after the fjord.

Figure 1.5. Johannes Gjerde and Marta Tuftene in front of Resaland farm in the Sogndal valley, near Kaupanger, ca. 1905. Nils Olsson Reppen, from the County Archives in Sogn og Fjordane.

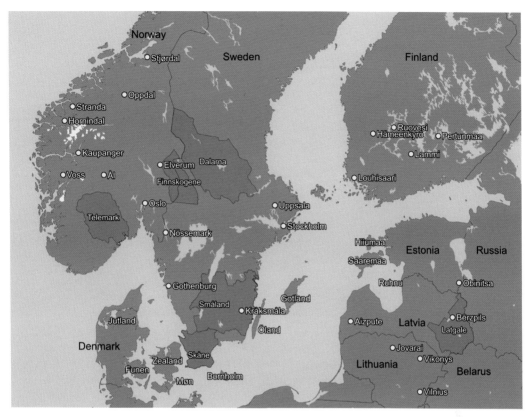

Figure 1.6. Map of the Nordic region with the main places and regions indicated. The white areas are glaciers.

The landscape of Sogn consists of narrow valleys flanked by steep mountains rising to about a thousand meters, often right out of the fjord. Farming here has always been difficult, but it is still an important vocation in the area.

Sogn has always been a very remote area, and the farming here remained primitive even into my own lifetime. Farmers largely subsisted by growing grain on every possible piece of land, and then feeding livestock on grass from the land that couldn't support grain. Because of the long winters it was necessary to produce as much as possible during the short summer and then store enough food and animal fodder to last through the winter. In the old days, fodder for the animals was pitifully scarce, so scarce that today you would face legal charges of animal cruelty if you tried nearly starving the animals that way. But the people on the farm did not eat much more than did their animals.

My grandmother acquired a farm outside Sogndal in 1974, in exchange for caring for an old couple already living on the farm. Even after my grandmother took over the farm, the husband spent the late summers on the narrow mountain terraces in the nearly vertical mountainside above the Årøy river, cutting the grass and storing it in small wooden sheds. Once the grass was dry, he carried it down from the mountain on his back. Not long ago this had literally been a matter of life and death, something that kept the animals alive during the winter. It was no longer necessary, but the husband could not bring himself to stop. He kept doing this until, one beautiful day in late summer, he had a stroke up there on the mountainside. My uncle, who was 20 at the time, was sent up to look for him,

Figure 1.7. The Barsnes fjord, seen from my grandmother's farm. The town of Sogndal is behind the low hill on the right.

and had to carry the old man, still convulsing, down the mountainside. This was in 1980.

It is hardly surprising that farmhouse brewing survived in an area like this. My mother says she remembers her uncle brewing for an outdoor wedding held at the Ølnes farm sometime in the 1960s. At this point, however, farmhouse brewing was in decline, and had been for some decades. The Swedish ethnologist Anders Salomonsson visited Kaupanger in 1974, when there were only four brewers left in the area. They made malt, brewed beer, and sold it to local customers, who wanted 100–150 liters of beer for weddings and similar celebrations.[8] The only malt mill available was in Lærdal, on the other side of the fjord, so the brewers had to take the ferry back and forth just to have their malt milled. The brewers complained that often more than half the beer would remain untouched after a wedding, because younger people preferred whisky or vodka. Salomonsson quite reasonably concluded that farmhouse brewing seemed unlikely to survive much longer.[9]

But somehow it did. Just before Christmas 2013, I was invited to come to Kaupanger to see a group demonstration of farmhouse ale brewing. I was just beginning to study farmhouse ale, so I jumped at the chance, never having seen it brewed before.

The brewer was Carlo Aall, who was not actually from Kaupanger. He moved there in 1992 and rented a house on the Amble farm in Kaupanger together with his fiancé. When Carlo told his landlord that he was getting married and that he was going to have an old-style wedding, his landlord suggested teaching Carlo how to brew traditional beer for the wedding. Carlo has been brewing ever since.

The brewhouse was a room at the end of a barn, with a concrete floor and two fireplaces large enough to accommodate two large copper kettles. The walls were darkened by soot, which made it look very dirty compared to modern kitchens and brewhouses. Water was supplied by a garden hose. At one end of the room was a large basin constructed from a section of concrete pipe. Other than that, there were two large plastic barrels, a small table, and a single chair.

Figure 1.8. The Amble farm in Kaupanger.

Figure 1.9. Inside the brewhouse at Amble farm. Part of the cooling basin can be seen on the right.

I had brewed with modern homebrewers before, so I was puzzled by the size of this brewery and also by the seeming lack of cleanliness. It turned out that Carlo planned to brew 150 liters of beer, so we did need equipment of this size, but I really could not understand why he wanted to make a batch this big. Later, I discovered that 150 liters is the most common batch size in Norwegian farmhouse ale, and seems to have been for a long, long time.

Figure 1.10. Making a juniper infusion.

Carlo filled the kettle with water and set about getting the fire started beneath it. Meanwhile, he asked me to go out and get some juniper branches from the plastic bag outside the door. Carlo explained that in Norwegian farmhouse brewing, the liquid used for cleaning and also for the brewing itself is not water, but a juniper infusion. You put juniper branches with needles in the kettle and heat the water to make an infusion of juniper. The result is a highly aromatic, very pale green liquid.

But before that, Carlo said, I had to take one of the branches and split it lengthwise, so that we could extract the sap from the wood. I had never heard of this before. "Why do you do that?" I asked.

Carlo just shrugged, vaguely embarrassed, and said, "I was told this was important, but not why." Then he was quiet for a while. Finally, he said: "When my mother taught me to cook pork steak, she told me I had to cut off the ends before putting it in the oven. When I asked her why she just said 'that's how we do it.' So, I always did the same. Many years later I asked my grandmother why. 'Oh,' she said, 'that's because our old oven was too narrow.'"

What Carlo was telling me, indirectly, was that when you learn farmhouse brewing you are learning a process, a sequence of steps that have to be followed precisely. But nobody knows why the process is exactly the way it is, and nobody knows for certain whether all of the steps are truly necessary or not. The reason is that the process has evolved over several millennia of trial and error and none of the people involved had any knowledge of biochemistry at all.

Figure 1.11. Carlo ladling the juniper infusion onto the grist.

Figure 1.12. The lauter tun. Inside is a filter of juniper branches and a piece of wire mesh.

So, I did as Carlo asked, and while the juniper infusion was heated in the kettle, Carlo found four plastic tubs, which he placed on the floor. We waited for the juniper infusion to reach 80°C. The temperature should not go higher, Carlo said, because unhealthy substances would be extracted from the wood. We filled the plastic tubs with ground malt and poured the 80°C infusion over that grist using a scoop, stirring it in with a mash paddle.

The malt all came from a homebrew shop, where it had also been milled. "Making the malt," said Carlo, "that's the really difficult part. For that you really need to be skilled." But people in the area are not making their own malt any more. Malting takes nearly two weeks of work, and also requires you to build and maintain a separate building just for malting. So, people just buy the malt from the shop instead.

Carlo said that when the mash paddle could just barely stand upright in the mash, the ratio of water to grist was right. And the temperature should be 72°C, he added. That is surprisingly warm, but, as we will see, it is by no means unusual in farmhouse brewing—farmhouse brewers like their beers sweet. It was cold in the brewhouse, so we placed some wooden lids and cloths over the tubs to keep the temperature up. Then we had an hour-long break.

The next step was to prepare a large, tall plastic barrel as the lauter tun. Carlo calls it *rostabidnet*, which he explained means "the tun with the grating." In fact, the Old Norse term for the tun was *hrosti*, so the word is more than a millennium old.[10] In the bottom we placed juniper branches, to serve as a filter, and then added a piece of wire mesh on top. Now the mash could be scooped up using a steel bucket and poured into the lauter tun.

Once that was done, Carlo placed the bucket under the tap at the bottom of the barrel and let out the first wort. It was steaming hot and deliciously sweet and rich. The first bucket, Carlo said, had to be poured back into the barrel. I asked why. Carlo just looked at me and said he did not know.

Figure 1.13. Hops boiling in the wort.

Figure 1.14. My cousin, Svein Ølnes, filtering the hops out of the wort as he filled the fermentor.

Carlo taught us that the wort should be allowed to run off slowly. The stream of wort coming out of the tap should be "as thick as a woolen thread." There was much fine-tuning of the tap to make the wort flow just right. Every time we poured one bucket of wort into the kettle, we would pour one bucket of juniper infusion into the top of the lauter tun.

Carlo told us that for the amount of malt we were using today he would normally take off about 20 buckets of wort. To count the buckets, he used a piece of sooty wood from the fire to make marks on the wall. There were lots of these marks from earlier brews, and some had dates next to them, "1992," "May 1993," "2012," "1989," and so on. Some had people's names, and in 2013 someone brewed weissbier and IPA. So even here, in Kaupanger, people were brewing modern beers alongside the traditional farmhouse ale.

Once there was enough wort in the kettle Carlo started the fire under it again, to boil the wort. When we were getting close to 20 buckets of wort, Carlo started tasting the wort to see when to stop lautering. Eventually he decided it was time. I tasted the wort and you could tell that most of the sweetness was gone. It still had some body, but it was not very sweet. This was Carlo's gravity measurement.

The wort in the kettle was boiled for an hour. Carlo added hops at intervals, measuring out the additions on an electronic scale he had brought. I asked Carlo which hops he was using, and he said he did not know. The homebrew shop had just given him some hops that were suitable for farmhouse ale. It was at this point that doubts started developing in my mind as to whether this guy actually knew what he was doing, and whether this beer would be drinkable.

Once the boil was over, we placed a primitive sieve made of cloth and wooden sticks over the fermentor, and ladled the wort into the barrel. Carlo used whole leaf hops, so the sieve filtered out the hops. Carlo said in summer he would normally leave the hops in until after fermentation, but there was no need for that in December.

I now discovered that the concrete basin was for cooling the wort. The barrel was placed into the basin and, once there was enough wort in the barrel, the basin was filled with cold water from the garden hose. Even so, cooling the wort took hours. In the end, it was getting on for midnight before the yeast was pitched.

The yeast in this case was a dry Safale yeast. Carlo had made a starter using some prepackaged "wort beer" in a saucepan many hours earlier.*

Figure 1.15. The finished beer in my kitchen.

A few weeks later, a sample of the beer arrived in a soft plastic container, something like a cross between a plastic bag and a plastic can. It had no real head, just a coarse froth around the edge, because the beer had very little carbonation. The body was opaque, nearly black, and hazy light brown along the edges. The aroma was dominated by notes of juniper and roasty, oily banana, and was really quite pleasant. The flavor was similar, but with an additional smoky element that I could not tell where it came from. It was sweet, and obviously strong, with a slightly rough bitterness in the finish. Overall, it was a lovely beer, sweet and strong but surprisingly drinkable. And quite different from modern beer.

At this point I should report the gravities, the ABV, and the IBUs, but this was a truly traditional farmhouse ale, so I don't have that information. From the recipe, I calculated an OG of 1.107 and an FG of 1.026, for an ABV of 10.6%. In reality, the finished beer was probably more like 8%–9%, because Carlo thought it tasted like "porter concentrate" and watered it down a little.

---

* This is a Norwegian thing. You can buy unfermented wort with CO_2 in bottles in the shops, basically as a soft drink. As it happens to have a gravity of 1.040, this prepackaged wort is perfect for yeast starters.

When I tasted the beer, I discovered that I could not detect any hop flavor whatsoever. Carlo used 270 grams of hops for 150 liters of beer. If these were Saaz hops, that would give 7 IBUs.* That is 7 IBUs in a sweet beer of almost 10% ABV. Clearly it did not matter what hops Carlo used, so he did not, in fact, need to know what kind they were. The hops were not there for the aroma or even for the bitterness, but to protect against infection. The actual balancing of the beer through bitterness, and the role of flavor addition, was assumed by the juniper, not the hops. Indeed, this is what many farmhouse brewers say about their own beers, for example, Jørund Geving and Pekka Kääriäinen.[11]

Later, I realized why Carlo had been taught to pour the first bucket back into the lauter tun. The first bucket tends to be full of haze from the malt dust, and pouring it back in serves to filter the wort one more time, making the beer much clearer. In other words, it was *vorlauf*—the recirculation of the first runnings—and he was definitely right to do so.

Visiting other farmhouse brewers, I learned why it was important that the stream of wort from the tap should be so narrow: the filter is just a fine steel mesh and juniper branches. If you allow the wort to run off too quickly, bits of juniper and even grain will be carried along with the fast-flowing wort and may block the tap. A brewer I visited had had to saw off the bend at the end of the tap and poke it open with sticks because they lautered too rapidly.[12] It also makes for clearer beer, and many brewers do it to ensure that their extraction efficiency is high.

Using larger juniper branches that must be split is unusual in Norway, but it is not something Carlo invented. A 1953 archive document from Jølster, not too far away from Kaupanger, says exactly the same.[13]

The visit to Kaupanger was a big lesson for me. Compared to the homebrewers I knew, Carlo seemed like he did not know what he was doing. And he clearly had no idea why he was doing many of the things he did. But he made excellent beer, because the process he had been taught did work. And, because he always brewed the same beer, and had been doing so for 20 years, he knew exactly what to do. The theory, and the reasons why he was doing everything he was doing, turned out to be unnecessary. The apparent lack of cleanliness that had bothered me was also not really an issue: soot may look bad, but it apparently has no effect on the beer.

Carlo is the last link in a very long chain of brewers before him. But how long is the chain, and how did it begin?

---

* Norwegian farmhouse brewers nearly always use old-school continental European hop varieties, low in alpha acids and with a relatively neutral aroma.

2

HISTORY

Nobody knows when beer brewing began in Europe, but it cannot have been before agriculture arrived, since without grain there can be no beer. Agriculture began in the Middle East, then started spreading into Europe around 6500 BCE, reaching the northernmost parts of Europe around 4000 BCE.

Figure 2.1. Rock carving depicting plowing using an ard, an older, more primitive type of plow. Ca. 1800–500 BCE, western Sweden. Drawing by Lidingo, Wikimedia Commons, CC-BY-SA.

As a rule, wherever people grew grain, they also made beer. What we do not know is how long after they started growing grain they learned about beer brewing. People in the Middle East were probably brewing beer by 6500 BCE, so it is highly likely that the knowledge of beer brewing spread together with the practice of farming, but this is not known for certain. Among archaeologists and historians, the "bread or beer" debate has been going on since the 1950s. The question is whether people started growing grain to make bread or to make beer. If it was beer then obviously beer brewing spread together with agriculture, but if the goal was bread then beer brewing probably developed later. Unfortunately, no consensus has been reached, so this is an open question.

The earliest definitive evidence for beer brewing in Europe comes from archaeology. In the Can Sadurní cave, just outside of Barcelona in Spain, a ceramic vessel was found with traces of what seems to be barley beer. It was dated to 3520 BCE.[1] There are many similar finds throughout Europe, many of them open to question and hard to interpret. All of this early brewing activity in Europe must have been farmhouse brewing, in the sense that the brewers grew and malted the grain themselves, and that the beer was intended for the brewer's own household.

Figure 2.2. Inside panel of the Gundestrup cauldron, a silver cauldron thought to have been used for ritual "hospitality." It is astonishingly large: 69 cm in diameter and 42 cm tall, weighing 9 kg. The cauldron shows scenes from an unknown Celtic mythology, thought to date from the first century CE. National Museum of Denmark, Copenhagen.

Mead was very likely the first alcoholic drink in Europe, but honey was so scarce that mead was always rare and precious, and could never play the kind of role that beer and wine did. It seems that beer came to Europe first, and that wine-making only arrived later. The earliest evidence of wine making in Europe is from around 2200 BCE, from Crete in Greece. It has been proposed that wine making most likely spread from the Near East to nearby areas around 4000–2160 BCE.[2]

For a long time, wine making and beer brewing coexisted in southern Europe, but eventually the Greeks and Romans developed a strong prejudice against beer, viewing it as a barbarian drink, and wine production seems to have driven beer brewing out of southern Europe.[3] Historically, wine grapes would not grow in northern Europe, so brewing continued in the north.

The reason wine replaced beer was probably not the cultural perception of wine as superior, but that wine making is far less work than beer brewing. Both require harvesting the raw materials and actually producing the drink, but to make beer it's also necessary to plough, sow, thresh, sort, and malt the grain. And wine is naturally stronger and will keep for longer, so those who had a choice would tend to prefer to make wine.

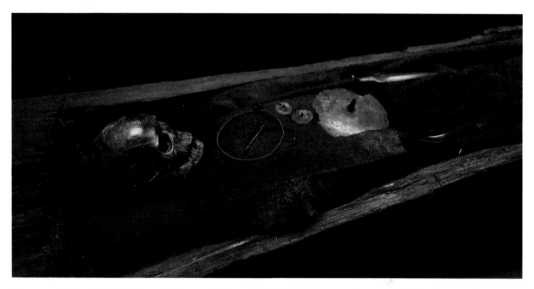

Figure 2.3. Oak coffin burial very similar to the Egtved girl's burial. Moesgaard museum, Århus, Denmark.

While proving beer was being brewed in northern Europe, the archaeological evidence is otherwise fairly thin and provides little additional detail. Several dried-up remains of mixed beverages have been found in Denmark dating from around 1500 BCE.[4] Evidence of malt being made around 500 BCE has been found in Germany and southern France.[5] Malting and brewing obviously began earlier in this area, but how much earlier is difficult to say. Although very little is known about how these beers were brewed, chemical analysis of the Danish finds showed that some were pure mead, while others were made from a mix of barley, berries, and honey. Finds from 2000 BCE show that malting was already known, so Europeans were also brewing true beer.[6] However, while we have some limited insight into the ingredients, the brewing processes that were used are largely unknown, since there is no direct evidence for most of them. To date, the issue of the brewing process has generally been ignored by most historians and archaeologists. What is clear is that by the start of the Common Era beer had already been brewed all over Europe for a long time, probably several millennia.

At this time, metal kettles, even those fashioned from copper or bronze, were extremely expensive and would make a fitting gift for a prince or a chieftain. Most brewers had no way to afford them, so it is not clear how they managed to heat the mash. It is possible that smaller and cheaper vessels of soapstone were used. From archaeological finds we know that heating the mash with stones was common. In Norway there are enormous deposits of fire-shattered stone, which are thought to be the remains of brewing stones shattered into fragments by being quickly cooled in the mash. Similar stones have also been found in other countries.

Figure 2.4. Handle of a bronze cauldron, third century BCE. As the decorations show, this was not an everyday kitchen utensil. From the Moesgaard museum in Jutland, Denmark.

Unfortunately, archaeologists have made no attempt to do systematic surveys of the stones, and archaeologists in different countries do not even agree on what the deposits actually represent. In Norway the deposits start to appear in the seventh century and disappear in the seventeenth century, but the full story is probably more complicated.[7] Unfortunately, not much more is known, except that the practice of brewing with hot stones is still alive. And, as we will see, there were other ways of heating the mash without a kettle.

The earliest beers did not use hops. What we know about the use of herbs in prehistoric beer comes mainly from pollen analysis, and it seems that sweet gale (bog myrtle) has been in use since the Stone Age. It is possible that juniper has been used for an equally long period, but the evidence for juniper is less solid. Hops begin to show up in archaeological finds in Germany and Scandinavia from the sixth century onward, but the evidence is so scarce that the use of hops could well have begun earlier.[8]

Originally, all beer brewing in Europe was farmhouse brewing, that is, farmers brewing beer from their own grain for their own use. The Roman Empire had commercial brewers in towns for military use, but the rural areas around them were filled with farmhouse brewers. So, farmhouse brewing was the overwhelmingly dominant form of brewing until the Middle Ages, which is when towns really started developing in northern Europe.

People living in a town cannot grow grain and will also have difficulty making malt. This situation created a market that led to the development of commercial breweries. Accounts of nineteenth-century brewing in relatively remote provincial towns, such as Goslar in Germany and

Klagenfurt in Austria, show this very clearly.[9] There were many very small breweries using the same techniques and equipment as those found in farmhouse brewing, such as filtering through juniper and straw. They bought their malt from small producers near the town, usually run "by widows and old spinsters."[10]

This development of farmhouse brewers going commercial began long before the nineteenth century, way back in the Middle Ages. However, around the twelfth century, something changed. German brewers in some of the larger towns in the northeast started boiling hops in their wort. Suddenly, they were producing a stable beer that could be exported. This meant that a single brewer could now serve a large market, which, together with increasing urbanization and trade, resulted in an explosive growth in commercial brewing. Within a couple of centuries, commercial breweries in the bigger towns were using copper kettles that held thousands of liters of wort.[11] Commercial brewing had now definitely parted ways with farmhouse brewing.

Over the centuries that followed, commercial brewing developed further. Lager brewing became established, and the eighteenth century saw the emergence of the great porter breweries in London. Also in the eighteenth century, new tools like the saccharometer and the thermometer appeared alongside the beginnings of modern chemistry. These developments put commercial brewing on a much firmer foundation. Then steam engines and refrigeration techniques appeared in breweries. And in 1883 Emil Christian Hansen, building on the research of Pasteur, developed the method and equipment for isolating and propagating pure yeast cultures, revolutionizing the use of yeast in brewing.[12]

Figure 2.5. Brewhouse in Voss with a copper kettle, 1855. Painting by Adolph Tiedemann.

Meanwhile, from Ireland in the west to the Urals in the east, and from the Alps to the Arctic Circle, farmhouse brewing continued. Practices and equipment were modernized, but very, very slowly. The most important modernizations in farmhouse brewing over the last few centuries are metal kettles, garden hoses, electric light, and, of course, the ability to buy the ingredients. Even today, hardly any farmhouse brewers use measurements beyond weighing and, perhaps, a thermometer. Pure yeast cultures have been adopted by most farmhouse brewers, but the original yeast cultures still live on in parts of Norway, Lithuania, Latvia, and Russia.

In the European countryside, malting and brewing were important parts of the annual life cycle of the farm up until the late nineteenth century, give or take. This was something everyone did, like baking bread or making cheese. Beer was brewed as an everyday drink where people could afford it, but also for celebrations. As we will see later, beer was a crucial part of many rituals and social functions. As a general rule, if people grew grain they also made beer from it. This applied all over the world, and also to types of grain not indigenous to Europe, like maize and rice. The exceptions were where either people had switched to wine, brewing was banned by religion, or governments placed restrictions on brewing for tax purposes.

In large parts of Europe, brewing was restricted by the landowners or the government. Landlords ran their own breweries and taverns, and to ensure that the peasants bought their products they either forbade brewing or levied a tax on it. These practices seem to have begun in the Middle Ages and varied from place to place. In Lithuania, in the area around Biržai, the instructions for tax collectors in 1674 stated: No subject of the manor can brew beer without first making known their intention and paying the brewing tax, 15 pennies per Vilnius barrel of malt, to the local tax collectors. The penalty was a kapa (60) pennies. Anyone celebrating a wedding in their home could make beer from one barrel without paying tax on it.[13]

In other places brewing might be forbidden entirely, or only allowed for specific festive occasions. This was a very effective form of taxation, which was common practice in parts of Germany, Prussia, Austria, and the Baltic states. In some parts of Europe, for example, the UK and parts of Germany, farmhouse brewing was taxed by the government into the twentieth century.[14]

In northern Europe there was little sun and the growing season was short. The farmers hastened the onset of spring by strewing ash and sand on the snow so that it would melt sooner, allowing them to sow the grain earlier. But there were limits to what could be done—the further north you lived, the harder it was to grow grain.

In Beiarn in northern Norway, just north of the Arctic Circle, one local reported: "Most people could not spend grain on malting. The village was mostly self-sufficient in grain, but in the old days there were often years of poor harvest." Buying the grain was far too expensive to be an option: "They had to save the grain in good years so they wouldn't have to eat bark bread in bad years. The old always told the young: 'Whatever you do, always make sure to have enough seed grain for next year'."[15] Bark bread was made from flour diluted with processed tree bark. It was a famine food to be used in extreme need.

The northern limit on brewing in Norway was roughly at the Arctic Circle. Areas starting at about latitude 63° north in Sweden, and areas of northern Finland and Russia, were too far north for brewing. Iceland was also too far north, once the farming of the early Norse settlers had eroded the soil. The northern limit for growing grapes was central France, southern Germany, Austria, and Hungary.

In the nineteenth century, life in rural areas altered dramatically, to the point that many observers felt that the ancient peasant culture was dying out right in front of their eyes. Agriculture became much more efficient and mechanized, so that far fewer workers were needed. Improved transportation made it possible to buy many of the things that people earlier had to produce themselves, making it possible for farmers to grow products for sale. Although the overall population grew, it dwindled in rural areas as people migrated to the cities and found work in industry.

One of the victims of this change was farmhouse brewing. Brewing was a lot of work, especially malting, and the beer could end up infected and sour. Many farmers stopped growing grain for their own food, and instead produced crops for profit, like fruit, meat, or milk. But without their own grain they would have to buy grain to make malt. With modernity, other drinks became more widely available, like milk, which was traditionally too precious to drink, and coffee. The arrival of coffee meant the farm could serve visitors something other than beer to drink. Religious temperance movements also did much to destroy the brewing culture in many places. In other areas, farmhouse brewing died out when it became easy to buy commercially brewed beer. This was partly due to bought goods being associated with higher status, because they were produced in the cities and buying them showed that you were wealthy enough to afford them. In north Jutland, Denmark, one local wrote that

> the brewing came to an end bit by bit. In the house where I was born beer was brewed as long as my mother was able to do it, until sometime in the 1920s. Many of the young who set up homes did not have the necessary vessels and might lack the experience. People had gotten used to buying ground ready-made malt, and when the small malt-makers could no longer sustain their business it became difficult to buy malt. The farms kept up the brewing the longest. The shops started selling malt substitutes, and packs of malt, hops, sweeteners, and so on, which were boiled in a big pot on the stove. (NEU 29999, 1973, from Lild, north Jutland)

Some farms took part of their grain and invented new methods to make a little malt from it, just enough to brew a small amount of beer with. "This had the flavor of real homebrew. The commercial Pilsner in casks never really appealed to the farmers. They said it was 'slack.' Some still do. My son and daughter-in-law still brew in this simpler way."[16]

In many places, when malting and brewing ended, people bought sugar or syrup, something that had not been affordable before, and brewed simple beer replacements from that. Or they bought ready-made kits with sugar and spices.

Today, grain growing has declined dramatically in Scandinavia because farmers there cannot compete with growers in more fertile areas. Very few farmhouse brewers grow their own grain any more, and home malting is also rare today. Classical farmhouse brewing, in the sense of the farmer brewing from his own grain, is now very rare. Which makes it harder to decide what counts as farmhouse brewing. The definition I have been using is whether the brewer makes a style of beer that is recognizably a farmhouse style, with similar methods, equipment, and mindset. Carlo, although a climate scientist by profession who buys nearly all his ingredients, is definitely

Figure 2.6. Ola H. Gjertveit and Martin O. Hovland brewing beer, probably around 1940. Hardanger, western Norway. Photo by Jon A. Bleie. Courtesy of Hardanger & Voss Museum.

a farmhouse brewer by this definition. Most of the commercial breweries who call themselves farmhouse breweries, or put "farmhouse ale" on their labels, would not be farmhouse breweries by this definition. Essentially, those are normal craft breweries that happen to be located on a farm, or use odd microorganisms in their beer. They have no connection with any ancient tradition of farmhouse brewing in their area.

Which raises the question of whether the brewers of *saison* in Belgium and *bière de garde* in France should be considered farmhouse breweries or not. It seems likely that both styles arose out of beers that were true farmhouse ales, but to what extent today's saisons and bière de gardes are like the original farmhouse ales is hard to say. Documentation of what the earlier beers were like has not surfaced yet, and until it does the question cannot really be answered with certainty. Most likely these beers are quite different today from the original farmhouse ales that they evolved from.

Brewing was so important to the farmers that it lived on far longer than anyone would have expected. As late as the 1950s, farmhouse brewing was still alive in England and Germany. It is still alive today in Scotland, Wales, Norway, Denmark, Sweden, Finland, Estonia, Latvia, Lithuania, Belarus, and Russia. More countries can probably be added to this list, although I have yet to find the evidence for it.

Pride in old brewing practices and a feeling of ancient traditions being carried on were not the only reasons to keep brewing—the flavor was also different from any beer you could buy. Together, these seem to have been the major reasons why this kind of brewing lingered on even after most of the rational reasons for doing so had disappeared.

By the 1990s, there was only a single traditional brewer remaining in the village of Balestrand, not far from Kaupanger in western Norway. He was diagnosed with cancer, and, realizing he did not have much longer, he announced to the village that he would teach brewing to anyone who wanted to learn, so that the tradition could live on. A single person volunteered, but she was a woman. In western Norway, there had long been a strict ban on women in the brewhouse due to superstition. It was believed that a female brewer would inevitably lead to sour beer, therefore, brewing was exclusively done by men.* The old man refused to teach her, and she had to return home disappointed.

By the next day, however, the old man had changed his mind. He realized that either he had to teach a woman or the tradition would die out forever. In the end, the two of them brewed together twice—the second time the old man was so weak he could no longer stir the mash, which gives some sense of how important he thought it was. The old man died not long after their second brewing session.

The woman still lives in Balestrand, and still brews in the traditional way.[17] Which is fortunate, because once the tradition dies it cannot really come back. A tradition that is documented can be recreated, but it will never be the same as the living tradition.

But if farmhouse brewing has been so widespread, and survives in so many places, why is so little known about it? One possible reason is that the beer was not commercial, so it was hard to find. Another possible reason was that this form of brewing was regarded as old-fashioned, strange, and connected with the shameful poverty of the old days. Several brewers have told me how their own family members refused to teach them brewing, seemingly embarrassed by it.[18] In many places, the people brewing today learned the craft from their grandparents, because their parents did not bother to learn farmhouse brewing, having never appreciated the tradition.

---

* This is well documented. See "Brewers or Brewsters" in chapter 6, p. 187.

Until the 2000s most people regarded any beer other than pale lager with deep suspicion, and farmhouse ale is very, very different from modern beer. It can shock even seasoned craft beer drinkers. So, it is not very surprising that these dinosaurs of the brewing world were misunderstood. For most people in the provinces, what came from the cities and from the major countries was what was fashionable. Farmhouse brewing was seen as something strange that old men out in the sticks were doing in their cellars.

There has been commercial production of farmhouse ale. Once farmhouse brewing began to decline, there was a market for the beer among the people who had a taste for the beer but no longer brewed it themselves. Many brewers failed to resist the temptation to sell illegally. This process began long ago. In 1886, there were old women selling strong and weak farmhouse ale to passing travellers along the road to Kalmar.[19] There are many more examples.

Today, some farmhouse brewers have gone professional and set up licensed breweries, but only a few of these beers are available outside the brewery's own immediate region. In Norway and Lithuania there are a couple of modern breweries that use techniques and flavors inspired by traditional brewers. Very, very slowly these approaches seem to be spreading. So it is possible that farmhouse brewing is about to experience a revival after two centuries of continuous decline.

3

MALT

Farmhouse brewers did not just brew with their own grain. Overwhelmingly, they also malted it themselves. And because these farmers were malting on a far smaller scale than modern commercial malthouses, they used completely different methods. The result was malt with flavors that none of today's commercial malts have. In technical terms, the quality of this malt was lower, in the sense that it yielded less sugar per kilogram. But in terms of flavor it is not clear that it was inferior at all, indeed, far from it.

The farmhouse ale festival in Hornindal, western Norway, in 2017 brought this home to me. Some 30 traditional farmhouse ales were entered in the brewing contest, of which five were chosen as finalists by professional judges, working blind. Only four out of those 30 entrants were made with farmhouse malt, and all four were among the finalists.

Malt is by far the most important ingredient in beer, and the malting methods used have a massive impact on the flavor of the beer. In my experience, farmhouse malt creates unique flavors that no other kind of beer has. This chapter will show how the farmers made, and continue to make, their malt.

Unfortunately, the descriptions of farmhouse malting are far from precise, and the grain varieties farmhouse maltsters worked with historically are largely gone or unknown. So an exact reconstruction of historical types of malt types is probably not feasible, but experience shows that the results of traditional malting methods are excellent even with modern grain. However, this uncertainty does mean that mapping historical descriptions of malting to modern malt bills is difficult to do with any real precision.

Stjørdal: Malt-Making Hotspot

Stjørdal is a farming community in central Norway, which is very different from the fjord country. The valleys are wide, with rich farmland flanked by small, wooded hills. The farms consist of large wooden houses around a central farmyard, exuding an air of respectable landed prosperity.

What is remarkable about Stjørdal is not just that it is home to what is probably the largest community of farmhouse brewers anywhere in Europe, but that they all make their own malt in the traditional way. Getting hold of the barley for malt is easy: many of them grow it themselves, or they buy it from a neighboring farmer.

Malt is made in a dedicated building, called a *såinnhus* in the local dialect, where *såinn* means the malt kiln itself. Building and maintaining a house like this is expensive and a lot of work, so most people find it difficult to justify since it is generally used only once a year. The local brewers have solved this by collective ownership, usually teaming up in groups of around 10 members who own and maintain a single building.

I visited Jørund Geving in Stjørdal while he was drying the malt in a small, red wooden house. The main room is quite cosy and welcoming, decorated on the inside with planks of dark, aged wood, plus some pictures and knickknacks. The building serves as both the brewery and as a place for the members to gather and drink beer. The other half of the building is occupied by the såinn,

Figure 3.1. Hegge farm in Stjørdal.

Figure 3.2. Jørund Geving standing behind the såinn, or malt kiln. The black rectangle on the lower right is the fireplace.

which fills the room, leaving just a little space to walk around it.

The green malt is spread out on top of wooden planks held in a wooden frame, raised to chest height on top of a concrete enclosure. Down on the floor is a small fireplace where alder wood is burned. And it must be alder wood specifically. The smoke and heat rise up through thousands of holes in the planks and through the malt itself, flavoring it powerfully with the aroma of alder smoke. Jørund himself was wreathed in smoke and steam as he turned the malt on top of the såinn.

The local style is known as *stjørdalsøl*, literally "beer from Stjørdal." These beers are powerfully smoky, much more so than German *rauchbier*, and brownish in color with a clear reddish hue. Alder smoke is highly distinctive, so the smoke flavor is clearly different from Scottish peat-smoked malt and German beech-smoked malt.

Figure 3.3. Jørund Geving drying malt.

Figure 3.4. Bottles of stjørdalsøl for a beer tasting out of the ordinary.

I had earlier made contact with local maltster and farmhouse brewer Roar Sandodden, and together with two friends I managed to get invited to taste a whole range of different stjørdalsøl. The three of us sat down at the table in his old farmhouse as Roar produced a strange collection of bottles. Two were proper glass bottles with nice, homemade labels. Most of the rest were plastic bottles with Post-it notes taped on, which bore the name of the brewer and some details about the ingredients. One was just a cola bottle with the name "Rimul" scribbled on the label with black marker pen.

The contents of the bottles were no less strange. Visually, they were much as expected. None of the beers had a proper head because of their very low carbonation. The color was a deep, dark, reddish-brown. Most of them were sweet, but some had a light acidity. And all were smoky, of course, but not in the same way as a rauchbier.

The first one had a massive aroma of barnyard, lingonberry, and campfire, with juniper notes and light acidity. It was good and interesting, but also a little rough and challenging. My notes on the second one: "Smoked toffee. Vast diacetyl. OMG. Ashy smoky vanilla fudge. Hugely interesting, but not very good." This was two and half years after the first brew with Carlo (chapter 1), and I had tasted many farmhouse ales since then, but these beers were still shocking, not just to me but to my friends as well.

The flavors were all over the map. Some were harsh and rustic, others clean and delicate, and one I described as "semi-clean in a bizarre way." Tasting notes for a beer just marked as "A": "Weird. Male sweat, smoke. Dryish sooty. I can't describe this. Extremely interesting. Roar says it's not untypical of stjørdalsøl. Lingering woody flavor. Faint acetone." Another set of notes for one that had a nice label of a red house: "Fruity phenolic lingonberry aroma, plus dung. Sweet fruity pine and smoke taste. Nice! Lovely. Does have notes of dung and barnyard, though."

Eventually, we were reduced to just shaking our heads in wonder. These beers were way beyond anything any of us outsiders had tried before. It got to the point where we had to admit that we did not really have the frame of reference necessary to say whether the beers were good or not. It was a bit like your first meeting with *lambic*—the beers were so different from everything else I had ever tasted in so many different ways that in the end it was just overwhelming.

The next morning, we were sitting at Roar's breakfast table trying to make sense of what had happened. In the end we agreed it had been like starting out all over again as a beer drinker, lost in a landscape where you do not know the landmarks and have to learn them all over again.

Although many of the beers we tried were quite extreme, not all stjørdalsøl was this way. One of the finalists at the 2017 festival in Hornindal was made by Håvard Beitland. He used no juniper, no hops, and fermented with lager yeast, because he wanted the malt alone to take center stage. Håvard's beer had a smooth, restrained alder smoke flavor with light toasty notes, fading out into a soft, velvety, soot-like smoke character. The light sweetness was delicately balanced by the smoke. The entire beer was a powerful demonstration of what a careful farmhouse maltster can do.

These experiences made it clear to me that the traditional malting methods have enormous potential for modern brewing. And although there was such enormous variety in the flavors that we were completely bewildered, all of these beers used malt that was made roughly the same way, on the same type of equipment, using only barley grown in this fairly small county. As you will see in this chapter, there has been vast variation in how malt was made in Europe, so even what we tasted in Stjørdal is just a tiny fraction of the full range that once existed.

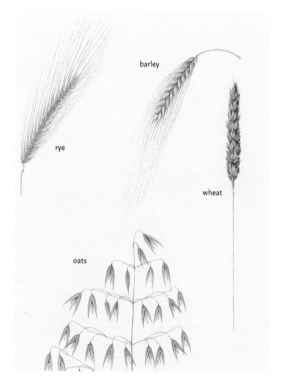

Figure 3.5. The four main types of grain in Europe. Oats can be recognized by their bell-like hulls, and wheat by their chubby, hairless appearance. Rye and barley are harder to distinguish, but rye generally has smaller grains.

Grain Types in Farmhouse Brewing

All of the four main European grain types— barley, oats, rye, and wheat—have historically been used in farmhouse brewing. By far the most common grain used was barley, because in most places it was considered to produce the best beer. The reasons were probably the same reasons modern brewers have for preferring barley today: it provides more sugar than other types of grain, tastes better, and has less protein.

Table 3.1 Accounts by Country that Mention Grain Type Used for Farmhouse Malting

	No. of accounts	Percentage of accounts mentioning specific grain type				
		barley	rye	oats	wheat	brome
Norway	221	99%	2%	19%	0%	0%
Sweden	202	97%	51%	24%	1%	0%
Denmark	108	100%	2%	2%	0%	0%
Finland	54	67%	81%	2%	0%	0%
Estonia	49	98%	33%	2%	6%	0%
Russia	11	18%	100%	9%	0%	0%
Lithuania	9	100%	11%	11%	22%	11%
Latvia	8	100%	0%	0%	0%	0%
Germany	6	100%	0%	0%	0%	0%
UK	5	100%	0%	0%	0%	0%
Belarus	2	100%	0%	0%	0%	0%
Austria	2	100%	0%	100%	50%	0%
Georgia	1	100%	0%	0%	0%	0%
Total	678	642	182	98	9	1
Percent total	100%	95%	27%	14%	1%	0%

Sources: See "The Database" section on p. 372 for explanation of sources.
Note: A single source may mention more than one grain type, so percentages will add up to more than 100%.

Barley is the most adaptable grain, and today it is grown in a large range of climates. It is especially good at tolerating dry and poor soils and the harsh northern climate. This hardiness is the reason barley was the main grain used for malting in northwestern Europe.

Just because the brewer preferred barley malt did not mean the beer would necessarily be brewed from it. Grain was the main source of food and wealth, so farmers had to grow the type of grain that would grow best in the local soil and climate. The farm might not produce enough barley to allow the beer to be made from only barley, or soil and weather conditions might result in low-quality barley. In these cases, the farmers had no choice but to malt what they had.

The Norwegian west coast had summers that were too cool and humid for barley, and so oats were the main grain there. Farmers may have set aside a small patch to grow barley for malting, or traded for the barley; or they may have brewed from oats alone, but oat was not considered a good grain for malting. "It's just oat beer," people said. Deeper inside the fjords the mountains kept the humid ocean wind out, and here farmers did grow barley.[1] The areas of western Norway where farmhouse brewing survives today are nearly all outside the oat belt.

Rye is the least demanding of the grains mentioned and will grow in soil where no other grain will grow. Perhaps the most extreme example is from the island of Fårö in Sweden, just off the northern tip of Gotland:

There are large parts of Fårö . . . where one wonders, when seeing the
stony fields, how in the name of all reason these fields, where a grain
of earth seems as rare as a diamond, can really produce any harvest.
One sees absolutely nothing but stone on stone. . . . But still rye grows
there. How is this possible? Well, on top of the stone cover is spread a
thick layer of kelp, which is allowed to rot, and always there is under
the stone layer some little earth. The fat from the kelp together with
the humidity that penetrates makes the grain grow in this earth.
(Salomonsson 1979, 34)

In Norway, rye was used high in the mountain valleys and on marginal land, but further east, in
parts of Sweden and Estonia, and even more so in Finland and the northern parts of Russia, rye was
the main grain. The reason was that the soil was usually not very good. In eastern Finland the Finns
were forced to use slash-and-burn methods to grow grain. In these areas, it was very common to brew
with either a mix of rye and barley or rye alone. In Sweden, Finland, and Lithuania, many brewers
considered that a little rye was good for the flavor and made the beer sweeter. Some even thought that
rye produced better beer than barley, or at least better than the barley they were able to grow.

Further south, in Denmark, England, the Baltic states, Poland, and Germany, the climate and soil
were more favourable, so farmers had enough barley for brewing. Even there the poor might use rye
or oats, but only rarely.

In Scandinavia and England, many farmers grew what the Norwegians and Danes called *bland-
korn*, which was a mix of oats and barley, known as *dredge* in English. This mix increased the
chances of a good harvest regardless of the weather. If the summer was cool and humid the oats
would dominate, but if it was hot and dry the barley would grow best. The farmers, however, were
not always aware that they were sowing a mix, and so a farmer might say that "the soil on this farm
was so excellent that the oats turned into barley." The grain did not change species, of course, but
the good soil made the barley win out over the oats, to the amazement of the farmer who thought
he had sowed oats.[2] The farmers not only wanted to sow what would give the biggest harvest, but
also had to guard against bad years. It was no good having a bumper crop in good years if three bad
years in a row would reduce the family to starvation.

Many have wondered why there has been so little mention of wheat in farmhouse brewing. The
reason is that wheat is a rather demanding grain. It needs a long growing season, plenty of sun,
and plenty of fertilizer, so it did not historically grow well in the north. Until about 1900, very little
wheat was grown in northern Europe. In Sweden, the harvest of wheat was next to nothing until the
eighteenth century, and even after that wheat made up only a very small part of the grain cultivated.
In nineteenth-century Sweden, wheat was often known as "regret grain" because the farmer would
often harvest less grain than he had sowed.[3]

So, it is not really surprising that very few sources mention even the possibility of malting
wheat. A very rare mention of wheat, from Småland in southern Sweden, says, "In my home
parish no more than two farmers grew wheat. One of them malted wheat once. The malt was
good, but too expensive."[4]

Out of 588 accounts of malted grain from Norway, Sweden, Denmark, and Finland, only two
mention the use of wheat, both from Sweden (table 3.1). Further south, in the rich grain country of

north Lithuania, Aldona Udriene told me: "Wheat beer? That was for rich people, like priests."

Due to its scarcity in northern Europe, and because barley and oats do not contain enough gluten to make leavened bread, wheat was very highly prized for baking bread. Even then, leavened bread was very rare into the twentieth century, something you might eat for Christmas, if you were lucky. It was only with the introduction of modern farming methods and grain breeding that it became possible to produce large amounts of wheat in northern Europe.

In summary, Europe can be divided into three major historic grain areas.[5] In the north, people grew mostly barley and oats, and therefore ate unleavened bread, such as the Nordic flatbread or the Scottish bannock. This area covered the British Isles, Norway, western Sweden, and the western parts of Finland. In the east, the main bread grain was rye, and the main bread was leavened or sourdough rye bread. Germany, Denmark, Poland, the Baltic states, Russia, eastern Sweden, and eastern Finland were all part of this area. This is also why rye bread is so common today in these countries. In the west and south, people grew wheat and only the poor grew rye. The wheat area lies around the Mediterranean, France, and also the westernmost parts of Germany.

The area for wheat growing started spreading in the eighteenth century, and today wheat is even grown as far north as Norway, although in Norway it is still difficult to produce good bread-quality wheat.

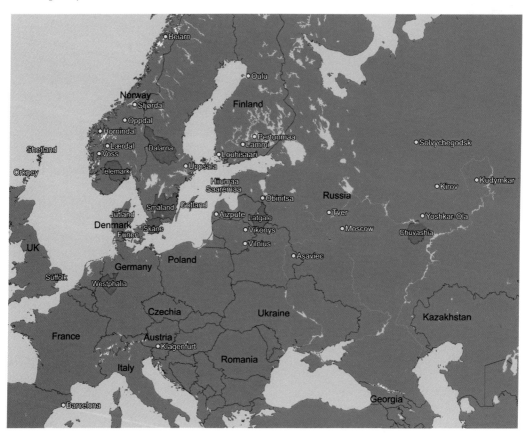

Figure 3.6. Map of European geographical regions and locations mentioned in the book.

More marginal types of grain have also been used, but very rarely. Millet was sometimes malted by the Chuvashians in Russia.[6] In Latvia, buckwheat was malted but only rarely.[7] Strangely, in the village of Salamiestis in Lithuania, the main part of the malt for the keptinis (lit. "baked beer") was from brome (L. bromus), a weed that was sometimes grown for fodder.[8] The reason seems to have been poverty. This part of Lithuania has poorer soil, and the keptinis malt was made from brome and low-quality barley taken from the corners of the fields.[*]

Barley Varieties

Barley can be either two-row, where the grains grow in pairs along the ear, or six-row, where there are six grains around the ear. Two-row produces bigger grains, since the grains have more room to grow. In Scandinavia, six-row barley dominated completely until the end of the Middle Ages, and even in the nineteenth century six-row was still the most common type of grain.

There is also four-row barley, but this is actually a variation on six-row barley where the grains are more loosely arranged. Because of this, many classify it as six-row barley. Four-row barley is relatively rare.

Some barleys are called hull-less or "naked," which means that the hull easily falls off after harvesting. There is also winter barley, which is sown in the autumn and spends winter in the ground before it sprouts in spring. The benefit of overwintering in the ground is that the growing season becomes longer, which means the grain can grow larger. The downside is that if the winter is too severe it can kill the grain. In the north, where the winters are harsh, spring barley is the most common. Both two-row and six-row barleys can be naked or require wintering.

Figure 3.7. Barley, both two-row (A) and six-row (B). (Otto Wilhelm Thomé, *Flora von Deutschland, Österreich und der Schweiz*, 4 vols., [Gera, 1885].)

The farmers of Scandinavia and the Baltic states generally preferred six-row barley for their malt, but some preferred two-row. The reasons given for the preference varied. Some preferred six-row because it sprouted faster, while others preferred two-row because the kernels were larger. Many brewers were vocal about the importance of large kernels in their malting grain. Others again thought six-row was best because the kernel sizes were more even.

Six-row was the old type of grain, and two-row a relative newcomer. Those who preferred six-row for malting may have done so out of conservatism, rather than because of any superiority in

[*] Simonas Gutautas (pers. comm.), based on Petrulis's hand-written notes in the Lithuanian National Library.

49

Table 3.2 Archival Accounts by Country that Mention Preferred Barley Types

	No. of accounts	Percentage of accounts that mention barley type		
		six-row	two-row	four-row
Sweden	26	69%	35%	0%
Denmark	12	75%	33%	0%
Lithuania	5	100%	0%	0%
Norway	3	67%	33%	0%
Finland	3	67%	33%	0%
Belarus	1	100%	0%	100%
Total	50	37	15	1
Percent	100%	74%	30%	2%

Sources: See "The Database" section on p. 372 for explanation of sources.
Notes: A single source may mention more than one grain type, so percentages will add up to more than 100%. At 50 total accounts, the data set is relatively small.

the six-row grain. The smaller grains in six-row barley mean that a given volume of grain will have a larger proportion of hulls and husks, so it produces less sugar per kilogram of grain. In Asarum, Sweden, they had a saying: "Six-row yields much in the sack but little in the drink. And two-row yields less in the sack but makes strong drink!"[9]

Today, farmers grow named varieties of grain, like Maris Otter. These varieties have been deliberately selected and bred by research institutes in search of optimal grain varieties. What the farmer sows today is seed grain where every grain is genetically identical to the others, but this is a modern and surprisingly recent phenomenon. Systematic breeding of grain and other plants only began in the last half of the nineteenth century. Originally, farmers took the seed grain from their own harvest, setting aside part of the harvest to sow again next spring. This grain had been grown in the same area for more generations than anyone could count. In fact, it might well descend from the grain grown in the same place in the late Stone Age. It was exquisitely adapted to the soil and climate in the specific place it was grown, which is why these grain varieties are known as landrace varieties, that is, varieties adapted to the land in a particular region.

In the highlands and islands of Scotland, farmers used the local landrace barley known as *bere*, an ancient six-row variety that is especially adapted to the Scottish climate and soil and grows very quickly. It is still grown in Orkney, where it is sometimes called "the 90-day barley" because of its extreme growth rate.* Farmhouse brewers on Orkney still make malt from bere, using it to brew the local farmhouse ale they call "corn ale."[10]

There are reports from Norway of communities that, because of disease or disastrous harvests, were forced to import seed grain from a different area and then found that it did not grow well in its new location. This was because the imported landrace was adapted to its area of origin, not to its new environment. It could take a long time for the imported seed grain to adapt to the new conditions.[11]

---

* Extreme in a British context. Norwegian landraces grow at about the same pace.

Figure 3.8. This black emmer wheat landrace from Gotland looks more like black barley than wheat. It was not unusual for landraces to have black coloring. Photo courtesy of Riina Noodapera.

Because landrace grains were never systematically bred, the farmer was sowing grains that were not genetically identical. This was, in fact, evident by the plants themselves, which grew to different heights and were visibly different from one another. The visible variation in landraces was enormous. Some were black, others yellow; some might have featherlike brushes sticking out of the hull, while others had none; and some varieties had no hulls at all.

The grains belonging to one landrace were also of different sizes, even when grown in the same field, which is why farmers carefully sorted them. The biggest grains were chosen as seed grain and for malting. By doing this, farmers were actively breeding the plants to produce bigger and more nutritious grain, and the results were quite striking. The original, wild plants that our modern grains descend from still grow wild in southeastern Turkey, but they produce much less grain than modern grain varieties. The wild grains also do not grow in anything like the variety of climates and soils that modern varieties do today.

In the nineteenth century, modern-minded landowners in Germany, France, and the UK started choosing grain more systematically. They selected promising plants from their fields and grew these separately. Those that were especially promising were given names, grown in large volumes, and subsequently spread far from the original farm. One example is the British barley Chevallier, which was grown in many countries in Europe.

The next step, which began in the late nineteenth century, was not just systematic selection of promising plants, but also systematic crossbreeding of different plants with each other to produce new candidates. The best of these were selected, bred with each other, and the process repeated.

Figure 3.9. Grain breeding at the Svalöf research station in Sweden. Photo by Bertil Wreting. Courtesy of the Nordic Museum.

Figure 3.10. Rye being harvested in Gustafsberg, Sweden, 1891. Note how tall the rye was. Photo by Per Gustaf Bergin, Bohusläns Museum.

This method was pioneered and made popular by the Swedish research station at Svalöf, founded in 1888. The varieties produced using these systematic methods were pure, that is, the plants within a single named variety were genetically identical, or at least nearly identical. This was slow and painstaking work. In Norway, systematic plant breeding began in 1905, but the first pure barley variety was not launched until 1916.

The landrace barleys, and also the first named varieties, were much taller than today's barley. The reason was that the grain needed to grow taller than the weeds, to beat them in the competition for sunlight. Growing this tall took energy that then was not available for the grain itself. The long, thin stalks were also vulnerable to being flattened to the ground by heavy wind or rain late in the season, which could cause the grain to be lost. In modern farming, pesticides prevent weeds from growing, and so modern barley does not need to be as tall. This is one of the reasons, together with artificial fertilizer and the effects of systematic breeding, that modern varieties can produce much larger yields.

What effect the transition from landraces to purebred varieties had on the flavor of beer nobody can really know today. In the eighteenth century, several Swedish authors claimed that hull-less barley produced the best beer. Landrace grains are still grown in eastern Finland, and farmers there say they prefer these varieties because they make particularly good bread.[12]

Maskin: Portrait of a Barley Variety

In southeast Norway, and stretching far into Sweden, are enormous tracts of forest with very low population density. They are called Finnskogene (lit. "the Finn forests") because large numbers of Finns settled there in the sixteenth century. The soil was not really suitable for growing grain using the usual methods, but the Finns practiced slash-and-burn agriculture as they had done in Finland and were able to grow rye and a little barley.

Researchers at the agricultural research station at Vang, Norway collected some landrace barley grains from the Bjørneby farm, near Solør in the Norwegian Finnskogen. Very likely the Finns had brought this landrace with them to Norway from Finland, because DNA analyses show that it is related to Finnish varieties. The barley grains performed very well in tests at the station, and a purebred variety was eventually developed from it. Because this first pure barley variety was, in its way, an icon of modernity, it was given the name *Maskin*, which in Norwegian means "machine" (pronounced "masheen").

In developing Maskin, the researchers had focused on the agricultural properties of the grain, but Maskin turned out to have another trick up its sleeve. Because the Finns' methods burned away all plant cover, the soil was bare in early spring when they sowed their grain. That made it hot in the sun, and so the grain needed to have enzymes that could tolerate high temperatures.[13] This heat tolerance made Maskin an ideal grain for malting and brewing, and it came to be dearly loved by farmhouse brewers all over Norway. In Stjørdal, many farmers still remember it with mixed feelings. Maskin produced excellent malt, like no other Norwegian variety, but it also had a flaw. One reason Maskin was such an excellent malting grain was its willingness to sprout, but it was so eager to do this that in wet weather it could start sprouting in the field before it was even harvested, which made the grain unusable.

Maskin had another flaw, too: once it was ripe, the grains could easily fall off the ear in a gust of wind, which would cause the harvest to be lost. So, when the grain ripened, it had to be harvested immediately. This worked fine until, ironically, machines were introduced. The first combine harvesters came to Stjørdal in the 1950s, at which point the farmers no longer needed large numbers of workers during the harvest. But, in these early years of mechanization, many farmers had to share a single combine harvester. This meant that one farmer's grain could ripen while another was using the harvester—if this happened, the irate farmer would see his entire harvest blown off the ear while he waited for the harvester. So, Maskin had to go. In Stjørdal, Maskin was replaced by other barley varieties in 1964, at least officially.

Another barley variety, Domen, was developed from Maskin, and this newer variety kept the excellent malting characteristics of Maskin. Somehow, Domen was exported to North America. Canadians quickly discovered how suitable it was for malting, so Domen became widely grown. The Canadians developed the variety Klages from Domen, and then Harrington from Klages. Into the 1990s, Harrington was the Canadian "gold standard" for malting barleys.

It turns out that some of the farmers in Stjørdal so love Maskin that, even though Maskin seed grain is not sold anymore, they still grow it.[14] They grow commercial barley varieties for their commercial output, but set aside a small field to grow Maskin for their own malt. By keeping some of the harvest as seed grain, these farmers have managed to keep the variety alive. Ironically, that means they are slowly turning Norway's first pure barley variety back into a landrace.

How the Grain Was Grown

Modern-day farmers use artificial fertilizer, but in the old days the fields were fertilized with manure from the farm animals. This meant that there was a close relationship between the size of the grain fields and how many animals the farm had, which in turn depended on how much pasturage the farm had. The farmer had to balance how much land to set aside for pasturage against how much was left for grain. In practice, there was never quite enough manure.[15] This was one reason why in many countries it was common to have a separate area of summer pasturage far away from the farm, often in areas too high in the mountains for growing grain.

Each field was not necessarily planted each year but instead might lie fallow for some years. Different regions had different systems for how often a field lay fallow, and this again was related to the amount of manure available, the type of grain grown, and the soil itself.

Once the fields were fertilized, the next step was to plough. In the north, this had to wait until the snow was melted and the frost was out of the ground. Plowing loosened the soil so the sowed grains could get deeper into it. Turning the soil buried the weeds, and also brought nutrients up from deeper layers. In the west, and in more affluent areas, this was usually done with the plow, but in the east and in more marginal areas it might be done with an ard, an older and more primitive instrument that did not turn the soil.

In many places, on smaller farms, the soil was turned by hand using shovels. For people who owned no horses this was a sensible solution, even if it was hard work. Shoveling the soil by hand went on in Norway at least into the 1950s. Partly, the reason was that people were cultivating fields too steep for any tractor or horse, but it may have also been out of sheer conservatism.

One spring morning in the 1850s, the story goes, three workers in western Norway were shoveling the fields. One of the hired hands thought this was ridiculous when two grown horses were walking free in the pasture nearby. He told the widow who owned the farm that he was not going to shovel anymore, but would take one of the horses and plow the field. The widow looked him gravely in the eyes and said: "Now you must ask God to preserve you and not speak thus. This field is going to be shoveled." The fields were literally what sustained life, and not a place to introduce innovations lightly.[16]

After plowing, a harrow was dragged over the fields to break up the lumps of earth and loosen the soil further; it also tore up the roots of any weeds. Those who shoveled the soil did not need to do this, as they would have already hacked up the lumps and torn up the weeds during the shoveling.

Once all this work was done, it was time to sow the field. Sowing was a significant moment. The sower should be bare-headed and started by declaring, "In the name of Christ." The seed grain was thrown out by hand and it was crucial to cover every part of the field, and cover it evenly. If the grains fell too far apart, the grain would grow thinly and the harvest would fall short. If they fell too closely together, the plants would end up competing and much of the seed grain would end up yielding little and reducing the potential harvest. Other workers followed the sower to turn the soil with rakes and spread fertilizer on top.

All this was terribly hard work, especially on farms where they had no animals to help out. Even so, this was just the beginning.

Once the grain was sowed, the farmers mostly turned to other work while the grain grew. The next major bout of fieldwork was the haymaking in late summer, then, in the autumn, the grain was harvested. The grain was cut with either a scythe or a sickle, and this was heavy work, often in uncomfortably cold and wet weather.

When the grain had been cut it was tied up on a pole in the field or stacked into what was known as a shock. The stack had to be very carefully constructed so that vermin were kept out, the rain ran off, and the grain dried. Landrace grain often ripened unevenly in the field while still in the ground, so a benefit of the shock system was that grain that was still green could mature in the shock before it was collected.

Now came the hardest job of all: threshing. In older times, threshing was done by literally beating the grains loose with a flail made from two pieces of wood connected with a rope. This was back-breaking work and could take all winter to finish. On winter mornings, the villages would often echo with the rhythmic sound of beating flails from every farm.

Then came the sorting. In Norway and Sweden this was done by sweeping the barn floor clean and then sitting on a low stool next to the pile of grain. You would take a small shovel and use it

Figure 3.11. Workers shoveling the fields in spring. The woman on the right is not shoveling: she is using a digging fork to break up the lumps of earth. Haus, Osterøy, western Norway. Photo by Hilmar Stigum.

Figure 3.12. Harrowing in Skåne, southern Sweden, 1909. Courtesy of the Nordic Museum.

to throw the grains over your back. For this to work effectively, the thrower had to take an equal amount of grain each time and throw it equally hard each time. This was a skill that took time to learn. The job could be quite exhausting, and the story is told of the man who went in for dinner after a long session of grain throwing. So ingrained was the throwing habit that the first spoonful of porridge was flung over his shoulder and onto the wall.[17]

The effect of the throwing was to separate the grain from the chaff. Dust, chaff, and other impurities fell to the ground behind the thrower's back. The poorer grain landed first; the heavier the grain, the further it flew. The best grain hit the wall and formed a neat row there, known in Norwegian as *veggeranda* (lit. "the wall row"). The seed grain and the malt grain were taken from the wall row.

In Hornindal, I met Rasmus Kjøs, a sprightly 85-year-old farmer who still brewed his own beer. His mother taught him brewing at the age of 14, during World War II when Norway was occupied by Nazi Germany. I asked him if he had ever malted his own grain, and he said that, yes, during the war they malted their own grain. "But we brewed from the light grain then," he added. This was the poor grain that did not make it to the wall.

"Why did you do that," I asked, stupidly.

"We couldn't afford anything else," said Rasmus quietly. Then I realized what he meant. The war was a time of hardship, when people were literally on the edge of starvation, so making beer from the best grain was out of the question.

With sorting done, the work was still not finished. In northern Europe, the grain that was to be ground to flour had to be dried first. (In France, Spain, and around the Mediterranean, drying the grain was not necessary because of the drier climate and longer season.) The drying was usually done with the same equipment that was used to dry the malt, which is described later in this chapter.

Given how much work went into growing the grain, you may wonder how people could possibly get more calories out of the grain than went into producing it, but the fact is they did. Growing grain was literally how people made their living. It has been estimated that in Sweden the farmers got 70%–90% of their calories from grain.[18]

All the work required to grow grain and then malt it is also the explanation for why everyone who could make wine did so instead of brewing beer. Wine making requires nothing more than picking the grapes and pressing them, and the result is as strong as the strongest beer. Of course those who could would prefer to make wine.

Steeping and Sprouting

Malting makes the grain start creating enzymes to turn its energy reserves, in the form of starch, into sugar that it can use to grow when planted in the ground. To start the process, the grain needs to be soaked in water and left to start sprouting.

In Norway, there was a rule of thumb that said "three days in the brook, three days in the sack." That is, you took a sack of grain and simply threw it into a running brook, or creek, then left it there for three days. Because the water kept running naturally through the sack, the grain had access to oxygen and there was no need to change the water. The running water also carried away dust and dirt. However, the grain would swell up quite a lot, so the sack could only be half full.

The other way to soak the grain was to use a watertight container of some sort. This could be, for example, a round tun-like brewing vessel. The grain was poured in and then water added on top. This method had the benefit that impurities and poor grain floated to the surface and could be removed. The downside was that the water had to be changed a few times a day.

The next step was to let the water run off. This could be done by simply leaving the grain in sacks somewhere for a couple of days, allowing the water to slowly run off. If the sacks were somewhere warm, the sprouting might begin right then and there, with the rootlets coming out through the fabric of the bag.

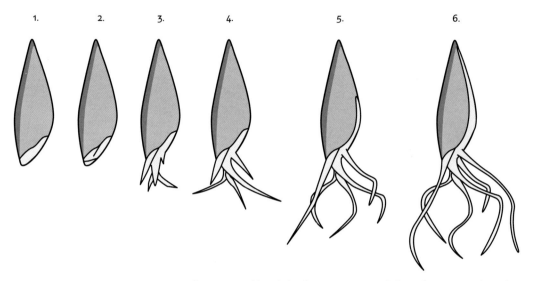

Figure 3.13. Stages of germination. Note the acrospire (shoot) slowly creeping upward along the grain on the right-hand side. The grain was usually dried when it reached stage 5.

Finally, the grain had to sprout, and this needed to happen somewhere that was not too cold. Many farmers had a wooden frame for this, onto which the grain was spread out in a layer about 10 to 15 centimeters deep. The grain grew hot to the touch and sprouted for real. During this germination stage, the shoot comes up along the side of the grain and multiple rootlets come out from the grain's base. The farmers knew that the grain grew hottest in the middle of the layer and would therefore grow faster there. To ensure germination was more even, many turned the grain once or twice a day. Regular turning also had the benefit of preventing the rootlets from matting the grain together in one thick mass.

In some areas, the practice was to actually allow the grains to mat together. Ågot Skrindo, from Ål in Norway, told me the rule there was that the grains should mat together like a cake, so that you could carry the whole mass on your back. As with all farmhouse lore, no reason was given.

The usual way to tell if the malt had finished sprouting was by looking at the length of the shoot inside the grain. The rules of thumb people used varied from place to place, but usually the sprouting was stopped if the shoot was two-thirds or three-quarters of the length of the grain, or if it was as long as the grain itself.

Not everyone followed the process described above. Some put the grains in heaps, watered them for a week, and then dried the malt. There were many other variations. Whether these variations affected the flavor, I really have no idea. Maybe people had to use different methods because their grain was different. It is difficult to know for sure, and hard to research, because so few people make their own malt today.

About half the maltsters removed the rootlets before brewing. Some accounts say the rootlets fell off during drying, while others say they needed to be rubbed off by hand. Rubbing was easy work, so it was often given to the children. Aldona Udriene, of Jovarai in Lithuania, told me during a 2015 interview that she started doing this at the age of four; she could remember her hands getting sticky from the malt. In places where they used a lot of malt, the entire family might join in the work.

In Stjørdal today, most of the maltsters have a wooden frame with steel netting in it, and they remove the rootlets by rubbing the malt against this netting. Malt cleaning machines have been built locally using the transmissions from old washing machines, which turn a cylinder of steel netting. With this machine you simply put the malt into the cylinder, let it turn for a while, and take out clean malt.[19]

Morten Granås from Stjørdal showed me a bag of rootlets removed after the malt had dried, and the bag smelled like a tobacco pouch. Many locals claim that beer brewed with the rootlets still on the malt is intensely smoky and has a disagreeable creosote flavor. If the malt is not smoked this may matter less, but there are accounts claiming that the rootlets cause beer to be murky.[20]

During germination and drying the maltster was always on the lookout for visible signs of mold. If anything like mold was spotted, the malt was usually thrown away because drinking beer made from it could be dangerous.

Malt Drying Methods

The moment sprouting is finished, the grains need to be dried to stop them from using up the sugar they are beginning to make. Wet malt is also highly prone to mold and infection, which is another reason it has to be dried. Wet malt is also very difficult to mill.

Today's brewers design a malt bill for the beer they want to make, but for farmhouse brewers that was a foreign concept. The farmer had one method for making malt, and that was how the malt was made. Generally, making another type of malt would have required either buying malt, which was expensive, or changing the equipment. It might even have required making changes to the building where drying took place or constructing a new one. One type of malt was in any case enough because malt made by traditional methods, with little temperature control, has much more complex flavors than commercial malt.

The method used for drying malt varied by geographical area, but even people in the same village did not always dry their malt the same way. A rich farmer made lots of malt, while a poor tenant farmer had very little.* So, while the rich farmer might need a large two-story building to dry his malt, the tenant farmer was able to dry his small batch in an iron pot.

---

* A tenant farmer rented a small plot of land from a landlord, typically a rich farmer. The tenant would usually pay his rent by performing work for the landlord. In *Täällä Pohjantähden alla* (Eng. *Under the North Star*), Finnish novelist Väinö Linna called the moon "the tenant farmer's sun," because after harvesting the landlord's grain by day, the tenant would harvest his own grain by the light of the moon. It is also, of course, a metaphor for poverty.

One thing that comes across very clearly in reading about farmhouse malt drying is that the only thing you really need to do is to get the moisture out of the malt. How you do it is, of course, going to affect the flavor; but, in the end, as long as you are fast enough to prevent mold and slow enough not to destroy the enzymes, it will work.

In general, farmhouse malt seems to have ranged in color from very pale to some level of brown, even darkish brown. Producing dark malt was harder, since malt tended to darken very quickly at the end of the process. Without thermometers this would have been difficult to control precisely, and managing temperatures accurately using a wood fire would in any case have been difficult. Specialty malts also have poorer yields. Thus, the type of very dark malts that are produced in modern malting were just not available. I know of no farmhouse brewer using this type of malt today.

The danger of fire runs through all accounts of drying malt with fire. People were acutely aware of the dangers posed by an accidental fire, and so wooden malt kilns were always built outside the farmyard itself, well away from the other buildings. In Denmark, insurance laws explicitly took this risk into account, so malt kilns had higher insurance costs than other buildings.[21]

It is often said that historically all malt was smoked, because methods that do not smoke the malt are a modern invention. As this chapter will show, that is not true at all. It seems that in the nineteenth and twentieth centuries about two-thirds of farmhouse brewers were using heavily or lightly smoked malt, and one-third were not smoked at all. Several of the very old malting methods do not impart any smoke aroma, so unsmoked malt probably goes back to the very beginnings of beer brewing.

Table 3.3 Accounts by Country that Specify Specific Malt Drying Methods

	No. of accounts	Percentage of accounts that specify malt type				
		Smoky, high heat	Very smoky, high heat	Low heat, not smoked	Caramel	High, un-even heat
Norway	137	48%	23%	23%	1%	4%
Sweden	129	47%	31%	5%	25%	0%
Estonia	36	0%	0%	53%	47%	0%
Denmark	34	3%	68%	24%	6%	0%
Finland	12	75%	0%	25%	0%	0%
Lithuania	8	0%	0%	63%	38%	0%
Russia	5	0%	0%	40%	60%	0%
Germany	4	0%	0%	75%	25%	0%
Belarus	1	0%	0%	0%	100%	0%
Total	366	137	94	78	61	6
Percent	100%	37%	26%	21%	17%	2%

Sources: See "The Database" section on p. 372 for explanation of sources.
Note: In this data set, each account specifies only one drying method, so rows sum to 100%.

Low Heat, Not Smoked

Traditionally, many brewers dried their malt by heating it very, very gently and providing lots of ventilation. If the malt was spread out thinly this would be enough to dry it, producing a very pale, unsmoked malt. These malting methods are quite rare today, so I have tried very few beers made with this type of malt. That makes it hard to say much about the flavor.

Figure 3.14. Malt being dried in the sun in the village of Kaisvere on Saaremaa in Estonia, 1964. Photo by I. Kala, Estonian National Museum.

The simplest and easiest way to dry malt was to simply spread it out on a cloth or a wooden frame to dry in the sun. This method is so simple it is possible this was how the first malt was dried. From Voll, in western Norway:

> In the summer they dried the malt in the sun and the wind. They spread it out on a carpet, a sail, or old bedclothes. The layer of malt could not be thick and had to be even. Now and again they'd stir it with a rake. In the evening they'd fold the cloth up and take it indoors. The next day it had to be carried back out. The children were given the job of keeping the birds away so they didn't eat anything. It was an easy job, which the children liked. (NEG 9187)

Similar drying methods are known from several places in northern Europe, such as Estonia[22] and Lithuania.[23]

The practice of drying the malt in the sun in western Norway puzzled me, because once you start steeping the grain it takes about a week until you can start drying. The summer weather in western Norway is notoriously unreliable—how could they know the weather would be

Figure 3.15. Meelis Sepp's malthouse.

Figure 3.16. A malt drying shelf, or *turkehelle*, in this case with fireplace underneath. Usually the shelf was next to the main fireplace. Sandane Museum, Norway.

suitable so long in advance? I asked Rasmus Kjøs in Hornindal, and he just laughed. "If the weather was bad, we'd spread the malt out on the floor of the loft and heat the fireplace," he said. In other areas, the locals knew that certain months of the year, like May in Voss, the weather would be suitable.[24]

The malt from this method of drying would be very pale, rather like Pilsner malt. Indeed, the brewers in Hornindal nowadays mostly use a mix of 50% Pilsner malt and 50% pale malt. I asked Rasmus why they used 50% pale. Would that not make the beer darker than it was before? He laughed again, and said that, in the old days, they usually browned some of the malt in the oven.

In Estonia, people say a final drying in the oven after the sun-drying was necessary to ensure the malt was sufficiently dry.[25] When the malt was dry enough, the kernels were supposed to make a cracking noise when bitten. In Norway, some maltsters considered the malt dry when they could write on the wall with a kernel as though it were chalk.

Drying the malt on the floor of a heated room, like Rasmus, was also common, and the malt must have come out much the same as if sun-dried.

We visited Meelis Sepp on the island of Saaremaa in Estonia. Together with his neighbor, Jüri Mesila, Meelis makes his own malt from barley that he grows right next to his malthouse. They dry the malt by spreading it out on the upper floor of the building and heating it using an oven on the floor below, which has a flue channeling smoke under the floor to a chimney. This type of kiln was common on the islands of Hiiumaa and Saaremaa in Estonia. Meelis's beer was excellent: sweetish, with a light acidity, it had a rough dusty hay and straw flavor, with light earthy pea notes, and traces of fruit and gooseberry. While the flavor was very complex, the beer remained light and refreshing, and amazingly easy to drink. What color his beer was I cannot say, because Meelis brought it in a plastic bucket and served it in an enamel mug.

Meelis brews in much the same way as his neighbors on the island, but the flavor of his beer really stood out to us. We were convinced it was because Meelis was the only one we met who still used homemade malt. Other brewers' beers had a far less complex malt profile than his beer did.

In western Norway, a similar arrangement to Meelis's malthouse, but on a much smaller scale, was common. Next to the fireplace there would be a surface of stone or mortar, and the heat and smoke from the chimney entered a hollow space underneath it. The drying surface was much smaller than an entire floor because these farmers had far less grain to malt, but the effect must have been much the same. Some people claim this produced lightly smoked malt.[26]

Archaeological excavations in southwestern Norway in 1933 found a similar type of kiln, this one made from rounded stones, with a small fireplace underneath a big, flat stone. The finds were dated to the fifth century CE—on seeing them, the district veterinary exclaimed that similar malt kilns were still found on nearby farms.[27]

There were many more drying methods that gave similar results. In Norway, Denmark, and Latvia it was common to use a wooden frame with a bottom made of metal mesh or woven from straw or hair. This could be attached to the wall above the stove, allowing the malt to be dried in small batches inside the living room. In Denmark, it was very common to have a wood or metal drawer underneath or above the stove.[28] Probably both methods produced very pale unsmoked malt.

In Estonia, Lithuania, and Russia, it was common to dry malt on top of the great stove.[29] It is hard to know what the exact temperature was, of course, but since this was also a common place to sleep, it could not have been that hot. I have tasted beer made from malt dried this way, but it was rye malt, so the exact effect of the drying was difficult to determine.

Overall, very pale, unsmoked malt seems not to have been common in farmhouse brewing. These malts were used in northwestern Norway, northern Jutland in Denmark, on the southern tip of Sweden, on the Estonian islands, in Lithuania, and in the northern parts of Russia. But in most places, people seem to have dried the malt differently.

Lightly Smoked, High Heat

Figure 3.17. Gregar O. Nordbø has lit the malt kiln (badstu) at the farm of Nordbø, Telemark, in Norway, ca. 1915. Photo courtesy of Bø Museum.

Historically, one of the most common types of malt used by farmhouse brewers was relatively lightly smoked and dried at temperatures that would be hot compared to sun-drying. Exactly what "lightly" means varied, and even more so "hot." Precise information on temperatures is not available, but from experience and other information in the descriptions, I assume the color of the beer was between an amber and a brown ale. The drying temperature seems to have been so hot that people could only just bear to touch the malts, which probably means it was usually around 45–50°C.

There are limited data on what people burned to smoke the malt, but it is clear that the fuels chosen were far from random. Several factors determined their choices. For example, in Orkney and western Jutland there was little firewood, so people were forced to use peat.

The maltsters wanted wood that burned evenly without too many sparks to minimize the risk of fire. Consequently, wood from coniferous trees was not suitable. These trees have large channels for resin running inside the wood, which the heat causes to boil so that the wood bursts with loud bangs and showers of sparks. The only exception I am aware of is an account from Gotland in Sweden that mentions spruce.[30] The Gotland kilns had a long stone channel leading up to the wooden boards under the malt, which may be why maltsters there dared to use spruce.

Different types of fuel produce very different smoke flavors. German beech wood and Scottish

Table 3.4 Accounts by Country that Mention Fuel Type Used to Dry Malt

	No. of accounts	Percentage of accounts that mention fuel type					
		Alder	Birch	Juniper	Beech	Peat	Other
Sweden	47	34%	36%	36%	11%	4%	2%
Denmark	23	39%	0%	0%	52%	4%	22%
Norway	22	32%	59%	14%	0%	5%	18%
Finland	4	100%	25%	0%	0%	0%	0%
UK	1	0%	0%	0%	0%	100%	0%
Germany	1	0%	0%	0%	100%	0%	0%
Latvia	1	100%	0%	0%	0%	0%	0%
Total	99	37	31	20	18	5	10
Percent	100%	37%	31%	20%	18%	5%	10%

Sources: See "The Database" section on p. 372 for explanation of sources.
Note: A single source may mention more than one fuel type, so percentages may add up to more than 100%.

peat-smoked malts are obviously very different, and the alder wood-smoked malt of Stjørdal is again different. As table 3.4 shows, other types of fuel were also used. What is striking is that the exact same types of wood are still in use today for smoking meat and cheese in some of these areas. In Norway, sheep's head is smoked with alder, and smoking food with birch is very common. In Sweden and Denmark, you can buy sausages smoked with alder, juniper, birch, or beech.

Birch is very common in Norway, and is very commonly used for firewood because it produces a lot of heat. Since the smoke aroma from birch is not strong, it is a good choice when you do not want too much smoke aroma in the beer. Gunnar Skare, the only brewer I know of who smokes malts with birch today, deliberately uses very dry birch wood with white bark, and tends the fire very carefully to ensure there is as little smoke as possible.

Beech has long been a popular choice for smoking malt on the Continent, but it generally does not grow in Sweden and Norway north of a line a little south of Oslo and Stockholm. This is very likely why there are so few reports of it being used in those two countries. Beech produces a rather subdued and clean smoke aroma that reminds many people of bacon.

Alder was very likely chosen not only for the aroma and color that it gives, but also because it grows almost like a weed and is therefore readily available. Alder burns evenly and produces little soot. It also emits relatively little heat, which makes it easier to control the amount of heat and avoid fire. It also means alder was not as valuable as a fuel for other purposes. The Finns still use alder in their smoke saunas because it is easily available and makes little soot. The smoke aroma from alder is powerful, funky, and earthy, often with overtones of barnyard.

Juniper has very likely been used for the aroma it imparts, being a very aromatic wood. Because the trees have mostly small branches, juniper was not a natural choice as a fuel, which is probably why nobody used juniper as a fuel alone. It seems many of the maltsters who used juniper did so specifically for the smoke aroma, with the main heating supplied by another type of wood fuel.[*]

---

[*] EU 13115 and 18612 are good examples, but there are others.

Figure 3.18. A *badstu* (lit. "bath cottage") in Morgedal, Telemark, Norway. The building is sited well outside the farmyard for safety.

Figure 3.19. Inside view of badstu kiln. The stone oven is in the middle and surrounded by two sets of shelves that run around the walls. Aga, Hardanger, western Norway.

Peat is the fuel used to smoke whisky malts, and peat-smoked malts are also used in some modern beers. The aroma is soft and rounded, smooth and elegant, reminiscent of toffee.

In the material I have found, there is only a single mention of oak, but it is likely that oak use was not unusual in areas further south where there is more available. Like peat, oak also has a very elegant and round aroma profile, with deep, powdery tones.

The most common drying method in Norway and Sweden was the *badstu* (Norwegian), or *bastu* (Swedish). The term literally means "bath cottage," and until the end of the Middle Ages this was a building used the same way as the Finnish sauna. Astonished visitors to medieval Norway from elsewhere in Europe reported how the entire household would strip naked in the main house and then walk to the badstu, there to take baths together. Obviously, the church did not much approve of this, and the practice seems to have disappeared toward the end of the Middle Ages. But the houses were still there, and still used for smoking and drying meats, and drying linen, grain, and malt. Some Norwegian farms still have these houses, but very few still use them for drying malt.

Badstu construction is very simple: a small log cabin with logs interlocking at the corners and no windows, but small openings in the walls that could be closed with wooden blocks. In Sweden, they were often made from stone or brick. In the middle of the badstu was a rough fireplace of stone, but no chimney. Around the sides were one or two levels of deep shelves with raised wooden ledges so that the malt and grain would not fall off. The ledges usually had little openings that could be lifted up to make it easier to scoop the malt out. Often, the steeped grain was sprouted on these shelves too because the bath house could be heated in winter.

Drying began by spreading the green malt out on the shelves. Usually the fire had been started earlier so that the house was already warm. Normal practice was to have the room hotter in the beginning

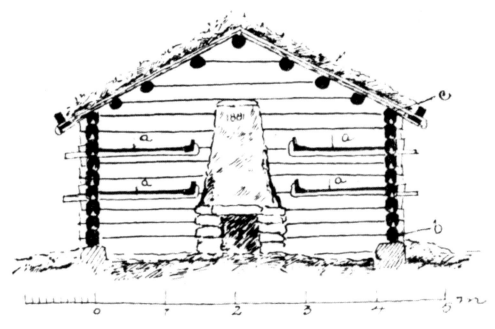

Figure 3.20. Drawing of a badstu from Ore in Dalarna, Sweden. Reproduced by permission from ULMA, the Institute for Language and Folklore, Uppsala, Sweden.

and then reduce the temperature as the malt began to dry. Many maltsters say that evaporation from the wet malt reduces the level of heat, but that later it can get too hot once the malt loses its moisture.

A Swedish maltster writes that "after the first day one couldn't heat so much, because one could get 'basta burned malt,' which had poor sweetness."[31] What he is describing is how heating the malt too much will destroy the enzymes in the malt, reducing efficiency later. In modern brewing this is not a problem, because brewers combine dark specialty malts with a paler base malt full of enzymes. But farmhouse brewers used only a single type of malt, so overheating had to be carefully avoided. Many would light the fire and let it burn itself out, then let the smoke escape by opening the holes in the walls. After some hours the temperature would have dropped a good bit, and so the fire would be lit again and the cycle repeat.

The temperature inside a badstu during drying varied dramatically from place to place. It was hot, of course, but exactly how hot varied. In many places, it clearly was not too hot, although going inside to check on the malt and stir it would have been unpleasant. As one respondent put it: "You would barely have time to go inside and stir the malt before you would fall out the door, ready for a heat stroke."[32] A villager from Rauland in Telemark, Norway said, "If it got so hot that the badstu burned down, but they were able to save the malt, they would have outstanding malt."[33] This implies that they really wanted to brown the malt as much as was safe. A few places specify it was always necessary to have two people stirring the malt. The second stayed outside, so that if the first person fainted, the second could drag them out by the ankles.[34] The person stirring the malt held his cap in his teeth, so the air was cooled a little before he breathed it in.

One respondent from Vislanda in Småland explained: "As long as the malt was in the bath house one of the family had to stay there at night, well shut and locked in, so that nobody would steal the malt. What risk to life and health it was to be locked in with the smoke and heat can easily be imagined."[35] Having someone stay with the malt at night was common in southern Sweden and Denmark, and this would usually be a young member of the household. A resident of Hov in Skåne described how "in the evenings the youths in the village would gather in the malt kiln to keep the maltster company. They sang songs, guessed riddles, and fried apples on the stone oven."[36] A different account describes a similar tradition in more detail:

> During the malt-drying we had the happiest times. Boys and girls gathered from all directions to keep the "lonely" maltster company. They sat on tree stumps, lay on straw and sacks, and talked and joked while they were served food and coffee. Every now and then one had to run outside when the smoke got overwhelming, to get some air and let the sweat in one's red eyes dissipate a little. Myself, I have many times in my boyhood sat for hours in the malt kiln and listened to the conversation, often with a certain tension when steps were heard outside or there was a knock on the door. One had no idea whether it was friend or foe coming, and many hot "battles" have been fought with outsiders who came to disturb the girl watching the malt. This girl should not be one who was easily frightened, and malt drying was so hard that, when she came home, she would usually go to bed and rest for a whole day. (LUF 11217, Önnarp, southern Sweden)

Figure 3.21. Classic Finnish sauna oven. Asikkala folk museum, Finland.

Sauna culture still lives on in Finland, the Baltic states, and Russia. In many parts of Finland, the sauna was also used to dry malt. Saunas of this kind consisted of a simple stone oven, wooden benches to sit on, and on one side a mezzanine where the green malt was laid to dry. It must have produced malt that was very similar to that dried in a badstu.

Further east, another method was used. In eastern Finland, parts of the Baltic states, Russia, Belarus, and Ukraine, the harvested grain was dried before it was threshed, that is, with the grain still on the stalk. This required a slightly different type of building that was taller than the badstu/sauna, with horizontal bars high up on which the straw was laid. This type of building was called a *ria* in Swedish or *riihi* in Finnish.[37] In eastern Finland, the riihi was used to dry malt by spreading straw over the bars and then the malt on top of that. In the Baltic states, where drying using a ria was less common, malt might instead be put into a box with holes in the bottom.[38]

Many people were not very fond of the smoke aroma from drying in a badstu. By the late nineteenth century, these malthouses were often modified by adding modern iron or steel ovens with chimneys to let the smoke out. This must have had the added benefit of making the drying process less uncomfortable, since those coming into the house to stir the malt would no longer have to deal with the smoke stinging their eyes and throats.

Those who did not want the flavor of smoke in their beer had another way of reducing it. By heating the house or kiln before the malt was in place, then allowing the smoke to escape, most of the smoke could be kept away from the malt. When the fire was lit later, the malt would be covered with thick cloth to keep the smoke away until it could be vented.[39]

Gunnar and Ivar Skare in Ørsta, western Norway, use a kiln rather like the såinn used in Stjørdal, but have installed a small funnel to let the smoke out. Gunnar says that the birch he uses for fuel mainly

Figure 3.22. Diagram of a ria in Gästrikland, Sweden. Reproduced by permission from Nordic Museum.

smokes when he is starting the fire, so he heat the kiln with no malt in it and lets the smoke out. Later he is careful to add more firewood before the fire burns down, to keep the new wood from smoking. This, together with using well-dried birch wood with white bark, keeps the smoke aroma at a minimum. Indeed, his beer has very little smoke aroma.

Heavily Smoked

Many of the traditional malt-drying methods produced heavily smoked malt similar to German rauchbier, although in many cases even more heavily smoked. The main survivor of this type of beer today is in Stjørdal, Norway, but *gotlandsdricke* is also made with this type of malt. In Latgale in eastern Latvia, a similar type of beer is still being made.

Many different kinds of malt kilns produced heavily smoked malt. One example is the såinn, the type of malt kiln that is used in Stjørdalen today. They were also used elsewhere in Scandinavia in the past. A såinn is simple, easy to build, and can dry large quantities of malt relatively quickly, but it takes up a lot of space and requires a building of its own.

The såinn is essentially a rectangular box of brick or stone, about one and a half meters high, 3–4 m wide, and 1–1.5 m deep. On top is a wooden frame with wooden planks that the malt lies on top of. Altogether, the planks have thousands of holes drilled into them, which, today, is done using a 6 mm bit. It is best to drill from above and down, because the planks often splinter where the drill comes out and you do not want the holes to close when you lay the malt on top.[40] Some people are concerned that the splinters sticking out can catch fire, and so remove them.[41]

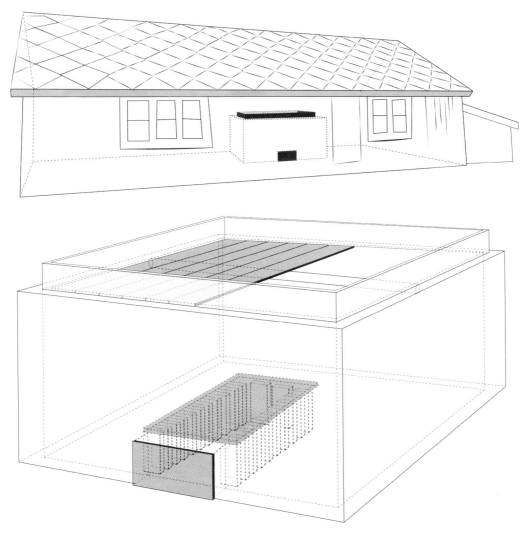

Figure 3.23. Diagram of a såinn at Hegge farm at Skatval in Stjørdal, thought to have been built late nineteenth century. Drawing by Silje England Garshol.

The planks must be replaced when the heat wears them out. To help with this, some use a type of jig, made up of boards with pieces of wood attached in the corners so that four to five planks can be placed on them and held in place by the pieces of wood. This way, several planks can be drilled in one go.

On the floor in the middle of the front wall is the opening for the fireplace, which is called *kjerringa*. This literally means "the woman," and, according to Odd Nordland, it is one of a group of words that were used in Scandinavia for "dangerous or especially potent objects." In Stjørdalen, several maltsters insist it is called that because you have to sleep beside it at night to watch the fire. In Sweden, it was called *galten* (lit. "boar"), which Nordland considered to be another word in the same class.[42]

The fireplace usually has a door, and inside has stones set at angles around the entire fireplace with small vertical openings between the stones. On top of the stones lies a flat stone roof, about

Figure 3.24. Planks with holes over the såinn. Stjørdal, Norway.

Figure 3.25. Kjerringa visible inside a såinn with the planking removed. Tautra, near Stjørdal, Norway.

30 cm off the floor. This arrangement prevents the planks directly above the fireplace from getting too hot and also from being hit by sparks. Still, drying malt on a kiln like this is prone to starting fires. I know of kilns in Stjørdalen that have burned down. The local maltsters say that when the planks start making cracking noises you are in the "danger zone" and need to reduce the fire immediately. In the beginning, when the malt is wet, this is not so much of an issue because of evaporation, but when the malt starts drying the risk grows.

It may seem strange that a building like this should catch fire so easily, but it really does happen. Antti Pahalahti in Hartola, Finland, told me how his family's smoke sauna burned down. His uncle had just come back to the house after a sauna bath. Everyone except Antti's grandmother had gone to bed, when she saw light through the window. She thought it was a car coming to visit their remote farm and went over to the window to look. It was then she saw it was the sauna burning. The wood in these buildings is very dry after years of use, and when it is hot a small spark from the fireplace can be enough to start a blaze.

Many of the traditional maltsters do not measure the temperature of the malt as it dries, instead using the popping sound from the planks to tell them that they need to reduce the fire. In one interview, a maltster told me that when he could only just keep his hand between the malt and the planks for a short time, the temperature was about right.[43]

Roar Sandodden, who uses a såinn, told me he starts with 200 kilograms of grain, and typically ends up with 160 kg of dried and cleaned malt. He has two drying periods of about eight to ten hours each with a ten-hour pause in between when he lets the fire go out. In the beginning, when Roar had just started malting, he measured his mash efficiency to be about 50%, but now it is higher.

In eastern Norway and southern Sweden, it was common when making heavily smoked malts to use a two-storey kiln known as a *kjone*. This had a rough stone oven with no chimney on the first floor where the fire was. In the middle of the second storey was a drying surface, rather like that of the såinn, through which the heat and smoke rose and dried the malt. The second storey was a

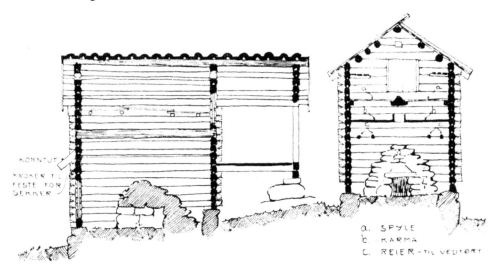

Figure 3.26. Drawing of kjone from Våle in Vestfold, eastern Norway. Reproduced by permission from the Norwegian Museum of Cultural History.

little wider than the first, forming a floor to walk on around the drying surface. The kjone was used because it could handle more malt than the såinn.

In Denmark, many brewhouses had an oven with a spark catcher inside the chimney, the spark catcher being shaped like a pyramid with holes in it. Above it were doors in the chimney where one could put in either mats woven from branches or boards with holes in them. The malt was dried on these, with the smoke and heat rising directly through the malt.

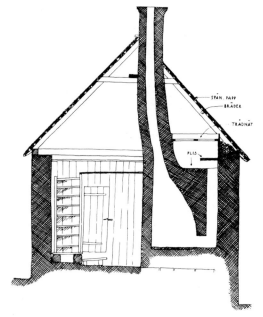

Figure 3.28. Drawing of Gotland-type kiln, from Öja on Gotland. *Bräder*, wooden poles; *Flis*, slate tiles (basically a spark catcher like in the såinn); *Papp*, roofing felt; *Spån*, wooden roof tiles; *Trådnät*, netting. Reproduced by permission from the Nordic Museum.

In Denmark and on the island of Gotland, a common type of kiln had a fireplace on the ground floor and a drying surface of wooden boards with holes in the loft. The fireplace was the normal type for cooking and brewing, but in addition to the regular chimney, there was a second chimney that led to the drying surface. A "door" in the chimney made it possible to control which way the heat and smoke went.

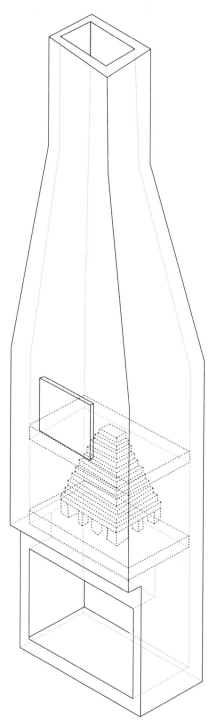

Figure 3.27. Diagram of a typical Danish chimney malt kiln. Drawing by Silje England Garshol.

Heavily smoked malt was common in southern Sweden, the Swedish island of Gotland, southeastern Norway, and most of Denmark except northern Jutland.

On Orkney, the farmers had barns built of stone, with a round tower-like kiln at one end. The kiln had a fireplace at the bottom, with a drying surface made either of wire mesh or sticks laid crosswise with straw on top. The kiln was fired with peat, and the smoke and heat rose through the malt, drying it.[44]

Caramel

In the east, drying the malt in a great oven was common. Marina Fyodorova demonstrated this method to me in Chuvashia, Russia. She lit a fire in her great Russian stove and let it burn out. This heated the brickwork in the oven, which retained the heat for a long time. The oven was then

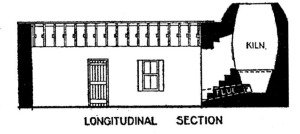
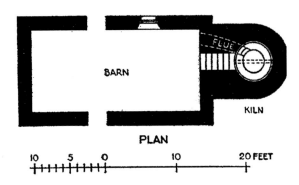

Figure 3.29. A drawing of the type of kiln found in the Northern Isles. Exnaboe, South Mainland, Shetland.

Figure 3.30. A great oven used for malt drying. Kshaushi, Chuvashia, Russia.

scrubbed free of embers and ashes with oak twigs, water, and a towel, until the surface of the oven was completely clean. Twenty liters of wet malt were then placed inside the oven in a layer 5 cm thick and left to dry. The damp air from the malt circulated out of the oven in the same way as the smoke. After 12 hours, the malt was taken out, the fire lit again, and the whole process repeated. In total, it took three fires to dry the malt.

We tasted Marina's malt and it was very like modern caramel malt, which is not surprising. Caramel malt is made by using high temperatures initially on wet malt, converting some starch to sugar within the grains, that then caramelizes to produce a caramel-like flavor. This is exactly what Marina's oven does, since it is hottest when the malt is added and then gradually cools until the next fire is lit.

This drying method was common in central Sweden, roughly from Gothenburg to Uppsala further north, and it was also used on the southwestern tip of Jutland in Denmark. I do not have exact data on Russia, but this method must have been common there, seeing as every peasant house had a great Russian stove. Apart from the Chuvashians, I do not know of anyone who makes malt in this way anymore.

Strong, Uneven Heat

An ancient method for drying malt was to use hot stones. Very little documentation survives of this method, although it may well have been widespread in earlier times. In parts of western Norway, people used what was called a *turkebrye* (lit. "drying trough") into the nineteenth century. This was a hollowed-out wooden log, about the size of a small canoe, sealed with wooden boards at the ends.[45]

Figure 3.31. A wooden trough for drying malt with hot stones. Sandane Museum, Norway.

Figure 3.32. An iron pot for drying malt with the traditional implement (*kare*) for stirring the malt. Mølstertunet Museum, Voss.

A pile of small stones was placed in a fire. When the stones were hot, they were taken out with a rake and spread out to cool down some, before being picked up with wooden tongs and dropped into the malt in the log. Another person stirred quickly so that the malt did not burn. The malt was said to let off steam and smoke.[46] This type of malting seems to have died out in the nineteenth century. What the resulting malt tasted like is anybody's guess.

Another method that was used into the twentieth century, and that must have given similar malts, was to sometimes "dry malt in an iron pot, while constantly stirring over a slow fire, but this kind of malt was never as good as that dried in a badstu."[47] Using a pot was tedious, because the malt had to be stirred all the time to prevent it from burning. What is more, only a small quantity of malt could be dried at a time. Still, for the tenant farmer who did not have much malt, or had no malt kiln, this was a practical solution.

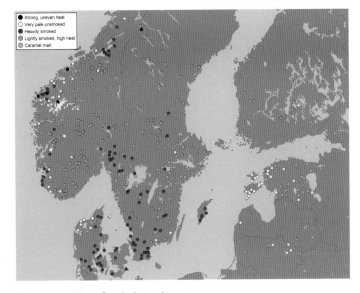

Figure 3.33. Map of malt drying by category.

Undried Malt

I brewed with Dmitriy Zhezlov near in the village of Shitovo, near Kirov, about 900 km northeast of Moscow. At the start of the brewing session, he brought out his homemade rye malt in a plastic sieve, along with an ordinary meat grinder of the kind used in home kitchens. While Dmitriy was grinding the malt, I asked him how he had dried it.

Figure 3.34. Dmitriy Zhezlov grinding undried malt. Shitovo, Kirov Oblast, Russia.

"Oh, it isn't dried," he said cheerfully, with a sly smile.

"It's not dried?"

"No, I haven't dried it."

Only the whirring of the meat grinder broke the silence, while I tried to process what I had just been told. Eventually, I worked it out. Dmitriy made a batch of malt for each brew; since it was used immediately, mould did not have a chance to grow in it. Traditional querns have a hard time grinding wet malt, but Dmitriy's relatively modern meat grinder served this purpose perfectly well. Rye makes dark beer even if the grain is not toasted at all, so why bother drying the malt? It is really just a waste of effort in Dmitriy's case.

In the past, brewing with undried malt seems to have been almost unheard of. A resident of Gloppen in western Norway[48] said he had heard of people doing it, but that is the only example I know of.

4

YEAST

Today, the word "farmhouse" on a bottle of beer tends to mean that it contains some kind of funky yeast. People seem to assume that farmhouse yeast must have been funky because farmers historically maintained their own yeast cultures and fermented in wood. *Brettanomyces* would have been living in the wood, the argument goes, and would have made the beer funky. And, besides, saison yeast is phenolic and kind of funky too.

This thinking was based on guesswork, and since very little was known about actual farmhouse brewing, guesswork was all that was available. Since 2014, many surviving farmhouse yeast cultures have been collected and analyzed and much more documentation of farmhouse brewing has come to light. This chapter tells the story of what we have learned, and how our understanding of farmhouse yeast has changed.

Voss: Discovering Kveik

When I started looking seriously into Norwegian farmhouse ale, I quickly found that in Voss in western Norway the brewers did not buy their yeast. Instead, they used what they called *kveik*. This was supposed to be the same yeast that had been used in the region's local farmhouse ales since before anyone could remember. Nothing more

Figure 4.1. Dyrvedalen, Voss. This small valley is a powercenter for the local farmhouse brewing tradition. Sigmund Gjernes's house is a few kilometers away. Bjørne Røthe's farm is on the upper right edge, with Sjur Rørlien's house behind it to the left.

seemed to have been documented, but on online homebrewer forums many people were skeptical about these yeast cultures. Many did not believe the brewers could have kept the cultures going for so long, and others thought they would have to be full of bacteria and wild yeast because they had never been purified in a lab.

I had no idea what the yeast would be like, but my trip to Kaupanger (chapter 1) had been so interesting that I was determined to visit Voss and learn more. That, however, meant finding a local brewer. For months I tried emailing every contact I could think of, but with no luck. The farmhouse brewers brew at home and they do not sell their beer, so there is no published contact information, no advertisements, and no real reason for them to accept a stranger into their homes. In the end, I thought I would have to travel to Voss and stand in the local post office with a sign saying, "I seek traditional brewers!"

Then one day I got in touch with Reddit user Eirik Steen-Olsen. He is from Voss and said his best friend's father was a traditional brewer who had his own kveik. Gradually, via Eirik, I managed to persuade them to let me and two friends brew with them. This meant letting us stay over in their house for 24 hours.

We did not really know anything more than that the brewer was called Sigmund, and that he had his own yeast and a huge copper kettle. So, it was with some uncertainty that we stopped at a small railway station outside Voss in May 2014 and called our hosts. Soon, a young man in a battered pickup truck showed up, presenting himself as Yngve. He was the son of the brewer Sigmund Gjernes. We were led a couple of kilometers along a narrow, winding road through pine forests, going steeply up the hillside. We were brewing on a farm, although it did not much look like one, since the fields were all out of sight, hidden by folds in the steep hillside.

Figure 4.2. Sigmund Gjernes's brewery. That is Sigmund stood on the right, preparing the juniper.

Eirik and Sigmund were both there to meet us, and took us to see the brewery, which was a room in the basement. A section of a large concrete pipe had been cut and turned into a fireplace, on top of which a huge copper kettle fit exactly. The kettle was a lovely piece of work dating from the eighteenth century, and could hold 340 liters. A big metal mash tun, which doubled as the fermentor, a plastic tub, and a big home-welded steel serving tank made up the rest of the brew kit. For me, it was instant déjà vu, being so similar to the brewhouse in Kaupanger where I had helped brew my first traditional beer just six months earlier.

We had been told beforehand that they had no more of last year's brew left, but, on checking the tank again, Sigmund was able to pour a glass of muddy brown liquid that looked more like mocha coffee than beer. This was just the dregs, not really meant to be drunk, but I eagerly dove into it to see what we were going to make. I could not really judge it very well from this sample, but one thing stood out: a strong aroma of orange peel and Christmas spices. I was completely baffled. Where did this aroma come from? The ingredients were supposed to be a juniper infusion, pilsner malt, kveik (the family yeast), and noble hops. The source of these unusual aromas had to be the kveik, but who ever heard of a yeast that makes orange-peel aroma? This had to be investigated.

I asked Sigmund where the kveik came from, and he told me that the people on the Gjernes farm, where Sigmund's family came from, used kveik from his uncle Brynjulv Gjernes. However, when Sigmund bought his own farm in 1987, he mixed his uncle's yeast with kveik from a neighbor. Since then, he has been reusing the same culture.[*]

---

[*] "#1 Sigmund" in table 4.1, p. 108.

Figure 4.3. Sigmund using a kitchen sieve to remove impurities from the juniper infusion.

They filled the big copper kettle with water and juniper branches and started a fire underneath. Unlike Carlo (chapter 1), Sigmund used only the tips of the juniper and no branches. On the subject of berries, Sigmund and Carlo were in full agreement: the fewer the better. Having started the fire, a quiet period followed. Heating 300 liters of water to 80°C takes a while, even if you are heating it over a big fire. While we waited, Sigmund now and then took out a kitchen sieve and removed things from the infusion. When I asked why, he grinned and said, "All sorts of things come with the juniper. Like spiders. You don't want that in the beer."

Eventually the infusion was hot enough and we could mash. Sigmund did this by putting a portion of grist in a plastic tub, pouring the hot juniper infusion on it, sprinkling some hops on top, and stirring for a good ten minutes. To make it easier to stir, Sigmund added lots of the infusion until the mash formed a loose porridge. The tub was quite small, so we had to fill it four times in order to mix all the grist, taking turns stirring the mash.

The mash was tipped into the mash tun, which had a metal mesh forming a false bottom with a bed of juniper branches on top. Once all of the mash was in, Yngve poured the hot juniper infusion into the mash tun to get the right temperature. The mash tun was then wrapped with a thick Styrofoam cover to keep it warm while it was left alone. To our surprise, mashing was to last a full six hours!

To mash for so long is risky, because if the temperature drops below 45°C any lactic acid bacteria in the grist can go to work and start souring the beer. It was to protect against this that Sigmund added hop pellets to the mash and insulated the tun. Indeed, putting hops in the mash is an old tradition in Voss.[1] I am not sure whether Sigmund was aware of the exact nature of the problem, but I find again and again that farmhouse brewers nearly always have very good reasons for what they do.

Figure 4.4. Sigmund holding the yeast ring with dried yeast on it.

By now it was midnight, so we went to sleep while the mash continued. Three to four hours of mashing is the norm in Voss, but in order to get more sleep Sigmund extends it to six. We were led to a small apartment on the second floor, where we quickly crashed into our beds and passed out. It seemed just moments later when I heard Yngve coming up the stairs to tell us brewing was starting again. Getting up was not easy, but somehow we did it. Later, Sigmund told me that one guy who visited him to learn how to brew had struggled with this part; the guy just could not get up in the morning, and so missed the first session. Six times he had been over to brew, and every single time he had failed to get up. The seventh time he solved the problem by not going to bed, which worked great until he fell asleep in a corner at 10 o'clock in the morning.

Figure 4.5. The kveik ready for use, with a visible column of bubbles.

Once we were up again, the first step was to start lautering the wort from the mash tun into a steel bucket. As I had seen with Carlo, it was important to keep a thin but continuous flow. Once the bucket was filled, it was emptied into the kettle and the fire underneath it was started again. You cannot start the fire without liquid in the kettle because that will turn the copper black and brittle, destroying the kettle. Running off was a slow process, taking hours to get the 300 liters of wort out of the tun.

We poured some of the runnings into a glass. The wort was deep golden and very sweet, which was confusing. This wort fit the malt bill of only Pilsner malt, but then why had the beer sample Sigmund given us been dark brown? The flavor was much as you would expect: sugary, syrupy and malty, with a dose of juniper flavor in the background that added some rough bitterness. No hint, however, of that orange-peel flavor.

Sigmund then brought out the kveik. The first thing he showed us was a traditional yeast ring, known as a *gjærkrans*, which looked like an intricate wooden necklace, or an animal's spine. The gjærkrans was used to gather yeast from the fermentor, which then dried on the wood. Because of all the little wooden links, the ring has a large surface area, so it is very effective at collecting yeast. The ring was then hung up somewhere until it was time to brew again. Yeast dried like this can stay good for years. Sometimes people would find mold had grown on it, in which case they would throw the yeast away and get kveik from somewhere else.

Sigmund does not use a yeast ring anymore, but he had prepared this old ring with yeast to show us how it was done. Outside he had the real yeast container, a big glass jar screwed tightly shut with a rubber band seal. Sigmund had kept it in the refrigerator since the last time he brewed, six months ago. Inside was a thick, muddy yellowish-brown substance: the kveik. On top, a deep brown liquid had separated out. Sigmund opened the jar and asked us to smell it. And there it was again! A deep, earthy, yeasty orange-peel and spice aroma washed over us. So, the kveik really was the source of that aroma.

In order to tell if the kveik is in good condition and fit to use, Sigmund tasted the liquid on top. If that is sour or tastes bad, Sigmund will get rid of the kveik and get some fresh from his brother, Gunleiv, who uses the same yeast. I had to taste it too, and the thick brown liquid was like an explosion in my mouth: intense yeasty earth, orange peel and spice, a flavor that just went on and on and on. Sigmund pronounced it excellent, so the kveik was clearly good to use.

Just a few minutes after opening it, the glass jar started bubbling quietly to itself, with little columns of bubbles running up the side of the glass. Sigmund said this meant the yeast was vigorous and ready to go, so he would not have to make a starter. Instead, he would just chuck half the contents of the jar into the wort and let it go. The other half he would keep in reserve, just in case. I stood there for a long time, staring at the jar in fascination, taking pictures and just watching. I had never seen anything like it—Sigmund had his own strain of yeast living in the fridge, like a prehistoric domesticated animal, unknown to science, a separate tribe of living creatures descending out of nobody knows what distant past.

Sigmund took a big saucepan, added a little wort to the bottom, then threw the yeast ring into it. That was all that was needed to get the dried yeast going again. Four hours later, the wort was covered by a foamy, bubbling layer. The kveik had obviously wasted no time in getting to work. And out of the saucepan rose again that unmistakable orange-peel aroma. There was none of that flavor in the wort, so the source could be nothing other than the kveik.

Figure 4.6. The kveik on the yeast ring has started fermenting. This is four hours after the yeast ring had been dropped into the wort.

Figure 4.7. Sigmund removing the "headache." The dark marks on the inside of the kettle show how wort has been boiled away.

By now we were getting very excited indeed. To see why, ask yourself how many really aromatic yeast types there are. There is *Brettanomyces*. There is hefeweizen yeast, obviously, and maybe some Belgian strains. But the number of strongly aromatic yeasts is quite limited. So not only did Sigmund have his very own private yeast living in his fridge, but it was actually a yeast producing a totally unique aroma. Now we were beginning to see how Sigmund could brew with low-aroma hops, straightforward pilsner malt, and juniper and still get an interesting beer. Yeast is often described as "the spirit of beer," and rarely has this been more fitting than with Sigmund's beer.

Sigmund, meanwhile, taking no notice of the dazed beer writer walking in shocked circles on his lawn, proceeded to boil the wort. Once we had recovered enough to pay attention, we were struck by another surprise. The boil, Sigmund told us, starts when the first wort is in the kettle, then carries on for a few hours as all the wort is run off, and after that the entire wort is boiled for four hours. All told, Sigmund boils away half of the 300 liters of wort he started with. Obviously, this long, evaporative boil, together with the wood fire and the copper kettle, adds both color and caramel flavor to Sigmund's beer. That was the explanation for the dark beer we tried before.

After a while, the hot break occurred, with protein coagulating out of the wort and forming a thick porridge-like foam on top. Sigmund took up his sieve again and scooped off the foam. "We call this the 'headache,'" he told us, "You have to remove the headache." In addition to protein, he said, the "headache" contains quite a lot of juniper oil, so removing it reduces the rough juniper bitterness and some of the juniper flavor. It also removes some unhealthy substances from the juniper, he said. "Now we're really making the beer," Sigmund added, showing how much emphasis the brewers in Voss place on the boil.

Now we were getting close to the point where the kveik was going into action, so I brought out the little plastic bottles I had taken on the trip in the hopes of getting kveik samples. Part of my plan was to get samples and send them to a lab for analysis so we could get a better understanding of what kveik really was. I asked Sigmund whether I could get a sample. Without hesitation, he said, "No problem." Later I discovered many local brewers get their yeast from Sigmund, so he was already used to distributing it. Sigmund took out a metal measuring cup and spooned some kveik into it, stirring it to liquefy it. We then carefully poured two samples into two of the small plastic bottles, which I tenderly wrapped up and stored in my suitcase.

Once the wort had finished boiling it was noticeably darker, and, as Sigmund had predicted, roughly half the volume had gone. The wort was transferred to the fermentation vessel, where a coiled copper immersion chiller was used to cool it down for fermentation. The copper kettle was then scrubbed with steel wool, and I was surprised to find that none of the wort had burnt onto the bottom. There was a thin dark layer of loose sooty particles on the bottom, but that was all.

The kveik cultures from both the ring and the jar were then added to the cooled wort, and Sigmund again insulated the vessel. When we asked him why, he said it was so the kveik would be warm enough. Puzzled by this, I asked at what temperature he pitched the yeast. "About 39 degrees Celsius," was the answer. Silence followed, as I stared at him. Many brewers consider 29°C, the temperature at which some Belgian yeast strains ferment, to be extreme, and here was someone going a good ten degrees Celsius warmer! Seeing my surprise, Sigmund calmly added, "My brother Gunleiv has measured temperatures during fermentation as high as 43 degrees Celsius."

Shaking our heads, we started packing our gear. The job was pretty much done at this point. The kveik would work for three to four days before racking and transfer of the beer to the serving tank. Even before we left, a delicate orange-peel aroma was wafting through the cellar, a last greeting from our mysterious friend, the kveik.

From Voss we drove north, winding through the maze of fjords and valleys that make up western Norway. About 300 km further north in Stranda, we met farmhouse brewing veteran Stein Langlo. He had gathered a group of brewers who would bring their beers and tell us about the local brewing traditions.

We showed up a bit too early, so Stein took us on a tour of Stranda in his car while we waited for his friends to get ready. I noticed a plastic box of sour cream in the door pocket of his car and thought to myself, "Who drives around with sour cream in their car?" Stein showed us stunning views of the fjords and the olivine mines, as well as the cabin of German publishing magnate Axel Springer, while we plied him with questions about brewing and yeast.

Suddenly, Stein asked me to take the sour cream box and open it. I was surprised to find pale beige-yellow dry flakes of some material that looked vaguely like concrete. "Taste it," Stein said. I tasted it, and recognized the flavor from childhood. It was dried yeast. "Take it," Stein said. So, within a few days I had collected two different kveiks.[*]

That evening we were talking with Stein and his friends and tasting their beers. They had started out as traditional farmhouse brewers using their own kveiks, but had gradually learned modern brewing and switched to modern brewing processes and laboratory yeast. So, they had a foot in each camp. Back when they used kveik, they also fermented very warm, typically pitching the yeast at 30°C or warmer. "But this shop yeast, it won't ferment above 27 degrees," said one of them, sounding equal parts puzzled and amused.

We returned to Voss a week later to try the beer we had watched Sigmund make. We sat down with Sigmund at a table outside the house in the May sunshine, where we were served a clear, deep reddish-brown beer with little head; so it had very low carbonation, obviously. The flavor was powerful, earthy, caramelly, with orange and spice, and a clear juniper character that balanced the fairly sweet taste. A very good beer, and very similar to the two other *vossaøl* we had managed to find in the meantime.

I came back from this trip with two small bottles of yellowish-brown sludge that could ferment at 40°C and make beer with orange-peel flavor, and a sour cream container with yellowish dry flakes that apparently could also ferment warm. What was this actually? I needed to find out.

First Laboratory Analysis

I sent both Sigmund's and Stein's kveik in for analysis at the National Collection of Yeast Cultures (NCYC) in Norwich, England. The analysis results came back for Sigmund's yeast first. They showed it consisted of three closely related strains of *Saccharomyces cerevisiae*. That is, ordinary top-fermenting yeast. No *Brettanomyces*. And no bacteria.

These results may be difficult to believe, but in the autumn of 2018 I visited Sigmund again. He threw a small party, serving cured meats and, of course, his own beer. Late in the evening he opened a bottle of the beer we had brewed in his cellar in May 2014. It was quite oxidized and the kveik flavor was mostly gone, but it was perfectly drinkable. There was not a hint of acidity, funkiness, or anything like that.

In 2009, Norwegian homebrewer Håken Hveem had collected kveik from Svein Rivenes, another brewer in Voss, and sent it to NCYC.[†] Chris Bond at NCYC now compared the genetic fingerprints

---

[*]   See "#3: Stranda" in table 4.1, p. 108.
[†]   See "#2: Rivenes" in table 4.1, p. 108.

of Svein and Sigmund's kveiks and saw very clearly that they were different but closely related. They must share a common ancestor "some decades in the past," Chris wrote.

Getting Stein's sample to grow was much harder. Chris tried several times with no luck, and eventually had to write back to say that the yeast was dead. It must have been a good while since Stein last used it. Then, a couple of days later, Chris contacted me again. He had scratched loose some dried material in a corner of the orbital shaker and tried again. This time the yeast grew, but Chris only found a single strain in it. Very likely the yeast was saved in the nick of time and only that single strain survived. Again, the analysis found only *Saccharomyces cerevisiae*. From genetic fingerprinting, Chris said he thought Stein's kveik might be related to the two from Voss, but he could not be sure. If they really were related that would be quite surprising, because the two places are nearly 200 km apart as the crow flies, separated by several mountain ranges.

I was very happy with these results, but also a bit frustrated. OK, so it was yeast. But what kind? Was it similar to other strains, or was kveik a new type of strain? Was there anything special about it apart from the flavor and the high temperature tolerance? I tried asking Chris, but the only answer I got was that it seemed to have "moderately well-developed pseudomycelia." That did not tell me much.

Many modern brewers were suspicious about these yeasts. Most brewers today are taught that you cannot reuse yeast more than 5–15 times, and yet here there were brewers claiming they had reused their yeast for many decades, maybe even centuries. Surely this would have to be wild yeast, people said, and not brewer's yeast. If it really was brewer's yeast, how was that possible?

I realized I did not know anything like enough microbiology to actually understand what questions I needed to ask. So, I started reading up and collaborating with more labs, and eventually a story emerged.

Yeast, Wild and Domesticated

Top-fermenting yeast, *Saccharomyces cerevisiae*, evolved as a wild microorganism somewhere in east Asia, probably an area of what is China today.[2] There it made its living fermenting tree sap, honey, fruit, and other natural sources of sugar. It seems to have a close relationship with certain types of tree, and also with fruit flies. The yeast gives off fruity smells that attract the fruit flies, which pick up yeast on their bodies when they land to feed and so carry it with them to the next food source.[3]

Figure 4.8. Yeast from the genus *Saccharomyces* have been found in plant galls like these. Modern *S. cerevisiae* strains used in fermented products likely originated from sources such as these. Photo courtesy of Diego Libkind.

Somehow, human beings started using this yeast for fermenting wine and beer. In the process we changed it, so that brewer's yeast is no longer the same as wild *Saccharomyces cerevisiae*, even though it is still the same species. The reason is that brewer's yeast has lived inside breweries for a long time, a habitat so different from nature that the yeast has had to evolve and change. Many of the changes are a result of natural selection, while others have been caused by direct human intervention.

Compared to its wild counterparts, brewer's yeast can tolerate more alcohol, is better at fermenting maltotriose (a sugar that is rare in nature but common in wort), and is better at flocculating. These three changes happened more or less by themselves, because yeast cells that mutated such that they could eat maltotriose and tolerate alcohol grew better in beer, outcompeting those that did not. Yeast that has gotten better at flocculating will also have had a better chance of being collected by the brewer, either from the bottom or the top of the fermentor. Yeast that remained suspended in the beer was consumed and so died, never making it into the next batch of beer.

Another difference between wild and domestic yeast is that brewer's yeast seems to have lost the ability to survive drying. Very likely mutations have destroyed the necessary genes. In nature, if a yeast cell loses the ability to dry it is at a big disadvantage. But not in a commercial brewery, where the brewers will keep the yeast in liquid for a short time before pitching it into a new batch of wort. So, the yeast lost an ability it no longer had any need for.

Wild yeast nearly always makes a phenolic aroma compound known as 4-vinylguaiacol (4VG). The yeast has no particular use for 4VG itself, but in order to get rid of ferulic acid and other harmful acids. These acids are found in nature, and probably serve as defensive mechanisms in trees who want to keep the sugar in the tree sap to themselves, but there are not enough of these acids in beer to be harmful for the yeast. Recent research shows that the yeast genes responsible for making 4VG were destroyed by mutations quite early on in the divergence of brewer's yeast from wild strains.[4]

In addition, brewers seem to have preferred non-phenolic yeast strains over those that are phenolic. Microbiologists call the phenolic yeasts POF[+]; the "POF" part means phenolic off-flavor, while the "+" is microbiology shorthand for "the strain has this property." Non-phenolic yeast strains are called POF[-]. Since most domesticated beer yeasts are POF[-] and nearly all wild ones are POF[+], this is a useful marker to differentiate domesticated yeast from wild yeast. Examples of domesticated yeast strains that are POF[+] are saison yeast and hefeweizen yeast.

Today brewer's yeast is kept frozen in yeast banks and very carefully maintained so that it will change as little as possible. So how did it become domesticated? The answer is that the use of yeast has been through a revolution, and that brewer's yeast was domesticated before that change.

The Yeast Revolution

In the mid-nineteenth century, just about every brewery on the planet had their own yeast culture, which they collected from the fermenting beer and pitched into the next batch. The main exceptions were the few breweries making spontaneously fermenting beer. When Josef Groll brewed the first Pilsner in 1842, he was repitching his yeast in much the same way as Sigmund; the same is true of brewing giants like Carlsberg (founded 1847) and Anheuser-Busch (founded 1852). Everyone did it this way because there was no alternative. Modern microbiology was just getting started, and yeast handling in breweries was technologically on about the same level as Sigmund in Voss is today. Brewer's yeast was domesticated before modern laboratory equipment and sanitation came into use, so it is clear that brewers back then had enough control over their yeast to keep the same strain going for many decades, even in those primitive conditions.

The yeast revolution was inspired by Louis Pasteur, who did extensive experiments on yeast starting in the 1850s. He showed that alcoholic fermentation was done by yeast, a living organism, not by a simple chemical reaction caused by protein sludge, as chemists had argued. Pasteur's research advanced the science of microbiology by leaps and bounds but had little practical impact on brewing, with one important exception: it inspired quite a few breweries to set up microbiological labs to study brewer's yeast using Pasteur's methods.

The actual yeast revolution was started by Emil Christian Hansen, a scientist at the Carlsberg laboratory. Breweries back then struggled with something called "the yeast sickness," which made the pitching yeast go bad. Since the yeast was recycled from brew to brew, yeast sickness was a disaster that could only be solved by getting new yeast from a different brewery. Carlsberg were proud of never having had this problem, but in the autumn of 1883 it was finally their turn. Carlsberg, however, did not get new yeast from another brewery, because Hansen thought he could solve the problem another way. Hansen split the yeast culture into single cells, then grew those in sterilized flasks. This allowed him to do experiments on the various strains and show that there were four strains all told in the Carlsberg pitching yeast. Two strains were "good," and both of them came from the original German lager yeast brought from Germany in the 1840s by brewery owner J.C. Jacobsen. These strains made good beer. However, if one of the two "bad" yeast strains was added, the beer went off in exactly the way the brewery's commercial products had started doing.

Hansen had now found the cause of yeast sickness, but he went even further and developed a solution that involved a new way of using yeast. The new method was to repitch as before but only for a few generations, after which the brewery went back to the stored, clean, single-strain yeast culture. To ensure that the yeast remained clean, Hansen developed an apparatus to grow the yeast under sterile conditions. Hansen's analysis had shown that the original Carlsberg yeast consisted of two strains that were very similar but had noticeable differences, rather like Sigmund's three strains. Hansen named these strains Carlsberg No 1 and Carlsberg No 2, and for a while both were used separately at Carlsberg.

Hansen's method cured yeast sickness at a single stroke, and also gave brewers better control over their product. It spread like wildfire, taking over in most big lager breweries in Europe and North America before the twentieth century began. It was quite literally the biggest revolution that had happened in brewing for many centuries.

You might think that this revolution would have brought an end to repitching top-fermenting yeasts, but, strangely enough, it did not. In Canada, Labatt were still repitching their ale yeast in the 1970s, and in Belgium many breweries did the same into the 1980s. The same goes for the UK, where Harvey's in Sussex is still to this day repitching their yeast.[5*]

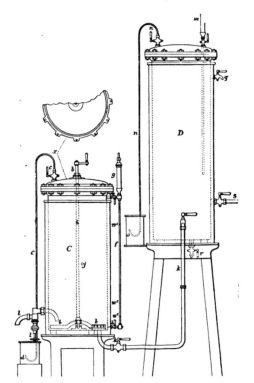

Figure 4.9. Hansen's yeast propagation apparatus. From Hansen (1888).

---

* Timothy Taylor has done the same since 1982.

So kveik is less of an anachronism than it might seem. Once you realize that until 1883 nobody was getting their yeast from a lab, it does not seem so extraordinary that farmhouse brewers should have been able to keep their own yeast cultures going from then until now. And if Harvey's can do it for 60 years without the use of lab equipment,[*] why should farmhouse brewers not be able to?

Yeast on the Farm

In the mid-nineteenth century, farms all over northern Europe had their own yeast cultures that they were repitching in exactly the same way commercial breweries did. And just like the breweries, the farmers maintained their own yeast cultures because there was no alternative. As one source put it: "There was no yeast to be bought in the countryside in the old days, and that was why people were so careful to take care of what yeast they could get hold of."[6] It was only in the second half of the nineteenth century that yeast became available for sale; even then, most farmers would have preferred to save their money and not buy it. Farmhouse brewers in Suffolk, England also had their own yeast:

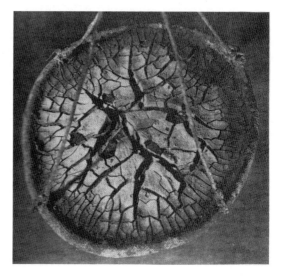

Figure 4.10. Yeast dried on a hair sieve, from western Norway.

> One pint of home-brewed yeast was obtained from a neighbour. Each household would arrange this beforehand. There was a yeast-chain in the village, and the wife would know before she started to brew which of her neighbours had brewed last and would have the freshest yeast. Prissy remembers being sent out by her mother to "borrow some barm." Borrow was a word used advisedly for after the brew the debt could be paid back with interest. (Evans 1972, 63)

In some places, as described above, the most important thing was to have fresh yeast. Stig Olav Lødemel, the mayor of Hornindal, told me he remembers having to run out to the neighbors to borrow dried yeast in a cup.

There was a saying in many places that went, "You cannot deny anyone yeast." Charging money for yeast was in most places just not done. However, in some areas, people tried their best to maintain their own yeast culture, only borrowing from their neighbors in an emergency. From Denmark:

---

[*] In fact, the culture itself has been in continuous use for even longer. Harvey's got the culture in 1957, but at that point it had not been separated into single strains and had already been reused for a long, long time.

> If, despite all care, the yeast had gone bad, one had to borrow, but for a housewife it was almost shameful to have to borrow yeast, so the yeast was guarded like a treasure. There were many who always had fine and plentiful yeast, and others one didn't so readily loan to. When the loan from such people came back it would be quietly poured out. (NEU 29001, Elling, north Jutland)

Farmhouse brewing died out in most places from the 1850s onward, and even in places where it did not die out most of the farmhouse brewers started buying bread yeast instead. The result was a mass extinction of brewing yeast cultures, probably without any equivalent in history. What amazing variety of yeast we lost can only be imagined, but from old documents we can learn some of the properties that farmhouse yeasts in different parts of Europe must have had, and how people used them.

There were many methods for preserving the yeast. The yeast ring Sigmund demonstrated was used in several places in Norway, Sweden, Germany[7] and Denmark. Strangely, not everyone used them for yeast. In Dalarna in Sweden, people say they used them as trivets, with no mention of yeast and brewing.[8] The exact same design is known from Hungary, where shepherds used it to support the conical pots. The shepherds called it *kutyagerinc*, literally "dog spine."[9]

Another piece of equipment people used was the yeast log, known as a *kveikstokk*. This could be a sophisticated piece of wood, cunningly constructed with holes in many sizes to catch as much yeast as possible. Or it could just be a section of tree trunk:

Figure 4.11. Yeast log, Upper Telemark Museum.

> They took a section of birch trunk with uneven bark and set it in the fermentor. The yeast settled in the folds of bark so the trunk was smooth on the outside when they took it out of the fermentor before shaking up the beer. Then they hung the yeast log in the crown of the wood stove until the yeast dried. Afterwards they hung it out in the food storehouse on the farm. Then it was ready to be used the next time they brewed. (Nersten 1950, 80–83, quoting a resident of Setesdal, southern Norway)

In southern Sweden, some people had another method. They collected the yeast and stirred in flour (mostly rye) to form cakes of dough. These were called *jästkakor* (lit. "yeast cakes"). They might stick a wooden rod through the yeast cakes and hang them up to dry, or dry them in the oven. When it was time to use the yeast, the cakes were broken up into lukewarm water and rye flour stirred in. Once the mix started fermenting the yeast was ready to use.

Figure 4.12. Plaster replicas of yeast cakes. Nordic Museum.

Much has been written about how people historically used a "magic stick" that would make the beer ferment, but what is striking about the actual historical accounts is the near complete absence of any magical thinking around yeast. Yeast was something people took good care of and made sure to handle well, but it did not seem to be treated with any more reverence or mysticism than other things. The only exception I know of is high in the Caucasus mountains in Georgia.[10] (See chap. 9, p. 340.)

As simple as these methods were, even this level of sophistication was not necessary. Many people simply dried the yeast on a piece of cloth, hot bricks, a straw ring, a wooden board, or even juniper branches. Svein Rivenes told me that his grandfather used a ring of straw, which he would pull back and forth in the yeast slurry to get it well soaked with yeast. Then he would hang the ring under the eaves of the barn, where it was airy, so it would dry quickly. "I can picture him now," Svein went on, "taking that ring down. The birds would shit on the ring, but grandpa would just scrape the shit off with a knife, then throw the ring in the wort," he said, laughing and shaking his head.

Others would keep their yeast wet, for example, in a jar. In summer, the jar might be stored in the ground, in a well, or in ice in order to keep it cool. In Denmark, it was common to change the water in the jar every few days.

In the north, in Norway and central and northern Sweden, nearly everyone seems to have dried their yeast. Further south, some seem to have dried the yeast while others kept it wet. The reason seems to be that people who lived further north could not produce as much grain because of the climate, so they did not brew as often. With only one to four batches per year, people had to dry the yeast between brews to protect it against infection. Their neighbors to the south could afford to brew when the beer barrel was emptied; with 12–36 brews per year, they could keep the yeast wet. Some seem to have dried it regardless, and probably the ones who had yeast that could survive drying would dry it, while those who could not kept it wet. But, further north, keeping wet yeast seems to have been unusual.

I have collected fermentation temperatures from about 250 different accounts, and these show that farmhouse brewers fermented surprisingly warm. Most fermented over 25°C, and the most common temperature described was "milk warm", which means the temperature of milk as it comes out of the cow, roughly 35–37°C. How high people went is hard to say—there are a few examples of 40°C, and, in Dyrvedalen in Voss some decades ago, the common pitch temperature used to be 43°C.[11] Some accounts say things like "so warm you could stand to keep your naked arm in it" or "somewhat warmer than milk-warm," which sounds intriguingly warm. Marina Fyodorovna, in Chuvashia, said she had tested how warm the water was when she could only just about keep her hand in it and found it was 45°C, which actually fits relatively well. Only a small number report temperatures of 20°C or lower, and very few of these brewers had their own yeast.

This information has been collected mostly from accounts from Norway, Sweden, and Denmark, but sparser data from Finland, Estonia, Lithuania, Russia, and the UK show the same picture. So, people probably fermented just as warm across most of northern Europe. This is striking, because if you tried fermenting at these temperatures with today's laboratory yeast, the yeast would either die or you would get a beer with massive off-flavors. So why did the farmhouse brewers ferment so much warmer?

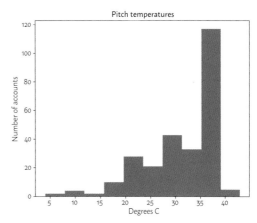

Figure 4.13. Pitch temperatures from around Europe. Diagram assumes "milk-warm" means 36°C. The very low temperatures are from modern sahti brewers (*see* p. 145). Source: see "The Database" section on p. 372.

Figure 4.14. Terje Raftevold harvesting his yeast. He says it is best to harvest after 40 hours, because when he racks the beer at 48 hours the yeast has often sunk to the bottom. Innvik, western Norway.

One reason is that, until the second half of the twentieth century, farmhouse brewers had no equipment for cooling the wort, so cooling a typical 150-liter farmhouse batch took a long time. And when you are cooling wort the temperature drops more slowly as the temperature of the wort approaches that of the surroundings. Cooling from 100°C to 40°C is much faster than 100°C to 20°C. In summer, it could take 20 hours or more for the wort to cool sufficiently.[12] Brewers were impatient to pitch the yeast so they could go to bed, and the longer they waited the greater the chance that an infection would make its way into the wort and take hold before the yeast could be pitched.

It seems, therefore, that there was a strong selective pressure on the farmhouse yeasts to handle warm fermentation temperatures and, clearly, the farmers had yeasts that could handle these temperatures. It is perhaps more of a mystery why commercial brewers have been fermenting so cold, ending up with yeast strains that could not ferment warm. This may be because commercial breweries had cooling equipment, and found that by cooling quickly to 20°C they reduced the chances of infection, since lactic acid bacteria grow better at 37°C than at 20°C.

Another surprise is how briefly people fermented their beer. Most people fermented just 12–24 hours before harvesting the yeast and kegging the beer, although a significant proportion waited 48 hours. A primary fermentation longer than 48 hours seems to have been unusual. Of course, a primary fermentation this short meant that there was often visible fermentation in the secondary.

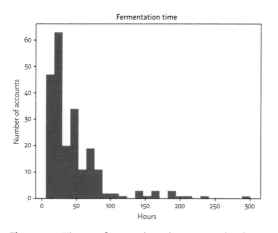

Figure 4.15. The time from pitching the yeast until racking.

This practice may seem strange, but there were good reasons for it. *Saccharomyces cerevisiae* grows rapidly, while competitors like lactic acid bacteria and *Brettanomyces* usually grow more slowly. If you have an infected beer it normally takes at least a week for the acidity to become noticeable. If the brewer collects the yeast within a day or two, the yeast will have grown much more than the contaminating microbes. By repeatedly harvesting early, the yeast outcompete their rivals which disappear, leaving only the yeast. Exceptions will be unwanted microorganisms that can grow as quickly as the yeast itself. If this type of infection gets into the yeast the only solution for farmhouse brewers is to throw away the yeast and replace it. Stopping primary fermentation as quickly as possible and then cooling the beer by storing it in the cellar also has the effect of slowing down any infection that may be present, so that the beer will keep longer. Which is another reason to keep the fermentation short.

The short fermentation may help explain why the farmhouse yeast did not become infected despite its rough treatment. Just getting wild yeast or bacteria into the yeast was not in itself enough. The contaminating microbes must also be able to grow faster than the yeast over a short time to increase their numbers. An infected yeast culture would gradually start tasting bad, until at some point the farmer would throw it away and get new yeast. Brewers thus avoided problematic off-flavors by being careful and throwing away the yeast early, before problems developed. Emil Christian Hansen himself described this progression very well:

The spent yeast is spilled in the yard, and carried down into the fermentation cellars on the boots of the workers, or it dries to dust out there, and is blown by the wind into the coolships. From here some of the organisms of disease reach the fermenters, where they start to develop. To begin with they develop slowly, so that there is no sign of danger, . . . but in the end there is so much wild yeast in the pitching yeast that the disease breaks forth. From that moment, the development spreads like wildfire, and soon all the beer in the brewery will be infected. (Hansen 1888, 101)

Origins of the Yeast

These warm-fermenting, fast-growing yeasts, where did farmhouse brewers get them from? When I asked Bjarne Halvorsgard, a farmer in Hallingdal, eastern Norway, where his yeast came from, he went quiet for a while, then said: "No, it . . . [*long pause*] No . . . [*long pause*] No, it . . . [*long pause*] From the previous beer." That I knew, of course, but where had he gotten it from originally? Bjarne had to admit he had no idea where the yeast came from originally. As far as he knew, it had always been on the farm. It was clear that he had never thought about where it came from and he was not really sure exactly what I was asking.

I have tried to trace the origins of most of the collected yeast cultures by asking the owners. If they got it from someone else, I call that person, and so on until the chain is broken. Lars Olav Muren, at the Norwegian ethnographic museum in Oslo, gave me one kveik. He got that from Einar Vestrheim, who brews together with Tor Ølver Helland near Oslo. Helland's brother-in-law is a farmhouse brewer in Hardanger, western Norway, named Hans Haugse. When I called Haugse, he said he used to get yeast together with malt from Johan Arnøy in Dyrvedalen in Voss. That is just a few kilometers from Sigmund's farm, in the same valley where Svein Rivenes (owner of #2 Rivenes) lives. Johan Arnøy is dead, however, so I was not able to get any further.

Every time I do this, the result is the same: the chain ends with someone who is now dead. Very often this is the owner's parent or grandparent. What happened before that nobody can say exactly, but from the ethnographic documentation we know that people shared yeast freely with each other. There must have been a slow diffusion of yeast strains across the brewing regions.

From the yeast logs and rings that have been preserved we know people have been reusing yeast for a long time. The oldest yeast log I know of comes from Morgedal in Telemark, eastern Norway, and has the year 1621 carved into the bottom.[13] Reuse of yeast in Norway began long before then. The book of Thorlak Thorhallson's miracles, written in Iceland in 1199, tells a story of how "when the yeast was added to the wort and everything was carefully prepared, fermentation did not begin, so that all their work had been in vain."* Saint Thorlak then performed a miracle, making the beer ferment.[14]

That yeast reuse in the north is a very old practice is beyond dispute. And we will see more evidence later. What we do not know is where the yeast originally came from to begin with. It must at some point have come from nature, obviously, but we do not know how or when.

---

* The word used for yeast in the original is *kveyk*.

Archaeological beer finds from before 1 CE are interesting, because they show beers made with not just malt, but also honey, berries, or other fruit. Honey and fruit add fermentable sugar, of course, but they also contain yeast. Was this how people added yeast before they figured out that they could reuse the yeast from the previous batch? It is certainly possible, and there are reasons to believe it.

Figure 4.16. Finnish poem singers Poavila and Triihvo Jamanen reciting Finnish folk poetry, 1894. Today the village is named Kalevala, and is in the Republic of Karelia, Russia.

The Finnish national epic, *The Kalevala*, is put together from sung poems that people in the countryside have been passing down for many, many centuries. It contains a segment that tells the story of a wedding, and a key part of the wedding preparations is the brewing of beer. The brewer has, implausibly, never made beer before, so she has to be told what to do and, when everything is ready, she does not know how to get the wort to ferment. She tries a few things before hitting on the idea of adding honey and, lo and behold, the beer suddenly ferments. This could well be a folk memory of an old practice of adding honey to make the beer ferment.

However, there was another way to get yeast that was used into the twentieth century. In southern Sweden, people made what they called "midsummer yeast" (*midsommarjäst*):

"Midsummer yeast" should be made in "Marstimman" (the hour
when the sun rose) on "midsummer night." That some superstition
according to old folk beliefs is involved is obvious. Silently, one went to
some water running north. Here one collected a bucket of water and
stirred rye flour into it, until it was like a thin porridge. This vessel was
then placed somewhere lukewarm without a lid, until the contents
started fermenting. When it had fermented for 24 hours it was mixed
with rye flour into a hard dough. The dough was picked apart into
small pieces and stored in rye flour in a container with a lid.

When needed, a little of the dried dough was wet with wort and
stirred in. It fermented excellently and could be used for any
fermentation. Moonshine wort, beer wort, and any kind of dough.

Whether the water for the midsummer yeast was collected from a
stream running toward the south or the east makes *no difference*, the
yeast is *just* as good anyway. But in older times it was thought that
waters running toward the north were *holy*.

The fact is that the yeast is made at midsummer. It seems as though
the yeast fungus is then the most *vigorous*, according to trials made
by *us*. The older folks here still use midsummer yeast for rye bread.
The lovely rye flavor from good rye flour ground with stone is kept,
but is lost when fermented with pressed yeast [factory-made baker's
yeast], which is poisonous. (EU 7725, a 1935 account from Kråksmåla;
emphasis in the original)

There seems to have been two main ways to collect midsummer yeast. One was to collect water
as described above, which could be from a well, river, or lake, but it had to be on midsummer
morning. The other was to take a bedsheet or other large cloth and drag it through the grass in a
field to collect dew. Whichever way you collected the water, it would then be mixed with rye flour
as described above.

People thought it was very important to collect the water on midsummer morning. However,

eventually they figured out that lake water collected when plants
are blooming had the same effect as midsummer dew. And that
ordinary well water also might work is shown by the following. On a
farm in the area the daughter had been given the task of collecting
midsummer yeast from her mother. However, her fiancée [or lover; the
text says "fästeman," which is ambiguous] was staying with her, so she
forgot. The sun was already high in the sky when she remembered.
But she thought of a solution. She dipped the cloth in ordinary well

water, and her mother made midsummer yeast from the water they wrung out of the cloth. It fermented, and her mother never discovered the fakery before her daughter long after told her the truth. (LUF 5257, a 1937 account from Vrigstad in Småland)

Essentially, the practice of using midsummer yeast seems like a way to make sourdough yeast with a healthy dose of superstition thrown in. Yeast strains in nature are more active around high and late summer, so it is not impossible that the time the yeast was collected could affect the results. It is known that ordinary beer yeast, *Saccharomyces cerevisiae*, exists in grain, so very likely the rye flour could have been used on its own. Zoran Gojkovic, of the Carlsberg Research Laboratory, told me that in the lab they tried finding yeast in grain, and actually found a *Saccharomyces cerevisiae* they were able to brew beer with.[15] The use of rye flour was also a good choice. People who make sourdough starters find that rye flour tends to be much easier to start a fermentation from, because the microbiota on rye are more active.[16]

There are also accounts of making brewer's yeast from rye flour from northern Norway and Latvia.[17] Starting yeast from rye flour was obviously common across northern Europe, but outside Sweden there does not seem to have been any superstition about where the water came from. A Norwegian cookbook from 1925 has a recipe for "making yeast":

4 liters water
125 grams hops
¾ kg rye flour
¼ kg sugar
40 grams salt

Boil the water and the hops about half an hour, sieve off the hops, and leave the water until cooled. Sieve the flour, sugar, and salt into the water slowly while mixing. Let the mix stand four days at an even temperature, stirring it a couple of times daily. (Erken 1925, 541)

This recipe shows very clearly that what is happening: the yeast is coming from inside the grain itself, and that all the various methods basically rely on this. The recipe above is interesting because it clearly uses salt and hops to repress bacteria and get a purer yeast culture. If you want to try this yourself it is important to buy a type of rye flour in which all of the microorganisms have not been killed.

The yeast cakes described in the previous section are similar to this method, since the cakes are made by mixing the yeast with a lot of flour. The yeast then has to compete with whatever organisms come from the flour. I saw something similar in Chuvashia in Russia, where Marina Fyodorovna stirred rye flour into her yeast to make a yeast starter. She would wait to pitch the yeast until the starter had begun working. Marina Ivanovna in Kudymkar, much further east of Chuvashia, did the same thing. This method was common in many places in western Europe too.[*]

---

[*] Example descriptions can be found in NEG.

Exactly what the rye flour contributes we still do not know, unfortunately. I collected raw rye from Kudymkar, Russia and sent it to a lab. They found only non-*Saccharomyces* yeast and abandoned the analysis.[18] So, for the time being, the question remains unanswered.

Clearly, the original farmhouse brewers got their yeast cultures from nature, somehow; and, presumably, now and then, some of them got new yeast from nature. These brewers shared the yeasts with each other, and those cultures that made the best beer tended to be the ones people preferred to borrow, reuse, and pass on. But how do the farmhouse yeasts we have collected over the past few years fit into the bigger picture of what we know about wild yeast and brewer's yeast? To answer that, I needed to understand a bit more about brewer's yeast and to find out more about what kinds of yeast exist.

Yeast Species

The yeast species we are interested in are those in the order Saccharomycetales that can ferment sugar to produce carbon dioxide (CO_2) and alcohol. As you can see in figure 4.17, nearly all of them are also members of the family Saccharomycetaceae, consisting of yeasts that reproduce by budding.

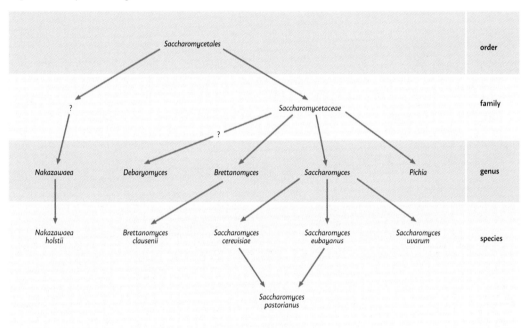

Figure 4.17. Taxonomic tree of selected yeast species in the order Saccharomycetales.

Species names in Latin consist of two parts: the first is the name of the *genus* (pl. genera), a family of closely related species. The second gives the specific species. In figure 4.17, the genera are shown on the third line, starting with *Nakazawaea*. Many of the "species" we refer to in everyday speech, such as "wheat" or "elephant," are actually genera and not species. Proper species would be common wheat versus emmer wheat, or Indian elephant versus African elephant.

Nakazawaea holstii is an obscure species, and not very much is known about it. It is not even clear which family within the order of Saccharomycetales it belongs to. Originally it was considered to be part of the genus *Pichia* and known as *Pichia holstii*, but in 2011 it was given a genus of its own and renamed to *Nakazawaea holstii*. It has been found in bark beetles, on dry-cured Spanish hams, and also in cider and on apples. And in Lithuanian farmhouse ale.

Another fairly obscure genus is *Debaryomyces*, and the best-known species is *Debaryomyces hansenii*. This yeast is unusual in that it does not require much water and can handle surprising amounts of salt. It is commonly found in cheese, sausage, and salt water. *Debaryomyces hansenii* is not a good fermenter, so it cannot be used as the primary yeast in beer. The pitching yeast at Harvey's brewery, mentioned earlier in this chapter, contains both ordinary ale yeast (*Saccharomyces cerevisiae*) and *Debaryomyces hansenii*. Their imperial stout is famous for cellaring well, and it is thought that the *Debaryomyces hansenii* may contribute to this.

Pichia is a large and well-known genus containing more than 100 species that mostly live on decaying plants, but they can also be found in cheese and can produce off-flavors in wine. In some cases, they can protect against mold. Like *Debaryomyces*, *Pichia* yeast are not good fermenters.

The genus *Brettanomyces* is also known as *Dekkera*, so every species in this genus has two names: one starting with *Brettanomyces* and another starting with *Dekkera*. *Brettanomyces* is very well known and was first described in 1904 by a researcher from the Carlsberg Laboratory.[*] *Brettanomyces* species are famous for the flavors they add during the maturation of beer and wine, but can also be used for primary fermentation. Brewers tend to refer to them as "Brett." In wine, they are often seen as unwanted infections.

The *Saccharomyces* genus is one of the most famous groups of microorganisms, and also one of the best-studied. It contains quite a few species, many of them little known. Most of the species in this genus are strong fermenters and could, in theory, be the primary fermenter in a beer. Far and away the best known in this genus is *Saccharomyces cerevisiae*, also known as "top-fermenting yeast." This is the main yeast used to ferment beer, wine, sake, mead, and all other alcoholic drinks. It is also the yeast used in baking, where it is often simply called baker's yeast. In brewing, it is often called "ale yeast" or brewer's yeast.

Saccharomyces pastorianus, also known as "bottom-fermenting yeast" or "lager yeast," is actually a hybrid of two different species. Compared to ale yeast, lager yeast can ferment at much colder temperatures, almost down to freezing point. It seems to have developed in German lager brewing. Very likely what happened was that the Germans started fermenting cold to avoid infections and produce stable beer, and when this hybrid was formed it outcompeted the original *Saccharomyces cerevisiae* and eventually took over almost completely in lager brewing.[19]

The yeasts used in farmhouse brewing could be from any of these species, although it would be expected that *Saccharomyces cerevisiae* would dominate. It would be reasonable to expect nearly all farmhouse yeasts to be either *Saccharomyces* or *Brettanomyces*, simply because these yeasts are better at fermenting than the other species and tend to win out when fermenting beer and other drinks.

---

[*] Other researchers found *Brettanomyces* before N. Hjelte Claussen, but they did not publish their findings. See Gilliland (1961, 257–61).

Knowing the species of yeast, however, is not enough. Top-fermented beer is nearly all fermented with *Saccharomyces cerevisiae*, but, as we all know, there are many strains of yeast within that species that behave differently and produce different aromas. So, in order to understand where the farmhouse yeasts belong, we need to dive deeper into that species.

The Yeast Family Tree

When the NCYC did the first kveik analysis in 2014, one reason they could not tell me where kveik fit into the landscape of brewer's yeast was that the landscape had no map. That changed in 2016 with a landmark paper that finally gave us an overview.[20] The researchers sequenced the genes of 457 yeast strains and assembled a family tree of all the strains. They looked at both brewer's yeast, wild yeast, sake yeasts, wine yeasts, and several other types of yeast, all of them *Saccharomyces cerevisiae*. They found that the yeasts clustered into separate groups, which they called "Wild," "Wine," "Beer 2," "Mixed," and "Beer 1."

Most of the yeasts that modern brewers use belong to the Beer 1 group. The Beer 2 group is considerably smaller, and consists mostly of Belgian yeast strains, especially saison yeasts, but also a few English strains. The Beer 2 group seems to be more aromatic, and most of them are also phenolic. Diastatic yeasts (STA$^+$) seem to all be part of Beer 2. Nearly all the beer strains studied in the Gallone paper belong to either Beer 1 or Beer 2, and these two groups seem to be descended from just two strains of yeast. Within the Beer 1 group the scientists found three subgroups: Belgium/Germany, UK, and US. So, the descendants of this single strain of yeast seem to have spread slowly over the centuries, leaving a clear geographic pattern.

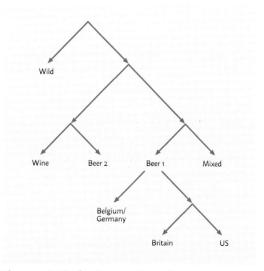

Figure 4.18. The family tree of brewer's yeast.

The above makes it seem as though all brewer's yeast comes from Belgium or Germany, but you have to remember that this tree was built from the yeast strains that are still alive. The native farmhouse and commercial yeasts that existed across most of Europe are now extinct, and therefore not in the tree. It seems likely that the Beer 1 and Beer 2 groups both came from continental Europe, but we cannot really conclude any more than that.

But it does raise the question of when brewers started reusing their yeast, which would mark the point when people started domesticating yeast. That people did not know yeast existed before Pasteur's work in the mid-nineteenth century is a myth. Accounts of beer brewing from the sixteenth and seventeenth centuries show very clearly that collecting yeast from the fermented beer and putting it into the next beer was common. There are no proper recipes from earlier centuries, but yeast is mentioned in many, many quotes from different countries and centuries, showing that people were deliberately using yeast in beer all the way back into the Middle Ages.

Logically, it makes little sense that people would have been using spontaneous fermentation. That method is slow and uncertain and takes a long time to produce drinkable beer. And, as we have seen, farmhouse brewers generally expect to have drinkable beer in a couple of days. They also usually brewed for specific occasions, like Christmas, weddings, and so on, so the beer needed to be reliably good and finished on time. Most farmers also did not have much grain to waste on bad beer, so if the beer turned bad on a regular basis they probably would not have brewed at all.

The other thing is how incredibly easy it turns out to be to keep your own yeast culture. A straw ring or a piece of wooden trunk is enough. It is not 100% reliable, but certainly far more so than spontaneous fermentation. So, you would expect brewers to have discovered yeast reuse very early, and to have continued reusing the yeast once they discovered it was possible. Looking at ancient sources, this is exactly what we find.

Pliny the Elder writes in 77 CE of the Iberians (Spanish) and Gauls (French) that they take the foam from fermenting beer and use it in bread, so that they have lighter and better bread than other peoples.[21] It seems very strange that they should have done that without also having realized they could use this foam to get their beer to ferment.

Greco-Egyptian sources from the same period mention pitchers of beer yeast, land-lease deals paid in measures of dry yeast, and even "yeast-maker" as an occupation. The yeast mentioned seems to have been used both for brewing and baking.[22] There also exists a short description of brewing that was inserted into the writings of Zosimus of Panopolis by some scribe copying the book by hand. We do not know exactly when the text was inserted, but it exists in a manuscript that dates to about 1000 CE. Max Nelson, a professor of Greek and Roman studies, thinks it "arguably reflects ancient practice" (pers. comm.). Unfortunately, the text in question is not very clear. It first describes malting, then says "grind the [grain] and make [it] into loaves, adding yeast as that for bread." The loaves are then heated and crumbled into water, and then the text ends. This sounds very like the Swedish yeast cakes, but it is fairly ambiguous. But, as Nelson says, "At least the passage shows that it was known that yeast was used to make beer."

So, it is clear that reuse of yeast began a long, long time ago, even if we do not know exactly when. In fact, we do not know for certain of any period when human beings brewed beer but did not know about the reuse of yeast. Yeast reuse may well have begun many millennia ago. We do not know how it began, but there is an enlightening example that gives us some ideas.

In parts of South America, the Quechua Indians still brew *chicha*, a farmhouse ale made from various types of maize. When he asked the brewers what they put into the wort to make it ferment, beer writer Martin Thibault was met with blank stares, until one of them suddenly lit up, excitedly saying, "One moment!" She came back with a block of sugar. Investigating more closely, Martin found that the brewers carefully reuse their fermentors without cleaning them, which of course ensures the yeast is reused in practice. But Martin remained convinced the Quechua brewers did not know what yeast was.[23]

Very likely, this was the first stage of the invention of yeast reuse: people found that not cleaning the fermentor after a good batch produced much better beer. The second stage, potentially much later, was when people realized that the sludge in the fermentor was the real reason the fermentor made good beer, and so they started deliberately reusing that. In Europe and the Middle East, the beginnings of the second stage must lie millennia in the past. The introduction of Emil Christian Hansen's techniques might be considered the third stage.

Intriguingly, the story of the chicha brewers did not end there, because some of them do harvest and reuse the yeast.[24] It seems that chicha culture in South America as a whole is in the middle of the transition from the first stage to the second, with brewers in some regions having made the transition while others have not.*

But what do the yeast cultures European farmhouse brewers reuse actually consist of? Are they wild yeast or brewer's yeast? Are they from group Beer 1, Beer 2, a new "Beer 3" group, or just from all over the family tree?

European Farmhouse Yeast: What We Know

Even where farmhouse brewing has survived, the yeast the farmers originally used are mostly gone. So, while many farmhouse yeast have been collected, they give us only a glimpse of what once existed. Still, that glimpse is very exciting.

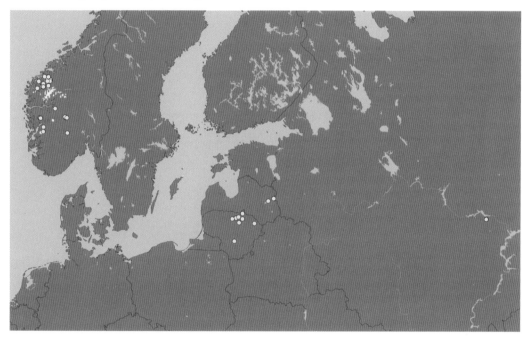

Figure 4.19. A map showing locations from which farmhouse yeast cultures have been collected. Locations correspond to cultures listed in table 4.1, except for #51, which is not shown because the location is unknown.

In total, to date, 49 cultures have been identified and about 40 have been collected (table 4.1). They come from quite a few different places:

- Most cultures are from western Norway.
- Two different cultures are from eastern Norway.
- Two different cultures were found in Latvia.
- Many cultures were found in Lithuania.
- Two different cultures are from Russia.

---

* Martin confirms what he has observed on two research visits to the region is consistent with this theory.

Analysis has been done on many of these, but not all, and what we have learned is both enlightening and confusing. These cultures that come from who knows where and have been reused for decades and probably centuries with no laboratory equipment could, in theory, contain just about any microbe capable of fermentation. But that is not what we find at all. Instead, there are clear patterns, but the patterns are not the same in different places.

Table 4.1 Currently Identified Farmhouse Yeast Cultures

Yeast	Origin	Kveik	Pitching temp. (°C)	Harvest	Dryable
#1 Sigmund	Voss, Norway	Yes	39	bottom, 84 hours	Yes
#2 Rivenes	Voss, Norway	Yes	37	top, 60 hours	?
#3 Stranda	Stranda, Norway	Yes	30	top	Yes
#4 Muri[a]	Olden, Norway	No	20	?	?
#5 Hornindal	Grodås, Norway	Yes	30	top, 40 hours	Yes
#6 Lærdal	Lærdal, Norway	Yes	30	either	Yes
#7 Granvin	Voss, Norway	Yes	30	bottom	?
#8 Tormodgarden	Sykkylven, Norway	Yes	30	bottom	Yes
#9 Ebbegarden	Stordal, Norway	Yes	28	top	Yes
#10 Framgarden	Stordal, Norway	Yes	30	?	Yes
#11 Lida	Grodås, Norway	Yes	33	top	Yes
#12 Nupen	Eidsdal, Norway	Yes	31	top, 30 hours	Yes
#13 Årset	Eidsdal, Norway	Yes	28	top	Yes
#14 Eitrheim	Bleie, Norway	Yes	37	either	Yes
#15 Nornes	Voss, Norway	Yes	36	?	?
#16 Simonaitis	Joniškelis, Lithuania	No	35	top	Yes
#17 Midtbust	Stordal, Norway	Yes	33	top	Yes
#18 Gausemel	Grodås, Norway	Yes	30	top	Yes
#19 Nystein	?	Yes	28	top	Yes
#20 Espe	Grodås, Norway	Yes	20	top	Yes
#21 Tomasgard	Grodås, Norway	Yes	29	top	Yes
#22 Stalljen	Grodås, Norway	Yes	31	either, 24 hours	Yes
#23 Otterdal	Otterdalen, Hornindal, Norway	?	29	?	Yes
#24 Unkown[b]	?	?	?	?	?
#25 Raftevold gård	Grodås, Norway	Yes	?	?	?
#26 Arnegard	Ål, Norway	?	35	top	Yes

Table 4.1 Currently Identified Farmhouse Yeast Cultures (Cont.)

Yeast	Origin	Kveik	Pitching temp. (°C)	Harvest	Dryable
#27 Skrindo	Ål, Norway	?	35	top	Yes
#28 Halvorsgard	Ål, Norway	?	32	top	Yes
#29 Løvoll	Eidsdal, Norway	?	29	top	?
#30 Markjene	Otterdalen, Hornindal, Norway	?	?	?	Yes
#31 Ner-Saure	Bjørke, Norway	?	25	?	?
#32 Jovaru	Jovarai, Lithuania	No	29	?	No
#33 Su Puta	Paliūniškis, Lithuania	No	?	?	?
#34 Čižas	Dusetos, Lithuania	No	?	?	?
#35 Wollsæter	Hellesylt, Norway	Yes	34.5	top	Yes
#37 Apynys	Kaunas, Lithuania	No	?	?	?
#39 Marina	Kshaushi, Russia	No	39	bottom	No
#40 Rima	Kshaushi, Russia	No	?	?	No
#41 Skare	Ørsta, Norway	Yes	32	top, 20 hours	Yes
#42 Pundurs	Briežuciems, Latvia	No	?	bottom	No
#43 Opshaug	Strandadalen, Norway	Yes	23.5	top	Yes
#44 Jordal	Jordal, Norway	?	32	?	Yes
#45 Rakstiņš	Bērzpils, Latvia	No	?	?	?
#46 Drąseikiai	Drąseikiai, Lithuania	No	32.5	?	?
#47 Folkestad	Nordfjordeid, Norway	?	?	?	?
#48 Hovden	Stranda, Norway	?	27.5	top	?
#51 ???	Vefsn, Norway	?	36.5	top	?
#53 Vinje	Stordal, Norway	?	27.5	top, 24 hours	?
#54 Mårem	Atrå, Norway	?	30	?	?

[a]   Not a farmhouse culture. See the discussion on page 137.
[b]   Believed to exist, but neither verified nor disproved.

Each culture turns out to contain several strains of yeast. The number of strains varies between two and at least ten.[25] The strains are usually very closely related to one another, but in some cases the strains seem to consist of groups. For example, strains 1, 2, and 3 may be closely related to one another, and 4, 5, and 6 are closely related to one another, but there is no relation between the two sets.

These cultures probably consist of even more strains than the ones that have been found by analysis, and some strains make up a much larger proportion of the culture than others. This means analyzing farmhouse yeast is a complicated proposition, and two different labs analyzing the same culture usually disagree on the number of strains. It appears as though there really is an uncountable number of different strains in the cultures, but that many of the strains are very similar to each other. Also, in any one culture, there are usually just a few dominant strains that make up the majority.

#7 Granvin

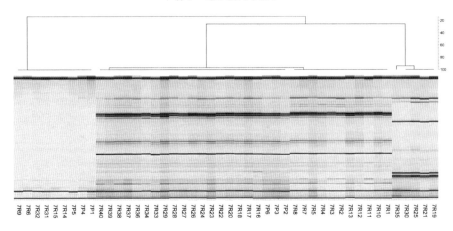

#17 Midtbust

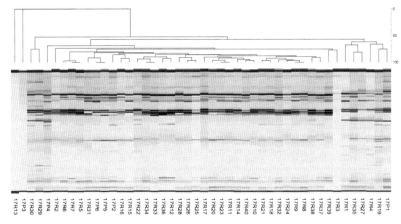

Figure 4.20. An analysis of strains in two kveik cultures by comparing genetic markers. These are family trees of the strains within each culture. The cultures are listed in table 4.1. Courtesy of Jan Steensels, KU Leuven.

The most detailed study of the strains in these cultures was done by the Catholic University of Leuven (KU Leuven). Most laboratories normally select perhaps 10 to 15 colonies, but in this case a much larger set was chosen and subjected to genetic analysis to build the family tree in figure 4.20. There are just a few strains in #7, and these can be divided into three main groups. #17 is far more complex, and it seems that there are probably even more strains than what the analysis found (fig. 4.20).

The next step is to work out what these strains actually are. Here we have to split the cultures into two groups: the western Norwegian cultures (which I will call kveik) and the others. We will start with kveik and come back to the others later.

Kveik

The kveik are all *Saccharomyces cerevisiae*.[26] Some contain bacteria, and NCYC found one that contained a little *Pichia*, but in most cases these contaminants do not seem to affect the flavor based on tastings I and others have done. It is possible that these kinds of contaminants are only temporary, sometimes growing to detectable levels, but being outcompeted by the dominant strains when the brewer continues using the yeast.

Why do these uncontrolled cultures all contain the same species of yeast? This is less surprising than it may seem. After all, the yeast strains used by brewers producing top-fermented beer are also all *Saccharomyces cerevisiae*, and those too were continuously reused yeast cultures of unknown composition, at least up until the breweries purified their cultures in modern times. So, it is not too surprising to find that farmhouse yeast is similar to commercial brewer's yeast.

The deeper reason is that *Saccharomyces cerevisiae* is naturally dominant in wort, simply because it is better than other species at exploiting this environment. It grows rapidly, and quickly adapts the environment to suit itself by reducing the pH, producing alcohol, and consuming oxygen and simple sugars. This is why beer is not usually infected, even though most homebrewers and smaller breweries make beer in conditions that are very far from sterile. Their wort contains other microorganisms besides yeast, but the yeast dominates anyway. This is perhaps most clearly seen in lambic brewing, where the brewery adds no yeast culture at all. Even so, microbiological analysis shows that, for the first three months, lambic fermentation is completely dominated by beer yeast.[27] This is precisely because it outcompetes other yeast species to the point that they really only gain a foothold after six months.

Still, many people feel it is surprising that there is no *Brettanomyces* in the Norwegian farmhouse yeasts. The argument is that Brett lives in wooden brewing equipment and is nearly impossible to remove. This turns out not to be the case. Steam and hot water can indeed kill Brett quite deep into the wood,[28] and farmhouse brewers sanitized their wooden vessels with a juniper infusion heated to boiling. Some even boiled the juniper infusion inside the vessel with hot stones (see chapter 6, p. 195). *Brettanomyces* is also relatively slow-growing, which means that even if there were a little Brett in the culture, it would probably be outcompeted by the main yeast over time. The Brett would probably also not survive the drying that has been standard practice with kveik.

As we saw with the family tree of brewer's yeast, the species *Saccharomyces cerevisiae* contains many different types of yeast (fig. 4.18). So, knowing the species is not enough. Many brewers and researchers have assumed that farmhouse yeasts must be wild, because the brewers have so little control over them. However, analysis has shown the exact opposite. Kveik are very clearly domesticated, since they can ferment maltotriose, attenuate wort sugars well, are highly flocculent, and are all POF⁻.[29]

Table 4.2 Properties by Yeast Type*

	Brewer's yeast	Kveik	Non-kveik	Wild
Alcohol tolerance	8%–10%	13%–16%	High?	Low
Phenolic	No	No	Yes?	Yes
Attenuation	70%–80%	75%–85%	Good	Poor
Flocculation	Good	Excellent	Variable	Poor
Drying tolerance	Mostly no	Yes	Mostly no	Yes
Heat tolerance	18–22°C	41–43°C	High	Unknown
Fast ferment	No	Yes	Yes?	No!
Aroma	Fruity	Tropical fruit	Aromatic	Aromatic

One point on which kveik differ from those of ordinary brewer's yeast is that they can all survive drying. The reason as explained earlier, is that Norwegian farmers all dried their yeast between brews because they had to, so yeast that could not handle drying never got established in Norway.

Another difference is that kveik strains seem to consistently ferment faster than modern yeast strains.[30] It is not unusual for a kveik fermentation to be done within 30 or 40 hours, even without a starter and even though the alcohol content is typically quite high (7%–13% ABV). When Richard Preiss received his first kveik samples, he rehydrated one sample in water, put it into a small tube with wort, and then went to lunch. Returning 40 minutes later, he was astonished to find it already fermenting. "That's when I first realized this wasn't normal yeast," he said.[31] These yeasts really are very aggressive. As one farmhouse brewer put it, "My kveik starts making hissing noises as soon as it sees sugar."[32] Exactly why these yeasts ferment so quickly is not clear, but it is not just because of the high fermentation temperatures. Comparisons at "normal" fermentation temperatures show the farmhouse kveik yeast still ferments more rapidly than commercial yeasts.[33]

Older accounts describe how brewers monitored the fermentor to see when the yeast started. Some used a wooden beer bowl placed in the fermentor so that they could hear it bumping against the side of the vessel when the wort began fermenting.[34] If nothing happened, they might attempt to find another yeast or try heating the wort. It seems people were impatient for the fermentation to begin, and they probably selected for yeast strains that showed activity quickly after pitching.

The alcohol tolerance of the kveik strains is also impressive. The various strains collected can handle from 13% up to 16% ABV,[35] which is considerably more than most brewer's yeast and far more than most wild yeast.

The flavors produced by kveik seem to have certain family resemblances: clean, aromatic, tropically fruity, and non-phenolic. However, even within the kveik family there is substantial variation. The Voss kveiks produce orange-like, slightly spicy flavors; #3 Stranda has deep tropical fruit, with some banana and melon; the Hornindal kveik cultures have milky caramel, fruit, some citrus, and sometimes mushroom; and #20 Espe gives warming alcohol and fruit, cognac and plums.

In general, the northern kveik cultures seem to have more strains than the southern ones, probably because brewers in this area have been taught that they must mix their kveik with another every five to ten years to keep it vigorous. Some say the kveik would get "weak" if it were not mixed, others that it would become "in-bred."

How do we know that these strains are actually the same farmhouse yeasts that were used in the old days? Farmhouse yeast strains are clearly domesticated, yet different from those found in yeast banks around the world. If what we have collected is not the original farmhouse brewer's yeast, then where did these domesticated strains come from?

Some of the collected yeasts stand out from the others, however. One of the first to be collected was named #4 Muri, after the farm it came from in Olden, western Norway. The last traditional brew on the farm was in 1991, after which the yeast was dried and stored in a food storehouse on the farm. When the kveik buzz started growing in Norway, the son of the farmer, Bjarne Muri, went back and found the yeast. He went through several cycles of washing and

Figure 4.21. The "#14 Eitrheim" kveik (table 4.1) in the brewhouse at Aga, Hardanger, western Norway.

Figure 4.22. The #4 Muri yeast.

growing, mostly getting "black stuff," but eventually the yeast did grow.[36] He shared the yeast with other brewers, and it was even sold commercially for a while by White Labs as WLP6788. This yeast stood out from the other kveik strains, however, because it was phenolic, and because it made a highly sulfurous aroma, rather like rubber boots fresh from the store. The aroma would disappear after some months of maturing, after which the yeast produced something like a fruity Belgian blonde.

Genetic analysis has shown that #4 Muri is not *Saccharomyces cerevisiae*. It seems to be a hybrid of *Saccharomyces cerevisiae* and *Saccharomyces uvarum*.[37] And it is clearly POF+. Some of the other Norwegian yeast strains we collected also turned out to be POF+. After a while, we started seeing a pattern. The ones revived from dried cultures older than about a decade were dead if a laboratory tried to revive them, and POF+ if amateurs revived them. It is likely that the amateurs were growing contaminants rather than the original cultures. The exception was any culture that had been stored in a freezer.

#4 Muri eventually proved to be the same yeast as White Labs WLP351, a hefeweizen yeast. Clearly, Bjarne Muri accidentally grew a contaminant that was somehow present in his apartment, probably from a previous hefeweizen homebrew.[38]

That many of the other farmhouse yeast strains are genuinely new strains, however, is evident from genetic analysis. Richard Preiss and colleagues at Escarpment Labs and the University of Guelph isolated many strains of kveik and built a family tree based on their genetic fingerprints. In the tree was also one Lithuanian farmhouse yeast and 11 well-known commercial strains. The result was fascinating: the kveik strains clearly stood out as a separate sub-branch of the tree, while the non-Norwegian yeast all ended up in another branch. This did not quite prove that the Norwegian kveik strains deserve a new "Beer 3" group of their own, but it certainly showed that kveik is a separate family of brewer's yeast. It also showed, again, that the farmhouse brewers had control over their yeast, since wherever you go in western Norway, every time you get farmhouse yeast from someone it always comes from this same family. In fact, it must once have started out as a single strain that gradually spread across all of western Norway.

But where did that strain come from? And where in the family tree does kveik belong? To find out, the researchers also had the complete genome of six of the kveik strains sequenced.[39] The results were then combined with the DNA sequences from Gallone et al.,[40] which gave us the tree shown in figure 4.23. To my surprise, it showed that kveik belongs to the Beer 1 family, splitting off quite near the root. In fact, the first division in Beer 1 has the kveik strains plus three hefeweizen strains on one side, and the rest of Beer 1 on the other.

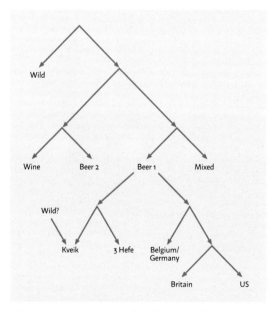

Figure 4.23. Brewer's yeast family tree with kveik inserted. Based on Preiss et al. (2018). Adapted from Preiss, Tyrawa, Krogerus, Garshol and van der Merwe (2018), *Front. Microbiol.* 9:2137.

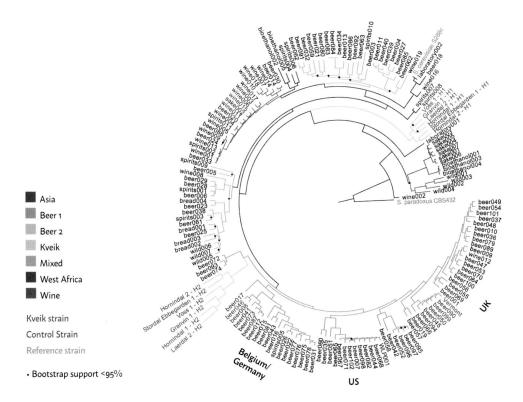

Figure 4.24. The full family tree, from Preiss et al. (2018). The two halves of the kveik genomes shown in red. Adapted from Preiss, Tyrawa, Krogerus, Garshol and van der Merwe (2018), *Front. Microbiol.* 9:2137.

As if that were not surprising enough, the story has another twist: the genetic signature of kveik indicates that it was formed by two very different yeast strains from the same species mating. So, the researchers split the two parts of the genome apart, then inserted them in the tree separately. One half ended up in the same place as before, but the other half ended up in a kind of no-man's land, not really related to anything else. The researchers think this means that kveik was formed by a domesticated Beer 1 yeast mating with a wild yeast. Whether the unknown ancestor really was a wild yeast or not is just a guess at this point. The reason the hefeweizen yeast strains were grouped with kveik is probably because they too show signs of being hybrids, and not necessarily because of any shared historical connection.

What this means is that kveik comes from the same ancestor that gave rise to most American, British, Belgian, and German top-fermenting yeast strains. An interesting similarity with lager yeast is that both kveik and lager yeast are hybrids, although kveik is a hybrid where both parents belong to the same species.

Whether the hybridization that created kveik happened in Norway or not we do not know, nor do we know when it happened. It is clear that the ancestor of kveik branched off from Beer 1 several centuries ago, but how many is impossible to say. It could be four centuries, or eight, or twelve. We also do not know how the ancestor came to Norway. It may have been by ship to the busy trading port of Bergen, or it may have been overland. Perhaps the farmhouse brewers in Denmark, Sweden, and eastern Norway were also mostly using yeasts in the same family? Or perhaps not, given that the southern Swedes seemed to often get new yeast from grain.

Figure 4.25. Sverre Skrindo's gong dried on cloth. Ål, eastern Norway.

Since all the yeasts from these areas seem to be dead, we may never find out. However, two cultures of yeast have been collected from eastern Norway that may give us some insight. High up in the valley of Hallingdal, in the mountains separating eastern and western Norway, Sverre Skrindo in Ål is using a yeast he calls "gong." It is preserved between brews dried on pieces of cloth and seems to have been in the village as long as anyone can remember.* But is gong the same thing as kveik? Early initial findings hint that gong may be related to kveik.[41] The other culture was collected very recently from Tinn in Telemark, about 80 km to the south of Ål.† Here, in the tiny village of Atrå, several families seem to have been maintaining yeast cultures they call "berm." Whether berm is related to gong and kveik, we do not know, but it is possible kveik was also used in eastern Norway. It looks like in the future we may have some chance of finding out at least what was used in eastern Norway.

Non-Kveik Farmhouse Yeasts

Kveik has so far been found only in Norway. What about farmhouse yeasts from Latvia, Lithuania, and Russia? This is where the story gets strange. These yeast strains behave in much the same way as kveik in that they ferment equally warm and fast, but many of these more eastern strains seem to be POF⁺, and they mostly cannot be dried. They are also not all *Saccharomyces cerevisiae*. One is pure *Brettanomyces*, while another is *Nakazawaea holstii*. One is *Saccharomyces uvarum* mixed

---

* #27 Skrindo seems to be the same as #28 Halvorsgard, which I mentioned on p. 99 in the conversation with Bjarne Halvorsgard.
† See "#54 Mårem" in table 4.1.

Figure 4.26. Marina Fyodorovna preparing a yeast starter (*see* "#39 Marina" in table 4.1). Kshaushi, Chuvashia, Russia.

with *Brettanomyces custersianus* and *B. anomalus*. Some seem to be hybrids. And of those that are *Saccharomyces cerevisiae*, some contain other species.

Why the Lithuanian and Russian yeast cultures are so different from the Norwegian ones is not clear at all. We need more yeast samples and more research to answer that, if we can answer it at all. Richard Preiss has proposed that by drying their yeast the Norwegian brewers may have helped to kill off species other than *Saccharomyces cerevisiae*, and that is why their cultures contain only that species. But at the moment, this is all speculation.

No sequencing of the entire genome has been done on the Latvian, Lithuanian, and Russian farmhouse yeasts, so current results are a bit uncertain. The two Russian cultures do not seem to be related to anything else. The Lithuanian and Latvian ones may be related to each other, and they may also belong to some family of brewer's yeast. Work is ongoing to tell us more about them.

Several of these yeasts come from commercial breweries, which means that tasting the original beers made with them is possible. One Lithuanian yeast, #16 Simonaitis, has been widely shared with homebrewers and is also available commercially. Apart from fermenting hot and fast, #16 Simonaitis is very different from the kveik strains. The original culture produces powerful fruity and phenolic aromas. However, the original contains lactic acid bacteria, which are probably kept in check by the huge amounts of hops that Julius Simonaitis uses.[42] When other people brew with this culture, they usually get sour beer. Commercial versions of #16 Simonaitis that have had the bacteria removed are reportedly very fruity. Saison yeast should very likely be considered farmhouse

Figure 4.27. Julius Simonaitis tasting his yeast (#16) to make sure it's good, just like Sigmund Gjernes does. Joniškelis, north Lithuania. Photo courtesy of Alastair Philip Wiper.

yeast similar to these more recently discovered yeast strains. Although it has not been conclusively proven, it seems likely that commercial saison brewing really did come out of an earlier tradition of true farmhouse brewing. Saison yeast also seems similar to other farmhouse yeast in its tolerance of high temperatures, even if it is quite different in terms of flavor.

What is striking is that all of these farmhouse yeast strains have properties that match the historic ethnographic descriptions of how people used the yeast in each area. That is, farmhouse yeast has a tolerance for high temperatures and high concentrations of alcohol and also ferments quickly. In addition, the ones that come from regions where the yeast was dried can still be dried. Some of the ones that come from regions of more mixed usage cannot be dried while others can.

It actually seems that one could predict some of the properties of farmhouse yeast from a specific area by looking at how farmers in that area brewed. This is another very strong argument that farmhouse yeast is domesticated.

Bread Yeast

Commercial bread yeast became available in the mid-nineteenth century, and apparently it was quite popular with those who could afford it: "The first commercial yeast came to Elverum [eastern Norway] in 1875/76. People travelled all the way from Våler to get hold of it."[43]

Bread yeast has a poor reputation among modern brewers, but, surprisingly, in the regions where the original farmhouse yeast has been lost the brewers have switched to using the local bread yeast.

In Stjørdal, Gotland, Finland, Estonia, as well as in parts of Latvia, Lithuania, and Russia, the brewers all use bread yeast. And not only do they use bread yeast, but they make good, often excellent, beer with it, although flocculation is often not as good as it could be. The scientific literature seems to agree these yeasts can make good beer.[44]

Strikingly, most of these brewers use the yeast in much the same way they used the original farmhouse yeast. That is, they often ferment nearly as warm and as rapidly. Bread yeast usually produces pleasant, clean aromas, often more aromatic than normal brewer's yeast. So, bread yeast as a rule seems to behave surprisingly like farmhouse yeast, certainly more like farmhouse yeast than like commercial brewer's yeast.

Microbiologist Kristoffer Krogerus investigated the brewing properties of the Finnish Suomen Hiiva bread yeast, which is used in both *sahti* and *koduõlu*. He found that it fermented slightly faster than the commercial brewer's yeasts he compared with, had higher attenuation, and produced similar aroma. Suomen Hiiva produced significantly more isoamyl acetate (banana aroma), which will surprise nobody who has tasted sahti. The yeast was clearly POF[+] and it flocculated rather poorly. His conclusion was that "it is evident that the Finnish baker's yeast is perfectly usable for beer fermentations."[45]

Interestingly, bread yeast in general seems to be well suited for brewing, since it can usually ferment maltose and maltotriose and has high sugar tolerance. Genetic surveys of yeast usually classify strains of bread yeast together with those of brewer's yeast. In fact, a recent, more comprehensive study by Fay et al. changed the name of the "Mixed" group from Gallone et al. to "beer/baking" because it seemed to consist mostly of a mix of brewer's yeast and baker's yeast with some distilling yeast as well.[46]

How can this be? In Scandinavian ethnographic accounts, people generally say that the yeast from beer making was also used for their baking. Where people had sourdough that was almost always kept separate from the beer yeast. People used their farmhouse yeast for baking because brewing produces yeast, in fact, more yeast than you can use, but baking consumes yeast. So when you have a household with both baking and brewing, it is almost inevitable that you will end up using some of the surplus yeast from your beer in your bread. In towns it was also common for bakers to get their yeast from the local breweries. To

Figure 4.28. Beer fermented with the Norwegian bread yeast Idun Blå, showing poor flocculation. Oslo, Norway.

take one example, in eighteenth-century Copenhagen, brewers were required by law to give yeast for free to the bakeries.[47]

The yeast companies that produce bread yeast must have gotten this yeast from somewhere. Some probably came from sourdough, but it seems likely that many of these yeasts came from farmhouse brewing. Since so many of the original farmhouse yeast cultures are dead, proving this is going to be difficult, but it fits well with what we know, and likewise it fits well with the properties these yeasts have.

Dying Out

Given how good these yeasts sound in theory—rapid fermenters, thermotolerant, easy to use, and highly flavorful—it does seem surprising that people stopped using them. However, maintaining your own yeast culture indefinitely means having to be careful and keeping backup cultures. It also means constantly running a higher risk of infection and having wort that will not ferment because the yeast has died. Many people who use kveik prefer to get it from a "kveik supplier" like Sigmund in Voss rather than maintaining their own culture, simply because it is easier and feels like a safer option.

Increasingly, maintaining your own yeast culture must also have seemed old-fashioned and strange. In western Norway, some early vendors of homebrewing supplies argued forcefully against kveik, claiming that it contained "all kinds of contaminants." Reportedly, everyone buying malt and hops from the local homebrew shop in Hardanger was told "and then you need yeast." In the 1990s, kveik was common in Hardanger, but twenty years later only a few families had it. It takes a good bit of self-confidence to stick to the old method while everyone says you are being absurdly old-fashioned.

Being the last brewer in a community to use your own yeast culture is the hardest of all, because then there is nowhere to turn if the yeast goes bad. The Eitrheim family in Bleie, Hardanger, in western Norway is one example. The family patriarch, Jakob Eitrheim, told me that he has kept cultures of his kveik dating all the way back to the 1990s, just to be absolutely sure that he is not going to lose the yeast if it goes bad.[48]

And, sometimes, accidents happen. Sigurd Johan Saure[49] said his family used to hang the yeast up to dry in fly netting in a house on the farm. One day, in the late 1990s, they pitched the yeast and found fly larvae floating up to the surface. After that, they switched to using a freezer, and a few years later they stopped using kveik altogether.

One brewer told me that the last time he used kveik he collected the yeast in two full glass jars, which he put in his cellar. One of the glasses exploded with such force that glass shards were embedded in the door on the other side of the room. "Had anyone been there they could have been killed," he said. Yeast slurry and glass shards covered the fruit and other things stored in the room. And it was not over yet, since there was still the other jar. Nobody dared touch the second glass, so they covered the shelf with a tarpaulin. A couple of weeks later, the other glass exploded too. "There was no more brewing with kveik after that," he said dryly.[50]

There were, of course, good reasons to keep using the yeast. Flavor was a major factor. Bjarne Halvorsgard bought dried brewer's yeast and tried it at 24°C, like it said on the packet, but the beer was "nearly undrinkable." He added, "It had a completely different taste." I heard similar complaints from other brewers too. Ove Kambestad said his group of four brewers had switched to lab yeast from kveik. One of the brewers complained that the flavor of the beer from the new yeast was not as good, but they changed anyway.

It is not clear when the use of farmhouse yeast died out in the various parts of northern Europe where it was common. It very likely was alive in England into the twentieth century. Räsänen thinks it died out in Finland in the 1950s.[51] On Gotland, Anders Salomonsson wrote that the last time he heard of "hemjäst" (homegrown yeast) was in the early 1970s.[52] A survey response from Bredstrup in Denmark from 1971 gives the impression the yeast was alive there then, but it is not definitive.[53] Several brewers I spoke with on the Estonian island of Saaremaa thought the yeast there died out in the 1990s. In Norway, Latvia, Lithuania, and Russia it is still alive. As far as anyone knows, those are the only places in Europe where farmhouse yeast is still alive in traditional brewing.

The farmhouse yeasts that have survived have also come very close to dying out. In Hardanger, there only seem to be two families who still have yeast. South of the Jostedal glacier most of the other surviving yeast cultures seem to come from Dyrvedalen in Voss, where there were 12 farms brewing into the 1990s. Today, there are only four farms brewing there.

Further north, although many farmhouse yeasts have been collected, just about everyone seems to have stopped using them. The exceptions are the 10 to 15 brewers in Hornindal and a handful in Stordal. We were lucky that many people in this area preserved their yeast in freezers, so that even when they stopped using it ten or twenty years ago, it was still alive and well preserved.

In Hornindal, Terje Raftevold took me to the small valley of Otterdalen where his uncle lived. His uncle had been brewing since 1944, but it turned out his beer had started turning sour on a regular basis, so Terje's brother had thrown the kveik away just a few months before I came. "I didn't know, or I probably wouldn't have let him," said the uncle sadly.

Figure 4.29. Three vintages of kveik from Hornindal, all dead.

Leaving that house, we drove some 100 meters to the next house. Terje said the family there had their own kveik, although it had also gone sour. We stopped the car, and through an open upstairs window we could hear a large family having dinner. Terje shouted some greetings through the window, then asked if we could have a sample of their kveik.

"We don't have kveik anymore. It went bad," was the answer.

"We don't care if it's good or not," shouted Terje. "We just want to check the genetics."

"One moment," came the answer. Then, in an aside to someone out of sight, "If they're going to study it on that level that's different."

A few minutes later, a man opened the door and brought out three large plastic boxes of yeast, labeled 2003, 2005, and 2007. Unfortunately, it was all dead.[*]

The situation seems to be similar in Lithuania and Latvia: very few people have their own yeast, and most farmhouse brewers seem to be using either baking yeast or commercial yeast.

People have suggested that the farmhouse yeasts in places like Stjørdal and Finland, where the original yeast died out, must not have been very good, since people were willing to switch to bread yeast. However, this is clearly not true. Ove Kambestad, mentioned earlier, is just one example. Writing about Stjørdal, Leirfall says explicitly that one does not get the same good flavor with baking yeast, but that people were switching anyway.[54] Until the early twentieth century, farmhouse brewers in Finland did not use bread yeast because their own farmhouse yeast was considered better.[55] But they stopped using it anyway.

Finland is something of a special case. The pitching temperature used to be equally high in Finland,[56] but after the traditional yeast was lost the brewers have changed their approach. The Suomen Hiiva bread yeast has to be handled very carefully to get clean flavors, and it also contains some lactic acid bacteria.[57] Because of this, many brewers now cool the wort to just a few degrees above freezing, pitch the yeast, and then let the wort rise to ambient temperature by itself. This way the yeast will start more slowly and produce cleaner flavors, and there is less risk of sour beer.

One has to wonder what the farmhouse yeast was like in the places where it has now died out. From the documentation I have, it must have been able to ferment quickly and warm, like kveik. But, based on the lab anal-

Figure 4.30. Petteri Lähdeniemi at the Finlandia Sahti brewery, fondly regarding his fermenting sahti. Sastamala, Finland.

ysis of the surviving farmhouse yeast strains, they could have been anything at all. Very likely they were domesticated and produced good beer. Given what has been written about how these yeasts behaved, they were probably much more like kveik than like modern commercial yeast.

So how did commercial brewers end up with a very narrow side branch of the domesticated brewer's yeasts that have been used in Europe? Most of the commercial yeast seems to descend from only two yeast strains, but the ancestry of the few farmhouse yeast strains that have survived is considerably wider than that. And why did the commercial brewers end up with slow and temperature-sensitive yeasts that are easily stressed? I cannot help but feel there has to be a reason, but, so far, I cannot think what it might be.

---

[*] It is still listed in table 4.1 as "#30 Markjene," but nobody has been able to revive it.

Kveik Renaissance

Kveik used to be viewed with considerable scepticism among modern Norwegian homebrewers, and also by the western Norwegian homebrew merchants selling supplies and providing training. But analysis has since shown that the kveik yeast strains are domesticated top-fermenting brewer's yeast and are highly suitable for brewing. The traditional cultures may contain some contaminants, but these rarely affect the flavor.

Kveik has recently become very popular among modern homebrewers, who propagate and exchange cultures with each other, posting their experiences in online forums. Many homebrewers say they prefer kveik over normal yeast, since it ferments so quickly and produces drinkable beer in a very short time.

Several yeast labs in the US, Canada, and Poland now sell kveik commercially, and I have counted at least 443 commercial beers brewed with kveik. One was picked by three expert judges as one of the 10 best Norwegian beers on the market in 2017.[58] In 2017, the overall winner of the American National Homebrew Competition, out of 8613 competing brews, was a beer produced with Sigmund Gjernes's kveik.

In several places around Norway, people have now become excited about trying to revive or find the old farmhouse yeasts from those regions. There have been calls for yeast in the newspapers and on the radio, and several enthusiastic brewers have been trawling through old farmhouses looking for old yeast rings, beer barrels, and fermentors. In particular, Jørund Geving in Stjørdal has been extremely active.

Many samples of old, dried yeast have been found, but, unfortunately, none of the attempts at reviving them have been successful. The closest so far are two strains of *Debaryomyces hansenii* that were revived from the dried foam around the bunghole of a beer cask from the Sve farm in Stjørdal. These strains have very low alcohol tolerance, so they cannot have been the main fermenting yeast, but *Debaryomyces hansenii* is robust and can survive drying for long periods. It very likely was a part of the original yeast culture, which makes for an interesting parallel with the Harvey's yeast.

The Word "Kveik"

I came back from my 2014 trip through western Norway thinking everyone there called their farmhouse yeast kveik, and this delusion persisted for many years. Eventually, I built a map of the dialect words for yeast in different places and was astonished to find that large parts of western Norway instead used *gjest(er)*, *gjær*, and *berm* for yeast.

The word kveik was used in Hardanger and Voss, southern Sogn, and in the inland districts of southern Norway (on the coast they used gjær). It was also used in the inner parts of Sunnmøre. But north of Voss, all the way up in Stranda, Stein Langlo grew up calling yeast gjær. He never corrected my assumption that he called it kveik, so it was only when I was creating the map that I realized my mistake.

In Sweden, people mostly called the yeast *jäst*, but some places (particularly the southern tip) people called it *gär* or *jäl*. In Denmark the word was *gær*.

Gjest, gjester, and jäst are all easily recognizable as coming from the same root as the English "yeast" and Dutch *gist*, which originally developed out of a word meaning "froth." Kveik, on the other hand, comes from the same root as the English "quick" used in the sense of being alive. In fact, in dialectal Norwegian, "kveik" is two different nouns. One is female and means the yeast, while the other is male and means to breathe new life into something. The male noun is used for the act of kindling a fire and, in a metaphorical sense, for inspiring people to work harder.[59]

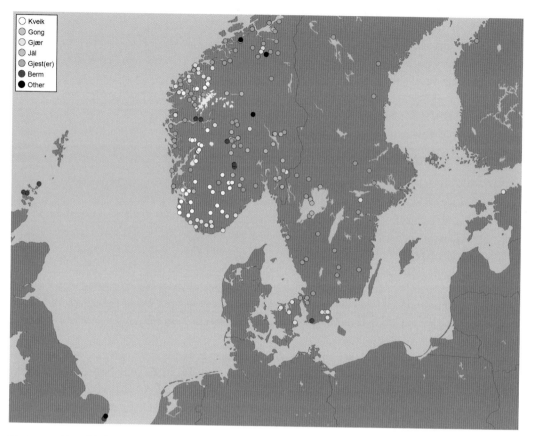

Figure 4.31. Map of dialect words for yeast. The yellow dot in Estonia is from the Swedish-speaking population on the island of Vormsi pre-1944 (EU 30584). Danish data have not been coded up, but Denmark would probably be 100% yellow.

In English farmhouse brewing, people seem to mostly have called the yeast "barm." It is interesting that in central Sogn in western Norway people used the word "berm" for the same thing.

Many people think kveik is a style of beer, but it really, literally means yeast and nothing else. The traditional farmhouse styles have other names. If you try asking a Norwegian farmhouse brewer for kveik, he is going to give you dried yeast chips, not beer.

Many non-Norwegians struggle with how to pronounce "kveik." The correct, Norwegian pronunciation is close to the English "quake" but with a "v" sound. If you try saying something like "qvake" or "kvike" you will get fairly close.

Today, the word kveik has come to mean any yeast that genetically belongs to the same family as the farmhouse yeasts collected from western Norway. So far, kveik has only been found in that region, but members of the family could still turn up in other places too.

5

FARMHOUSE BREWING PROCESSES

In modern craft brewing, everyone mostly uses the same process with a few minor variations. The farmhouse world, however, has mind-bending variations in the way beer is made. Many farmhouse brewing processes produce flavors that are very different from those you get from normal brewing practice, so farmhouse brewing has great potential for new and interesting beers.

People recreating ancient and historical beers usually ignore the process completely. They tend to focus on getting the same ingredients, thinking the ingredients make the beer, and then forget that old brewers used completely different methods. Such recreations will be nothing like the originals; instead, they usually taste like modern beer with a couple of extra ingredients.

The problem with these older processes is that having the process documented on paper is a very different thing from having it as part of a living tradition. There are many tiny details in each process that together make the final flavor. One example is the Finnish speciality *taari*, which everyone thought had died out. Several Finnish sahti brewers have tried to recreate taari from older documents. One Finnish brewer, Jouko Ylijoki, tried, but was frustrated because of "a lack of reference—[Jouko] does not know what taari should taste or look like. He has made taari two or three times . . . and he has gotten different results each time."[1]

Therefore, it is difficult to write about brewing processes we only know from documents, which is why I have taken care to travel to visit brewers, see how they brew, and taste their beers. If you have not tasted the beer and do not know the full recipe, it is nearly impossible to understand what the beer tastes like and what the process actually contributes to the whole.

Hornindal, Norway

On my Norwegian road trip in 2014, I met a group of farmhouse brewers in Stranda who had modernized their own brewing process and stopped using kveik (*see* chapter 3, p. 41). They told me there were still people using the traditional process in nearby Hornindal. You could taste the difference between the modern process and the traditional one with a single sip, they said. Also, they added, the people in Hornindal did not know how to take care of their kveik, so the beer had gone sour, although the people there claimed the beer should be that way.

I did not quite know what to make of this, but it sounded interesting. Later on, I was given a sample of a kveik from Hornindal. The sample was sent to NCYC for analysis, and the immediate response was that this kveik contained bacteria. Not very surprising, given what I had been told in Stranda. I asked the people at NCYC if they could send me back the kveik cleaned of bacteria, which they promised to do.

Meanwhile, I was offered a bottle of the beer made with this kveik. My expectations were low, but I figured there is such a thing as good sour beer and, in any case, I was curious. I opened the bottle at a tasting with friends where we all brought our best beers. We had just had Cantillon's Lou Pepe, a *gueuze* that had been received with much oohing and aahing. Now people were looking at glasses containing what looked like a hefe-weizen with no head.

And then complete silence fell in the room. People were simply stunned by this beer, which was unlike anything any of us had ever tasted. The aroma and flavor were an improb-able mix of fresh fruit, milky caramel, and

Figure 5.1. Terje Raftevold's beer at the tasting in Oslo. Note the gray tinge the beer has; this is typical of raw ale.

shiitake mushroom, all meshing perfectly. The background was made up by minerally, straw-like notes and a fresh, green juniper character. It was fairly sweet, but not overly so, and I could detect no hops in it, nor any acidity. The bitterness from the juniper was what was balancing it. And we all agreed it was better than the Cantillon we had just had.

There was one hint in the flavor, though, that gave me some ideas as to how the beer had been brewed. The straw-like, mealy, green flavors were very similar to some of the Lithuanian farmhouse ales. Could there be some common tricks shared between the farmsteads in north Lithuania and this beer from an isolated valley in the fjord country of western Norway?

I realized I had to learn what on earth the brewer had done to make this beer. I tried to get the recipe from him in writing. I got the ingredient list, but details on things like mashing proved impossible to ferret out. After some persuasion, he agreed to let me come brew with him in Innvik, near Hornindal. The brewer turned out to be Terje Raftevold, a tall, athletic man with piercing bright blue eyes and a shaved head. He looked, to my mind, like a professional soldier, but it turned out he was a teacher at the local high school.

Figure 5.2. The brewhouse used by Terje Raftevold, on Ørjan B. Skåden's farm, with the stream running underneath it.

Terje learned to brew from his uncle when he was 17, during a long summer holiday on the family farm in Hornindal. His uncle in turn had learned to brew from Terje's grandmother at the age of 14. That was in 1944. Now Terje brewed in a small *eldhus*, literally a "fire house," which is a traditional rough kitchen for tasks like brewing, flat bread baking, sausage-making, and so on. The brewhouse had a small brook literally running underneath the floor with steps inside leading down to it, which was quite handy.

Terje filled a copper kettle with water from a garden hose, then started a fire underneath. He took some juniper branches from a garbage bag and cut them up to make them fit in the kettle. The mix was then boiled to make a juniper infusion.

Once the infusion had boiled a while Terje ladled it into a big plastic tun and let it stand a while to cool down. He brought out another big plastic tun and poured some malt grist from a bag into that, using a bucket to pour the scalding juniper infusion on top. Then he started stirring it with a mash paddle. At intervals, he would add more grist, then more of the infusion, stirring all the while. Finally, he was satisfied and walked away.

Figure 5.3. Terje, left, moving the mash into the lauter tun. His assistant, right, adding more water to the kettle.

I looked at Terje's retreating back, wondering what had made him suddenly decide he was done. I had seen no thermometer. I had, however, brought my own, so I ran over and measured the temperature. It was 73.8°C. "So," I asked Terje carefully, "that's a pretty warm mash temperature, isn't it?"

"Well," said Terje carelessly, "I don't usually brew in the middle of summer, so the malt is probably warmer than usual now. I guess it might be a little warmer than usual." He added that this was actually the first time anyone had measured his mash temperature. When Terje brewed again in November, I had an accomplice measure the temperature again: 74°C. When Terje brewed in March, they just sent me a photo of a thermometer showing 73.9°C. So, Terje might not have known the correct mash temperature in degrees, but he does seem to be able to hit it consistently.

Terje now refilled the kettle with cold water to heat more of the infusion. I asked him how long he intended to mash, and the answer was, "Until the kettle starts boiling." That turned out to be an hour and a half.

Suddenly Terje brought out a long piece of wood with lots of holes drilled in it. "We call this a *rustekuse*," he said, with an embarrassed grin. The first part of the word is the western Norwegian dialect word for the lauter tun. The second part is pretty rude. It turns out to have a more polite name too: *rustesko*, with the second half this time meaning "shoe." The rustesko was laid directly over a tap near the bottom of the lauter tun, with juniper branches going on top. As usual, this is to support the filter bed in the lauter tun. At this point, Terje did something I had not seen before: he did not just lay the branches directly in the tun but dipped them in a bucket of scalding juniper infusion first. I watched him as he stood there laying the branches down in a cloud of steam.

Figure 5.4. Terje dropping flakes of dried kveik into wort.

Figure 5.5. Terje's yeast starter, 31 minutes later.

Eventually, the mash was transferred by ladle to the lauter tun and laid carefully on top of the juniper branches. More scalding hot juniper infusion was added, and, after a quick recirculation, we started the traditional slow running. The wort was run off into steel milk cans, in which a small muslin bag with hops was floating. The milk cans were put into a plastic basin of cold water to cool, before being emptied into the fermentor, a big insulated square steel tank originally intended for milk. It may seem like I am forgetting something here, but I am not. Terje does not boil the wort at all. That is traditional for the farmhouse brewing in this area.

While we were running off the wort, Terje brought out a plastic bucket and a small plastic box. The box contained his kveik, retrieved from his father-in-law's freezer that morning, and was now thawed. Terje poured some wort into the bucket and let it cool, before sprinkling the dried yeast flakes directly into the wort. The time was now 2:30 p.m. precisely. Terje covered the bucket with a cloth and put it away.

Exactly 31 minutes later, we went back to the bucket and lifted the cloth. The surface of the wort was now covered in what looked like brown porridge, full of bubbles. Clearly, the kveik had needed less than 30 minutes to turn from dried flakes into visibly fermenting yeast.

"Here in Hornindal we call this *mariaue*," said Terje. This made me curious. Literally, it means "Mari's eyes," and Mari is a common Norwegian woman's name. The part about the eyes I could understand, because the bubbles in the starter look a little like eyes. But who is Mari? A Norwegian dialect dictionary by Aasen gave me the answer:[2] it is the Virgin Mary! Norway has been Protestant since 1537, so clearly this is not a new word.

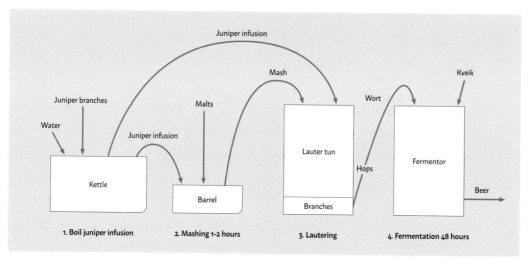

Figure 5.6. Terje Raftevold's brewing process.

Figure 5.7. Party in the brewhouse. Oppskåke is always held in the brewhouse.

Once all the wort had been run off and cooled to 30°C, Terje took the bucket and poured it into the fermentor. Apart from the cleaning up, we were now done with the brewing. Three and a half hours later we came back and checked on the fermentation, and the beer was now covered by a thick hat[*] of foam. Terje always tastes the beer at this point to check on it, so I did the same, and in my mouth it was as warm as blood The taste seemed fine so far.

Exactly 40 hours after pitching the yeast, we came back to collect the yeast by skimming off the foam on top of the beer. Terje said it is important to do it around this time, because if he waits until 48 hours the foam tends to have collapsed, making it harder to collect the yeast. The yeast then goes to his father-in-law, who washes it in water before drying it on baking parchment and putting it in the freezer.

Terje normally racks the beer 48 hours after pitching, because the beer is usually done fermenting then. I measured the gravity of the batch we had just made at 40 hours, and again at 48, and found no change. It did seem the beer was pretty close to done.

At this point it is traditional in western Norway to have a party in the brewhouse for friends and neighbors. The party is known as *oppskåke*, which literally means "shaking up." Basically, it is racking.

So, there I was, in a rough old brewhouse in a green field right underneath the white-capped mountains, about a kilometer from the fjord. Around me were Terje, a bunch of farmers, and Terje's father-in-law, Oddvin, who was the former mayor of the county. We were seated on plastic folding chairs around the rough wooden table where the lauter tun had stood during brewing.

The beer was served by ladling it directly from the fermentor into plastic cups. It was flat, with hardly any carbonation, and sweet, with citrus, earth, and pea flavors. Rather different from the matured beer, but good. I could feel the alcohol warming my mouth. Even this early, it was a great beer, almost too drinkable at 7.5% ABV.

The talk around the table at the oppskåke turned to energy production regulations, a subject of intense interest to the locals, many of whom use the abundant streams and waterfalls in the area to produce electricity for sale. Then the conversation moved on to cherry growing, local politics, and, later, outrageous stories about drinking, farming accidents, drinking accidents, and so on.

Terje and Oddvin were not satisfied with the beer, however. They did not think the taste of the beer was good enough, so they decided not to keep the yeast from this brew. This is another aspect of the reuse of kveik: the best brewers are careful about which batches they reuse, thus selectively breeding their kveik. And they were right about this beer, because it turned sour after about a month. That was the second time it had happened to Terje in 20 years of brewing.

So how is Terje able to make a good beer that is not sour when he does not boil his wort? And how would he ever come up with trying something like this in the first place? Farmhouse brewing processes are the result of local traditions slowly evolving over many centuries, as brewers learned from their neighbors and, very rarely, tried new things. The process evolved by pure trial and error. These brewers had no scientific basis for what they did, but anyone can taste what works and what does not.

But how did people come up with the idea of brewing raw ale in the first place? Actually, raw ale is a fairly obvious development from an earlier type of beer. To understand it, we need to first look at that earlier beer.

---

[*] Hat is a common expression in western Norwegian dialect. The poet Olav H. Hauge also used it in one of his poems.

Stone Beer

In the summer of 1851, Norwegian sociologist Eilert Sundt was walking across a field in Hedmark, eastern Norway, when he noticed a pile of stones. They caught his eye because they looked peculiar. They were small, about the size of a fist, with obvious signs of burning, and they had been chipped and cracked somehow. He asked a farmer working nearby what the stones were.

"Brewing stones," said the farmer.

"Brewing stones?"

"Yes, boiling stones."

"Boiling stones?"

"Yes. They were used for boiling in the old days, when people didn't have metal kettles."[3]

Sundt noticed these piles of burned and cracked stones could be found on many farms in Hedmark. Other farmers told him the stones were used for brewing in wooden vessels in the old days, by dumping hot stones into them. Now why would people do that instead of using a kettle?

Metal kettles have been around since the Bronze Age, which began around 1500 BCE in the Nordic countries, but they were extremely expensive. And the price remained high. In 1350 CE, the owner of one of the biggest farms in western Norway, Finnen in Voss, died and the document that describes the division of his estate lists three copper kettles among his possessions. Those three kettles were valued at eight cows, more than two per kettle.[4] Even centuries later, a tenant farmer would be lucky to have a single cow, much less two. So, for a period of literally millennia just about every farmer brewed beer, but kettles were something that only the very rich had.

How would people have brewed beer using hot stones instead of a kettle? As we saw above, even today many farmhouse brewers do not boil the wort, for the simple reason that you do not have to. What you really do need is to heat the mash. Without a kettle to heat the brewing liquor, the solution is fairly obvious. To heat the mash, simply put hot stones into the mix of water and grist. Add stones at intervals, and, after an hour or two, you are ready to run off. At this point you could boil the wort with hot stones, but that is hard work and completely unnecessary. Stones in the mash are necessary, but stones in the wort are not.

In the summer of 2015, I visited Ugis Pucens in Aizpute, western Latvia, to see how he brews. Ugis did not grow up in the farmhouse brewing tradition himself, but he and his wife

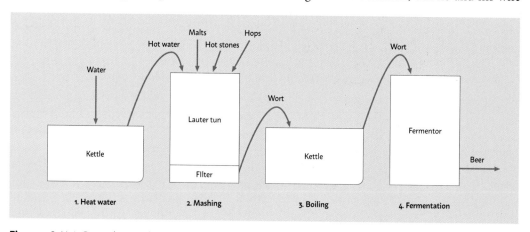

Figure 5.8. Ugis Pucens's stone brewing process.

Signe have interviewed many Latvian farmhouse brewers and recreate their beers using exact replicas of the traditional brewing gear.

Figure 5.9. Ugis and helper tying the "witch's broom."

Ugis had a wooden mash tun with a drainage hole in the bottom and a false bottom with relatively large holes. A pole with a tapered tip passed through the false bottom and was used to close the drainage hole. Lifting the pole made an opening for the wort to run out. Juniper branches were tied to the pole above the false bottom to form what Ugis called "the witch's broom". Tying the branches like this made it possible to stir the mash in the tun using a second pole without disturbing the filter.

Ugis then started a fire underneath a pile of stones on a steel grating in a temporary brick "oven." While the stones were heated, Ugis mashed in the usual way by putting the malt in the mash tun, then pouring hot water on them. He stirred carefully with a stick, making rotating movements in the mash so as not to disturb the filter, then left it for an hour.

Then it was time for the stones. Ugis used huge iron tongs, maybe a meter long, to lift each stone and dip it in a steel bucket of water to rinse off the ash. Every time a stone approached the water I cringed, because these glowing stones were intensely hot objects. Dipping the stone into the water set off a fierce hissing, like a thousand cats fighting, and hid the bucket in a cloud of steam. Sometimes, the sudden cooling made the stone split in two with a loud bang, like a pistol shot.

Figure 5.10. Pile of stones being heated with fire.

Figure 5.11. Ugis adding a hot stone to the mash.

Figure 5.12. A big stone makes part of the mash boil.

When the stones were dropped in the mash, the hissing started again and steam enveloped the mash tun for a moment. Then the stone disappeared into the mash. The smaller ones sank without a trace, but the larger ones made the mash boil for a few minutes above where they sank. I saw this again when Vykintas Motuza demonstrated the stone brewing of Andrioniškis in Lithuania. His stones were bigger and really did glow red when they came out of the fire, leaving the mash boiling furiously around them for several minutes.

The hot stones in the mash of course caramelize it, but I have to be honest and admit that I have not actually tasted any of these beers, so I am not sure what the resulting flavor is actually like. Clearly, the hot stones must cause Maillard reactions in the mash, but exactly what it tastes like I do not know.

Much has been written about the importance of choosing stones that do not fracture, but, as we saw above, some of Ugis's stones cracked in two. Vykintas's stones did the same. This was normal. The stones that caught Eilert Sundt's eye were also shattered from being dropped red hot into cold liquid. Hellenius[5] wrote that "the stones mostly shatter and leave gravel on the bottom of the tun." Deposits of fire-shattered stones are found in many places in northern Europe. Norwegian archaeologist Geir Grønnesby has studied the remains of brewing stones in eastern Norway and found that the deposits seem to begin in the seventh century, then start dropping off sharply in the sixteenth and seventeenth centuries.[6] That is nearly a millennium of stone deposits. The end probably coincided with the time metal kettles became more affordable.

You would think that a millennium of stone brewing would leave a good bit of stone behind, and you would be right. These deposits are so big that many old Norwegian farmhouses are built

Figure 5.13. Cracked stones. Note the sharp fracture lines from heat shock.

right on top of them, literally using them as the foundation. One farm in Trøndelag, Norway burned in the late 19th century. When a farmer in 1978 tried ploughing the area where the farmhouse had stood, he struck black earth and fire-shattered stones. The volume of the stone deposits was estimated to be over 1300 cubic meters, which would fill more than 35 standard 20-foot shipping containers.[7]

Similar deposits of shattered stone seem to exist in most northern European countries, but no systematic surveys exist.[8] Historians in other countries seem mostly not to have considered the possibility that they might be remains of stone brewing, with a few exceptions.[9] In the British Isles, the deposits take the form of so-called "burnt mounds," which in Ireland are known as *fulacht fiadh*. There is no consensus about what they were used for.[10]

Most people have assumed that stone beer was made by using the stones to boil the wort, but, as we have seen, that is not what one would logically expect given how farmhouse ale is normally brewed. I have collected 25 first-hand accounts of stone brewing (not counting the two mentioned above) from Denmark, Norway, Sweden, Finland, Austria, Russia, Belarus, Lithuania, and Estonia. In every single case, except one, the stones are used in the mash, not in the wort.

The exception was Marina Fyodorovna in Chuvashia, who threw hot stones in the wort after it was run off before she put it in the kettle to boil it. The why was never explained, but she was using an open outdoor hearth to heat her kettle that probably was not very effective. Using hot stones was probably an effective way to reduce the time it took to bring the wort to a boil.

All of these brewers had metal kettles but continued to use hot stones, most likely out of a combination of conservatism and a preference for the toasted, caramelly flavor from the hot stones. Some brewers said straight out that the stones "are used mostly for giving the beer a darker color and for a better taste."[11] In parts of Estonia and Finland, stone brewers might sprinkle rye flour on the hot stones before dropping them in the mash in order to get some extra burnt flavor in the beer.[12]

Every conceivable variation in brewing process has been used together with hot stones, including varying the grain type and other ingredients. So, it does not really make sense to talk about stone beer as a single style. Stone beer was probably the main branch of beer styles right up until the end of the Middle Ages.

Two examples can illustrate some of the variation. The first is the process used by the Swedes on the island of

Figure 5.14. Woman sprinkling rye flour on a glowing stone. Suure-Jaani, central Estonia, 1937. Reproduced by permission from Estonian National Museum.

Ruhnu in Estonia. They used barley dried in a ria (a malt drying kiln common in eastern Europe; see p. 69), with the wort filtered through wooden sticks and straw. Brewing began by pouring hot water over the grist, then stirring and waiting. Glowing hot stones or metal balls were added to the mash "to give the beer a beautiful brown color," causing the mash to boil. Hop tea was boiled and poured into the lauter tun and the mash added on top of it. The wort was run off, cooled, and the yeast pitched.[13]

The second example is the stone beer brewed in Solvychegodsk, near Kotlas in the Russian north. It was not said explicitly, but the malt was almost certainly made from rye, since all other accounts in this area mention nothing but pure rye. Hot water was first poured over the grist. Meanwhile, cobblestone-like stones were piled up on top of firewood and heated until they glowed red. The red-hot stones were picked up, using tongs made from spruce sticks split at the end to form a Y shape, and lowered into the mash, bringing it to a boil. (I saw Vykintas Motuza do exactly this, and the tongs caught fire where they touched the stone. Seeing him wield the burning sticks holding red-hot stones was quite a sight in the dark.) The mash was then left half a day. To see if it was ready, the brewers took rye straw, made a triangle of it, then dipped it into the wort. If the wort was ready a transparent film would form in the triangle. Once ready, the wort was scooped up and boiled in a kettle with hops. Finally, it was filtered, cooled down, and the yeast was pitched.[14]

Today, stone brewing is still alive in Lithuania, Finland, Belarus, and Russia, at least. Hollolan Hirvi in Hollola, Finland, sells a true stone sahti, the only authentic commercial stone beer I am aware of. Stone brewing has been rare for the last two centuries, accounting for only about 3% of the recipes I have analyzed. Most brewers seemingly abandoned stone brewing for some other method, which is not surprising given how awkward and inefficient brewing with hot stones is.

Figure 5.15. Used brewing stones, and the tongs used to lift them. Hollola, Finland.

Raw Ale

In the late Middle Ages, and for some time after, the same scene must have repeated itself: the farm has just acquired a metal kettle and it is time to brew again. Should they try using the kettle instead of the stones? And if so, how? Of course, most people will have looked to their neighbors, but, in every village, someone must have been the first to try brewing with a kettle. Figuring out how to use it must have taken some thought.

To us, perhaps the most obvious way to use the kettle instead of stones would have been to heat the strike water (or juniper infusion) in the kettle and then pour it over the grist. Lautering, cooling, and pitching of the yeast would have been as before. If you were to do that, you would be following the most common raw ale brewing process, exactly as Terje showed me in Hornindal.

Dealing with the hops must also have taken some thought. The simplest solution is the one Terje showed: just run off the hot wort through a bag of hops. While that would give some hop aroma and some protection against infection, it would not make full use of the hops. To fully utilize the hops, they must be boiled so that the alpha acids in the hops are isomerized to become water-soluble. Otherwise, the alpha acids will behave like oil in water and not dissolve in the beer.

A simple solution is to make what the Lithuanians call *apyny arbata*, literally "hop tea." Simply boil the hops in a liter or two of water while mashing, then add the hop tea to the wort later. Usually the tea is added before fermentation, but some Danish brewers added it to taste after fermentation was complete. This was a clever way to solve the problem that the sugar yield from homemade malt was variable, not to mention variations in the alpha acid content of homegrown hops.

A Danish woman wrote that if anyone "who didn't know brewing came by while we poured the hop tea through the lauter tun, we would offer them a taste of the new beer. But how they spat and made faces! The hop tea is of course very bitter. They didn't want any more new beer after that."[15]

Another solution was to boil what the Norwegians call *humlebeit** by taking a liter or two of wort and boiling the hops in that. The humlebeit was always mixed back in before fermentation. Both methods save a lot of time and energy and preserve the special raw ale flavor.

In technical terms, what happens in a raw ale is that the long, hot mash effectively pasteurizes the mash. For milk products, 63°C for 30 minutes, or 72°C for 15 seconds is enough for pasteurization; the mash, however, is a lumpy mix of grist and water and will take longer to be pasteurized. The mash will not be sterile, but boiled wort is not either, once it has been cooled down. Whatever microorganisms remain will be overwhelmed by the yeast and the hops, so raw ale is very rarely sour. You do have to be careful when brewing it, though, which is why Terje cleaned the juniper branches for the filter in the boiling infusion.

With no boil, there will be no hot break, so protein from the malt will remain in the beer. This has the effect of filling out the body even if the beer is relatively dry, making the mouthfeel rounder and smoother. The effect is not too different from using oats or wheat in the grist, allowing raw ales to be attenuated further than other beers without feeling thin and dry. An extreme example is Jovaru Alus, a commercial farmhouse ale from Lithuania. When Martin Thibault took a bottle back to Montréal to share with experienced beer-tasting friends, they ended up in a heated discussion over whether the beer was sweet or dry. One of them eventually found a hydrometer and measured the specific gravity of the beer as 1.003.[†] There was almost no sugar in the beer! And yet many drinkers on Ratebeer.com and Untappd reject the beer as too sweet. The full mouthfeel and lack of hop bitterness fools them into thinking the beer is sweeter than it really is. The proteins and other compounds remaining in the beer give it a slightly abrasive feel in the mouth, which can often have the effect of balancing the sweetness of the beer. As a result, compared to boiled beer, less bitterness is needed.

Of course, when the wort is not boiled, many of the chemical processes that occur during the boiling of wort simply do not happen, which will lead to the overall flavor profile being different. A good equivalent from cooking is tomato soup versus gazpacho—the ingredients are much the same, but the flavor is different because gazpacho is not boiled.

Raw ale has a characteristically different flavor compared to beer brewed from boiled wort. The difference is hard to describe. The character of the malt tends to stand out much more, often in a straw-like, grainy kind of way. In addition, a "green," sometimes pea-like, flavor will come to the fore. Once you are familiar with it, the raw ale flavor is quite easy to recognize.

Also consider that the enzymes from the malt will not be deactivated by the boil, so the original gravity you measure before pitching yeast may not actually capture all of the sugar in the beer. More sugar may be formed during fermentation by enzymes that are still active. Many of the farmhouse brewers sparge with a boiling juniper infusion, which probably deactivates the enzymes. This does not worry the farmhouse brewers, of course, who do not measure the gravity in any case. The alco-

___
* The first part means "hops," but the second part is not clear. It may derive from the verb *beita*, in the sense of "to sharpen" (Aasen 1873), so that boiling the hops sharpens them, as indeed it does by making them bitter.
† I later measured the gravity with a refractometer and computed a corrected gravity reading by taking the ABV on the label. The result was a final gravity of 1.004.

hol level I computed for Terje's beer when I helped brew it is very similar to the alcohol level that was measured by chemical methods for one of his later brews. So, the effect is probably small.

Many have thought that dimethyl sulphide (DMS) would be an issue in raw ale, but it is not. The precursor compound to DMS, S-methylmethionine (SMM), converts very slowly to DMS as long as the temperature is below 85°C, and in raw ale the mash and the wort will normally not go above that. In addition, DMS is volatile above 50°C, so what little has formed will most likely evaporate during the long mash and runoff.

Raw ale has historically been extremely widespread in farmhouse brewing. In fact, out of 555 analyzed recipes, about 60% did not involve boiling the wort. Note that there is a difference between what is basically a normal beer where the boil has been skipped and a stone beer (or other strange types of beer, as described below) where the wort is not boiled. The 60% figure includes all of these variants.

In general, a classic raw ale is one that starts with a one- or two-step infusion mash, lautering, cooling, and finally pitching; this is essentially what Terje did. This is the classic brewing process for styles like *kornøl*, *koduõlu*, *kaimiškas*, and *landøl* (these are described in chapter 9), and it has been used over most of northern Europe.

Historically, Berliner *weisse* was also a raw ale before brewing processes changed in the nineteenth century. This has probably been the case for other commercial beer styles too.

Boiled Ale

An obvious development from raw ale is to start boiling the entire wort with the hops in it. This is what north German brewers started doing in the twelfth or thirteenth century, and it enabled them to export their beer to nearby towns because it would keep better.[16] Many farmhouse brewers do the same thing, as we saw with Carlo (chapter 1) and Sigmund (chapter 4).

The boiled ale brewers in western Norway were well aware that there were places where the wort was not boiled.

> To the people of Sogn this is a barbaric custom that spoils much of the pleasure of meeting people from Nordfjord and Hordaland. There is therefore more than a little suspicion and expectation of disappointment in the story of the man from Sogn who visited his relative south of the county border, and on a warm summer's day was given the traditional welcome bowl of beer on the steps. He looks in the bowl, drinks, and face shining, sends the bowl to the others while exclaiming: "Well, you certainly don't brew raw!" Still the emigrant hadn't left the family, and here one could look forward to drinking their beer. (Nordland 1967, 138)

"Left the family" is an attempt to translate Nordland's literal "*or ætta komen*," which means to have left the larger family group (much like a noble house). In other words, whether the wort was boiled or not was a powerful identity marker, and a single sip was enough to tell whether the wort had been boiled.

Of course, the people who brewed raw ale saw it differently. They boiled the juniper infusion before mashing with it, so to them the wort boilers were *oppatkokarar*, or "again-boilers." It was only poor hygiene, they claimed, that forced these people to boil the wort.[17]

The *Brulosophy* blog did an experiment where they boiled half of a Berliner weisse wort, and left the other half raw. In the ensuing triangle tasting test, 31 out of 37 tasters were able to tell the difference, which is one of the strongest results they have ever had. So, there is no question that the flavor difference is clearly noticeable. Interestingly, 15 tasters preferred the boiled version, 13 the raw version, and three had no opinion, even though they could tell the difference.[18]

Many people in the modern homebrewing community have been skeptical of the long boil to reduce the wort volume that is common in Voss and Hardanger in western Norway. A common claim is that the Maillard reactions in the wort will reduce the fermentability of the wort. These reactions cannot be reducing it very much, because Sigmund aims for an OG of 1.080 and an FG below 1.015, which means he expects at least 81% apparent attenuation.

The Mash Boiled

However, the infusion mash and wort boil were not the only ways to make use of the kettle. In the summer of 2017, I was interviewing a Chuvash family in the village of Kshaushi in Russia. We had gone through malting, cleaning the vessels, and grinding, but when I asked about their mashing suddenly a long discussion broke out between my translator, Aleksandr Gromov, a professional brewer, and the family. Eventually, Aleksandr turned to me, with shock on his face, exclaiming, "They boil the mash!" I just smiled and explained that this was completely normal. Aleksandr shook his head but carried on with the interview.[19]

Boiling the mash may sound like a strange brewing technique, but it is actually perfectly logical. Think back to the stone brewers who have just bought a kettle and wonder how to use it. The most direct way to imitate what happens when you heat the mash by putting stones in it is by pouring malt and water into the kettle and starting the fire. Since the stones boiled the mash around them, many unscientific brewers will have done the same with the kettle because that seemed like an important part of the process.

It may sound as though this process should destroy the enzymes in the malt and produce no sugar, but the process of heating 150 liters of grist and cold water is sufficiently slow that the mash goes through all the mash temperatures. You can think of it as a step mash, except there are no defined steps with pauses and the heating goes all the way to 100°C.

Boiling the mash was a common method in southwestern Denmark, southern Sweden, parts of Finland, and eastern Norway. Overall, about 25% of brewers reported using this method (see "The Database" at the end of this book on p. 372). Unfortunately, farmhouse brewing has died out in nearly all of these areas, except Finland. In both Ål and Morgedal in eastern Norway, older descriptions said the mash was boiled, but when I traveled there to brew with the locals they only heated the mash in the kettle without boiling it.

An account from Morgedal warned against doing more than just bringing the mash to a boil "or the whole thing would turn to porridge."[20] That is, it would be impossible to lauter the beer. Other accounts said boiling the mash at all would make it impossible to lauter. And yet others said the mash was boiled, in some cases for hours. I assumed all this meant what it often means: those who have not tried something convince themselves it could never work, while those who have grown up with it have no idea what the problem is supposed to be.

Preparing for the Finnish expedition with Mika Laitinen in 2018, I tried to make sure that we would brew with at least one brewer who boiled the mash, but this turned out to be difficult.

Figure 5.16. The barn where Olavi Viheroja brews with hops climbing the wall.

Figure 5.17. Olavi Viheroja stirring the mash in the kettle. The fire is lit underneath.

Figure 5.18. The mash beginning to swell and bubble at the surface.

Nobody seemed to know for certain who boiled the mash and who did not, but I was told that we would get to see it for sure so I should not worry about it.

Our first brew session in Finland was with Olavi Viheroja. Olavi lives on the family farm in a fairly remote area in Hämeenkyrö in the west of the country. We drove for 30 minutes on dirt roads ever deeper into the forest to find the farm. Olavi is a local brewing legend, and we were lucky that one member of the group had gone to school with his daughter, making it easy to set up a brewing session.

Olavi began by first adding warm water in steps over several hours to raise the mash temperature, then transferred the mash to the kettle and started heating it. While it was heated it had to be stirred constantly. He then waited for the mash to become covered in foam and to start exploding in little bursts at the surface. When this happened, Olavi declared that "it's now at 80 degrees Celsius," and, to my disappointment, stopped the fire under the kettle. We brought out thermometers and measured the mash temperature as 79.9°C.

We asked Olavi about boiling the mash, to which he replied he did not want to do that because it would go all lumpy and it would not be possible to lauter it. Olavi had said beforehand that he boils the mash, but he clearly meant only the heating that we had seen, which did look like a form of boiling. Mika Laitinen said it was the same with many other sahti brewers: they heated the mash until it started moving and called it boiling, but it never reached 100°C. Mika also told me that a friend of his had tried boiling the mash and found that with his modern lauter tun made from a coolbox he had not been able to lauter the wort at all. His friend actually had to give up entirely and produced no beer from that batch.

At this point, it seemed like the contradiction between the sources could be reconciled by assuming that the ones who said you cannot boil the mash were right and those who claimed they boiled the mash only heated to 80–90°C but called it boiling. Without a thermometer, how were they to know that the simmering mash was not really boiling?

The day after, we visited Seppo Lisma in Ruovesi while he was brewing, and it was the same story there. He step-mashed by adding water first, then transferred to the kettle and heated the mash further by gently heating with wood until the mash started rising to the surface in spurts. He called this boiling the mash but, in the end, the temperature was 89°C.

At this point I was getting worried, since we had only planned one more brewing session, but Mika told me he had hopes for our last stop. We were going to brew with Eila Tuominen in Pertunmaa, and Mika said that in this region people believe that if the mash is not well boiled the drinkers will get stomach trouble. If anyone was going to actually boil the mash, surely it would be Eila.

Eila met us in the farmyard between her house and the barn where she brews. Her brewery is in the room the Finns call a "cow kitchen," although no food is prepared there. Instead, it is used to heat water for cleaning utensils and so on, so it is suitable for a brewery because it has a kettle, drains, and running water. On the door was a notice announcing that Eila sells sahti wort, with instructions on how to ferment it.[*] On the sign was also a guarantee: this mash is properly boiled, if you get stomach trouble you get your money back.

Eila started at six o'clock that morning, mixing the warm juniper infusion with malt and then heating the mash in the kettle. She returned at intervals to start the wood fire under the kettle again. Like Olavi, she did not use a thermometer for mashing. When we arrived at 8:00 a.m. the mash was at 49°C and Eila was just coming back to start the second fire. After an hour of heating, she stopped with the temperature at 53°C. Then, at 11:30 a.m., she restarted the fire, this time really piling on the firewood.

Figure 5.19. Eila Tuominen stirring the mash.

---

[*] Selling wort is much simpler than selling sahti, because the wort is not alcoholic. You still have to meet food safety standards, but you avoid all the complex regulations and taxation around alcoholic drinks.

It was a hot and muggy day in the Finnish lake country, so we were already warm outside. Inside the brewhouse the heat was stifling. None of us could stir the mash more than five minutes without breaking into a sweat, yet Eila was stirring almost constantly. She wore shorts and a t-shirt, sensible given the weather, but she had added an apron and thick rubber boots on top, which seemed a strange choice to me.

The mash went through the steps we had seen brewing with Olavi and Seppo, but Eila did not stop there. By 12:20 p.m., bubbles started appearing around the side of the kettle, giving the impression of a kind of boil. Excitedly, we measured the temperature around the edge and got 98°C, but in the center the temperature was just 91°C. We looked at each other: should we consider this boiling or not? But Eila kept on adding wood to the fire and stirring, and the mash kept moving more and more. She told us she would keep heating the kettle until the mash sank and the foam disappeared, then she would let it rest for a good while. That did not sound like boiling, but at least it should be hotter than what we had seen before.

Then things started developing very rapidly. While we were excitedly chattering away and taking photos, Eila stood in the heat, stirring the mash and looking at our excitement in indulgent bemusement. At 12:24 p.m., the bubbles around the edge began getting more violent, and the mash began heaving in the center just a minute later. Soon, gobs of mash were literally flying out of the kettle, spattering onto the wall, the kettle itself, and the floor. Wearing an apron and rubber boots suddenly seemed like a reasonable precaution.

At 12:30 p.m. the mash collapsed, the surface literally sinking down five centimeters and going very dark. This was what Eila had been waiting for, so she closed the flue and let the fire die down, then covered the kettle with a thick paper sack. We went off to have lunch. Returning at 1:30 p.m. when the "mash rest" was over, we found the mash was still gently simmering from the residual heat in the mash and kettle.

Figure 5.20. The mash boiling during Eila Tuominen's brewing session.

Figure 5.21. Eila sparging by ladling hot juniper infusion onto the mash.

Eila ran off the wort in a *kuurna*, a lauter tun shaped like a hollowed-out log that has been closed with boards at the ends. There was a hole in the board at one end, out of which the wort ran, filtered through juniper branches on the bottom. This is the standard lauter tun in Finland. Olavi and Seppo also used kuurnas. After running off was finished, Eila cooled the wort to 4°C, then poured it in the fermentor and pitched the yeast, letting the temperature rise to ambient temperature while the yeast got started.

That evening we tasted an earlier batch of Eila's sahti. It was hazy, quite pale, and cold. In some ways it was reminiscent of a German weissbier, being fruity, full, and mealy; but Eila's beer was fuller and thicker, almost viscous. It was quite sweet and seemed mainly to be balanced by the slightly abrasive raw ale character, so it felt balanced, harmonic, and drinkable. I could not taste the juniper at all, and there were no hops.

Figure 5.22. Eila with a glass of her own beer.

It was a very good beer, but also a major disappointment because there did not really seem to be any clear flavor contribution from boiling the mash. Her beer tasted like many sahtis, except that the lack of roasted rye malt meant the flavor was fruitier and clearer. Suddenly, the pursuit of boiled mashes seemed kind of pointless, but, in retrospect, I do not think it was.

We learned two things from this visit. The first is that it is possible to lauter even when the mash has been boiled. It is very likely true that it becomes harder, but the Finnish kuurna is perfectly designed for lautering difficult mashes because it is horizontal. The mash forms a thin layer on top of the filter, allowing the sparge water to be sprinkled on any part of the mash and giving the wort a much shorter distance to run inside the mash.

It should be added that many people have used the boiled mash method in other areas where the kuurna is not found, instead relying on the more familiar-looking vertical lauter tun. They generally used a complex arrangement of alder branches, straw, and juniper. When carefully arranged, this type of filter can probably also handle a boiled mash. It may require more skill than with ordinary mashes, however.

The second thing we learned was that boiling the mash for the flavor was not what matters. Sahti tastes quite different from its very close cousin Estonian koduõlu for two main reasons: the mash regime and the use of rye. The mashing and the rye together give sahti a thick, viscous texture that is unlike any other beer style I know of. The important thing seems to be that the grist is mashed with a long, slow step mash over many hours and then strongly heated in the kettle. Whether the heating in the end goes to a full boil is not the important thing.

Probably these long, complex procedures need to be treated as a separate form of mashing, because of the effect on the flavor. Unfortunately, this is not as fully explored as it should be, so we do not know the exact effects yet. I have brewed with brewers who heated the entire mash in the kettle, with several steps over many hours. They used only barley malt and got very clean malty flavors, but no viscosity like the sahti brewers.[21]

Complex Mashes

Many farmhouse brewers use only simple infusion mashes. This is the norm in western Norway, on the Estonian islands, and in the central part of north Lithuania. However, that is only one of the many mashing techniques brewers used. Even boiling the mash is just a part. The full range of variation is essentially too large to describe here, but we can review at least a few of the main alternatives.

Many brewers actually start mashing the evening before the brew day by adding a little cold water to the mash; not very much, because hot water will be added the next day. The cold water is typically 4–5°C, and the brewers generally take care that the mash stays cold (between 0°C and 10°C) throughout the night, because if not the mash will sour. The brewers give no reason for why they do this, but the reason is that it probably reduces the pH of the mash, giving better mash efficiency. Cold mashing has mostly been practiced in east and central Norway, and in Sweden. It can be combined with all the other mashing methods.

As for the warm portion of the mash, one method is a relatively simple infusion mash with one or two steps, as mentioned above. There are three additional methods. One is the long step mash, where hot water is added in increments over a considerably longer period; rather like a modern step mash, except there are more steps and the temperatures in each step are probably not being hit consistently. Since there is such a range of temperatures, the mash works anyway, even without a thermometer.

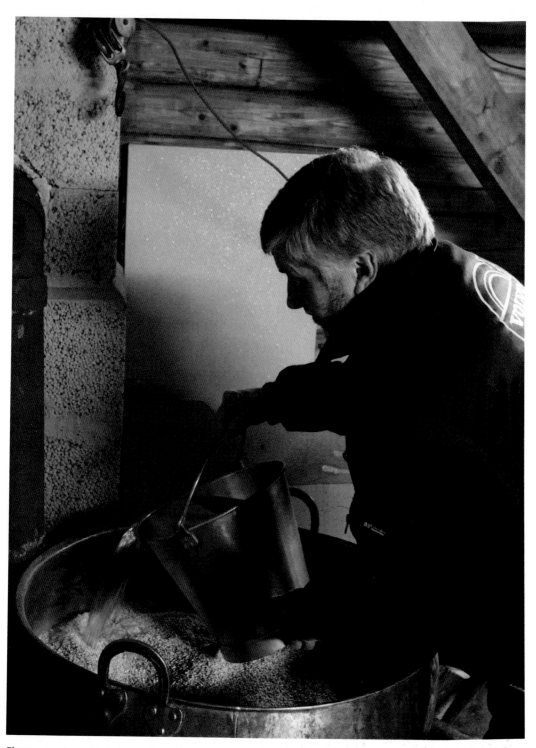

Figure 5.23. Sverre Skrindo pouring cold water on the grist the evening before brewing. Ål, eastern Norway.

Second is the kettle mash, which is similar to the long step mash. The great thermal mass of the grist and water in the kettle means that the temperature rises slowly, and so the mash goes through all the necessary temperatures. By the time the mash boils (or nearly boils) at the end, the sugar has already been extracted. The downside of this method is that the brewer must stir the mash all the time while it's being heated to avoid burning the mash. As Sverre Skrindo put it, "If you have to go to the toilet while you're firing the mash you'll just have to do it in your pants, because you can't leave the kettle for one moment."

The third method is very similar to German decoction: run off wort from the lauter tun, heat it in the kettle (not necessarily until it boils), then pour it back on. Just as with the other two methods, this would slowly take the mash up through all the appropriate temperatures. The constant circulation of wort would also mix the mash well.

These four basic approaches—simple infusions, long step mash, kettle mash, and decoction—could be combined with the cold mash and with each other in innumerable ways, such as starting with a cold mash, doing a couple of step infusions, and then boiling the mash in the kettle. Many variations are described in archive documents.

On top of that, mashing could be combined with a whole range of different ways to use the hops: boiled hop tea, humlebeit, first wort hopping, just adding hops to the mash, boiling the hops in the mash, and so on and so forth. The full range of complexity here is basically too large to even attempt an explanation, and the effects on flavor are not fully understood. Unfortunately, for now, we will have to leave the story there.

What we can say is that complex mashes dominated in eastern and central Norway, in Sweden, on Funen in Denmark, and in large parts of Finland. Infusion mashing dominated totally in western Norway, most of Denmark other than Funen, the southern tip of Sweden, and in the Baltic states. With more data, it may be possible to work out how these patterns came to be.

There was another approach to brewing, however, that was radically different from these western methods.

Keptinis

In northeastern Lithuania, the farmers have traditionally brewed what they call *keptinis alus*, which literally means "baked beer." I first encountered it when I met Ramūnas Čižas (see the introduction) and tasted his unusual beer. Unfortunately, I was never really able to work out the details of how he brewed it.

I eventually found a Lithuanian ethnographic paper describing keptinis brewing.[22] It described how the grist was mixed with hot water, formed into bread-like shapes about 17–19 cm thick, and placed on a layer of straw before being baked in an oven. It was baked until black and crisp on the outside. Ethnographic videos show "loaves" that seem charred on the outside and brown inside.[23] After baking, the mash was taken out and crushed with mortar and pestle, before being mashed in the normal way with hops and lime tree bark for four to five hours. Then it was run off, cooled, and yeast pitched; there was no boiling.

Martin Warren of the Poppyland Brewery in Norfolk, England tried to brew a beer according to the description I had put together, and failed miserably. The baking in the oven destroyed all the enzymes in the malt, and he wound up with black, unfermentable water with no sugar in it.[24]

Figure 5.24. Vytautas Jančys looking out of the brewhouse.

Figure 5.25. Vytautas Jančys mashing in with help from his son, Ignas.

The Lithuanians have brewed this way for centuries, so it has to be possible somehow. But how? I was confused about this method for years until I was invited to visit Vytautas Jančys to see him brew keptinis on the family farm in Vikonys, northeastern Lithuania. One small brick building on the farm holds the brewery. A rough, tiny room has two kettles and a small table. The next room has a brick oven, built by Vytautas's father specifically for brewing keptinis.

Vytautas and his son, Ignas, started by boiling water in one of the kettles. They brought out a large wooden barrel with no lid, into which they poured the grist. Once the water had been heated, they started adding some to the grist, stirring, adding more water, sometimes adding more grist, stirring again, and so on. Vytautas repeatedly poked the porridge-like mash with a stick, then added more water. He lifted the mash paddle and watched the mash and wort drip off it, then stirred some more. Eventually he was satisfied, even though I had seen no thermometer. I immediately went over with my thermometer and stuck it in: 65°C. Vytautas hit the perfect mash temperature simply by judging the consistency of the mash. He knew that when he had added the right amount of water, the temperature would be right for mashing. Later, I realized this was why Carlo, and many other Norwegian brewers, had this rule about the mash paddle not being able to stand in the mash. They were trying to reproduce the right mix of water and malt, not because it mattered in itself (you just need enough water), but because that was how people judged the mash temperature in the old days. Nowadays they have thermometers, but many of these brewers still follow the old rule, even if only half-heartedly.

Once Vytautas was satisfied, the mash was left for an hour. This clearly solved the enzyme problem: the sugars were produced during this hour-long wait. However, not all oven brewers mash first, as we shall see later on.

Meanwhile, Vytautas had been firing his brick oven to heat it up for baking. Once the hour was up, he and Ignas took four shallow open steel boxes and ladled the mash into them, packing it closely to make as much as possible fit, then smoothing the surface. Vytautas removed the red-hot embers from the oven and placed them into a bucket, while the four boxes stood on top of the oven. The oven was then left a while to cool down. Finally, some more water was added to the mash to get the right mix, before the four boxes were inserted into the oven to bake for three hours.

I did not dare try to measure the temperature of that oven with my thermometer because it was clearly very hot. Vytautas was wearing a plexiglass face mask and huge gloves when inserting the boxes. Simonas Gutautas[25] believes the temperature was probably 350–400°C. Three hours later the temperature had dropped quite substantially.

Figure 5.26. Vytautas carrying the mash boxes to the oven.

Figure 5.27. Vytautas's baked mash.

When the boxes were removed three hours later, we could see what it is that makes keptinis so distinctive a style of beer. Vytautas and Ignas had started with pale malt, but the mash had baked a deep, dark brown. The mash had clearly boiled in the oven, because sugary wort had run down the sides of the boxes and dried into hard globs of toasted sugar. On top of the boxes a hard, dark crust about a centimeter thick had formed. Once Vytautas broke it with a wooden spoon, we could see that underneath there was a softer, paler mass of baked mash. Breaking off chunks with my fingers, I tasted it. It was sweet, toasted, and caramelly sugary with earthy, honey-like notes. It tasted really good. So good, in fact, you could probably make and sell sweet mash cookies baked this way.

Porter, dunkel, stout, and schwarzbier are dark because they are made from malt that is dried at high temperatures. But that is malt; what is roasted during drying is starch. Keptinis is darkened because the mash is baked, but, in this case, there is true caramelization of the sugars in addition to Maillard reactions. So, the unusual flavors in a keptinis come from the caramelized sugars. This sets keptinis apart from all the other dark beers, making it a very distinct style.

Stone beer is similar, since the red-hot stones will caramelize parts of the mash. In fact, Vykintas Motuza told me that when the brewers in Vikonys need to brew large batches of beer, for example, for a wedding, the oven is not large enough to bake the entire mash.[26] In these cases, the brewers will instead make what they call *mistinis*, where the mash is darkened using hot stones held with tongs in the mash. In Estonia, people did the same thing.[27]

It is clear that the shape of the mash will affect how the mash is roasted and also the flavor. The surface is baked much harder than the inside, so the surface-to-volume ratio is important. Vytautas's boxes were 6 cm high, 35 cm long, and 28 cm wide. In an ethnographic video, I have seen what looks like a normal-sized round loaf of the usual European type.[28] Petrulis describes simply "loaves."[29] So separate loaf-sized chunks of mash seem to be about right.

With the mash boxes out of the oven, Ignas started soaking small blocks of wood in a porcelain basin. These blocks, about 10–15 cm long and 2 × 2 cm square, were going to be used in the lauter filter and had to be soaked so that they would not float up through the mash. Vytautas went over to the barn to retrieve a huge plastic bag full of wheat straw, which was hung under the ceiling to prevent mice from getting at it. Vytautas now brought out his lauter tun, a steel vessel with three stout legs and a hole in the middle of the bottom. He built this because it was easier to use and clean than the normal wooden lautering tun. The wooden blocks were spread over the bottom in a loose heap with lots of wheat straw packed on top. This was the filter.

The mash was broken up with a large wooden spoon and then dumped from the boxes into the mash tun. Meanwhile, water that had been heated was poured onto the mash very carefully so as not to disturb it. After a short pause the tun was opened and black wort started running out. Because they baked the mash, the Jančys family were able to make a beer the color of porter entirely from pale malt. The first runnings were poured back on, before the running off began in earnest. Hop tea was made by boiling 150 grams of hops for 30 minutes and added to the mix. Eventually, they ran off about 100 liters of wort, which was cooled using a copper coil with cold water running through it. Once cool, Safale S-04 was pitched.

Vytautas served us an earlier batch of keptinis, brewed six months before. It came out of his steel keg looking almost like whipped cream because of the high pressure inside the keg. It slowly settled into a liquid state, but now with very low carbonation. It had a massive toasty, earthy flavor, like a softer, less burnt and deeper-flavored porter, with lots of caramelized sugar and toffee notes. It reminded me of a very malty brown ale. The aroma hops were surprisingly noticeable. An aftertaste of caramel and coffee lingered for a long time after each sip.

Figure 5.28. Ignas Jančys dumping the baked mash into the lauter tun.

Figure 5.29. Vytautas and Ignas checking the first lautered wort.

Figure 5.30. The six-month-old Jančys family beer being poured in the cellar. It is initially poured into buckets to allow the creamy foam to subside.

I tasted several other homebrewed batches of keptinis and eventually concluded that this style is like a softer, rounder porter with stronger, deeper caramel and toffee flavors. I have tasted three commercial keptinis brews, which really are made by baking the mash, but they have much less flavor, even if they were all very interesting. Two of them had only 30% of the mash baked because of the problems with finding large enough ovens. The Lithuanian brewery Dundulis has recently produced new batches of keptinis that have 55.6% of the mash baked, which had more of the right keptinis flavor.

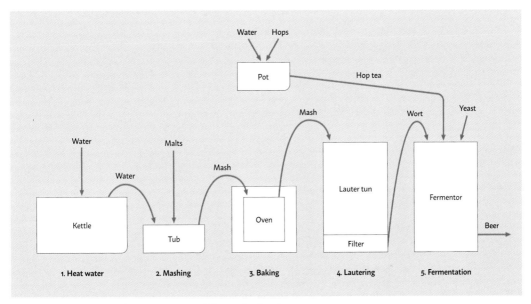

Figure 5.31. The keptinis brewing process of the Jančys family.

This caramelization from baking is reminiscent of the way brewers like Sigmund Gjernes in Norway darken their wort by boiling it for many hours (chapter 4, p. 89). Boiling produces less color, however, and gives more of a toffee flavor with less depth. The three brewing methods of reduction boil, heating the mash with stones, and oven-baking after the mash all produce related flavors. Drying the malt in the oven probably had a similar effect.

I tried brewing keptinis myself with the oven at 180°C for three hours. By the end, the mash had not dried out and the center of the boxes were at 95–98°C. The resulting beer tasted like vossaøl because I had not been able to get the temperature above 100°C. Clearly, this method requires less water in the mash and a higher oven temperature.

My opinion is that keptinis could become an important new beer style if commercial brewers take it up. There are three Lithuanian brewers producing this style of beer commercially already. Dundulis's version has two logos on the bottle, since it is a collaboration brew with Biržu Duona, the local bakery, whose large ovens were used to bake the mash.

The Great Stove
After the brew session in Vikonys, I went to the Lithuanian national museum in Rumšiskes, which has a huge outdoor exposition of Lithuanian traditional houses. I was astonished to discover that every single house, without exception, had a huge brick oven. The sizes and shapes varied, but typically they

were at least 1.5 meters high, 2 meters long, and 1 meter wide. Many had a large opening like a traditional pizza oven, with a smaller metal door on the side below it. This way one could either heat the main oven compartment or use the lower oven to heat the cooking surface inside the compartment.

Figure 5.32. Four examples of duonkepis ovens from the open-air museum in Rumšiskes, Lithuania. The long pole with the metal hoop at the end is used to insert and retrieve pots.

Figure 5.33. A Vepsian man taking a sauna bath inside the great oven, probably in Karelian Republic, Russia. Photo by A. O. Väisänen. Reproduced by permission from Finnish Heritage Agency

The ovens are constructed so that the hot air must move through a labyrinth of passages inside the oven. This pulls as much heat out of the air as possible, transferring it to the bricks in the oven, which means that the oven remains warm for a long time. In winter, when it is really cold (−40°C to −20°C) it is enough to heat the oven two or three times a week.[30] A side benefit is that the house maintains a very even temperature.

In Lithuania, these ovens are known as *duonkepis*, which literally means "bread baker." I had seen a similar oven in Setomaa in eastern Estonia the year before. And a few months later, I was in the Russian Ethnographic Museum in St. Petersburg where I saw lots of examples of these ovens from all over Russia, and even Tajikistan.

Later on I learned that in Russia this oven is called *pyech*,* but usually affectionately referred to with the diminutive *pyechka*.† The oven was a major part of Russian traditional life and appears in many folk tales and stories. It was really the center of the traditional peasant hut, the *izba*, and was used for cooking, heating the house in winter, washing, drying linen and grain, and so on. In places where they had no sauna, people would even take their hot baths by lying inside the oven.[31] This shows that they must have had good control over the temperature of the oven, very likely good enough to hit mash temperatures fairly accurately.

One has to wonder how brewers ever came up with the idea of making beer using their ovens. It could be that brewers who had no kettle figured out that they could use the oven to heat their mash instead of using hot stones. If that was the case, there should be evidence somewhere of brewers putting a cold mash in the oven and heating it. So, in the summer of 2017, I set out on a journey through Russia to see what I could find.

Vsekhsvyatskoye, Russia

We travelled to the Kirov region, about 800 km east of Moscow, to brew with Dmitriy Zhezlov. In the 1990s, Dmitriy lived in the nearby village of Vsekhsvyatskoye, a small place deep in the forest, well off the main roads, known for hop growing and farmhouse brewing. There he learned to brew Russian farmhouse ale in the traditional way, and he has continued doing that at his dacha.

Figure 5.34. Dmitriy's dacha in Shitovo, a tiny village in Kirov Oblast.

---

* In Lithuanian it can also be called *pečius*, clearly derived from the Russian.
† Similarly, the Russian for water is voda. *Vodka* is the diminutive of water, so it literally means "little water."

Figure 5.35. The korchaga with its wooden plug.

Figure 5.36. Dmitriy laying the straw filter in the korchaga.

Figure 5.37. The korchaga in the oven, with clay packed around the wooden plug.

Figure 5.38. The wort being lautered from the korchaga in Dmitriy's banya (Russian sauna).

Dmitriy has no brewery, but instead brews outside because the weather in this area is fairly stable. He makes his own rye malt and picks wild hops in the forest. The key item in his brewing kit is a large ceramic jar known as the *korchaga*. It has a small hole closed with a wooden plug near the bottom, and it serves as both mash tun and lauter tun.

Dmitriy began by cutting rye straw to the right length, then laying it crosswise in the bottom of the korchaga to serve as the filter. The wooden plug was inserted and a layer of clay was smeared on the outside, because if the plug shrinks and falls out in the heat the entire beer will be lost.

Once the korchaga was prepared, Dimitriy poured the grist on top of the straw. He had preheated the pyechka oven with a fire and let it die down, although the embers were still glowing. Dmitriy added cold water to the korchaga, more or less filling it, then placed the korchaga in the hot oven to be left overnight. Dmitriy believed the oven was at about 150–180°C. We took the korchaga out of the oven after the first hour and measured the temperature to 80°C, so the contents had already been through something like a normal mash by that point. The mash had also run over, most likely because of the heat and because the mash had swollen up.

The next morning the mash temperature had fallen to 63°C. Dmitriy carefully removed the korchaga and carried it into his sauna, setting it on top of a wooden tray with a channel for the wort to run in. He placed an enamelled metal pot under the end of the tray, scraped away the clay, and took out the wooden plug. The wort started running out into the tray and from there into the pot.

Watching Dmitriy brew, it was quite impressive how simple the process was. Compared to mashing with stones this was really straightforward. In fact, it was considerably simpler than the normal brewing processes in farmhouse brewing today. It was easy to see why people might prefer this method over the more common methods. Although, without stirring and careful temperature control, mash efficiency might not be the best, and the use of the pyechka oven clearly limits the size of the batches.

Once all the wort was run off, Dmitriy put the enamel pot on top of a small outdoor oven made of steel and started a fire. He threw in some handfuls of hops and boiled for about an hour. Then it was time to cool the wort and pitch the yeast. Dmitriy used French baking yeast. I asked him what temperature he pitched the yeast at, but he did not know it in degrees. "Like the bathwater of a small child," he said, then measured it with his elbow. Once he was satisfied, I measured it: 37°C.

The evening before, we had tasted Dmitriy's beer from an earlier batch. It was dark, with little carbonation, and had a straw-like, fruity, foresty aroma. The taste

Figure 5.39. Dmitriy with the pitched yeast bag floating in the wort.

was quite dry, with clear rye flavor, surprisingly clean, and ended in a long, astringent finish that made it very drinkable. The astringency may well have come from oven-mashing, but it was hard to be certain. It could also have come from the rootlets still on the undried malt. The astringency was a major part of the character of the beer and balanced it very well. A lovely fruity character merged very well with the rye and the foresty flavor. Overall, a very good beer, probably around 6%–7% ABV.

Understanding Oven Beers

Reportedly, the great stove was developed in what is now Russia sometime in the fifteenth century and gradually spread outward from there. It seems to have reached eastern Finland in the late eighteenth century. This means the stove will in most places have been introduced before metal kettles became affordable, which will have made the oven an attractive alternative to hot stones.

There are two main types of oven-baked beers: one where the oven is used to heat the mash, as in Dmitriy's beer. The other is where the malt is mashed first and then baked in the oven afterward, as in keptinis. Heating the mash in the oven will create flavors more like a kettle mash, while the second creates massive caramelization of the sugars. If the oven is hot enough to caramelize the mash, it will probably be too hot for the enzymatic processes necessary for starch conversion. because the enzymes are destroyed by the heat.

Of course, it would have been possible to heat the oven once, mash the malt in the oven, take it out, and the heat the oven again to bake the mash. However, since this requires starting two fires, it seems likely that brewers would think of these two processes as conceptually different. The flavor would also be different, so these are two clearly distinct types of oven beer that probably have some clear pattern of geographical distribution. Unfortunately, I do not have enough detailed material on oven-based beers yet to say much more.

The Jančys family brew a baked-mash beer, but there are also Lithuanians who heat the mash in the oven.[32] In Estonia, many brewers made the malt "loaves" by mixing cold water with crushed malt and then put these loaves in the oven. Since they were lautered immediately after, the baking in this case must have taken care of the mashing. This process probably required heating the oven more gently than what Vytautas Jančys did. That this process was so common would seem to indicate that the original motivation for oven-based brewing really was to heat the mash. The Tver Karelians in Russia used to heat the strike water in pots in the oven, which is further indication that this theory is probably correct.[33]

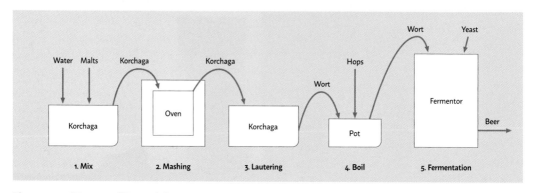

Figure 5.40. Diagram of Dmitriy's brewing process.

Figure 5.41. Commercial malt "loaf" from producer Louna Pagarid. Obinitsa, Setomaa, Estonia.

Northern Lithuania is divided into two brewing regions: in the east the brewers make keptinis; in the west they make raw ale. When plotted on a map, the accounts create a fairly clean dividing line. However, with the fertile farmland of the northern Lithuanian highlands being largely flat, there is no clear geographical feature that could explain the boundary. It may have been created by kettle-based brewing slowly spreading from the west, and the great stove (together with oven-based brewing) slowly spreading from the east. It is not implausible that they met on the current dividing line and that conservatism then made each side stick to "their" method.

In classic oven-mashed beers, and also in keptinis, there was no actual bread involved. Despite all the talk of ovens and "loaves," the beers were made from malt, just like ordinary beer. One exception is eastern Finland, where grain was used, but it was still not edible bread as we understand it. The oven was used simply as a source of heat, to either heat the mash or to caramelize the sugars from the mash.

Estonian Seto koduõlu (see chapter 9, p. 280) uses "malt loaves," or "beer bread" as it is called, but this is not bread. I tried a bite of it and found I could not eat it. It was far too dry and heavy for chewing, which is not really surprising since it is basically baked malt.

Many have compared keptinis with *kvass*, but kvass is not actually a beer. Instead, kvass is made from leftover bread—yes, actual bread—and perhaps a little flour or sugar to make it ferment better. (Kvass is discussed more in chapter 8, p. 254.) As we will see later on in chapter 8, there are variants called kvass that straddle the line into beer, but there is still no clear relation between kvass and the oven beers.

Another parallel is the Mesopotamian *bappir* and Egyptian *bouza*, both of which seem to have been made from some grain-based objects that were baked in ovens. No reliable description of these brewing processes seem to exist, so it is not clear what the role of the "bread" was, or even if it was bread. The best description I have found is in Lucas,[34] which seems to imply that the oven is used to heat the mash and that the yeast comes from the bread. How both can be possible is not clear.

Could the Russian and Baltic oven-based beers be related to those earlier examples from the Middle East? It is not completely impossible, but it does seem very unlikely given that the great stove was invented in the Middle Ages. Of course, it developed out of more primitive ovens, but the distance in time and space is still enormous. What seems much more likely is that bappir and bouza were the result of convergent evolution: people in the Middle East came up with the same solution to the problem of how to heat the mash without metal kettles. In any case, it seems that the original brewing process in Europe was much more primitive.

The Mash Fermented

I first came across this kind of beer when reading the Norwegian survey response from Vanylven in western Norway. The author follows the numbered questions in the questionnaire until he gets to question 44, where he writes in frustration, "The procedure when brewing here was different from what the questionnaire assumes, so I will depart from the numbered questions."[35] To my astonishment, he then wrote a crystal clear description of mixing the boiling juniper infusion, malt, and hops in the mash tun, then cooling the mix until it was "milk-warm," and pitching the yeast. No, this was not just raw ale. Notice that there was no lautering. This beer was fermented in the mash tun with the malt and the hops still there.

For a long time, I was not sure whether to believe this or not. But his response was so clear and definite that it did not seem possible that he could be wrong, especially as he made it clear that farmhouse brewing was still just barely being practiced. And yet, it did not seem possible to make a decent beer this way. Maybe it could produce a kind of kvass, perhaps, but not real beer; except the account even said one barrel of grain should yield one barrel of beer, which would definitely put it in the realm of strong beer.

Years later, going through Danish archival material, I came across a response dated 1973 from Øls in northern Jutland.[36] The respondent was describing how his mother had brewed beer sixty years before, and how, on this particular farm, the grain quality was so poor they had to buy malt. But what really piqued my interest was that, once again, there was a description of the brewing process

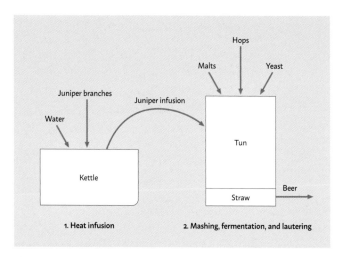

Figure 5.42. The brewing process described in NEG 7329 from Vanylven.

where they pour hot water over a mix of malt grist, hops, and wormwood, wait for it to cool, and then pitch yeast. The next day the yeast was skimmed off and the beer lautered. The respondent could, of course, have been mistaken when describing something so long after, but his account was detailed and otherwise completely believable. Maybe he confused lautering with draining the finished beer, but it really did not sound that way, because he wrote that, when lautering the finished beer, they had to be careful to avoid the spent grain coming out together with the finished beer. This made the story more believable. But was this a real beer, or just kvass? The respondent had written that they had to buy the malt, but only in small portions. Later, he wrote that for Christmas, Easter, and parties, they wanted better beer and so they used more malt, but there was no mention of any change to the brewing process.

Then, going through the Swedish archives, the same process turned up again in no less than four separate accounts.[37] One account ended with: "This beer was good and strong."[38] Then were a further four accounts of Swedish speakers in Finland, reporting the same process from the western and southern coasts of Finland.[39]

Clearly the man from Vanylven had not been making it up. But how on earth would such a beer have tasted? The problem was that in all these places the brewing was long dead, so it did not seem possible to find out more. For a long time, I toyed with the idea of trying it out myself. But if it tasted terrible, how would we know what we had done wrong? As I mentioned at the start of this chapter, Jouko Ylijoki in Finland has tried making this three times, and eventually produced a good beer. But whether it has the correct flavor or not, nobody can tell. Ivar Husdal brought a beer fermented in the mash to the Norwegian farmhouse ale festival in 2019. That beer had a powerful flavor of butyric acid, so it's clear that this brewing process presents some challenges.

Eventually, someone using this process who was still alive turned up. Jury Pleskačeŭski found Lidzija Babkova in the village of Asaviec in eastern Belarus.[40] Unfortunately, Lidzija was getting old and had developed problems with her memory, so it was too late now to learn from her.

It seems there I must leave the story, which shows how important it is that brewing traditions are kept alive. For beer fermented in the mash, it seems like time ran out before anyone could document the process and results in enough detail to reproduce them. If raw ale, keptinis, and the boiled mash had died out, we would only know about these processes from old documents and everyone would assume that evolution had killed off these strange processes because they produced terrible beer. But because they are still alive, we know that they have huge potential for making interesting beers, and we can learn first-hand how to do it right from the brewers themselves.

The Evolution of Brewing Processes

Michael Jackson classified beer styles according to fermentation: top-fermented, bottom-fermented, or spontaneously fermented.[41] For modern beer, where there is little process variation, that makes good sense. The main process distinction is between infusion mashing and decoction mashing, which, had Jackson adopted that as a classification method, would have given him much the same split as dividing ale and lager by fermentation. That is not the only way, however. In farmhouse brewing, there are no known systematic differences in fermentation or yeast, but there are massive differences in process. Since the brewing processes really seem to match cultural shifts and divides, it makes sense to use a process-based classification.

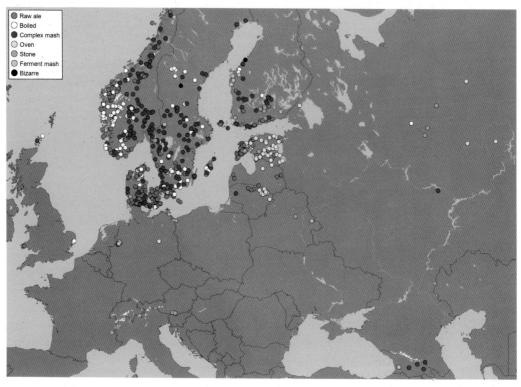

Figure 5.43. Simplified overview showing the geographical distribution of farmhouse brewing processes in Europe, based on the database.

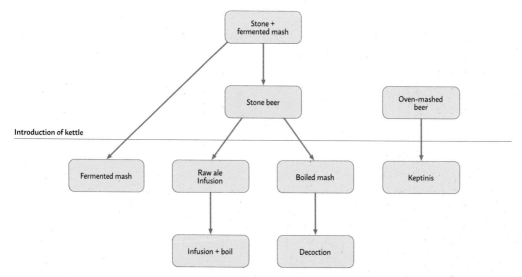

Figure 5.44. A possible evolution of brewing processes. Arrows indicate how a process may have developed from an earlier process. Processes that arose after the introduction of the kettle are, to some extent, all kettle-based. Further details are explained in the main text.

The treatment of the wort is a relatively superficial issue, whether it is boiled or not is a change that is more easily made than a change to the mashing process. The main heat source during mashing seems to reflect more fundamental issues, so I classify the processes by the heat source during mashing. That gives us three categories: stone-heated, oven-heated, and kettle-heated beers.

In this scheme, keptinis is a hybrid between kettle-heated and oven-heated beers, while most modern stone beers are stone/kettle hybrids. Dmitriy's beer would be a pure oven-heated beer. Since all brewers today seem to use kettles, a more practical approach is to ignore the hybrid nature of some of these beers when dealing with styles of beer still alive.

There is no direct evidence for the brewing processes that were used in ancient times, but we can make some guesses as to how these processes evolved. Stone brewing has been practiced over most of northern Europe, perhaps even all of it. The fermented mash process also seems to have been used most places. Both processes are evidently very old. Given this it is tempting to suggest that the original brewing process was to simply mix crushed malt and cold water in a suitable vessel and heat it up with hot stones. After that, the brewer simply waited for the mix to cool before pitching the yeast. Once fermentation was finished, the beer could be run off through the filter. Or, if one did not have a filter, the beer could be drunk through straws, which would serve as a filter. This was done in Mesopotamia, and is still done in some parts of the world. This would have been a simple and quick brewing method that used relatively little energy and required hardly any technology at all.

In fact, a description of almost exactly this process exists. The recipe is undated but is thought to have been written in the 1770s or 1780s. It comes from the Louhisaari Estate, an aristocratic manor near the southwestern coast of Finland.[42] The process it describes is as follows: pour boiling water over the grist; then heat grey stones until they glow red and drop them into the mash while mixing well; add rye flour while stirring; keep stirring while the stones keep the mash boiling and until the mix is cool enough that the yeast can be added. After fermentation, the beer is sieved through a cloth.

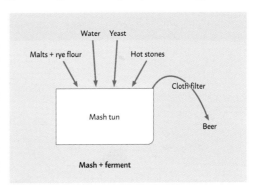

Figure 5.45. Diagram of the Louhisaari brewing process.

And there you are. Omit the boiling water at the start and you have what could be the original brewing process. It must, however, have been difficult to hit consistent mash temperatures with that method, and some of the enzymes must have been destroyed by the heat from the stones. Hot stones are, of course, also unpleasant to work with. Once the technology improved, people were probably very willing to switch to better methods.

Unfortunately, there is one problem with this story. The deposits of brewing stones in Norway appear to begin in the sixth century CE, but we know people were brewing for millennia before that. Where are the brewing stone deposits from those brewers?

The intriguing thing is that the appearance of brewing stone deposits coincides with a major historical change: the transition from the early Iron Age to the late Iron Age. The archaeological record clearly shows there was a massive societal change at this time, with major changes to farm structure, building methods, the arts, and so on.

There are deposits of shattered stone from the early Iron Age, but they are different. In these layers, the stone is shattered not by being dropped into cold liquid, but simply through being heated over and over again. People cooked their food by heating stones, then laying food wrapped in leaves or something similar among the stones and covering both with earth.[43]

The archaeological finds are therefore not consistent with stone brewing as we know it, which seems to indicate that people brewed some other way. What method they used we do not know, but British archaeologist Merryn Dineley did a series of experiments on what she calls "hearth mashing," looking for possible ways to brew using stone-age technology. She worked with simple hearths formed by rings of stones, with some stones inside as well. This is exactly the kind of cooking—not necessarily brewing in particular—that would leave the sort of deposits that archaeologists have found. She was able to mash successfully in flat ceramic bowls of a type that existed in the stone age.[44] Clearly, with patience and experience, small batches of beer could be made that way.

Merryn was also able to mash crushed malt mixed with cold water and formed into flat "cakes" on top of flat stones heated in the hearth. The idea was to replicate how bappir might have been made and used, and again it is clear that small batches of beer could be made this way.[45] This method is intriguingly close to oven beers where the malt "loaves" are mashed in the oven.

So, it is possible that originally, before the introduction of kettles, there were several primitive brewing processes besides stone beer. The benefit of stone beer is that it would scale more easily to larger batches of beer. A benefit of the methods demonstrated by Dineley above is that they do not require staved vessels like the mash and lauter tuns found in farmhouse brewing. Constructing

Figure 5.46. Merryn Dineley's experiment with hearth mashing. Orkney, UK, 1997. Photo: Merryn Dineley.

staved vessels without metal tools is difficult. However, the Finnish kuurna, which can easily be made by hollowing out a log with stone tools, shows that this need not be an obstacle.

There is fairly direct evidence for stone brewing methods, but none for the methods proposed by Dineley. However, although archaeological traces from hearth mashing specifically are impossible to distinguish from those left by cooking in general, right now this process seems like the best explanation available. Either way, all of these methods were clearly awkward and difficult to scale. Brewers must have been eager to abandon them in favor of something more practical.

In eastern Europe, the evolution of the great stove must have revolutionized cooking, since it was now possible to heat ceramic pots containing food in the stove. People making beer must then have quite quickly realized that the mash could be heated the same way, and very likely the various kinds of oven-mashed beers developed from this as use of the great

Figure 5.47. A woman brewing stone beer. Painting by Thorolf Holmboe. Photo courtesy of Mjøsmuseet.

stove spread. This form of brewing was only possible in areas where the great stove was used, so it is found in eastern Finland, the Baltic states, Belarus, Ukraine, and Russia.

In western Europe, stone brewing was probably the normal brewing method until metal kettles became cheap enough that ordinary farmers could afford them. In Norway, this seems to have happened around 1600, so it probably happened a little earlier in the rest of western Europe. It is possible that alternatives to the use of a kettle other than stone beer and oven beer existed, but so far there has been no trace of them. Once kettles became available, brewers had to figure out how to use them in brewing beer, and they seem to have come up with different solutions.

The main difference was how the mash was heated: infusion mashing, either as a single step or multiple steps, kettle mashing, or by circulated heat. The biggest difference is between the simple infusion mash and the more complex mashes. It is possible that these two separate approaches arose out of an earlier difference between those who heated the mash with stones and those who heated the strike water with stones. Another possibility is that complex mashing is a later improvement on infusion mashing, developed for better efficiency.

If people ever heated the strike water with stones, however, there is remarkably little trace of it in the documentation available. The reason could be that the need for stone brewing disappeared centuries ago. Those who continued to brew with stones probably did it because of the way the hot stones flavored the beer. But heating the strike water will not have affected the flavor much, and so that method probably died out more quickly. There is one account from Vormsi in Estonia of people heating the strike water with stones, but that is the only one to mention this method

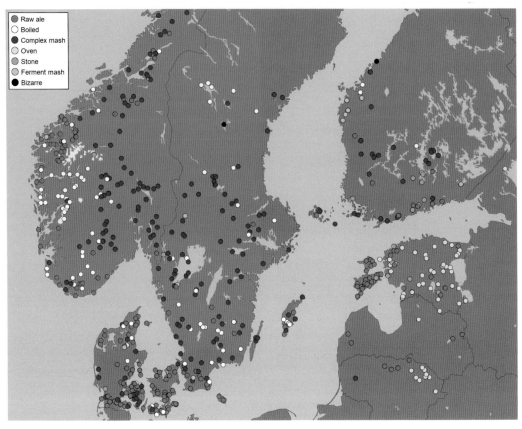

Figure 5.48. Simplified overview of farmhouse brewing processes in the Nordic and Baltic regions. Note the Jostedal glacier in Norway separating the raw ale brewers to the north from boiled beer brewers to the south.

at all.[46] (Interestingly, that account matches the present-day geographical distribution of mashing methods, if we accept that simple infusions descended from earlier stone brewing, since the brewers on the Estonian islands today use infusion mashing.)

Boiling the wort seems to have developed later, and while by the nineteenth century everyone seemed to have kettles, boiling the wort never really took over in farmhouse brewing. Of the 555 brewing processes I have analyzed, only 38% report boiling the wort. And those who boiled the wort often did not boil it with hops, they boiled hop tea separately instead. This seems to indicate that they took to boiling the wort relatively recently, and had not yet realized they could simply boil the hops in it.

Some have suggested that it was the introduction of hops that caused brewers to start boiling the wort. This does not seem to match the timeline, since hops have been used since at least the sixth century (see chap. 7, p. 221) and were widespread in farmhouse brewing even before the kettle was introduced. As we have seen, it is not necessary to boil the wort in order to boil the hops, since one can boil hop tea or humlebeit instead. It is also possible that the hops were originally boiled in small containers made from soapstone before large metal kettles became affordable.

The evolution of farmhouse brewing processes is still continuing today. In the town of Ørsta, western Norway, mountain climber and author Dagfinn Hovden developed an interest in brewing. He tried interviewing the local farmhouse brewers to learn how they brewed but found that they could not tell him details like mashing temperatures. In frustration, he ordered Ludwig Narziss's massive, technical book on scientific beer brewing, and spent a whole winter reading it.[47] Dagfinn then started brewing his own beer based on what he had learned. In 1991, together with local farmhouse brewers, he started an annual seminar on beer brewing.* Based on Dagfinn's technical reading, presentations from professional brewers, and intense discussions among the brewers, the farmhouse brewers gradually modernized their brewing practices. They started boiling their wort and stopped using kveik. Today, their beer is recognizably similar to the kornøl they originally brewed, but now the fruity flavor comes from dry hopping and the raw ale flavor is gone. The color and carbonation remain the same.

Together with vendors of homebrewing supplies, this same group has been trying to persuade the local farmhouse brewers to adopt more modern brewing practices. One local homebrewing vendor taught a course where his students clearly strongly disagreed with him on how to brew. A visiting journalist was told: "This is a bad habit they have, not to boil the wort. Nobody else in the whole world brews like this."[48] The clear implication was that this was wrong, old-fashioned, and these people had better come to their senses and start brewing modern beer.

Clearly, there has been considerable pressure on farmhouse brewers in many areas to give up on their traditional methods and instead switch to more modern brewing practices. Many farmhouse brewers in the Stjørdal area have also changed their brewing process, and boiling the wort is clearly becoming more popular. Very likely the processes are still changing in other places too.

---

* Stein Langlo was, and is, one of the driving forces behind these seminars.

6

BEER AS PART OF FARM LIFE

The most dramatic and far-reaching social change of the
second half of this century, and the one which cuts us
off forever from the world of the past, is the death of the
peasantry.

— Eric Hobsbawm, *Age of Extremes:
The Short Twentieth Century, 1914–1991*, 289

Historically, farms were mostly self-sufficient, producing nearly everything the people there
needed. Cheese, butter, meat, bread, drinks, and so forth were all made on the farm from the
farm's own produce. Even clothes, tools, kitchenware, and similar items were made on the
farm. Farmers lived mostly outside the money economy, only spending money on things that
they could not make themselves, like advanced metalwork, glass items, and so on.

A good example is rope. Today, rope is something you buy, but on the farms in the old
days people made three types of rope themselves. One was ordinary rope, made by braiding
fibers from hemp, animal hair, or even certain types of bark (linden bark could be prepared
through a quite complicated process to make rope). Another type of rope was made from

leather. Finally, for some uses, including the kind of thing you often see steel wire used for today, young shoots from birch or willow were twisted and dried to form a kind of stiff rope.[1] In Norway this was called *vidje*, in English "withy."

Of course, the farmers produced all their food themselves. This was literally how they made their living. Grain was the most important source of food: estimates indicate that in Sweden people got 70%–90% of their calories from grain.[2] In Finland, Sweden, and Norway, most farmers lived in places it would be difficult to transport enough grain to, so they had to grow their own. Even if transport were feasible, very few farmers could have afforded to buy enough grain to last them a whole year.

Transportation really was the key: farms produced goods that could be sold, but transporting them to a place where people might buy them was mostly too difficult. Similarly, transporting most products that farmers were interested in buying to the farms was also difficult. Hawkers made their living by walking around, carrying their wares on their backs. Only some products could be sold profitably this way, one of which was hops.

Figure 6.1. Section of the road that Ole of Kjørro walked, not far from Kaupanger. The road was improved in 1873. Another, much improved, section of the same road is shown in figure 1.1. Drawing by Johannes Flintoe, 1845. Reproduced by permission of the Nasjonalmuseet.

The year 1860 saw poor harvests in Norway, and Ole of Kjørro, a poor farmer in Valdres, eastern Norway, was forced to buy grain. He walked 100 km across the mountains to Lærdal by the fjord in western Norway, where he bought a barrel of grain. This was too much for him to carry, so he split the barrel into two sacks. He carried one sack some distance, put it down, went back to get the other sack, and kept switching like this. This method of carrying forced him to walk 300 km to get home.[3] That the Norwegians had a word for this method of transportation, *tvibæring* (lit. "twice-carrying"), says it all.

There were two main kinds of farm: farms owned by the farmer living on the land, and the tenant farm. The tenant farmer rented his farm from the owner and paid for it in either cash, farm produce, or work done for the owner. The farmers who owned their own property were the richest; tenant farmers were much poorer. What rights the tenant farmers had varied. In Russia, they were serfs, while in Norway and Sweden they were quite independent.

The farm itself largely determined how well-off the farmer was. While a smart and enterprising farmer could get the most out of the farm, there were limits to what was possible. Someone working a small farm in a high valley in Norway would never be rich, because the soil and climate made it impossible to produce very much from the land. If the farm was particularly small or poor, the family might live on the edge of starvation in years when harvests were bad. In Norway, there were farms named "Sveltihel," which literally means "starve-to-death," because they were so poor.[*] In northern Sweden, mixing the flour with tree bark to make it last was not unusual.[4]

A small farm usually had only family living there, and older children might be sent off to serve at larger farms to reduce the number of mouths to feed. Larger farms might be so big that the family could not work all of it themselves, and so these farms might have accommodated quite a few non-family employees. The farmhouse ale was brewed for the household, whether that was a single family or a family plus workers. On larger farms, people often thought that having good ale for the hired hands helped to attract and keep good workers. Others were stingy and deliberately brewed weak, sour beer for the hands so the workers would not drink so much of it.[5]

In Norway, Sweden, and Finland, summers were short and the winters long, so the warm period was spent trying to produce and conserve as much food and fodder as possible so that the family and their animals could survive the winter. It was necessary to have a backup store of food to get through the bad years, which could come at any time. This was extremely important, and visitors might well be taken to the food storehouse where the owners could proudly show them how much was stored there, how well run the farm was, and how safe the farmer and his wife felt.[6]

Beer was made in every home outside the towns, which meant that just about everyone was a brewer or at least lived with one. As a result, all the technical vocabulary that modern brewers have developed also existed in every local dialect in northern Europe. The farmers had their own words for the yeast starter, the spent grain, the filter in the lauter tun, sprouted but undried malt, and so on and so forth. These were everyday terms, as necessary as the words "rope" or "threshing." In fact, brewing was so much a part of daily life that malting and brewing made it into many everyday sayings and expressions. In Telemark in Norway, they said of people who were a bit slow on the uptake that "he arrives later, like the oat malt."[7] This referred to how oats sprouted a day or two after barley when oats and barley were malted together. On Gotland in Sweden, if one farmer started blaming his neighbor for a girl becoming pregnant, a third person might attempt to stop the argument by telling the first "just watch yourselves, you may also get green malt in the loft."[8] The grain was sprouted in the loft, and it was important to stop the sprouting before the shoots turned green, otherwise too much of the sugar would be used up.

---

[*] The official guideline to the Norwegian law on place names suggests farms should be allowed to change their name if it can be considered derogatory, and "Sveltihel" is given as an example.

Harvest Ale

Farmhouse ale was especially important for the hardest bouts of work in the heat of summer. In Aurland, western Norway, the farmers brought in beer in big two-and-a-half-liter cans for fieldwork in the heat, because "if they drank only water they would feel weak."[9] Even if you are extremely fit, doing very hard physical work all day requires calories to keep going. Farm workers needed both liquid and calories, and beer provided both.

In the UK, the concept of harvest ale is well known, and I thought summer farmhouse beer was also brewed for laborers working on the grain harvest. The reality turns out to be more complicated, however. There was another heavy bout of fieldwork in the summer: the haymaking, and haymaking came before the grain harvest. Haymaking was the cutting of grass from fallow fields and every piece of land on which grass could be found. From the accounts I have read, it seems that in the UK the farmhands were served beer for the harvest, but in Scandinavia the beer was used for haymaking. Exactly why the difference was so stark is not clear to me at all.

Harvest ale was an important part of the work rituals and was part of what kept the workers going during weeks of backbreaking labor.* As a Swedish woman put it, "For haymaking, there

Figure 6.2. Grain harvest in Mittet, Romsdalen, western Norway, roughly 1910. Reproduced by permission from the Romsdalsmuseet.

---

* I use the English term "harvest ale" here to also mean beer for haymaking.

was a demand for drink like no other time of year."[10] The importance of ale for farm workers is clear from countless descriptions from Wales,[11] England, Norway, Denmark, Sweden, and Finland, among others.

There were two kinds of harvest ale. One was somewhat weaker than normal beer and intended to be drunk during the work day. The other was stronger than normal beer and was drunk for celebrations in the evening after the day's work was done, or for the celebrations when the work was over. Traditionally, a region would stick to brewing either weak or strong harvest ale. On larger farms, which hired outside workers to help with the work, beer was part of the pay.

A common view was that "it wasn't good to have the beer too strong [for the haymaking]. The work suffered then."[12] But it seems it did not have to be that way: "Thirty to fifty years ago, there was a farmer here who always brewed for haymaking, at least one barrel each time, and the beer was all for his own mouth. He always made the beer strong, and during the haymaking he was often two sheets to the wind. But then, he worked furiously too. 'The beer cask is my best workman,' he said."[13] This expression about the beer cask being a good worker is repeated many places, and seemingly not without reason. On August 24, 1883, at Beacon Hill outside Amesbury in England, a strange competition took place. Mr. Turrell, a corn dealer, challenged Mr. Abbey, a visiting temperance speaker, to see who could harvest the most grain, with Turrell drinking beer and Abbey drinking only water. Mr. Turrell held a large lead right from the start, and at 4 p.m. he was declared the winner.[14]

Clearly, drinking beer did nothing to harm Mr. Turrell's ability to work, but if the beer was too strong that could happen. One account relates how J.W. Thörnblad, a teetotalling farmer on Öland in Sweden, brewed strong beer in March in preparation for haymaking, burying it until the rye harvest. When the time came, Thörnblad bid his workers drink up the good, strong beer, "But that experiment he never repeated, because he had no benefit from the workers, since they lay dead drunk in the field, unable to perform any work at all."[15]

In the end, mechanization of agriculture killed off harvest ale in several ways. The work was no longer so physically demanding and far fewer workers were needed. Furthermore, having tipsy workers handle machinery in many cases led to accidents.[16]

Brewing harvest ale was an eminently practical concern, but there were other reasons to brew that, while perhaps not as practical, were important too.

Ritual Beer

The toast, when the beer bowl was sent round the table, was a solemn occasion, and in the old days it meant a lot more than just having a drink. The grain, which was the foundation of all life, was treated with reverence. Even today, people in Norway sometimes refer to it as *gudelånet*, "the loan from the gods."[17] In Sweden, at least in some places, the term meant the beer.[18] In many parts of Europe, the last grain to be harvested would be kept as a separate bunch, called *kornmora* (lit. "corn mother"; in English it was known as the corn dolly). The corn mother was venerated and in some places the corn mother would be plowed back into the ground in spring.[19]

Sverre Skrindo[20] told me that, into the twentieth century, people in Ål in Hallingdal, eastern Norway, would take their hats off to sow the grain in spring, because "this was a holy act. It was to

Figure 6.3. Man sowing, unknown location in Norway. Photo by Olav Lorck Eidem.

be or not to be, if it failed." One local man was known for being particularly skilled at sowing, and he always wore a white shirt when sowing. Customs were similar across the rest of Norway. Usually, the sower was bare-headed and began sowing with the words, "In the name of Christ."[21]

Beer held such importance not only because it was made from grain, the most precious of all commodities, but also because it altered your state of consciousness. Many societies, both tribal and modern, use intoxicating substances in their religious ceremonies precisely because of these mind-altering properties. The high point of Christian church services is literally the veneration of bread and wine. Imagine how people would react to something that was the "loan from the gods" transformed into a mind-altering drug, which is precisely what beer was. In late eighteenth-century Telemark in Norway, the priest Hans Jacob Wille showed the connection quite clearly:

> The farmers here are highly reverent when they brew beer for feasts, out of a fear that the beer will not turn out strong, which is held a great disaster. When they hold feasts and there is a guest who does not become drunk, they consider it a sign that the curse of God lies upon the person, of whom it is said that "God's mercy upon whom the gifts of God do not bite." Should it happen that a guest at a feast does not become drunk the host is so saddened as if his farmhouse had burned down. Therefore, many guests pretend to be drunk, even if they are not, so as not to offend the host, and to show that the curse of God does not lie upon them. (Wille 1881, 30–31)

It is not at all surprising that people used beer as a ritual drink. That this custom goes back a long way is shown by the thirteenth-century writings of Snorri Sturluson on the subject of the pagan midwinter sacrifice. Every participant had to bring beer to the gathering, and the high point of the feast was the saying of toasts, when the beer bowl would be passed around the fire. The first toast was for the gods, followed by toasts for "their ancestors, those who were dead and laid in barrows [burial mounds]." There would be toasts to the king, for good harvests, and so on. The last toast could be a *brageskål*, a toast in which the drinker promised to perform some great deed in the coming year.[*]

This toasting was called *minni* (memory), and something similar to it could be seen into the late nineteenth century in a custom called "drinking minni to St. Eldbjørg." The church accepted this since it was dedicated to a saint . . . except there is no St. Eldbjørg, and the name literally means "fire-saving." The family gathered round the fire, then drank a toast "that the red cock may never crow over my house," continuing "so high my fire, but no higher nor hotter." Then beer would be poured on the fire. It was essentially fire worship, and note the way the beer was used together with formulaic phrases to turn it into a sacred ritual.[22] Used in a similar way, beer was a necessity for all major celebrations on the farm. Solemn toasting rituals, usually slowly degenerating into partying, were a key part of celebrations like Christmas and weddings.

---

[*] Sturluson, "Håkon den Godes saga," *Heimskringla*, para. 14.

Beer was also required for funerals. Into the early twentieth century, farmers in western Norway who knew they did not have long left to live might set aside a portion of grain for their own funeral beer.[23] There are several stories about farmers recovering and drinking their own funeral beer three, four, even five times. And beer really was necessary for funerals, as this story from Saaremaa in Estonia shows:

Figure 6.4. Sigvalde Jarl, performing a brageskål in which he promises to avenge his father by killing the king. Drawing by Halvdan Egedius, 1899, but depicting a scene from Viking times.

E. Kõpp, parish priest, related how one man from Tagamõisa came to him to register the death of a relative. The priest asked on what day he should hold the funeral. "Well," said the man, "if there is wind then Thursday, but if there is going to be a calm, then I don't know when we can do it." The priest was from the mainland, so he didn't understand the connection between the wind and the burial. He asked the man what he meant. The explanation was simple: without wind the mill can't grind the malt, and no malt, no beer. No beer, no funeral. (Jakovlev 1997, 118)

Figure 6.5. A bridal procession arriving at what would be the home of the bride and groom from this point onward. The man next to the door is ready to welcome them to their "new" home with a toast of beer. This was a custom in many parts of Norway. Painting by Adolph Tiedemand.

Enormous quantities of beer might be consumed at peasant weddings, which could last several days. At the Mølster farm in Voss, 1200 liters were brewed for one wedding, and well into the late twentieth century it was common to see 650–800 liters brewed for weddings in the Sysmä area of Finland.[24] In the past, the authorities repeatedly tried banning extravagant celebrations to reduce the amount of grain used.

Coming together as a group to drink beer, even if just two people, symbolized agreement and good will, and was used symbolically several ways. For example, when two families agreed two young people should marry, the betrothal was marked by drinking *festarøl*, which literally meant "betrothal ale."[25]

Very similar was the Norwegian custom of drinking *kjøpskål* (lit. "purchase toast") to mark an important sale. In the old days, neither the seller nor the buyer could write, so it was impossible to draw up a contract and then formally sign it to signify agreement.[26] Instead, the two parties would drink kjøpskål to mark that they had agreed. This might be done for many different transactions, from buying a load of fish, a horse, or a farm. Norwegian theologian and government minister Nils Hertzberg recalled that, as a 10-year-old in 1837, he happened to be at a horse market in the mountains, and, as the only person present who could read and write, he wrote purchase contracts for the horse traders who normally drank purchase toasts.[27] That must have been quite a sight.

This was not just a Norwegian custom. Many medieval Nordic towns had laws

Figure 6.6. Drinking kjøpskål. Wall decoration at the Hansa Borg Brewery, Bergen, Norway.

requiring a purchase toast be drunk for a sale for it to be legally binding.[28] In Lithuania, there was the same thing, called *magaryčios*: a toast drunk between the buyer and seller with two or three witnesses present.[29] The custom also existed in Germany, where it was known as *leikauf*, so it may have been a general European custom.[30]

These "purchase toasts" had real legal significance. And they were not the only examples of beer drinking with legal implications. When a farmer died, his relatives would gather to agree how to divide up the estate and, when they were finished, they would drink a toast to symbolize that they had reached agreement. Similarly, it was customary to take part in celebratory beer drinking when a child was born. In Viking-age Norwegian law, there were provisions stating that if someone had been born abroad and there was uncertainty as to whether they were actually in a position to inherit, they must support their claim by putting forth witnesses who were present at their childbirth beer celebration.[31]

There were also a whole range of social customs around toasting. For example, there was a separate type of small beer bowl intended for two people to share while toasting each other. An invitation from someone to drink like this was considered a mark of high favour, particularly from someone rich and powerful. It could serve many purposes, from wooing women to creating alliances.[32]

The toasting that people do at parties and in pubs today is a remnant of the extremely elaborate and, in the old days, important culture of ritual drinking and toasting.

Toasting was not the only ritual use of beer, however, because it was also used in ways that were downright superstitious, even semi-religious.

Superstition

Imagine being taught brewing on a farm at the turn of the nineteenth century. It would have seemed a fairly mysterious process, first taking several steps to turn grain, which is not sweet at all, into a sweet liquid, and then adding some grey sludge to start a strange process that looks like boiling, except it is not hot. At the end of all this, suddenly, inexplicably, the liquid has gained mind-altering properties. Why did it become first sweet and then intoxicating? What was actually going on? Nobody really knew. Furthermore, sometimes the process failed and you produced something that tasted off or may have even been undrinkable. Why? Again, nobody knew.

Everything in life was like this. You were taught to make rope, sow grain, and brew beer in specific ways. Sometimes there was a clear reason why things had to be done a certain way, but often not. What you did know was that if you repeated exactly what your parents had done you usually got a good result. Over time you also learned that any deviation, no matter how small, could be disastrous.

Today's modern, educated brewers know that some of what people were taught before is completely unnecessary and has no effect at all on the final beer, and so nowadays we call those things superstition. The line between knowledge and superstition, however, is something new. In the old days, there was only lore, the common knowledge held in the local community and passed on from person to person. You learned the craft of brewing as a whole, and some of what you learned was pure fiction. What was fiction was not at all clear.

The separation between real and fiction is not as clear as it might seem even today. When I met Terje Raftevold on the quay in Innvik before brewing with him, one of the first things he said was, "I was taught that we shouldn't brew during the 'dog days.'" He meant the warmest part of summer, from late July to late August. "But," Terje continued, "I've done it several times, and it's never been a problem." Except this time, it was a problem. The beer turned sour a month after we brewed it.

There are more microorganisms in the air during midsummer. It does not mean you cannot brew in midsummer, just that it is risky when brewing raw ale in an old-style open brewhouse with a dirt floor. The old-timers were right that it should be avoided, but how was Terje to know that? He tried it, it worked several times, and then it did not work.

Similarly, Sigmund Gjernes in Voss removes the foam from the boiling wort because of the oils from the juniper that, he has been taught, can give you a headache. Is that superstition or knowledge? I honestly do not know.

On the *Brülosophy* blog site, a team of homebrewing bloggers have done seven semi-scientific experiments to determine how the amount of yeast pitched changes the flavor of the beer. To their astonishment, what they have found does not at all match what the textbooks say. Does this mean using empirically determined yeast pitching rates on a homebrewing scale superstitious? I do not know. They do not know either.

Bear this in mind when you read what follows on brewing practices that clearly *are* superstitious. These superstitions are all from a time when most people had no education at all and could not even read and write.

When the beer failed or would not ferment, the blame was usually put on the *vetter*. These were supernatural creatures of many different kinds and with many different names. They were basically spirits that had to be mollified to prevent them from doing all kinds of mischief, not just to the beer, but also to humans, animals, and other things.

In many places, people were taught that when brewing or preparing to brew, there were certain things that couldn't be called by their right names. Collecting the juniper you could not call it *brakje*, you had to call it *eine* so that the vetter did not realize you were about to brew. If they knew you were brewing, they would either want some of the beer for themselves or simply spoil it. Similarly, you could not say that the juniper infusion or the wort was boiling, you had to say that it was "playing." This was a very strict rule. In the summer of 1872,

there was to be a wedding on the Blom farm in Hardanger, western Norway, and a local was hired to make the wedding beer. When the wort started boiling one of the bystanders thoughtlessly remarked that "now it's boiling." The hired brewer took his jersey under his arm and left without another word. The people on the farm had to run after him and beg him to come back and finish the brew.[33]

A custom that confused me for a long time was the "yeast scream" (in Norwegian: *gjærkauk*). This was the custom of screaming very loudly into the fermentor just as the yeast is added. The farmhouse brewers in Stjørdalen still do it, and it was still practiced in western Norway in the last few decades of the twentieth century as well. The local radio station in Stjørdal even had a competition to see who had the best gjærkauk.

If you ask them why they do the yeast scream, the brewers say it is so the beer will be good and the people who drink it will be happy. Jørund Geving, who is from Stjørdal, screams "oooooiii,

Figure 6.7. The farm's protective spirit, the *nisse*, was also a bit of a trickster. Here he has stolen the cat's food and is laughing at the animal's distress. Drawing by Theodor Kittelsen, 1887.

---

* A Norwegian word, singular *vette*, or *nisse*. In Swedish, it would be *troll* or *vätte*; in Danish, *vætte*; in Finnish, *tontu*.

good beer!" That kind of fits with the explanation given. But Roar Sandodden, another local, had the impression that it was to protect the beer, perhaps from the vetter, because many brewers shouted things along the lines of "shoosh, go away!" Roar had spoken to an older brewer who seemed to think this was the case. To explain why he kept doing it, the older brewer added: "I'm not sure it works, but it costs so little." Later on, I found this story from southern Sweden:

> A story is told about a farm where the trolls [in this part of Sweden, "troll" means vetter] would always take the wort just as the yeast was added. They therefore asked a wise old man for advice, and he told them that, just as the housewife pitched the yeast, someone else in the brewhouse should pretend to be frightened and scream "There's a fire on Killingeö" [Killinge Island]. When they later followed the wise man's advice, a troll woman ran out of the brewhouse, shouting in fear, "Oh dear me! Then all my children will burn!" From that day on the trolls never took their Christmas beer. (LUF 2954)

I found other variations on this story, and many more claims that the purpose of the screaming was to frighten away evil spirits from "infecting" the beer. So, it seems pretty clear that this really was the reason for the yeast scream.

The same practice shows up all over Norway, and also Sweden and Finland. In 2016, when we brewed with Paavo Pruul on the Estonian island of Hiiumaa, he told us that when he added the wort he had to say the names of every angry dog in the village, otherwise the beer would not ferment. A year earlier, I had asked Ugis Pucens in Latvia whether people did anything special when adding the yeast. He laughed and said old people had told him a woman should scream when the yeast was added, which is surprisingly close to the Swedish story above.[34]

Marina Fyodorovna, in Chuvashia, Russia, had also learned that when pitching the yeast she must pronounce a formula in her mind, without saying it out loud. She had no fixed words but would say something along the lines of, "Thank you to the universe, make the beer healthy, let the strength of the beer make us stronger." This seems to have been common practice in Chuvashia.[35]

It is not really very surprising that brewers see the pitching of the yeast as a particularly crucial moment and want to do something to make sure it comes out right. Even today, pitching the yeast means handing over the brewing process to mysterious, invisible creatures who, you hope, will finish the job. It is, in a sense, the moment of truth.

Many believed it was important to stir the mash in the right way. That is, you had to stir either in the direction the sun traveled or in a cross-like shape. People believed this about cooking in general, but in brewing the belief seems to have lasted longer. I have a recipe from southern Norway from 1996 that contains an explicit warning to stir the mash with the sun or in a cross otherwise the beer will turn sour.[36]

I visited the Nordic Museum in Stockholm in January 2017. Looking in their index catalog under brewing, I found the subheadings you would expect, including superstition. Under superstition I found "noa names" (referring to things by pseudonyms, as discussed above), "screaming," and so on. Weirdly, there was an entry for "men's trousers," which made no sense to me. In the documents I brought home from the museum I found the following record, from Dalsland in southwestern Sweden: "The fermentor was then covered up . . . and if the covering included a pair of men's trousers the old folks thought that the harvested yeast would be particularly good."[37] People report the same thing from Denmark and Norway, too: putting a pair of men's trousers over the fermentor would make the fermentation better.[38] Why, I do not know. None of the accounts give any reason, and I have not been able to figure it out myself.

Another way to protect the beer from the vetter was to just give them some. Since the vetter wanted the beer so badly, you could offer up a small amount to them in the hope that you could then keep the rest for yourself. An account from my mother's hometown of Sogndal in western Norway told how "the first drops [of wort from the lauter tun] were not for oneself. The brewer opened one door and flung the first ladle of wort through it and said, 'There you have yours.' Then he opened the other door and shouted, 'And there you have yours, too!' Then he would mutter that now he wanted the rest for himself."[39]

If you did not mollify them, the vetter could sabotage your entire batch in different ways. This story is from Evje in Setesdal, southern Norway:

A woman from the farm of Lund was brewing for Christmas, but could not make the beer "go" [ferment], no matter how hard she strove. Something like this she'd never seen before, so it had to be some kind of witchcraft that was blocking her. As it was getting late, she laid on her bed to rest. She was tired and dispirited and did not know how she was going to get the beer to go. So it would just have to turn out as it would. As she lay there half-asleep, in came a woman she thought she recognized, but just then she couldn't say who it was. They started talking about this, that, and the other, starting with the weather and ending with beer brewing. The Lund wife told her she had been struggling for days, but could not get the beer to go.

"Have you given to the årevette [fireplace vette]?" asks the stranger.

"No," says the Lund wife.

"Can you then expect the beer to go?" said the stranger. "You must always, when you are brewing, pour some wort on the stone in the fireplace if you want the beer to go and the brew to turn out successful."

"But you sleep now, and I will take care of the beer," said the stranger.

And the Lund wife slept. When she woke, the beer was fermenting so hard it ran over the fermentor and onto the floor. But the stranger was gone and nobody ever saw her again. (Galteland 1920, 10–11)

There were many kinds of vette, not just the one in the fireplace. Particularly frightening were the ones that lived in burial mounds, and terrible stories were told about what could happen if they did not get their annual tribute of beer on Christmas Eve. However, this was not the original belief. In really olden days, the vette in the burial mound was not a stranger, but rather a member of the family. Originally, people thought the person buried in the mound was the first farmer who had cleared the farm, and that he now protected the farm against all evil. In many places, people still remembered the name of the original farmer and revered him. Some even had human-like statues carved from wood, with metal buttons for eyes; on top of the head there was an indentation where the beer bowl was set. There were celebrations where everyone toasted the ancestor and asked him for good harvests. For each toast, the beer was taken from the ancestor's statue, served around, then put back, as if the beer were a gift from the ancestor himself.[40]

In remote parts of Norway this type of ancestor worship was practiced up to the late nineteenth century. At a burial mound in Slinde, western Norway, a beer sacrifice was made to the sacred tree atop the mound until the tree was blown down in a storm in 1874. In other areas, this type of practice continued as late as World War I.

Under the impact of Christianity, the worship of the ancestors faded. In popular imagination the ancestor merged with the vetter to become just another set of spirits in the landscape around the farm. But this type of belief lingered longer than you might think. Halvor Nordal told me that his grandmother would never enter a door in the most obvious way.[41] She would always open the door,

Figure 6.8. The birch on the barrow at Slinde, near Sogndal, western Norway. Beer sacrifices were offered to the tree until it blew down in a storm in 1874. Painting by Johan Christian Dahl.

step aside as if letting some invisible being out, then go through the door. When Halvor brewed his first farmhouse ale after learning the craft from other locals, his grandmother was present at the oppskåke. When Halvor got ready to pour, Grandma pushed her way to the front and made sure to get the first drops in a ladle. She then went out into the farmyard, over to the big stone in the middle of the yard, shouted "step aside" even though there was nobody there, and threw the beer onto a small stone on top of the big stone. This small stone had been on the farm as long as anyone could remember. It was shaped like a phallus and used to stand upright on the big stone. As a concession to modern sensitivities, it has been placed lying down for the last few decades.[42]

Brewers or Brewsters?

In the past, brewing was a part of housekeeping, like baking bread and washing clothes, and so it was women's work. In areas where beer was an everyday drink, brewing had to be done once a month or maybe even every other week. As one Swedish woman put it, looking back from old age, "Brewing we had to do so often, so often."[43] It was a chore, and one that involved two full days of work for each brew. Even the malting was mostly work for women, which added even more to an already heavy workload.

Figure 6.9. *Woman sieving the wort in Dalarna, Sweden, 1937. Photo by Ingalill Granlund, reproduced by permission of the Nordic Museum.*

Much has been written about how brewers in the olden days were mainly women, but there is more to the story. In Telemark, Halvor Nordal told me that his mother and grandmother brewed. In his family, the menfolk had died young, he said, which was why the women had to brew.[44] At one time, his mother worked as a servant on a nearby farm, but the man on the farm was a drunk and so she often had to do the brewing. Though it was traditionally supposed to be done by men, she was essentially forced to do it. And so she did. But pitching the yeast, that was such a momentous step that she, a woman, did not dare do it. In the end, Halvor's grandmother, a respected and self-assured woman, had to come over and pitch the yeast for her.

Listening to Halvor, I was puzzled. Everyone knows that brewing was done by women historically. So what was this stuff about women not being supposed to brew? It did not make sense.

The Norwegian farmhouse brewing survey has a question about whether brewing was a job for men or women.[45] I noticed that many of the responses were very clear that brewing was done by men. But many other responses said it was a job for women. This was confusing, so, on a long train journey, I plotted the answers on a map, shown in figure 6.10. When I opened it, I was astonished to see a very clear geographical divide. In western Norway, the brewers were men, and in eastern and central Norway, women. A few remote, isolated places in eastern Norway were exceptions, where the brewers were men. The brewers seem to have been men in northern Norway too. The farmhouse brewing survey answers were written in the 1950s and basically describe brewing as it was in the late nineteenth century and the first half of the twentieth century. Could it be that this split was a new thing?

Later, I discovered that in western Norway there was a strict superstition against having women in the brewhouse—that meant sour beer. I had heard hints of this from several places, so when I visited Svein Rivenes in Voss I tried asking him. He smiled and said the relatives that had the farm before him had told him very emphatically, "You have to make damn sure there are no women in the brewhouse or the beer will be sour!" If the reason men were brewing was superstition, that does not sound like a modern phenomenom.

In the late seventeenth century, a nameless Danish administrator wrote about upper Telemark in eastern Norway: "Up there . . . the menfolk brew all their beer themselves,"[46] so it has been going on for three centuries, at least in Norway. That the administrator should have remarked on it implies that in Denmark women were the brewers at that time.

Confusingly, in the Viking sagas both men and women are referred to as brewers. Old Norse society generally had very strictly defined gender roles, and a man who spent time on typically feminine activities could expect to be ridiculed and lose status. It is a bit strange, therefore, that brewing should seemingly be both a male and a female task. There is also no sign of any superstitious ban against women brewing.[47]

In Sweden and Denmark, the brewers were all women, and this seems to have been the case for Russia and Great Britain too. Georgia offers an instructive example half-way between the two: for ritual purposes brewing was done only by men, but when the beer was brewed for domestic purposes women were very much involved.[48] In Estonia, brewers were traditionally only men. The belief was that "if a woman somehow happened to intervene or step in to help in the brewing process, the beer would go bad," which is exactly the same belief found in western Norway.[49] This gender divide disappeared during the twentieth century, and women also started brewing on the Estonian islands. Farmhouse brewing seems to have died out on the mainland at some point after the 1930s, but exactly when is not clear.

Confusingly, in some cases the situation seems to have been reversed. In Lihula, western Estonia, "Men mostly do the brewing. However, there are farmsteads where women always do the brewing and men are not even allowed to watch."[50] Why this was the case, I do not know.

Curiously, Finland had a similar east-west divide, but the other way around to that in Norway: in the west women were the brewers, in the east it was men.[51]

Are western Norway, Estonia, eastern Finland, and Georgia the only places that preserved an ancient superstitious ban against women brewing? Or is it just a coincidence that these places ended up with the same superstition? I do not know.

Where beer was the daily drink, it would be difficult to maintain a semi-religious cult around it. When beer was brewed every other week, men would be more inclined to leave the brewing to women. It is definitely no coincidence that the places where men were the brewers are places where there was a lack of grain. In eastern Norway, it was only in a few remote places that men only were the brewers. One possibility is that this pattern shows originally it was men brewing everywhere, before the custom of letting women do it spread and eventually displaced the old ways in all but a few remote locations. However you would then expect to see the same in remote places in neighboring Sweden, but in Sweden brewing seems to have been work for women everywhere.

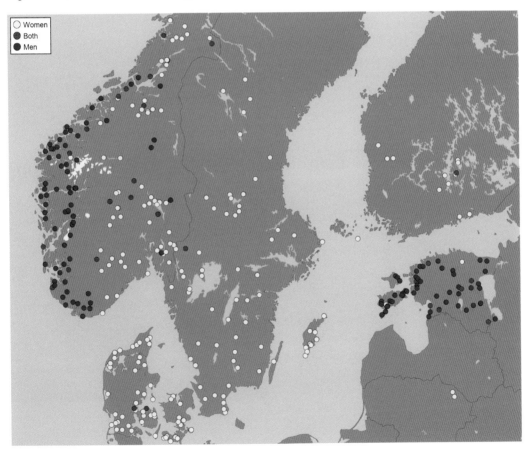

Figure 6.10. Map of which gender had the job of brewing: red for women, blue for men, pink for either/both.

There are a couple of tantalizing hints that may offer some explanation. In Denmark, Sweden, and Finland, malt was made by women, but in Norway men made the malt, even in eastern Norway. Is this an indication that men used to make the beer in eastern Norway too? It may simply indicate that Norway was somehow the anomaly. Another curious hint is that, while in most places bread was made by women, in some parts of western Norway men made not just the beer but also the bread. There are several old texts and names that indicate that "the bread protector" was a title used by local chieftains. Indeed, the English word "lord" derives from Old English *hlāfweard*, literally meaning "bread-guardian." Were these traditional gender divides remnants of a time when grain was so holy that the main grain products, bread and beer, had to be made by men? The oldest sign of beer in Norway is the Tune Stone, a rune stone from southeastern Norway dated to 250–400 CE. According to the inscription, the stone was raised in memory of Wodurid "the bread protector," who was buried underneath it. However, Wodurid's funeral beer, says the inscription, was brewed by his three daughters. It may very well be that we will never learn the full story of men and women as brewers.

Today, however, farmhouse brewers are nearly all men, regardless of whether men or women were traditionally the brewers in that area. The exception seems to be Russia. As Salomonsson pointed out, the reason for this male dominance is probably that farmhouse brewing is no longer a necessary part of housekeeping in modern life, but a hobby instead.[52] It is also something that, at least in part, is done to show off for guests and neighbors; generally, men are the ones who undertake these types of activity.

For farmhouse brewing to survive, men largely had to take it over from women once the job no longer made economic sense. It is possible this is one reason why farmhouse brewing has survived in large parts of western Norway but in only a few places in eastern Norway. Strikingly, the two places in eastern Norway where farmhouse brewing has survived are places where the brewers were traditionally men.

Equipment

The equipment used by farmhouse brewers varied, but everywhere it was primarily made of wood, except for the great copper or iron kettle. Those who brewed raw ale had to have one lauter tun and a separate fermentor, while those who boiled the wort could use the lauter tun for fermentation. In addition they had wooden buckets, a large wooden ladle, and a mash paddle. Finally, there was the beer keg, and perhaps a wooden rack to place it on.

Figure 6.11. Jarand Eitrheim (*left*) and Jakob Eitrheim adjusting the tap of an S-type lauter tun. Note the beautiful brewer's ladle next to it. Aga, Hardanger, western Norway.

There are only so many ways to make a kettle or a beer cask, but the lauter tun was a different story. In photos, the lauter tun is instantly recognizable because it is the vessel that stands on something, usually about 30–50 cm off the ground, so that the brewer can get a bucket underneath to collect the wort being run off. In Denmark and Sweden, the lauter tun usually stood on a curious U-shaped stand made especially for this purpose; the stand leaned slightly to one side to make it easier to get all the wort out.

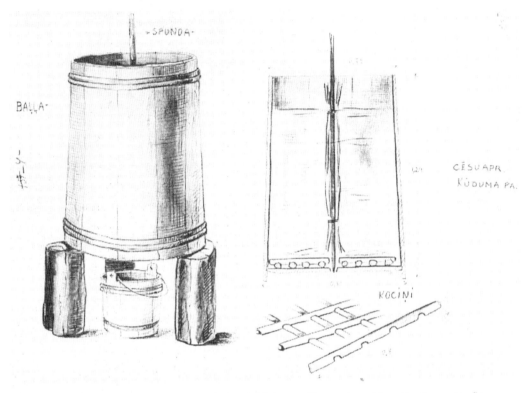

Figure 6.12. Drawing of B-type lauter tun with the witch's broom. The wooden grid enables the wort to flow underneath the filter. From Rideļi, western Latvia. Courtesy of the National History Museum of Latvia.

In western Europe, there were two main types of lauter tuns. The type that seems to be the oldest had a hole in the bottom, usually off to one side, which could be closed with a long rod that stuck out of the vessel. The rod was tapered at the end so that lifting it would let wort run out, allowing the brewer to easily control the flow. This was the type of lauter tun that would be placed on the U-shaped stand. I call this the "B-type." This lauter tun was almost the only type used in Denmark and most of the Baltic. It was also used in the UK, Germany, and southern Sweden. In Norway the B-type tun was quite rare, only found in a few places scattered around the country. This was because it had been replaced by a newer and more practical type, which I call the "S-type."

The S-type was a new type of lauter tun that had a hole in the side near the bottom, which was closed with a simple wooden tap that could be turned to open the flow. In later times, the wooden tap was often replaced with one of brass. There were two main sorts of S-type tuns: one that looked like a barrel with no lid; and another that was made from wooden planks joined together, where

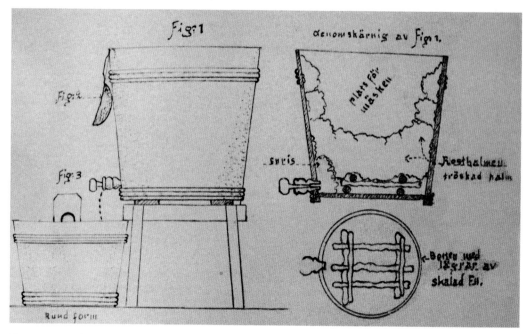

Figure 6.13. A classic S-type lauter tun. Peeled sticks of juniper on the bottom, to allow the wort to flow along the bottom. Juniper just in front of the tap, covered with straw. Drawing from EU 7779, Gammelgarn, Gotland, Sweden, dated 1935.

three of the planks were longer than the others, raising the lauter tun so that it did not need a stand. The S-type was the normal lauter tun in Norway as well as in central and northern Sweden.

The Finns, however, used a different design: a low wooden trough made by hollowing out a log. The trough had a hole at one end and, typically, wooden spiles would be placed over the bottom with straw and juniper laid on top. This created an open space underneath the malt where the wort could run to the hole at the end. This vessel was called the *kuurna*. The same vessel was also used in eastern Latvia, where it was known as *zlaukts*. Further in the east of Latvia, people used a variant that combined the hole in the middle with a tapered rod for opening and closing.[53]

Exactly what people used in Russia is not clear, but in Kudymkar, just west of the Urals, I saw a Komi woman brewing with a vessel shaped exactly like a kuurna. In Chuvashia, midway between the Urals and Moscow, Marina Ivanovna used a vessel like the Latvian zlaukts with a rod for opening and closing the drain. Further north, people used the B type lauter tun. Those doing the entire mash in the korchaga, like Dmitriy Zhezlov in Shitovo, west of Kudymkar (chap. 5, p. 161), can use the korchaga for lautering as well by preparing it with straw on the bottom. Once the mash comes out of the oven, the plug at the bottom of the korchaga is removed and the wort is run off. Some brewers among the Komi use the same technique.

Brewing equipment has seen dramatic change over the last few decades, with many farmhouse brewers shifting from wooden vessels to plastic or steel. Many have introduced steel milk cans, copper cooling coils, and other innovations in their breweries. Particularly in Scandinavia, brewers have modernized their equipment, while older wooden vessels are still very common in the Baltic states, Finland, and Russia.

Figure 6.14. Seppo Lisma lautering from his kuurna in Ruovesi, Finland.

Figure 6.15. Marina Ivanovna lautering through a kuurna/B-type hybrid. Kshaushi, Chuvashia, Russia.

Figure 6.16. Old wooden B-type lauter tun (*center*) next to Vytautas Jančys's modern steel lauter tun (*right*), with the hole underneath clearly mimicking the old B-type. Andrioniškis, Lithuania.

When farmhouse brewers build new lauter tuns using steel or aluminum, they could, in principle, choose any shape they want, but they do not. Instead, the brewers mimic the shape of the original wooden vessel. Sverre Skrindo in Ål, eastern Norway, had a steel lauter tun built and placed the tap on the side in the traditional way. Vytautas Jančys in Vikonys, Lithuania, had a similar steel tun built, but chose to put the hole in the bottom, as is common in that area. In Finland, many brewers use steel or aluminum kuurnas, but they are all canoe-shaped like the wooden originals. Matti Punakallio, at the commercial Sahtikrouvin brewpub, built a highly automated sahti brewery with a rotating mash and lauter tun, but even his tun is a horizontal cylinder.

This conservatism in the shape of the lauter tun is useful, because it makes it possible to trace deeper cultural connections. Lithuania seems to be divided between boiled mash brewers in the west (the region of Samogitia), and raw ale/keptinis brewers further east. The boiled mash brewers seem to have used the S-type lauter tun, but further east the B-type was common. More data will allow us to dig deeper into the historical influences.

Sverre Skrindo told me that, although the flavor of the beer was a little different, he was very happy with the switch from wood to steel, and he thought that had steel been available to people in the old days they would have used it. Then he was quiet for a moment, before saying that, back then, all the buckets for water and milk were made from wood and they were heavy and awkward, and usually leaky. When zinc buckets became available, some people did not simply throw the wooden buckets away—they literally smashed the old wooden buckets to pieces first because they hated them so much.

Preparations

A week before we were going to visit and brew with them, the Eitrheim brothers in Hardanger, Norway, sent a photo of the wooden lauter tun they were going to use. They had filled it with water, upon which the water leaked in every direction, making the tun look like a poorly constructed lawn sprinkler. In areas where people brewed only a few times a year the wood in the vessels would dry up, making the wood shrink and causing the vessel to leak. The solution was to fill it with water, so that the wood would swell up and close the leaks again. Incredible as it might seem, a week later that leaky lauter tun was watertight and perfectly fine to use for brewing.

In farmhouse brewing, nobody ever lined their barrels or brewing vessels with pitch or anything like it, as far as I know. In Latvia, Ugis Pucens showed me that if the leaks did not close by themselves one could make "bread putty" to close them with. He simply took ordinary wheat bread and soaked it with water, then rubbed it between his hands to turn it into a putty-like substance. This could then be stuck into the leaks to seal them.

In Telemark, Norway, Halvor Nordal had pestered his grandmother for years to teach him brewing, but she refused, saying she was too old for that kind of work. Halvor went to a brewer in a nearby village and learned from him instead. Coming home, he brought out the old brewing equipment and soaked the vessels to make them ready for use. Once the leaks had been sealed, he set up the brew kit in the yard of the farm and started preparing to brew. Then grandma came out. She was too old to brew herself but not too old to give advice.

Figure 6.17. Ugis Pucens making bread putty. Aizpute, western Latvia.

"What are you doing?" she asked.

"I'm ready to brew," he said.

"Hah, that's what you think! No, son, you have to *briskebaka* the vessels, and then *steinbaka* them, too."

What she was saying was that before Halvor could use the vessels, they had to be thoroughly cleaned. Not simply scrubbed with warm water like he had done, but essentially almost sterilized. The first step was to boil a juniper infusion and then fill the vessels with it while it was still boiling (this was briskebaka, lit. "juniper baking"). After that, the infusion was poured out and the vessels made ready for steinbaka, literally "stone baking." Juniper branches had to be placed on the bottom of the vessels, which were then filled with cold water. Stones were heated in the fire until they glowed, before being dropped into the vessels to heat the water. The branches were there to cushion the stones and keep them from knocking the bottom out. More stones were added until the water literally boiled inside each vessel, while the branches turned the water into a juniper infusion at the same time. Only when these two steps were done were the vessels ready for Halvor to use.

People cleaned their vessels in various ways in different places, but in just about every place where there was juniper the wooden vessels were cleaned with boiling hot juniper infusion. It was common to scrub the wooden vessels with brushes made from thin juniper or spruce branches; the kettle was usually scrubbed with sand or ash. In Denmark, while a few people used the juniper infusion for cleaning wooden vessels, the most common method was just boiling water.

Cleaning everything properly was crucial, and it was something everyone knew to do. A typical comment: "My mother's beer was hardly ever sour, and she said it was because she always took good care that the vessels, troughs, buckets, ladles, and casks were clean before they were used."[54]

Mold often grew in the wooden vessels after brewing. Farmhouse brewer Tor Vik in Stjørdal, Norway, is unusual in the area because he brews in wood. Although his lauter tun was full of white and green mold, his beer tasted great. Sjur Rørlien told me it was the same in Voss: the wooden vessels typically became moldy when not in use. His grandfather always cleaned them as carefully as possible after brewing and set them out so they would dry quickly, but even so there was always a little mold. It seemed to do no harm to the beer, though.

Milling

Once the malt had been dried, the next step was to mill it. There were two main ways to do this. The most common was using a rotary quern, which consisted of two circular stones mounted on top of each other and a wooden handle for turning the stones; in the middle of the upper stone was a hole to pour the malt into. The ground malt would come out between the stones. This was the subject of a Norwegian riddle: "What is it that eats through the eyes and shits through the side?" The answer is, of course, the malt quern.[55]

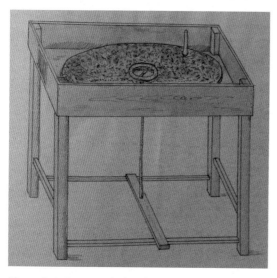

Figure 6.18. Drawing of a hand quern from EU 7814. Alster, Värmland, western Sweden.

Quernstones were made from very specific types of stone, because they had to not only be soft enough that they could be carved out, but they also had to have harder grains of stone sticking out of the grinding face. You could not find this type of stone just anywhere, so throughout the ages these stones have been traded over long distances. In Norway, they often came from Hyllestad in Sogn, Selbu in Trøndelag, or upper Telemark.[56] The Hyllestad area had a large number of quernstone quarries, from which the stones were exported large distances by ship. During the German occupation of Norway in World War II, all grain was requisitioned by the Germans due to scarcity. To prevent farmers from hiding grain, the Germans confiscated the quernstones as well. In Hyllestad, the story is told of how a father and son watched the Germans leave their farm with the quernstone. Once they were out of earshot, the father turned to the son and said, "Well, son, I guess it's time to make a new quernstone." It had not occurred to the Germans that the farmers could just make new ones.[57]

In Chuvashia, I was told that they could not get the right type of stone at all, and so the quern wheels were made of wood. What looked like large iron staples were stuck into the wood, and these did the job of actually crushing the grain.[58]

When milling malt, the quern had to be adjusted by moving the stones further apart to avoid the malt being ground to flour. The brewers knew perfectly well that milling too fine would make lautering difficult. The ideal result was to break each malt kernel in two but leave the two parts whole.

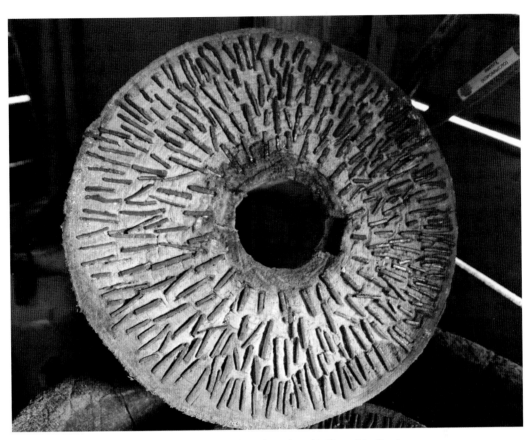

Figure 6.19. Chuvash hand quern wheel with metal staples. Kshaushi, Chuvashia, Russia.

A Swedish woman wrote that, as a young girl in Brösarp in Skåne, she would go with one of the serving girls to take the malt to a nearby farm and use the quern there. One girl would take fistful after fistful of malt and drop it into the hole on top, while the other turned the stone. After a while they would swap, then later swap again. For a normal batch of beer this took about two hours, but for a bigger batch it could take several extra hours. If the malt was slightly moist, it would stick to the quernstones and the whole process would take longer. She thought the whole thing was "fun."[59] Another account says milling malt was "not hard work."[60] I was surprised by this description, so, when I met Raija Syrjä, who said she had ground the malt by hand when young, I asked her if it was hard work. Her instant response, "Of course it was!" There need not be any contradiction here: what was considered hard work in the twentieth century might not be hard by nineteenth century standards.

Sometime in the Middle Ages, water-powered querns came to Norway and replaced hand querns. They used water from a stream to turn the quern, which saved a lot of hard work. In Norway, the landscape is so hilly that most places had a stream that was steep enough to drive a quern. In many places, up to 10 or 15 water querns would be standing, one after the other, where the stream was suitable. In other areas, people used windmills to mill the malt. How common this was I am not sure.

Figure 6.20. A farmer and his wife beside a water mill. Sogn, western Norway, ca. 1900. Photo by Nils Olsson Reppen, from the County Archives in Sogn og Fjordane.

Figure 6.21. Interior of a water quern. Sandane Museum, western Norway.

Water

One of the biggest recent technological advances in farmhouse brewing was the introduction of the garden hose. People often laugh when I say this, but consider how much water was needed to clean the brewing vessels, then to brew 150 liters of beer, and then clean again. All this water had to be hauled up from the well by hand and carried to the brewhouse. And the well was often surprisingly far from the house. From Haram in western Norway:

> It was a great happiness for the women that there was an end to the water-carrying. . . . The big water buckets took 16–17 liters each. They were waterlogged and heavy in themselves. Filled with water I think the whole burden must have been 60 kilograms. To carry such a burden, often a long way, could wear down anyone in storm and bad weather. It was no joke to be a serving girl on a farm in those days. . . . My mother told me from when she served that her skirt stood by itself when she took it off, because it was frozen stiff from the water splashing from the buckets when she carried them in frost, snow, and drift.* (Weiser Aall 1953, 4–6)

---

* "Drift" is an attempt to translate *rennefok*, literally snow carried on the wind.

In general, farmhouse brewers did not worry much about what water to use for brewing. One exception is in Denmark, which, excluding western Jutland, has very hard water. (In Denmark, it is usual to wipe the spray off of the tiles after showering, otherwise the tiles become covered in limescale.) Some Danish brewers say they just used well water. Others preferred the water from a marsh or field ditch, which some thought was softer and resulted in a better fermentation.[61]

> For brewing one needed above all water, and if the beer was to be particularly good, like *gammeltøl* and *gildesøl*, it was important to get the right kind of water.
>
> What property this water should have I don't think one had any real knowledge of, but I assume the choice of the place where they got it was based on the tradition, which again was based on experience formed long ago. People generally assumed that water that was good for boiling peas was good for gammeltøl. That might indicate that they wanted soft water.
>
> For the ordinary brewing of daily beer the water was taken from the well in the garden, but for the better beer it was taken from a spring-like source in a little hollow down by the beach. (NEU 8823)

Well water was probably used for everyday beer because it was easier than having to get water from outside the farm and transport it back. That people were willing to go further afield for water indicates that the softer water really made a noticeable difference for the beer, because just collecting water from the well was hard enough.

In Chuvashia in Russia, the water contained so many minerals that a white scum formed on the surface of the boiling water when we brewed with Marina Fyodorovna. She said brewers try to avoid water from the waterworks in favour of spring water, which has less minerals. According to Naumov, Chuvashians use water from snow melt in spring, or lake or river water where it is available.[62] They may also alkalinize the water with ashes to remove the minerals, although what those minerals are exactly, I do not know.

Professional brewer Simonas Gutautas had wondered why Julius Simonaitis (chap. 4, 117) insisted on first boiling his mash liquor and then cooling it afterward. Why heat the water hotter than the temperature you want, then let it cool? He tried asking, but Julius just said the water "needed to rest." Looking more closely at the water, Simonas found the reason: boiling had caused the carbonate in the water to precipitate out.[63] This little trick enabled Simonaitis to brew a good pale beer despite using hard water.

Norway generally has very soft water, around 3 dGH,[*] and Sweden is generally in the range 2–5 dGH. Denmark is a different story: parts of Copenhagen have water with a hardness over 30 dGH, about half of the islands have 18–24 dGH, and the rest 12–18 dGH; meanwhile, western Jutland has 8–12 dGH and central Jutland 4–8 dGH. Two water measurements from north Lithuania found 8 and 19 dGH.[64]

---

[*] A degree of General Hardness (dGH) is equivalent to a "German degree" (deutsche Härte, °dH); 1 dGH equals 17.85 parts per million (ppm).

Carbonation

One thing common to nearly all farmhouse ales is their very low carbonation levels. As a rule, farmhouse beer should not be completely flat, but the carbonation is much lower than in modern beer. In fact, it is very like British cask ale. The reason is obvious: producing highly carbonated beer without sugar and measuring instruments was technologically very challenging. In any case, beer was just about the only drink with any carbonation at all, so people were not used to carbonated drinks. However, farmhouse brewers had a more sophisticated approach to carbonation than one might think.

I used to wonder why the farmhouse brewers I had met had such short fermentation times, like Terje Raftevold, who fermented his beer for just 48 hours. According to my database, most brewers fermented for a period of 24 hours or less, and very few fermented longer than 48 hours. Surely the beer cannot have been finished fermenting that quickly?

Like me, Roar Sandodden had puzzled over why farmhouse brewers did not ferment their beer longer.[65] There would still be sugar left, he said. Roar knew this because he had been to a wedding where they served stjørdalsøl out of a milk can. Toward the end of the night, he had lifted the lid and looked down to see the beer was fermenting enough to be covered in foam. The fermentation had restarted when the beer came up from the cellar into the warm ballroom. Later, Terje Raftevold told me that in Hornindal the old men said that "a well-made beer could stand in a bowl with a rose of foam all day." Now how could that be possible?

Sometime after this, I learned that in the old days the beer was collected from the cask in the cellar using something that looked like a wooden gardening can, then poured into a huge bowl on the table in the living room. Ladles, often shaped like ducks, floated in the beer. When it was time for a toast, the toastmaster ladled beer into a bowl and sent the bowl round the room. If you did this with modern beer it would be totally flat by the time you got to drink it. Eventually, these pieces of information connected up and I realized what was going on.

When the beer is racked after 12, 24, or 48 hours, it has obviously not finished fermenting completely, but removing most of the yeast and transferring the beer to a cold cellar stops the fermentation process or at least it slows down. Once the beer was brought up to the warm living room, fermentation started up again in the bowl. This produced gentle carbonation that was sustained all day and night. For farmers a century ago, this was probably the only carbonated drink they would ever taste, so this level of carbonation probably seemed sufficient.

Today's farmhouse brewers are well aware that carbonation comes from secondary fermentation and will move their beer containers around between rooms so that the beer can "work itself up," as they put it. This means that it develops the

Figure 6.22. Terje Raftevold's farmhouse ale in my shed toward the end of Christmas. Outside temperatures have risen, causing the beer to start fermenting again.

amount of carbonation they want, which is still very limited. Getting this right can be difficult, of course, which is why when you get a traditional Norwegian farmhouse ale in a bottle, it is nearly always in a plastic bottle to prevent bottle bombs. Terje Raftevold told me how he had given a square plastic growler of beer to a friend, who had put it away in a room that was not cold enough. One day his friend called and said Terje had to come over. "The growler had swollen up so bad it was looking like a football," Terje said, laughing. They could barely get the cork off to relieve the pressure.

The approach to carbonating farmhouse beer is roughly the same in most places, although in Estonia the koduõlu brewers try to build up some carbonation in the keg.[66] In Lithuania, the brewers go further and allow massive pressure to build in the cask. When served, the beer is usually all foam, and has to settle for a good while before it becomes drinkable. There is still carbonation in it when served, but not very much. The high level of carbonation meant that kegging the beer at exactly the right time was very difficult. In Lithuania, it was common to invite neighbours over to help decide whether it was time or not. This high level of carbonation also made it difficult to serve the beer from cask, therefore, at celebrations, one person would be responsible for serving the beer. This person was not to drink at all but, even so, things could easily go wrong—it could happen that the cask master and several guests ended up showered in beer.

The low level of carbonation when the beer is drunk is a very important part of farmhouse ale and one of the things that most distinguishes it from modern beer styles. To a modern beer drinker, it makes the beer seem sweeter than it really is, but it also helps emphasize maltiness and brings out more complexity in the flavor. Unfortunately, most modern drinkers, and even barkeepers, think nearly flat beer is bad beer, which makes it near-impossible to sell something close to authentic farmhouse ale.

It is difficult to give exact guidance on how to replicate the carbonation level. For one thing, it does vary. For example, most people want carbonation, but in Dyrvedalen outside Voss people expect the beer to be completely flat.[67]

Oppskåke

When the beer has finished fermenting, the brewer has to transfer it to the cask, harvest the yeast, and clean up. This takes a couple of hours, and meanwhile the brewer is there with beer that is completely drinkable. Of course, the brewer is curious how the beer has turned out, so he is going to taste it. He might even have a pint or two.

In western Norway, the brewhouse is usually a separate building and the neighbors will have seen first that the brewer was cleaning the vessels, then the tell-tale smoke from the brewhouse chimney. They will have known how long the brewer usually fermented, and so they could work out when the brewer would be there racking the beer, and so forth. And, if they turned up right at that moment, of course they would be offered some beer. Sjur Rørlien said of Voss in the 1990s, "Nobody was ever invited to oppskåke. Fifteen to twenty people would just show up."

Paavo Pruul, on Hiiumaa in Estonia, told me how for 40 years, every time his grandfather's beer was ready, the neighbor would come by to ask if he could borrow their ladder because it was longer than his own. Of course, he was offered beer, and, of course, he stayed all evening, drinking and talking.

In western Norway, this custom developed into a tradition known as *oppskåke*. The word means "to shake up" and refers to the racking of the beer, but it also came to mean the party

Figure 6.23. Oppskåke in Svein Rivenes's brewhouse, Voss, 1991. Photo courtesy of Håkon Bonafede, ViMenn.

Figure 6.24. Former mayor Oddvin Drageset making a point at the oppskåke. Innvik, western Norway.

held in the brewhouse when the beer was racked. The tradition was not the same everywhere: in some areas the neighbors would simply show up because they knew the beer was finished, while in others they were specifically invited; in one village in Hardanger, western Norway, the brewers went a good bit further in the 1990s, setting off dynamite charges to announce that it was time for oppskåke.[68]

At the oppskåke all the drinkers were brewers themselves, and among the other talk they would often be judging the beer. There were well-known euphemisms for saying the beer was weak, like "you sure didn't have far to go to the well, when you brewed this." To tell the brewer that he lived near a big lake meant the same thing. Or people could say, "There's one flavor to this beer, and that's more-flavor," meaning the beer makes you want to drink more.

On Saaremaa in Estonia you would get very similar feedback on your beer. If someone said "his well was too close to the *paargu* [an outside kitchen where the beer was brewed]" that meant the beer was too weak. Today, racking parties like oppskåke seem to be informal,[69] but in the old days it was clearly a more formal custom, at least on the mainland.[70]

In some parts of Sunnmøre, northwest Norway, discussing the beer in front of the brewer was considered too sensitive, so the drinkers would avoid saying what they thought of the beer. Instead, when leaving the brewhouse that night they would stop and scream. Louder screams meant better beer. In some areas, there would even be a specific location where it was customary to stop and do the screaming. This was called *ølhauking* (lit. "beer shouting"):

> The problem was when the beer was unsuccessful. Once, in Valldal the guy in front stopped at the first shouting spot and turned to the others.
>
> "Was this anything to shout for?"
>
> They were all sober, and after a so-called "sober discussion," they decided they would have to shout, despite everything, to not offend the host too much. They did so, but not very enthusiastically. Beer shouting when sober could never be very impressive. (Tveit, 1986, 66)

People living in small, tightly knit communities sometimes disliked one another, and the oppskåke was one place where alcohol could cause ill feelings to spill over into violence. In Årdal in Sogn, western Norway, village custom required all neighbors to be invited, no matter what you might think of them. In one case, for some reason, only the hated neighbor turned up for the oppskåke.

> So, then they sat there, these two, swearing at each other. And the more they tasted, the angrier they got. And then it broke loose. One fist to one cheek, then to another. And the other hit back. The next morning, they were found peacefully sleeping in the potato bin. But one had a good-sized tuft of hair in his fist. (Krossen 1978)

In eastern Norway and in parts of Sweden and mainland Estonia, the custom was instead that a member of the household, usually a child, would be sent to each of the neighbors with a bowl of beer. In Norway, this was called *skokubolle* (lit. "shake bowl"). Lithuania had a very similar custom called *koštuves*. In some areas, koštuves was the same as skokubolle, but elsewhere it was the same as oppskåke. Vincas Vaitekunas wrote lyrically about koštuves:

> As the crows smell the rotting of decaying animal flesh . . . so do beer aficionados instinctively sense where the beer is. Just look around and here comes a couple of loafers, lost on some mission (to borrow a chisel, a drill, a harrow tooth; ask for advice; offer something). If the brewer is a generous one, sometimes the whole house fills up with these idlers. They try the beer, roll their eyes one way and the other, smack their lips. Appraisal. One wants to analyze the taste of the beer, give their compliments to the brewer, point out a shortcoming or two (bitter-ish! Too many hops?) and deliver further advice. They are the first to hear the brewer's mishaps, all the challenges and problems (the stuck mash, etc.). A few jugs later (a drink to the straight leg), (and if the amount set aside runs out—people start drinking the beer from the tun), people hurry on with their days—the work is awaiting, needs to be finished ("a drink for the road"). The brewer gets their word that they'll return another day. The invitation is made in turn. (quoted in Astrauskas 2008, 150–51)

The issue of visitors drinking more than expected of the just-finished beer has come up more than once. Several people from Hardanger have told me the story of how at one oppskåke all the beer was drunk. That is quite impressive when you consider that a normal batch is 150 liters and the local beer would probably be 8%–12% ABV. This probably explains how the brewer came to forget that all the beer had been drunk. The next day he sent his wife down in the cellar to get him a beer, but she came back saying it was all gone. "Well," says the man, "you can't expect it to last forever."

Cellaring

The beer cask was kept in the cellar, because that was the coolest place in the summer and people were well aware that keeping the beer cool helped to prevent it from going sour.

In places where they brewed often, beer did not need to keep very long, but Norwegian farmhouse brewers might keep the beer for months to have it ready in case guests should come by. In the UK, Denmark, and Lithuania there was a tradition of brewing in March and serving the beer in the autumn. It seems people were able to make the beer keep, but it is clear that it often soured when stored for a long time, especially once they had started tapping from the cask.

Jakob Eitrheim told me that once he started tapping the beer the upper staves in the barrel tended to dry out, which made them shrink and let air in.[71] He and his friends had figured out that they could solve this problem by slowly rotating the barrel so that all the staves remained wet. He said this only worked until the barrel was half empty.

Figure 6.25. The bowl from the Høstad find near Trondheim. Dated 800 BCE. Photo: Åge Hojem, NTNU Vitenskapsmuseet.

Figure 6.26. Beer bowl with portion markings inside. Sandane museum, western Norway.

Drinking Vessels

In the old days, the beer drinking vessels were surprisingly ornate, much more than one would expect. The vessels for serving and eating food were quite simple, but not those for beer. This was because beer was more than just a drink. As we saw earlier, beer drinking was an important ritual.[72]

In Scandinavia, the most common vessel was the beer bowl, and it has been in use for a very long time. In 1899, a man was digging for peat near Trondheim in Norway when his shovel hit something hard. Further digging revealed 13 objects made in wood, one of them a wooden bowl with a lovely ornamental meander pattern carved into the rim. The find has been dated to 800 BCE, and archaeologists believe the bowl was used for drinking beer.[73]

Older bowls had carvings, and later examples also had designs from burn marks made with metal stamps in different shapes. More modern bowls were painted, often with extravagant designs involving animals and, more recently, flower designs in many colors.

The first time I drank from a beer bowl was when I visited Stein Langlo in Stranda, western Norway. Stein and his friends drink their farmhouse ale from traditional wooden bowls. When they poured the beer into the bowl, I was surprised to note that with the low level of carbonation there was so little foam I could actually see the color and clarity of the beer. You have to drink carefully from a bowl because the beer sloshes around very quickly in such a low, wide vessel. The next surprise was that there was text in Gothic lettering around the rim. Carefully turning the bowl, I read

> I stood in green groves
> Now I slake thirsty mouths.[*]

The bowl was talking to me! This was common for beer bowls. They often had text stating the name of the owner and the year they were painted, but there would also be a rhyme, often with the bowl (or, more rarely, the owner or the drinker) speaking in the first person.

A common theme is that the drinker is welcome to the beer, as in this one, which also clearly references the view that the grain and the beer are gifts from god:

> Drink your fill
> Thank god for his gifts.

Getting drunk was seen not as a problem, but as the goal:

> Carry me to the right barrel
> And let good beer into me run.
> I will serve you so
> That you roll between tables and chairs.

---

[*] It rhymes in the original Norwegian: Før sto jeg i grønne lunder / nå slukker jeg tørste munner.

Another on the same subject:

> Good beer in the bowl
> Goes straight to your head
> From me drinks both man and wife.

However, you still had to behave:

> Drink, but don't swear
> Or you'll get nought but blande.*

Of course, as people were well aware, drinking too much had consequences:

> A man drank of me last night
> He forgot both cane and hat
> Now he lies in the corner asleep
> And I stand here alone.

Or this one:

> When the beer is in the man,
> The wisdom is in the can.†

And this small gem:

> I am but small to see, but can bring you to your knee.

This type of bowl was extremely common in Norway and Sweden, common to the point that just about every household must have had several. Today, Norwegian and Swedish museums have literally thousands of them of many different types and shapes. The bowls were usually plain and round in shape, but there were also variants with carved handles. The *kjenge*, much used in southwestern Norway, had two handles shaped as horse heads.

Bowls were carved out of a single piece of wood, often from burrs on the side of trees. Another way to construct a drinking vessel was to form it from staves, much like the lauter tun. Drinking mugs with wooden handles, and often lids, were very common and usually decorated with burn marks. These were common in Norway, Sweden, Estonia, and Latvia, at least.[74]

When we visited Aarne Trei on the Estonian island of Saaremaa, he served us his beer in a traditional *õllekann* made from juniper wood. We smelled it while it was empty and the mug was filled with a lovely aroma of juniper wood. The aroma of juniper wood lasts many years and, if it fades, sanding the inside makes it come back. Drinking beer from the õllekann was quite an experience: your hand gripping the hefty handle of the big mug, your lips curling around the thick, grainy rim,

---

* The acidic soured whey and water mix that people used as the daily drink.
† Meaning the watering can-like vessel used to serve the beer into the bowl.

Figure 6.27. A two-handled kjenge. Mølstertunet museum, Voss, western Norway.

Figure 6.28. Ølstaup. NF.1934-0590. Photo: Anne-Lise Reinsfelt © Norsk Folkemuseum.

Figure 6.29. Wooden õllekann. Pihtla, Saaremaa, Estonia.

Figure 6.30. Haarikka drinking mugs for sale. Karvia, western Finland.

and the aroma of beer blending with juniper from the wood itself. Of course, it helped that the beer itself was ridiculously good.

In Finland, the most common traditional drinking vessel today is the *haarikka*, a cup-shaped vessel made from wooden staves, where two of the staves are longer to form handles, often curving away from the main cup. In the Orkney Islands, a very similar drinking vessel is called a *cog*, but the shape of the handles there is a little different. In Lithuania, the traditional vessels seem to have been made of clay, usually glazed, with decorations in various colors. Simonas Gutautas explained this is because in Lithuania the right type of clay is very easy to find. "Just dig a hole anywhere," he said.[75]

A completely different type of drinking vessel was the horn. Caesar mentioned drinking horns being used among the Germanic tribes, but they fell out of favour during the Christianization of Scandinavia in the ninth to eleventh centuries, presumably because they were associated with heathen religious practices. The horns were often magnificently decorated with metal fittings and even feet so they could stand on the table.

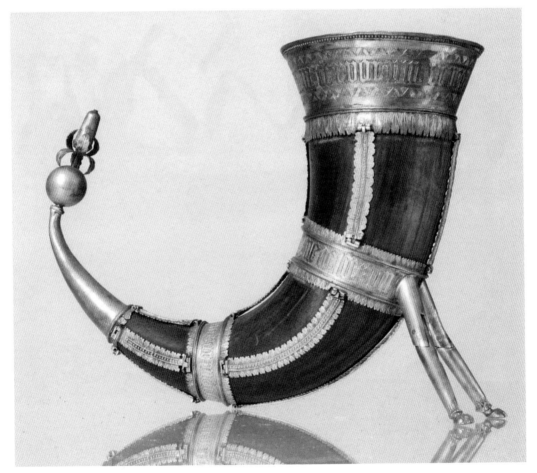

Figure 6.31. The Nersten horn, from southern Norway. Its age is unknown, but a legend about how this horn was originally stolen from the vetter in a burial mound was recorded in 1830. AAM.05177. Photo: Hannele Fors, Aust-Agder museum og arkiv KUBEN.

Most drinking vessels were purely practical, if decorative, but there is a strange variant known as the trick cup. These are constructed so that if you try to drink from them in the normal way you end up spilling the drink on yourself. The cup is actually a puzzle you have to solve in order to be able to drink. I was talking about these cups with friends at Prie Uosio, a wonderful pub in Panevežys, Lithuania, when the owner's face suddenly lit up and he left the table, coming back with a strange-looking ceramic mug. The neck of the mug, about three-quarters of the way up, had three rings of holes round the entire mug, and another set of holes around the rim.

While I was studying the trick cup, one of my friends impatiently lifted it and tried to drink, spilling the contents all over his lap. He jumped up in surprise, to laughter from around the table (politeness had required us to drink vodka.) This, of course, was what the cups were for: fun and games to while away long days and nights of drinking in the old days. Thankfully the owner had had the good sense to fill it with water.

Figure 6.32. Trick cup from Filefjell, in the mountains of central Norway. Every tip has a small hole and one of them can be used to suck out the beer. Photo: Stine Dornfest © Universitetsmuseet in Bergen.

I had read about several variants of trick cups, so it did not take me long to figure out the solution. On the inside of the handle, near the top, was a hole. This, and one of the holes around the rim, had to be covered with a finger. Once this was done, the contents could be sucked out through another of the holes around the rim.

Another type of trick cup is known in English as a "fuddling cup." This is several cups in one, which means that if you try drinking from one, the drink will spill from the others. The purpose is the same: to have a foolish person create drama by spilling beer before the group tries to figure out the solution together. A fuddling cup is designed so that it is possible to drink without spilling by arranging the individual cups in the right order.

Figure 6.33. Estonian kolmikkann, 19th century. From Käina, Hiiumaa, Estonia. Reproduced by permission of the Estonian National Museum.

A curious variant of the trick cup is the Estonian *kolmikkann*, literally "three-mug", which has three of the ordinary Estonian õllekann linked together. These were used in a peculiar drinking ritual during Estonian weddings, where the bride, groom, and mother-in-law had to drain the three cups together without spilling.[76]

Serving Beer

Today everyone gets their own glass, but in the olden days people shared a bowl of beer. A toastmaster or the head of the family poured the beer into the common bowl and sent it around the table for a toast. To make sure that everyone got their portion, there were often marks inside the bowl to show the portions. These could be ridges down the side or little metal buttons. In those days in Norway and Sweden beer was scarce, and this ensured that nobody took more than their fair share.

I only know about these marks from Norway, but they must have existed elsewhere. In medieval England, similar markings were used, and in 1102 the bishop of London forbade priests to "drink to pegs," apparently because this had developed into a drinking game.[77] This suggests the practice must have been widespread in earlier times.

The strength of farmhouse beer brewed today varies dramatically, and must have done so even more in the past. Sjur Rørlien in Voss told me that he used to get his vossaøl analyzed by his brother, who then worked at an industrial lager brewery. It was nearly always between 10% and 12% ABV. Svein Rivenes, who lives in the same valley and uses roughly the same recipe, said that today many brewers have started adding sugar. "Now I'm becoming known for making weak beer," he said, wistfully.

Historically, much of the beer was deliberately made very weak, so that there would be more of it and you could drink your fill without getting blind drunk. Although, like today, it is difficult to generalize about the strength of historical farmhouse ale, it is not impossible. Combining modern measured original gravities with those computed from malt/wort ratios in older documents, and creating an overview from the entire database (see p. 372 in the bibliography), it seems that about 30% of what was considered good beer was below 1.045 and about 50% was between 1.045 and 1.080; the remaining 20% was over 1.080, and while most of those beers were below 1.150, apparently not all of them were.* The reason many beers were so strong was clearly the value placed on intoxication, and the fact that the reputation of the farm was closely tied to the strength of the beer.

In Norway, there is another way to serve the beer, which is called *å belje ølet*, or *brøle ølet*. This literally means "to roar the beer." People did this with beer that had gone stale, to freshen it up, or if they wanted warm beer.

Ståle Raftevold, from Hornindal, once showed me how roaring the beer is done using his own kornøl. You take an empty saucepan and heat it on the stove. Then you take it off the heat and pour the beer into the hot pan. The beer immediately foams up powerfully with a hissing noise (hence the "roaring"), and the foam stays a long time. You pour it back in a glass and drink it. The immediate impression I had was that the beer had become almost

Figure 6.34. Ståle Raftevold demonstrating roaring of the beer. Norddal, western Norway.

impossibly soft and creamy, and, of course, lukewarm. The mouthfeel was a little like Irish coffee, and it really did taste more fresh and vivid, very different from the original beer.

I have tried roaring the beer once with a modern brown ale, and that did not work as well. The resulting mouthfeel, after roaring, was not the same from modern highly carbonated beer as from farmhouse ale. But maybe it will work better for other modern styles.

Beer Flaws

The most common problem with farmhouse beer of the past was that it could be sour, just like today. This was a known problem, and people were well aware that the most important thing they could do was to clean their equipment carefully and to cellar the beer well.

In earlier days it seems people drank the beer, unhappily, even if sour, because they had no choice. Over the last few decades, it seems that in most places people have come to consider sour beer undrinkable and pour it down the drain.

In 2018, I was asked to judge three beers made with kveik on live television. When I found one of them was a sour beer (deliberately so), I immediately discarded it, saying farmhouse brewers would consider this undrinkable. The year after, I was interviewing Ivar Skare in Ørsta when he suddenly said that he had seen a guy on television say that farmhouse brewers would just pour out sour beers, and added that he really liked that comment, because it is exactly what they would do. Ivar did not seem to realize he was telling this to the same guy he had seen on TV.

Despite all of the precautions, the beer often went sour anyway. In Zealand, Denmark they said "beer wives" had gotten into the beer. One woman wrote that she heard about these beer wives as a

---

* These numbers are based on how much malt was used per liter of beer, so these numbers are quite rough.

child and it made her afraid to drink beer, so she always looked carefully into it "in case there was a beer wife in the beer."[78]

People had various remedies for the beer going sour. From Denmark: "To remove the sourness, every time the beer was poured in the mug a teaspoon of natron was added. That removed the sourness, but the good beer flavor was spoiled. Pulling a face, the last beer was drunk with an 'ah.'"[79] The satisfied sigh once the last drop was drunk was because this meant they could start on the new beer, which was not sour. At least not yet.

But a little sourness was not the only problem in the past. Various microorganisms could grow on the grain while it was still in the field. The most dangerous was ergot, which could make people quite seriously sick, with vomiting and diarrhea, and even psychosis and gangrene. Other fungi could also cause problems. This was well known in Norway, and was one of the reasons why the brewer tasted the wort the moment it came off the lauter tun. If the wort made the brewer feel sick, the entire batch was thrown away instantly. Beer that made people sick was called *skjæksøl* (shakes-beer), *spyøl* (vomit beer), or *magøl* (stomach beer) in Norwegian.

A landowner in Kråksmåla in Sweden hired six workers for the haymaking and served them harvest ale. But the beer was sour, so the workers got stomach trouble. On top of that, the field was stony, so the scythes had to be whet frequently. A man coming by told the landowner, "Today you certainly have many workers!" The landowner replied that "Well, it doesn't help much, because two are hanging on the whetting rod, two are shitting, and then there's only two left to cut."[80]

Some thought that if the malt got too warm during germination it would produce vomit beer, which "was a great shame for he who had brewed it."[81] Others said if the grain lay too long in heaps before threshing, it could go moldy and make people sick. The same could also happen during germination.[82] In Setesdal, they would say that if one served stomach beer, "The young ones made a lot of noise, then," meaning they would taunt the unlucky brewer.[83]

In Denmark, and for some reason only in Denmark, the accounts mention one more problem. The beer could grow "long," by which they meant the beer was ropy. Very likely the cause was infection by *Pediococcus*, although the brewers did not know that:

> Niels Bjerg told me that he had experienced the beer growing "long," and he added that apparently nobody knew what the cause was. Even if the beer turned "long" the taste was not really bad, but the beer could be pulled out into long threads like cobwebs. (NEU 23283)

Another had ideas about what the cause might be:

> People used to consider the cause of ropy beer to be that the malt had not been boiled, but only mashed. Or it could be because they used wheat straw for the filter instead of rye straw.
>
> Today, there is good reason to believe that the cause is to be sought in the barley for malt containing too much protein. (AFD Frederik Dahlkild, 1969)

Figure 6.35. Various types of grain parasites. 5a and b show the dreaded ergot.

In another story about ropy beer, a husband angers his wife by commenting on the beer she had brewed:

> There was a farm where the man came in to drink. The beer mug was on the table all day long. When he had drunk, long threads hung from his face to the mug. Further inside the house, the servant girl sat, spinning linen while his wife was knitting. He took the mug and went over to the girl, saying, "Can you spin such pretty threads as these?"
>
> His wife was angry, which is not so strange. (NEU 2608)

People did not like ropy beer and had various remedies for it. "If the beer started turning long and sticky, the barrel was opened and 1.0–1.5 kilograms of wheat bran were poured into the beer and mixed in. In the same way, three to four eggs were added to the beer. This was intended to resolve this unwanted phenomenon."[84] Others added rye or barley flour.[85]

Whether these remedies worked is not clear, but it seems that there was a solution that really did work:

> After a few days, it might happen that the beer grew "long," a strange slimy condition. This happened rarely, only twice in my time. It could, however, be cured by quick action. These two cases happened in my boyhood and both times I was instantly sent off to a tenant farmer in Falsled. In his garden grew the plant [unreadable squiggle]. (NEU 28980)

I struggled a good bit to see what he had written. It looked like "frop," "jkop," or something like that, but none of those are actual plants. It took a good while before I realized the first letter could perhaps be an uppercase "I." I looked up "irop" and "ikop," neither of which exist, before I got to *isop*, which does exist. In English, it is called hyssop, in Latin *Hyssopus officinalis*. The account continued:

> Eight to nine stalks of hyssop in the beer barrel caused the beer to within four to five days become normal again. (AFD Frederik Dahlkild)

He went on to describe the plant as 20–30 cm tall, bush-like, with red-violet or blue flowers. The description fits hyssop exactly. But whether hyssop can actually cure ropiness in beer has never been tested, as far as I know.

7

HERBS, SPICES, AND ADJUNCTS

The spices in farmhouse beer were part of the tradition and not something the brewer played around with. It was very rare for the ingredients in the beer to change with the seasons, although it did sometimes happen. Strength aside, for the most part, the beer was the same no matter when it was brewed.

Somehow an image has become established of farmhouse brewers using "whatever was to hand" when making their beer. Personally, I only know of a single example. Marina Ivanovna, outside Kudymkar, just west of the Urals in Russia, said people often used berries in beer. When pressed about what kinds, she said, "Whatever they can find." The brewing in that area seems to have died out and been revived, however, so it is possible that this approach to ingredients is something new.

Farmhouse brewers used ingredients they could find locally, with very few exceptions. One exception was hops, and another was bitter oranges. This is why wild rosemary was never used in brewing in Norway: it only grows in areas where people had no grain for beer.

Many people have a romantic image of ancient farmhouse beers as brimming with all sorts of herbs, and herbal literature tends to support that by claiming that just about every herb known to man has been used in traditional brewing. Actual accounts reporting that

Table 7.1 Archival Accounts by Country Mentioning Herbs Used in Farmhouse Brewing

	No. of accounts	Percentage of accounts mentioning use of herb															
		Hops	Juniper	Sweet gale	Wormwood	Bitter orange peel	St. John's wort	Wild rosemary	Caraway	Yarrow	Tansy	Bay laurel	Tobacco	Potato	Juniper berries	Other	None specified
Norway	254	96%	95%	5%	0%	0%	6%	0%	5%	3%	2%	0%	1%	0%	1%	7%	0%
Sweden	200	87%	49%	8%	0%	10%	0%	2%	0%	1%	0%	0%	1%	2%	0%	4%	3%
Denmark	139	99%	1%	4%	19%	0%	1%	0%	0%	0%	0%	0%	0%	0%	0%	2%	0%
Finland	70	61%	53%	0%	0%	0%	0%	0%	0%	0%	0%	7%	0%	0%	0%	0%	7%
Estonia	55	96%	58%	25%	4%	0%	0%	18%	2%	0%	0%	0%	4%	0%	0%	7%	0%
Russia	12	100%	17%	0%	0%	0%	0%	0%	0%	0%	0%	0%	0%	0%	0%	0%	0%
Lithuania	9	100%	0%	0%	0%	0%	0%	0%	0%	0%	0%	0%	0%	0%	0%	22%	0%
UK	6	100%	0%	0%	0%	0%	0%	0%	0%	0%	0%	0%	0%	0%	0%	33%	0%
Germany	6	100%	17%	0%	0%	0%	0%	0%	0%	0%	0%	0%	0%	0%	17%	17%	0%
Latvia	6	100%	17%	0%	0%	0%	0%	0%	0%	0%	0%	0%	0%	0%	0%	0%	0%
Belarus	2	100%	0%	0%	0%	0%	0%	0%	0%	0%	0%	0%	0%	0%	0%	50%	0%
Austria	2	100%	100%	0%	0%	0%	0%	0%	0%	0%	0%	0%	0%	0%	0%	0%	0%
Total	761	694	416	47	28	19	15	14	13	8	6	5	5	4	3	40	10
Percent	100%	91%	55%	6%	4%	2%	2%	2%	2%	1%	1%	1%	1%	1%	1%	5%	1%

Sources: See "The Database" section on p. 372 for explanation of sources.

Notes: A single source may mention more than one herb, so percentages will add up to more than 100%. Every herb mentioned in the source is included, even if the source is uncertain whether the herb was actually used.

brewers in one specific area used herbs in their beer, however, are quite rare. In the nineteenth and twentieth centuries, it seems that the use of herbs other than hops and juniper was not common.

There are several sources that claim the use of herbs was more common before the nineteenth century, which may well be true.[1] Several herbs have Norwegian dialect names indicating they were commonly used in farmhouse brewing, even if there is little sign of it in modern accounts. Many of the respondents to the Swedish special questionnaire on sweet gale and hops (SP98) say they remember hearing about gale beer, even if they themselves never tried it. Many more hints can be found that herbs were perhaps commonly used in beer in the Middle Ages; unfortunately, they are just hints, and it is hard to say anything very specific based on these alone.

From the recipes I have analyzed, it is clear that two herbal ingredients were overwhelmingly dominant: hops and juniper (table 7.1). By comparison, all the other herbs were rarely found. Out of 784 recipes, hops appears in 653 and juniper in 397. The next most common, sweet gale, appears in only 36 recipes. These statistics cannot hope to capture exactly what people were using, but the rough estimates are no doubt correct. Although it is not always clear which time period a source is describing, these data likely cover the period roughly between 1850 and 1950. Since it appears herb use today is similar to the 1950s (except in Stjørdal), it is possible there have been no significant changes in herb use from the mid-nineteenth century through to the present day.

> ⚠ **WARNING** ⚠
>
> If you intend to pick any of these plants yourself, take care to identify exactly what you find. If you pick the wrong plant you can end up poisoning yourself and others.

Herbs, Spices, and Other Flavorings

Hops

Hops most likely evolved over a million years ago in what is now China and have grown wild in Europe for thousands of years. For most of that time, people brewed beer without making use of hop plants. No one is certain when European brewers started using hops in beer. The first definite evidence of hops in beer is from Trossingen in south Germany, where a flask with dried beer residue from 579 CE was found to contain grains of hop pollen.[2] Of course, this was not the first ever beer brewed with hops, but exactly when and where that was is hard to say given how sparse the archaeological record is.

There are other early archaeological finds of hops in a brewing context, for example, from Sweden and Denmark in the seventh century and Russia in the eighth century. It looks like once hops started to be used in beer it slowly displaced the alternatives. Hops appear to have been domesticated in the eighth century, and from the ninth century onward archaeological finds of hops become more common.[3]

Despite being adopted so late in the history of brewing, hops quickly became widespread, from the UK to far eastern Russia, northern Norway to Austria, and even high up on the south side of the Caucasus mountains in Georgia.[4] By the sixteenth century there was already a brisk trade in hops along the rivers of Russia. The British Isles were relative latecomers to the use of hops. Hop usage seems to have begun there in the fifteenth century, not becoming dominant until the eighteenth century.[5]

Figure 7.1. Hops growing up a pole in Isojoki, western Finland.

Hops never took over in northern Europe completely. As recently as the late nineteenth and early twentieth century, 15%–35% of farmhouse ales in Finland, Sweden, and Estonia seem not to have contained any hops at all. Even today, it is common for farmhouse brewers on Gotland and the Estonian islands to use less than 1 gram of low-alpha hops per liter of beer, producing beers that are generally below 10 IBU. And quite a few Finnish farmhouse brewers still use no hops at all.

Hops have been grown at least as far as 65° north in Sweden, 66° north in Finland, and north of the Arctic Circle in Norway, where brewers just outside of the city of Bodø grew their own hops.[6] Strese and Tollin found hop plants with cones growing in the Lofoten Islands in Norway, Kvikkjokk in Sweden, and Akureyri in Iceland. Reliable hop growing well inland above latitudes of 62°–63° north would have been difficult, however.[7] Of course, the limit for viable commercial cultivation must be much further south.

Hops were used for purposes other than just brewing beer. In northern Sweden, there is an old tradition of using hops to make both rope and cloth. Hops were also used in folk medicine; interestingly, one use was to fight infections, where hops may well have worked against Gram-positive bacteria. They were also widely used against sleep problems, and many people stuffed their pillows with hop cones. In Sweden, this practice went on into the twentieth century.[8]

In southern Sweden and Denmark, there was even a custom in the sixteenth to eighteenth century of burying people with hops. It was said that the reason was to prevent the corpse from rotting. In 2014, the grave of bishop Peder Winstrup in Lund, southern Sweden, was opened: he was found to have been buried on a bed of hop vines and his pillow filled with hop cones.[9] There was also the belief that a farmer should be buried with some hops, "lest he take the hop luck with him in the grave."[10]

One enormous advantage hops had over their competitor, juniper, was that they could easily be grown on a larger scale and readily transported by ship or horse and cart. Hop cones can be compressed into a small, light package. Juniper grows slowly and the branches are awkward to package and transport. A large trade in hops quickly flourished across northern Europe, but there has never been any similar trade in juniper branches. Hop farming may not be easy, but juniper farming seems next to hopeless.

The reason farmhouse ale was so widespread was that every farmer could make it, because every farmer had the necessary ingredients. It followed that farmers who could grow grain could also, as a rule, grow hops with little effort. Most farms seem to have used less than five kilograms of hops per year, which means that 20–50 plants would be enough for an annual supply. Those who could afford it often bought hops to save time and effort. In many places, it was even possible to just pick wild hops and use those, although Strese and Tollin[11] conclude that hops have never grown truly wild in Scandinavia. Where hops do seem to grow wild, they originated from hops that were deliberately planted centuries earlier and then became abandoned. Once the hops were planted they could spread slowly but surely, meter by meter.

Growing hops on a farm could be a very low-key affair. Paavo Pruul on the Estonian island of Hiiumaa told me that the only tending he did of his hop plants was to tear some down from time to time to prevent them from overwhelming the garden. He did not even plant them, his grandfather did. Many farmers are recorded as saying the hops "grew like weeds"; one Danish woman said her grandfather tore up the hop garden but, 50 years later, hop plants were still coming up between the linden tree and the main house where the hop garden used to be.[12] In Norway and Sweden, people would usually just grow hops next to a wall of the main house or a pile of rocks, generally on the south side so the hops would get more sun and warmth. They also tried to shelter the hop plants from the wind. The hops were fertilized with horse manure as they were planted. After picking, the hop cones could be dried in the sun or in paper bags in the loft.

On Funen in Denmark, especially the western part, farmers grew hops on a commercial scale. In autumn, these growers travelled all over Denmark selling their hops to farmers who needed them for their own brewing. One woman from Hårslev village on Funen described how her grandfather grew 400 kg of hops per year on 1.4 acres of land. Three times she went with her grandfather on the annual hops-selling trip. They packed the hops in large canvas bags, piled so high on the wagon that she and her grandfather were almost invisible.[13] The trip took a couple of days, and they made roughly 1000 Danish kroner by selling the hops, about 10,000 US dollars in today's money.

The same hop traders came back to the same villages every year, and many of them told the exact same joke every year: "Excellent Funen hops! My wife has brewed with them twice and they are still just as good." One woman says, when she heard this for the first time at the age of twelve, she replied, "Then we can brew with them a third time." She goes on, "For that I was given a good whack."[14]

Commercial hop growing on this scale was too much work for a single family. In spring, hop poles needed to be set out, for which workers had to be hired. Later, when the plants had grown enough, the women tied them to the poles using straw. The hop plants might get lice, in which case the growers hoped for thunderstorms because the old folks said that lightning killed the lice. The hops matured in early September and were picked when the seeds grew yellow.

The hop harvest lasted three weeks. The men cut the hop plants and tied them in bunches, then carried them over to the house to be picked. Every day, neighboring women came and picked the hop cones off the plants and collected them in big wooden containers. In the evening, these women would be joined by the village young folks and tenant farmers, who came to help out with the picking, which went on until 10 o'clock at night. While working, the pickers told stories and sang, drank coffee, and ate Christmas cake. Once the work was over, everyone went inside for wheat bread, schnapps, and beer. If one of the workers had a harmonica there might be dancing too. The hops from the containers were put in large canvas bags and stored in the loft. Later they were dried in the malt kiln, which was in the cookhouse chimney, so the hops were probably smoked.

When Bavarian hops came on the Danish market around 1900, farmers started using those in place of Danish hops and the Danish hop trade declined. In 1915, the trade was still going on, but at a much reduced level.[15]

The hops that farmhouse brewers grew had never been through systematic commercial breeding, or traded on a sophisticated hop market like those for commercial breweries. As a result, farmhouse hop plants had no named varieties. They were landraces like the grain varieties grown before systematic breeding began (chap. 3, p. 50). It is difficult to be precise about what these hops were like, but the examples I have tasted were similar to Continental noble hops in aroma. They were definitely not similar to hop varieties commonly used in modern craft brewing like Cascade and its successors. Cascade was the first hop variety to have the citric/tropical flavor profile we associate with modern craft beer, and only came on the market in 1972. Some northern European farmhouse brewers have used these hops over the last decade, but very few, and hardly ever in amounts sufficient to dominate the aroma.

Genetic analysis of Swedish hop plants collected from all over Sweden show much greater genetic variation than what is found in commercial varieties from the traditional hop-growing areas of Europe.[16] This is what one would expect when comparing landraces with systematically bred commercial crops. In fact, this is the same phenomenon we saw in chapter 3 when comparing landrace grain varieties with purebred varieties.

It is very likely that farmhouse hops are closer to wild hops, because they have been through much less breeding. Analyses of Norwegian farmhouse hops have found an alpha acid content ranging from 1.9% to 7.2%, with most in the range 2.0%–5.0%.[17] An earlier analysis of Lithuanian farmhouse hops found an alpha acid content from 0.7% to 4.0%.[18] In Swedish hops, the alpha acid content ranged from 0.3% to 8.6%, with an average of 4.6%.[19] In general, farmhouse hops appear to have been rather like noble hops from central Europe as far as alpha acid content is concerned.

There were various ways hops were used in farmouse brewing and these methods were sometimes combined.

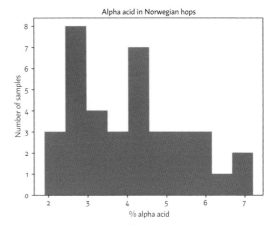

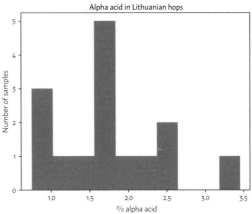

Figure 7.2. Alpha acid content analyses of Norwegian and Lithuanian hops.

- Obviously, it was quite common for the hops to be boiled in the wort, but, as we saw in chapter 5, that was far from the only method of adding hops.
- In Norway, some brewers boiled *humlebeit*, meaning they boiled the hops in a small portion of wort.
- The hops could be boiled in water to make hop tea, and the hop tea could be added with the yeast or after fermentation. In Chuvashia it could even be added according to personal preference when serving the beer.[20]
- Hops could be added to the mash. The effect would be different if the mash was boiled, but often hops were added to the mash as a way to prevent the wort from souring during long mashes. If the beer was raw, the effect might be similar to dry hopping.
- Hops could be used in the filter in the lauter tun, which would be much like having it in the mash. In Denmark, it was quite common to boil hop tea and then pour it through the filter. This would filter out the hop cones and also extract more from the hops during lautering.
- Dry hopping, that is, adding hops in the fermentor, was also practiced, especially in summer.
- Julius Simonaitis adds hop tea to the cask after fermentation, varying the amount of hop tea in different casks so people can choose how bitter they want the beer to be.

Figure 7.3. Lithuanians doing a demonstration brew, boiling hop tea in Söderbärke, Dalarne in Sweden.

Hops have played different roles in farmhouse beer in different places. Many farmhouse brewers used hops simply to protect against infection, and the aroma and bitterness from the hops would have been barely detectable in the beer, if at all. In these beers, juniper usually assumed the role of the flavoring and bittering agent. This was probably the most common way to use hops. Most brewers seem to have used 5 grams or less per liter. Some brewers used much greater amounts of hops than one would expect. In the Hardanger and Sogn districts in western Norway, several brewers reported using 10–13 grams of hops per liter

of beer (giving 80–110 IBU, if we assume Saaz with 2.8% alpha acid). From Jutland and Funen in Denmark, some people reported 10–15 grams per liter (80–126 IBU), and Funen beer seems to have had a reputation for being very hoppy.[21] These high hopping rates are only partly borne out by the data, however, as four accounts report only 3.6–5.5 grams per liter, although one does report 12.5 grams and, to be fair, the data available are very sparse. The Fyodorov family in Chuvashia, Russia uses 0.5—1.0 kilograms for 50 liters of beer, which is on average 15 grams per liter.

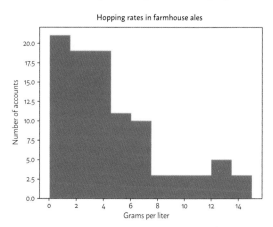

Figure 7.4. Hopping rates in European farmhouse ale.

Unfortunately, hardly anyone seems to brew with these amounts of hops anymore, so it is nearly impossible to say what these beers would have tasted like. I have only ever tasted one: a farmhouse ale brewed by Julius Simonaitis in Joniškelis, north Lithuania, using his own hops. He uses 8.3 grams per liter, which came as a shock for visiting craft brewer Per Kølster.[22]

Julius's beer really is a hop bomb, but not like an IPA. I tasted it from a traditional wooden cask at a beer festival in Sweden. When first poured, it came out looking like white porridge because of the high pressure inside the keg. It took some minutes for it to settle down to a clear yellow liquid that could be drunk. It had a massive, earthy, straw-like hop aroma, which blended excellently with the green, straw-like flavors from the lack of a boil, and the powerful fruitiness of Julius's farmhouse yeast (see #16 Simonaitis, table 4.1). The finish was a sharp, almost biting, hop bitterness that lingered for a long time. The hop profile was not unlike Brouwerij De Ranke's hoppy Belgian beers. Once the foam settled, the beer had very little carbonation. Truly an excellent beer by any standard.

Picking and drying the hops took time, so once they were able to afford it, farmhouse brewers started buying the hops instead. Opinions seem to have differed on whether local or purchased hops were best, but it did not matter in any case for beers with low hop rates. The pharmacies sold hops intended for use in folk medicine, for example, for their purported sedative effect, and farmhouse brewers used those into the twenty-first century.

Now, however, with the modern craft beer revival, there is a new emphasis on hops and on local ingredients. Many farmhouse brewers are rediscovering their local hops, often hops that are growing on their own land. Bjørne Røthe in Voss told me he was considering starting to use his own hops once again and took us to see his hop plant. It grew 10 meters from his brewhouse and had large healthy-looking green cones. We rubbed them in our hands and found that they had a nice fruity and resiny aroma. There was no reason at all not to use them in place of commercial hops.

It is possible to make good, authentic, hoppy farmhouse ales, but difficult, since there are so few examples to learn from and the hops themselves are so hard to get hold of. If you want to try, wild hops will probably be your best bet. Alternatively, European noble hop varieties would also be acceptable. At the same time, it must be added that in most farmhouse ales, and especially today, hops seem to play a fairly minor role. Unlike the next spice.

Juniper

Juniper re-established itself in northern Europe relatively soon after the end of the last ice age and has remained widespread ever since. In fact, *Juniperus communis* has the widest range of any woody plant. It grows in most of northern Europe and in mountainous areas of southern Europe, right across Russia into Japan, and across parts of North America. Unfortunately for Americans, *J. communis* mostly grows in Canada and only a few places in the United States. It is the only species of juniper in northern Europe, and so this is the juniper farmhouse brewers have used. There are three distinct subspecies. The most widely used is *Juniperus communis* ssp. *communis*, but there is also alpine juniper (ssp. *alpina*), which is a low shrub with boat-shaped needles that grows at higher altitudes. There is also a hybrid of these two subspecies. Nearly everyone seems to have used the ordinary juniper, however, including into the present day.

In much of northern Europe, juniper is easy to find. It prefers some shelter from the wind, but it likes sunlight, so forest glades with openings toward the south, or south-facing hillsides, are good places to look. In Denmark, Lithuania, and the UK, juniper is relatively rare. In the UK, juniper is a

Figure 7.5. Juniper in a field. Fårö, off the northern tip of Gotland, Sweden.

protected species so there are restrictions on picking it. On the islands in the Baltic, it grows out in the open and is extremely common. On the Estonian islands, juniper grows into quite large trees, as it can do in other places; in Østfold in southeastern Norway, one juniper grew to a height of 17 meters.[23] In the past, when most farmers kept animals, juniper would often be left alone to grow in the pasture. The animals could not eat it, and the farmer would let it grow because juniper was one of the most useful of all wild plants. If the juniper seemed like it would grow straight, the farmer might remove the lower branches to encourage that form in the hope of getting a fence pole out of it.

Juniper can adapt to the environment and will grow very slowly if necessary. In 1979, in Trysil, eastern Norway, a wood-carver found an alpine juniper with an unusual shape that he cut down and took home. Only when he started working on it did he realize that the tree rings were only 0.2 millimeters thick, so the tree must have been ancient. Researchers using a microscope at the Institute of Forestry Research concluded that the oldest preserved tree ring must be from 971 CE, but that several hundred rings were missing, possibly many hundreds.[24]

Historically, juniper was a very important plant, and it has been described as "the most useful plant in Norwegian nature."[25] Botanist Ove Arbo Høeg wrote a book on juniper covering its many uses. In Norway, juniper was sometimes used for parts of a house that needed to be durable; branches with needles were also used to form a covering for weather-exposed walls. It was fashioned into many types of wooden poles, such as fence posts, shock poles, runners for sleds, and also into nails for boats, rake tips, shoe pins, and row locks. It was also used for fish hooks, hooks in sails, clothes knobs, bows, and so on.[26]

Juniper branches were strewn on the floors of houses as a festive decoration, partly for the aroma. They were also used as scrubs for cleaning, and juniper infusions were used for washing hair* and bathing. Juniper wood was used to smoke many types of food, and also to air out bad odors. Juniper wood and berries were widely used as a spice and in folk medicine.[27] In Ove Arbo Høeg's book the list of uses for juniper takes up no less than 104 pages.

Throughout most of Europe, a juniper branch infusion was used to clean wooden vessels, not just for brewing, but also for making comestibles like cheese and butter, and so on. In the old days, people believed that it was good for removing bad smells from the wood. As one wrote: "A juniper infusion has an unusual ability to remove bad smells and make wooden vessels fresh and clean."[28] Today, people from western Norway to central Russia believe that it has antimicrobial effects.

Traditionally, juniper was also used to make juniper berry "beer," which was a weak alcoholic drink made with dried juniper berries as the sugar source. Another way juniper was used, at least in Norway, was to make what was called *treak*. This was made from juniper berries that were boiled down to a kind of syrup, which was then reduced further until it turned solid.[29] In modern times, people add sugar and cream during this process. The result is a black bar that looks like a cross between caramel and licorice but tastes strongly of juniper. Treak is hard work to make but is an excellent candy. It is still produced in Ål in Hallingdal.[30]

Note that what was used in farmhouse beer was juniper *branches*, possibly with the berries still on them, possibly not. Juniper berries were also used, but far more rarely. The flavor of juniper berries is different from that of the branches, so the two are not interchangeable.

Researchers used to think that juniper branches in beer was a recent innovation, because the main 18th century sources on farmhouse ale do not mention juniper at all.[31] Juniper also failed to show up in archaeological analyses of ancient beers. A closer look at the evidence shows a very different picture, however. There are eighteenth century sources on farmhouse ale brewing from Norway, Denmark, Sweden, and Estonia that describe the use of juniper.[32] In the early nineteenth century juniper was also used in Austria.[33] So the use of juniper must go back at least several centuries.

It also turns out that juniper pollen has thin and unstable walls, which means that even if juniper had been used in ancient beers, pollen analysis would not find any traces of it.[34] Nearly all the analyses of ancient beers had been pollen analyses, until Patrick McGovern's group analyzed two Danish beers from 800 BCE and 200 CE by chemical means and found traces of juniper in both.[35] This suggests juniper could be found in other ancient beer samples if appropriate methods of analysis were used.

The use of juniper is probably a very old tradition, but it seems to have been limited to farmhouse ale. This is not surprising, because collecting enough juniper for large-scale commercial brewing would have been difficult. This is probably also why there is so little mention of juniper in the beer literature: most of it covers only commercial brewing. The growth of commercial brewing very likely caused juniper to be pushed to the margins. There seems to have been no trade in juniper.† In Estonia, during our brewing session in 2016, Paavo Pruul told me that his grandfather always said that "nobody ever paid for juniper or stones." Now it is different with the

---

* My grandmother did this. Ågot Skrindo did too (interview, February 2017).
† That is: no trade in juniper branches as a flavoring. There was a limited trade in western Norway of juniper poles for fences (Høeg 1996, 17).

stones. Big construction companies pay for the stone for use in harbor construction, so people do not give them away for free any more. Juniper, on the other hand, still grows everywhere on the islands and nobody sells it.

In Norway, juniper has always been as common as hops in brewing and used by nearly everyone. While juniper has been widely used in Sweden and Finland, there were many brewers who did not use it. In Estonia and Latvia, it has clearly been in common use. There also reports of it being used in Germany, Austria, and Russia, and also rarely in Lithuania. In Denmark and the UK, people seem not to have used juniper, probably because it is relatively rare.

Juniper is a distinguishing characteristic of several types of farmhouse ale, so when three annual international competitions in farmhouse brewing covering Finland (sahti). Gotland (gotlands-dricke), and the Estonian islands (koduõlu) were arranged in the early 2000s, they were called the "World Championship in Juniper Beer."[36]

Norwegian, Finnish, Estonian, and Russian farmhouse brewers all say that juniper has antimicrobial effects, but whether it actually prevents bacteria and mold from growing is an open question. Sopp claimed a juniper infusion had a mild effect against lactic acid bacteria.[37] In 1979, professor Solberg at the Norwegian dairy institute carried out an informal experiment and found no effect.[38] In 2015, professor Jan Karlsen claimed to have found a clear effect,[39] but his paper appears never to have been published. So, unfortunately, the jury is still out on this issue.

Figure 7.6. Juniper in the lauter tun. Sõru, Hiiumaa, Estonia.

Apart from cleaning, there were two main ways to use juniper in brewing: to make a juniper infusion to use as the strike and sparge water, and/or using juniper branches as support for the grain bed in the lauter tun. Both methods add a clear juniper flavor to the beer as well as bitterness. Using juniper in the lauter tun has been much more common than using a juniper infusion. In Norway, nearly everyone used a juniper infusion (called *einerlåg*), but in Sweden people only did it in the northern half of the country and on Gotland. In Finland, juniper infusions seem to have been rare, while in Estonia they are relatively common. Juniper was also used in Russia, but how common that was is hard to say.

People picked juniper in different ways. Nearly everyone seems to have picked lowland juniper a day or two before brewing. Some wanted only the tips of the branches, while others took thicker branches. In parts of Sogn, at least one branch had to be split lengthwise, a practice still followed as we saw with Carlo Aall in chapter 1. Aave Nystein, in eastern Norway, used to dry the branches for months,[40] but I have never heard of anyone else doing that. People also disagree on whether the branches should have many berries or few. What is clear is that branches with berries are more aromatic. The only thing everyone seems to agree on is that the juniper should be green and fresh.

Sverre Skrindo preferred to go high up to pick his juniper, which means he must have been looking for alpine juniper. Since it is a different subspecies to *J. communis* ssp. *communis*, alpine juniper has a slightly different internal biochemistry and may produce a different flavor, but I have not verified this.

Nobody seems to have cared what season it was when they picked the juniper, and I have seen no mention anywhere of seasonal differences. In any case it did not matter much, because if you wanted fresh juniper you would have to pick it when you were going to brew and any seasonal variations would just have to be accepted.

Hops have usually been considered to hold a special position among the spice used in beer, since it is the only one that is used in just about every beer. In the world of farmhouse brewing, juniper holds a similar position, in that it seems to be used in just about every place where there is enough of it. But why was juniper so widely used in farmhouse brewing? It is generally accepted that the use of hops became so ubiquitous due to the flavor and aroma and their antimicrobial effect. It does not seem too much of a stretch to assume that the same is the case with juniper. That people continued to use juniper to make weaker berry-based "beers" indicates that people really liked the flavor. Given that you have a plant that produces excellent aroma, is useful as a filter and cleaning agent, and is easily available for free, why would people not use it?

It is also interesting that juniper is even more widely employed for cleaning wooden vessels—for brewing, milk products, and other uses—than it is as an ingredient in the actual beer. The reason people give is that it's very good at removing bad odors from wood.[41] In Finland, they also claim that resin from the juniper coats the pores in wood, protecting it against infection.[42] So, it is possible that the use of juniper for cleaning came first, and that people decided they liked the aroma of the infusion they used for cleaning. If that is how it started, then, as Nordland[43] pointed out, when brewers decided they would try it in the beer, it would have been a very small step because the juniper was already to hand, gathered for cleaning the vessels.

Many of the herbal ingredients in beer are very simple in terms of flavor, in that they contribute one flavor component and that is it. Juniper is a much subtler and more flexible ingredient that can lend many different flavors depending on the juniper and how it is treated.

Juniper's base flavor is a green, foresty, pine-like flavor, often with citric notes, but there are also moss-like and minerally components. It adds more than just that, though. Juniper also adds bitterness, and it is generally a smooth and round bitterness. Sour farmhouse ale has generally been frowned upon, but acidity can actually help the juniper flavor stand out more and be perceived as brighter.

As with hops, there are several ways juniper has been used in farmhouse beer, all of which can contribute different flavors:

- A juniper infusion could be used for mashing and/or sparging.
- Juniper branches could be added to the mash, for example, as it was boiled, although this was quite rare in practice.
- Juniper branches could be used in the lauter tun, which has been far and away the most common use.
- Juniper branches could also be boiled in the wort, but this was very rare.

There are various ways of making the juniper infusion, each producing different flavors. Heating the infusion to between 80°C and 90°C makes a light, delicate juniper infusion with a very pale green color. If the infusion is boiled it becomes a little darker and more bitter, and adds a flavor of boiled wood. Some brewers boiled the branches for hours to get an infusion that was deep golden in color, even dark brown. Boiling the branches can in some cases extract a sharp, solvent-like flavor. Some people let the branches steep in warm water overnight.

Figure 7.7. A juniper infusion that has been boiled until it turned brown. Sõru, Hiiumaa, Estonia.

The flavor from the juniper can be used in many different ways. If you are not sure how to use it, it is important to either follow a traditional recipe to the letter, or carefully change one thing each time in order to find what works in each individual beer. In traditional farmhouse ales, juniper can play the role of hops in several ways. It can add bitterness to balance the beer, or the flavors can be at the forefront, with green, foresty, mossy flavors that really pop out and dominate the beer.

For some styles, the juniper flavor is a large part of what makes the beer. Lammin Sahti, one of the major Finnish commercial sahtis, really showcases a delicate green minerally juniper character. At the 2017 Norwegian farmhouse ale festival, Gunnar Skare's beer was a real revelation of what juniper character can be like, prompting one of the judges to compare it with "running through the forest with your tongue against the green moss." Skare does not boil the juniper branches, but steeps them in near-boiling water for roughly three hours.

Sweet Gale

> I have such pain in my head
> I cannot bother for my limbs to move
> I have drunk the strong gale beer
> That comes from Dalarna.

—**From *Gustav Vasa och dalkarlarna*,** a sixteenth-century Swedish folk song

Sweet gale, also known as bog myrtle, is a small flowering shrub that grows in acid bogs and in sandy soils near water. Its Latin name is *Myrica gale*; in Scandinavia its common name is *pors*. In many places, sweet gale was used to protect clothes against vermin, especially moths. Sweet gale has definitely been used in beer brewing for a very long time, as there are many archaeological finds of the plant in a brewing context going all the way back to pre-Roman Iron Age.[44] It is very likely the third most important spice to have been used in brewing, but a distant third.

In the Middle Ages, local governments in the Low Countries and northwest Germany required brewers to buy a spice mix known as *gruit* from local monopolists, essentially as a form of taxation. Gruit seems to have usually contained sweet gale.[45] Sweet gale was also used in brewing in Scandinavia, the Baltic states, and other places outside the gruit area.

One experiment found that, when boiled, sweet gale had a clear antibacterial effect against *Lactobacillus* and *Pediococcus*, but not *Acetobacter*.[46] The effect seemed to be weaker than with the same amount of hops.

Unlike juniper, sweet gale seems to have been outcompeted by hops when hops entered brewing. In commercial brewing this is not very surprising, since sweet gale is even harder to farm and collect than juniper. But sweet gale seems to have also become much less common in farmhouse brewing, although why is not clear. Sweet gale did have a reputation in many countries for giving drinkers a headache, and many people considered it unhealthy, so these might be some of the reasons. In quite a few places, sources report that no gale grew in their area, which probably explains why it was not used in the beer there.

In the last century or so, sweet gale seems to have been used in Scandinavia and in Estonia, but only rarely. In Denmark, usage seems to be limited to Jutland, especially north Jutland. In Norway,

Figure 7.8. A sprig of gale floating in the hop tea. Sōru, Hiiumaa, Estonia.

it seems to have been used the most in Telemark. Close by the cluster of people who report using sweet gale is the town of Porsgrunn, which literally means "sweet gale grounds," so probably this use of sweet gale is very old. Unfortunately, because it was used so little there is hardly any documentation that mentions how people used it in modern times.

Three accounts, two from Denmark and one from Sweden, all agree that sweet gale was harvested in autumn and dried.[47] One source reports using the flowers, the other two claim the stalks were used. Most seem to have used sweet gale in every beer, but in Voer in Denmark the respondent said it was used for a special beer, *porseøl* (sweet gale beer), served to especially distinguished guests and used as a gift to women who had just given birth. This particular beer was made by taking some of the wort and boiling it with sweet gale, then bottling it separately. The porseøl was a good bit more bitter and spicy than the ordinary beer.[48]

In August of 2016, I was lucky enough to participate in a brewing session with Paavo Pruul on the Estonian island of Hiiumaa. Paavo used sweet gale in his beer. Paavo learned to brew from his grandfather, who did not use sweet gale, but there is a tradition of using it on the islands and, anyway, Paavo liked the flavor.

Paavo brewed a standard koduõlu using a two-step infusion mash and no boil. He used a hop tea that included a bunch of sweet gale, stems and leaves. The sweet gale was boiled for about an hour, just like the hops. Other modern brewers I know of who have used sweet gale have done the same.

It is not necessary to boil sweet gale, however. One of the accounts mentioned above, from Øls in Denmark, described putting the gale in the mash.[49] This brewer also fermented in the mash (*see* p. 165), which means the sweet gale would have stayed in the beer during the course of fermentation, only being removed when the beer was lautered after fermentation.

One Estonian account describes browning the sweet gale cones in a pan and using them as a hop substitute.[50] The description contains no further detail than that.

I have spoken to many modern brewers who have used sweet gale in their beer, and none reported any issues with headaches or other bad side effects. Mika Laitinen, in his book on sahti, says the same.[51] Why sweet gale historically had such a bad reputation when modern brewers have no problems is not clear. It is possible that the persistent stories about sweet gale giving headaches are wrong and that the headaches really came from consuming too much alcohol. Another possibility is that boiling deactivates the toxic agent or evaporates it away, which is why modern beers do not produce headaches, but older ones did. Or perhaps people used much more sweet gale in the past. I can find no indication that sweet gale is toxic.

The flavor of sweet gale is quite strong, peppery, woody, and lime-like, with a relatively sharp bitterness. The taste comes from the oil that's present in all parts of the sweet gale plant. The flavor is not the most subtle or flexible, so use sweet gale with caution. But, used right, it can impart good hop-like flavor to beer.

Both the stems and leaves of sweet gale seem to have been used. For quantity, 2–5 grams of dried plant per liter seems to be reasonable.

Wormwood

Wormwood (*Artemisia absinthium*), or grand wormwood, is best known for being used to make absinthe, but it was also used across Denmark in farmhouse brewing, including on the island of Bornholm. It was also used in Estonia, but not as widely. Wormwood also seems to have been used as a substitute for hops in eighteenth-century England.

In Denmark, almost every garden had wormwood, but some of it was picked in the wild. It was cut in late August when in bloom but before the seeds developed. It was tied in bunches and hung under the eaves of the house to dry, and then hung in the loft afterward. Some say the bunches had to be kept out of the sun while drying, otherwise the plant would be too dry and the buds would fall off.

In Denmark, some people used wormwood to make an infusion to clean the brewing vessels, which is an interesting parallel with the way juniper infusions were used. Wormwood was also taken for stomach trouble, especially intestinal worms, in both humans and farm animals. It was also used to fumigate chests, cupboards, and living rooms to remove foul odors, and also laid in bedding straw.

People seem to have used both the stalks and the leaves when brewing, with most seemingly adding them to the mash before the hot water was poured on. Others added only the leaves in the mash, putting the stalks in the beer barrel when the beer was stored. Very few brewers who used wormwood boiled their wort.

Wormwood is intensely bitter, so not much is needed to flavor beer. It contributes the menthol-like aroma that is characteristic of absinthe.

Wormwood is toxic, and it is possible to overdose on it. The main culprit is the compound thujone. European Union regulations allow a maximum of 5 milligrams of thujone per liter in beer, while the US limit is 10 mg/L. If you use wormwood sprigs in the beer you are very unlikely to exceed these limits.

Caraway

Caraway (*Carum carvi*) was definitely used in Norwegian brewing, where I about 5% of accounts mention it. Strangely, caraway is not mentioned outside of Norway. In Norway, where most other herbs are vaguely mentioned as "some have used it" or "I have heard it was used," caraway is actually found listed as part of the recipes themselves. It also does not seem to be limited to any one part of Norway, appearing in accounts all over the country.

Caraway grows wild in Norway and is so easy to find that people seem not to have bothered cultivating it. It was so widely used as a spice in cheese and bread that it was often known simply as *krydd* (spice). People also made caraway tea. Generally, the seeds were used, and these were also collected and sold, even exported.

In beer brewing, however, the accounts are unanimous: it was the caraway stalks that were used, usually dried. Nearly everyone says the same thing: the stalks were placed in the lauter tun, together with juniper and/or straw, with the purpose to extract the flavor. A single account from southeastern Norway, said the stalks were used together with juniper to make the mash liquor.[52]

How much was used is not exactly clear. "A sprig," says one account. "A layer in the lauter tun," says another. "Some." "A little." They clearly used less of caraway than juniper, but it is impossible to give any specific amounts.

The flavor of caraway is reminiscent of fresh coriander and has that clear herbal signature common to many of these well-known beer herbs. It works very well in wheat beers, and probably also in styles like koduõlu and kornøl. If using seeds, 2 grams per liter is probably suitable.

St. John's Wort

St. John's wort refers to any member of the genus *Hypericum*, which contains nearly 500 species. In brewing, probably only *Hypericum perforatum* and *Hypericum maculatum* have been used. The two are so similar that traditionally people seem not to have distinguished between them.[53] St. John's wort was widely used in liquor and also in traditional medicine.

St. John's wort is both aromatic and bitter, so it is suitable as a hop substitute. It has definitely been used in farmhouse brewing, but mostly in Norway, it seems. Unfortunately, no recipes that include St. John's wort have survived, and there is hardly any information at all about how it was used. The aroma is classically woody and herbal.

From Denmark, we are told that people picked it in summer in ditches along the road and dried the stalks.[54] Danish brewers seemingly added the stalks to the cask with the finished beer. That may explain the anecdote, from Meldal in Norway, about an old priest who loved beer but whose eyesight had begun to fail. Unable to see that dead flies had collected in his drink, the priest happily crunched through the beer, saying, "Oh, all this St. John's wort in the beer is just lovely."[55]

One Norwegian account from Telemark explained that St. John's wort was "mixed with the grist."[56] This suggests it was used in the mash.

Sixty grams of fresh, flowering plant per liter may be suitable.

Bitter Orange Peel

The bitter orange (*Citrus × aurantium*), in Swedish *pomerans*, is a type of orange originally from southeast Asia. If the scientific name looks strange, that is because this tree is a hybrid; citrus trees easily produce hybrids, so their taxonomy is nightmarishly complex. Bitter orange has been grown around the Mediterranean for about a millennium. It is the main ingredient in British marmalade, has been used for flavoring liquor, and, in Sweden, it is used to flavor gingerbread. In beer, bitter orange is mainly known for its peel being used to flavor Belgian *witbier*.

Surprisingly, nearly 10% of Swedish accounts say bitter orange peel was used in farmhouse ale, whereas accounts from elsewhere appear not to mention it at all. There is no clear geographic pattern: it seems to have been used as a flavoring in beer all over Sweden, even on Gotland. Exactly how, why, and when Swedish farmhouse brewers started using bitter orange peel is not clear at all. Laura Grubb's Swedish cookbook from 1888 mentions bitter oranges in several recipes,[57] although not the one for beer, so the fruit has been available in Sweden at least that long.

One account says the peel was boiled. In general, the peel seems to have been added to the beer barrel before the fermented beer was poured into it. It is clear that not everyone had access to bitter oranges, and some only had them at Christmas. This is unsurprising, since it was an ingredient people had to buy because it was imported.

Twenty grams of dried peel per liter of beer may be suitable.

Yarrow

Yarrow (*Achillea millefolium*) is only reported in a few accounts of farmhouse ale from Norway, and one from Sweden. The Swedish account at least explains that yarrow was boiled in water, like hop tea, and added to the beer after mashing. The wort was not boiled.

Yarrow must have been used more widely in the past, because in many parts of Norway the local name for yarrow is either *ølkong* (lit. "beer king") or *ølkall* (beer man). Yarrow grows wild pretty much everywhere, including in the ditches just 50 meters from my house. It was often used as a spice in sausage and blood dishes, as well as in bread and other foods. It was also used to make herbal tea.

Yarrow has a fresh, herbal aroma with piney, citrus notes. Four grams of dried stems per liter is suitable.

Tansy

Tansy (*Tanacetum vulgare*) has been used in beer in Norway, but the evidence is pretty thin. A few accounts say they have heard of people using it in beer, but there is no detail at all. The exception is an account by Hans Jacob Wille, who says it was used "in the filter, so that the beer may be strong and bitter."[58] It was very likely that the stems and leaves were used, possibly dried.

Figure 7.9. Tansy growing in a traffic island. Rælingen, eastern Norway.

Tansy has probably been used in more places in Norway than records suggest. In many places in Norway, locals referred to the plant as *ølkong*, literally "beer king," the same name that people in other regions gave to yarrow. Tansy has been cultivated since ancient times for its alleged medicinal properties, especially against intestinal parasites and as a treatment against lice. Today, tansy grows wild in Norway and can be found in nearly any roadside ditch, but it is not clear if it grew wild here originally.

When fresh stems are rubbed between the hands, they produce a strong and pleasant aroma. Tansy is quite bitter, so 1 gram per liter is enough.

Since it contains thujone, tansy is mildly toxic. If you decide to brew with it, treat it with caution.

Bay Laurel

Accounts of the Swedish-speaking population along the western and southern coasts of Finland report that they used the leaves of bay laurel (*Laurus nobilis*) in beer.[59] In no other country, not even in Sweden itself, is this mentioned.

Exactly how the leaves were used varies. The most common was to boil hops and laurel leaves in water, as with the hop tea. Some boiled them in wort instead. But the leaves could also be added to the fermentor or to the filter.

Marsh Tea

Marsh tea (*Rhododendron tomentosum*; formerly *Ledum palustre*), or wild rosemary, has a flavor similar to sweet gale (see above), being woody and lime-like, but is somewhat sharper and more bitter, more like a sharp, powdery bitterness. In much of Scandinavia, marsh tea has names ending with *-pors* because of its similarity to sweet gale. It is probable people in many cases have confused the two with one another. One Swedish account says the local name *getpors*, literally meaning "goat gale," was because "those creatures were mad for this plant."

In continental Europe, the marsh tea plant only grows in Germany and areas further to the north and east. In Norway, it only grows in areas where there is little to no grain growing, so it was probably never used in brewing. Marsh tea also grows in the eastern parts of Sweden and there are a few reports of it being used. The main users, however, seem to have been Estonians, where one in five accounts report using it.

An unpublished study tested the antimicrobial effect of marsh tea but found no effect.[60] Marsh tea is toxic to humans, but Swedish brewers appear to have been aware of this.[61] Consuming marsh tea while pregnant is strongly recommended against. In a 2016 interview I had with farmhouse brewer Aarne Trei, who lives on the Estonian island of Saaremaa, he claimed marsh tea has a narcotic effect, then added drily, "It gives you a nice headache as well." According to Wikipedia, the smell of the plant alone is enough to give some people headaches. So, in theory, using this plant sounds quite risky.

In Latvia, the Labietis brewery has made a barley wine with marsh tea that I personally quite liked. The brewer, Reinis Pļaviņš, says he has brewed with marsh tea for a long time and never noticed any bad effects from it, even up to 3 grams per liter. Using more than 3 g/L is too much and makes for an unpleasant flavor, says Reinis. He went on to say that, if you drank three bottles of their marsh tea barley wine "you will have a strange hangover with a bit of a dizzy feeling in the head, but that could also be the effect of drinking one-and-a-half liters of strong beer with 11.4 percent alcohol."

According to Reinis Pḷaviņš, ledol, the toxic component in marsh tea, is most abundant in new shoots that are present on the plant in August/September. If these shoots are used in beer they produce a "toxic" aroma. Harvesting the plant in late May or early June imparts less ledol and a rounder, more pleasant aroma to the beer. According to Simonas Gutautas, boiling without a lid makes the toxic components evaporate off.[62]

A similar North American species, Labrador tea (*Rhododendron groenlandicum*; formerly *Ledum groenlandicum*), grows in Canada and Alaska and is less poisonous.[63]

Heather

In Scotland, there are ancient legends about the so-called heather ale of the Picts, but it is not clear what it actually was and whether it ever really existed.[64] The Williams Brothers Brewery in Scotland brews a modern recreation called Fraoch.

Heather (*Calluna vulgaris*) has, however, definitely been used in beer. John Firth writes of Redland on Orkney in Scotland that it was common there to filter the beer through either heather or straw.[65] The *Zythophile* blog quotes John Bickerdyke in 1889 as saying the same practice had been common all over Ireland.[66] So, using heather in the filter was probably common in the British Isles, but the documentation is missing.

Other Flavorings

There is a long, long list of various plants being used for brewing that are mentioned in one or two accounts. The full list is too long to go through here, but I will describe some of the most interesting.

In Wales, gorse was used in the filter,[67] which very likely added some flavor. How common this practice was is difficult to say. There is no gorse in Norway, so I have not been able to test it myself.

Two Norwegian accounts say the green part of the potato plant was used to give a brown color to the beer. The grass could be boiled with the initial juniper infusion.[68] It is probably not a good idea to use it because one account says: "This didn't give any good flavor, but the color was so lovely."[69]

Using spruce in beer is relatively popular in modern craft brewing, but there is little sign that it was ever traditional. One Swedish account mentions that the hop tea was filtered through spruce branches.[70]

Wild radish (*Raphanus raphanistrum*) was used in the beer from Salamiestis in Lithuania. The seeds were added to the wort "for good aroma."[71]

On the island of Ruhnu in Estonia, a juniper infusion was used together with the flowers of chamomile (*Matricaria chamomilla*) described as giving the beer "a pleasant aroma and taste."[72] Chamomile has a very subtle aroma, so how much its flavor it really added to the beer is uncertain.

According to Rae Philips, in the past people on Orkney used bogbean (*Menyanthes trifoliata*) as a substitute for hops. According to Wikipedia, bogbean "has a characteristic strong and bitter taste," so it may be well suited for this purpose.

On Gotland in Sweden, walnut leaves were sometimes used as a substitute for hops, "as these are very bitter."[73]

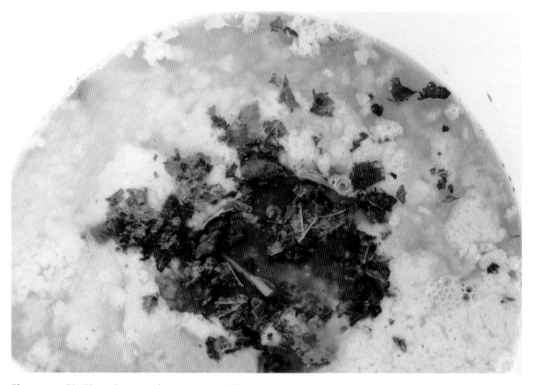

Figure 7.10. Blackberry leaves in the yeast starter. Sõru, Hiiumaa, Estonia.

In Tinn in Telemark, eastern Norway, "those who wanted particularly sweet beer" used common polypody (*Polypodium vulgare*). The polypody was dried, peeled,[*] and boiled before being added to the mash.[74] From my time in the boy scouts as a child, I remember walking in the woods when someone suddenly pointed and said, "Oh, look, polypody!" They explained that the root tastes of licorice, so we pulled them up, removed the earth, and ate them. It did, indeed, taste of sweet licorice. Interestingly, a 1971 research paper describes the identification of a compound they named osladin in the roots of common polypody. According to the researchers, osladin tastes 500 times sweeter than sugar by weight.[75] This suggests polypody may actually have made the beer sweeter, as osladin is not consumed by the yeast.

Paavo Pruul, on Hiiumaa in Estonia, had learned from his grandfather that blackcurrant leaves should be crushed in a mortar and added to the yeast starter. He had no idea why. When seven or eight leaves were added to 50 liters of beer in this way, the result was a lovely, delicate herbal fruitiness.[76]

Salt has been used in farmhouse ale in Estonia. According to one account, which said some brewers added salt so the "drinker's heart wouldn't go watery."[77] Apparently, this meant that he or she would not want to eat so much after drinking.[78] Another account by Paavo Pruul said the wells near the shore on Hiiumaa would go salty in the summer because the water table would be lower, allowing seawater to seep in. Salty well water made salty beer, although only slightly salty.

---

[*] At least, I think so. The verb "skarva" is obscure to me, but is probably a typo for *skava*.

In September/October, the rains come, the wells fill up again, and the water goes back to normal. Both accounts of adding salt are from brewers on the Estonian islands, near the sea.

Two Norwegian accounts mention using tobacco. Only one gives any detail: "Some laid tobacco on the bottom of the beer cask . . . , but those beers were not drinkable. They made you vomit."[79] This sounds like an exaggeration, as many modern craft breweries have made beers with tobacco without any ill effects. A single account from Estonia also mentions tobacco.[80]

Adjuncts

In modern times, people started using sugar and syrup to make the beer stronger, but these adjuncts are of course new, because in the old days people could not afford to buy sugar or syrup. However, there are quite a few other adjuncts that have been used in farmhouse beers. People diluted the malt with other starch sources, so that the enzymes from the malt could produce more sugar. Unfortunately, the accounts generally do not say why the adjuncts were added, just that they were. Whether this was done out of poverty or because people liked the flavor is not clear, but it is probably a bit of both.

Adjuncts seem to have been much more common in Sweden than in any other country in northern Europe. The reason is probably that Swedish farmers were using weak beer as an everyday beverage and this stretched their supply of grain to the limit, forcing them to add adjuncts to make it last all year. It may also be that, since the beer was generally weak and for everyday use, taste was not considered that important and so adjuncts were acceptable.

In Denmark, there does not seem to have been a need for adjuncts, and a Norwegian farmer would probably have been bitterly ashamed to dilute his malt with potatoes or anything like it. The Lithuanian attitude seems to have been more pragmatic.

Potatoes

The most common adjunct in Sweden was potatoes. They seem to usually have been grated and boiled, or boiled and mashed, before being added to the mash. Some brewers peeled raw potatoes, then cut them into tiny cubes.

Figure 7.11. Woman mashing boiled potatoes for the beer. Kurkijoki, formerly eastern Finland, now Russia. 1939. Photo P. Kyytinen.

Potatoes came to Europe from South America, so their use in European farmhouse brewing cannot be very old. They were grown by aristocrats in Sweden from the seventeenth century, but it was only in the nineteenth century that it became common to grow them in Sweden.

Potatoes do not sound promising at all as a beer ingredient, but based on a recipe from EU 8761, Lucy Clarke and Marcus Brand brewed a beer from Öxabäck where the grist was about 10% potatoes. To my surprise the beer was very good, with no detectable potato flavor or related off-flavors. The recipe is given in chapter 9 on page 319.

On the use of potatoes in Mälsa, Sweden, one commentator wrote:

> It was considered that, at most, 6% potatoes could be added to the mash, but often only half of that was used. The reason people added potatoes was partly that they wanted stronger beer, partly that they wanted it to foam. The latter was probably the most important, since people were very proud of beer that had a large head when it was poured. People seem not to have liked speaking of using potatoes in their mash, because many of the old folks in this region have no idea that people ever did so. They do remember, however, that some people had very foamy beer. (Nerén 1944, 292–93)

This account seems to fit the facts well: people were ashamed of using potatoes because it implied they could not afford to brew all-grain beer. But potatoes did the beer no real harm, and the protein in the potatoes may well have contributed to the head.

A couple of Norwegian accounts also mention potatoes as an adjunct.[81] The same is shown in an ethnographic video from Kurkijoki, formerly in Finland, but part of Russia since 1945.

Bran

Bran is the dark outer layers of the grain, which is removed from refined flour, but is retained in whole-grain flour and gives it its darker color. Bran has much more protein and fiber than the white part of the grain (i.e., the endosperm) and also less starch. It also contains some oil, which means it can go rancid. What the effect on the flavor of beer was I do not know, but rye bran in beer was very common in Sweden, and wheat bran was also used.[82]

Carrots

Carrots were another common adjunct in Sweden, and they have also been used in Denmark. The Danish account is from Revninge on Funen,[83] which is a very rich agricultural district. It therefore seems unlikely that carrots were added because the brewers did not have enough grain, which suggests carrots in the beer might actually be good.

The Swedish accounts strengthen the impression given by the record from Funen.[84] In general, they seem to agree that carrots made the beer sweeter, darker, and, in general, better tasting. The carrots could be either grated raw or boiled and mashed before being added to the mash. They sound like an ingredient worth trying.

Peas

In Lithuania, there is a tradition that involves adding peas to beer, which brewers claimed improved the foam on the beer.[85] The protein probably did do that. It would have filled out the body of the beer as well. There would also have been some sugar from the starch, which was probably desirable.

Remarkably, pea beer has been brewed commercially in Lithuania for at least two decades.[86] Today, Biržu Alus brews a pale lager named Širvenos, where the grist is 15% fresh green peas from nearby farms.[87] On draft, the peas give Širvenos a strange spicy,

Figure 7.12. Biržu Alus Širvenos, commercial Lithuanian pea beer. Vilnius, Lithuania.

floral character and a mealy mouthfeel. Unexpectedly, it is actually a very good beer. The peas can be tasted in the unfiltered bottled version too, but not as much.

I was told that commercial breweries started using peas as an adjunct in beer during the Soviet period (1944–92), because in the Soviet economy it could be difficult to get enough malt for the beer.[88] However, the commercial breweries probably got the idea from the existing farmhouse brewing tradition, because using peas in farmhouse ale is well documented from the 1930s.[89]

What is surprising is that farmhouse brewers describe adding the peas to the grain when it was steeping to make malt. In other words, they malted the peas in much the same way that grain was malted, except the peas sprouted sooner than the barley.[90] The amount of peas farmhouse brewers used has varied from 1%–2% to as much as 10% of the grist.[91]

Honey

Using honey to add flavor and strength to farmhouse beer has been a relatively common and long-standing practice in Sweden. There is also a tradition of doing so in Lithuania, where most of the farmhouse breweries today produce a version of their house beer with added honey. In Sweden, there was a tradition for brewing *mölska*, beer with honey, in medieval times.

Other Adjuncts

The full list of adjuncts that have been used in farmhouse beer is quite long, although it is not clear how significant some of them were or whether they are interesting enough flavor-wise to use today. Flour from various types of grain has been quite common. Beetroot and sugar beet have been used, and even birch sap. The use of raisins in bottles to provide carbonation is recorded in Denmark. Raisins were added to the cask in Sweden, probably for flavor.

Filter Materials

When laying the filter in the lauter tun, farmhouse brewers often used juniper, which we consider an ingredient because it flavors the beer. But farmers also used other things in the filter, though to what effect is not entirely clear.

Straw

Perhaps the most common material of all in the lauter tun was straw, often in combination with other things, such as juniper. The purpose of the straw was to support the grain filter bed that helped separate the wort from the grist. Much has been said about what effect this might have had on the flavor.

For some reason, rye straw massively predominates as the filter straw, dwarfing the use of barley and oat straw, even in places where people grew little rye. Nordland[92] claimed rye straw was more solid and therefore easier to tie into the elaborate rings and other shapes people often formed with it. Another source claimed it was because rye straw was longer.[93]

It seems to have been common to either wash the straw first or to pour a few buckets of boiling water through it before the mash was placed on top of it. This way, the straw would be disinfected before use. It probably also made the straw softer and easier to tie.

I have only tried a single traditional beer filtered through straw and, in that case, hot water was poured through the straw before use (this was with Vytautas Jančys, *see* "Keptinis" in chap. 5). I cannot really claim to have picked up any flavor from the straw but, on the other hand, that particular beer was a keptinis so the flavor may have been drowned out.

Alder Sticks

Another common material used in the filter was alder sticks, typically placed underneath the straw or juniper. One might use sticks of other woods too, quite often juniper, but alder was by far the most common. Clearly, the purpose of the sticks was to make it easier for the wort to flow along the bottom of the lauter tun by preventing the more fine-grained straw or juniper from lying directly on the bottom.

As for why alder exactly was so popular, the sources are confusing. "Because it added no flavour," says one.[94] "Because it gave a lovely aroma," says another.[95] "Because it added colour," says a third.[96] Alder bark produces a strong red color, so that last part is definitely true. Coloring was probably the main motivation because the brewers generally wanted the beer to be dark, which was seen as an indication that the beer was strong.

As for the flavor, I have tasted only a couple of beers using alder sticks, so it is difficult to tell. I did think I picked up a woody flavor in one. Two reliable sources claim it makes the beer more bitter.[97]

Sopp also claims to have done (unpublished) experiments showing that alder wood extract has clear antimicrobial effects, provided the wort is not boiled.[98]

While there are some reports from Dalsland in Sweden, just across the border with Norway, strangely, alder sticks seem to have been used only in Norway and Lithuania.

Other Materials

In Lithuania, the Piniavos brewery still makes a beer lautered through raspberry canes, following the family tradition. This was also done in Latvia,[99] and Petrulis says it was also used in Salamiestis in Lithuania.[100] Interestingly, Salamiestis is not too far from the area that Piniavos brewer Vidmantas Perevičius comes from. The Piniavos beer has a peculiar, tannic bitterness, very likely from the canes. It is also quite dark, possibly also because of the canes. Piniavos makes another beer lautered through red clover, which is another local farmhouse tradition.

8

THE DRINK PROBLEM: MAKING IT SAFE

Water alone was a despised drink. It was different when malt and hops came into it.

—Fredrik Grundtvig, *Livet i Klokkergaarden*, 172

The farmers in northern Europe just a couple of centuries ago had surprisingly little choice in what to drink. Tea and coffee were too expensive, wine even more so. Juice was not really available. Milk was safe to drink, but in winter the cows were fed too little to produce any milk at all, and in summer they would be away at the mountain pastures. And what milk there was, was needed for butter and cheese. But people had to drink. So, what did they choose?

Water was available, of course, but there were several reasons not to drink it. There is no nutrition in water and at a time when people did hard physical labor every day, it was often difficult getting enough calories as it was. Water also has little flavor and people preferred something with taste. And, finally, untreated water was not safe to drink. There was every reason to be afraid of supposedly pure water, with untreated sewage and other problems. Sigurd Johan Saure had the water in the well on his farm tested and found coliform bacteria in it.[1] Even today, people sometimes get sick from water treated at professionally operated municipal water supplies. In 2004, the city of Bergen in western Norway had an outbreak of giardiasis.

Were people aware that drinking water was not safe? That is not entirely clear. On one hand, there is no lack of medieval sources showing that people did drink water, and in some cases even preferred it.[2] On the other hand, there is also quite a bit of evidence that suggests people took the opposite view. In 1939, the Norwegian Ethnographic Survey sent out a questionnaire asking what

Figure 8.1. On the Markeset farm in Sogn, western Norway, 1951. The farmer would go up to the mountain pasture every Saturday to collect a week's worth of sour milk, then transport it back down to the farm by horse. If they wanted any kind of milk to drink this was the only way.

people had as their everyday drink. Regarding water, the answers largely repeat the same thing, over and over again: "We didn't drink water, we were afraid of the water."[3] Of course, this does not mean people avoided water completely, because they knew there are different kinds of water. However, it is evident that people overwhelmingly preferred other drinks, and that they went to surprising lengths to make sure they had something other than water.

Without question, the preferred beverage was beer. As one Dane put it: "People drank a lot of beer, and only beer. Nobody would think of drinking water or milk."[4] Many people have disputed that farmers in the Middle Ages drank beer every day and dismiss it as mere myth. The reality is that those who had beer drank it every day, not just in the Middle Ages but far into the twentieth century as well.

In Denmark and southern Sweden, farmers had enough grain that they could afford to drink beer as their daily beverage, and the fact that they did is beyond dispute. In various ethnographic surveys the responses repeat this endlessly. One respondent in 1951 described life between 1872 and 1914 thus: "We were given small beer* the whole year round, and the beer one drank between meals was always small beer. Seen with today's eyes, it seems that people drank incredible amounts of beer in those days."[5] Literally dozens more quotes from Denmark and southern Sweden like this one can be cited, all from independent sources where people describe what they did in their own homes. Most of them also describe the same custom: "In my home there was always a beer mug on the dining room table, where we all went many times a day to slake our thirst. . . . It was filled as often as it was emptied during the day, and at times that happened quite often."[6]

How completely ordinary and unremarkable this was is perfectly demonstrated by a quote from a different respondent. After writing about the same custom with the beer mug on the table in the living room, he added: "The mailman, when he had placed the newspaper on the

---

* *Dagligøl,* literally "daily beer," but the meaning is small beer.

table and saw the mug, would often come over, blow the flies aside and drink, before going on to the next house. This entire scene was so natural and straightforward back then."[7] It may sound incredible that the mailman would just go into the living room like that, but on Møn, in southern Denmark, Lotte Vinge told me that when she was a child the family would go into the barn to tend the cows every morning. At 9:30 the mailman would come, go into the house, and start the coffee. Once it was ready, he would go into the barn to let the family know it was ready, and everyone would gather around the kitchen table for coffee and beer. This, of course, was in the 1970s, when other drinks like coffee were available, which is why the mailman considered it a particular treat to stop at this farm.

The situation in the UK seems to have been very similar. Evans writes of Blaxhall in Sussex: "Beer was the usual drink in most households in this parish right up the beginning of the [twentieth] century." He goes on to say that people also drank tea, but it was expensive.[8]

Am I really saying that the entire household quenched their thirst every day with beer? Yes. Yes, I am. The documentation is just overwhelming. From late twentieth-century Gotland:[9] "Juice was not on the table. Such things are not served for an ordinary meal. Soft drinks had not yet been invented, and often there was not enough milk. Guess, then, what the five-year-old drank with the food."

In short, at least in Denmark, southern Sweden, and parts of the UK, beer was the everyday drink right into the twentieth century. The reason was simple: people had enough grain to make it, beer tasted good, and it was healthy and nutritious by the standards of the time. But even in these relatively rich areas there was not always enough. Højrup writes about Denmark:

> The wayfarer who asked for a sip of beer learned much about the area and the farm by tasting the beer. In poor areas one had to save, which was done by using less malt and fewer hops. Then the beer was thin, and it quickly soured. But the beer was not poured out. Instead, milk was poured into the mug, where it separated out into little lumps.[*] Then it was stirred with a spoon, before being drunk. The milk at least took away some of the sourness, and it slaked the thirst, but of course it wasn't good. It just made the beer last longer.
> (Højrup 1966, 60)

To the north and east life was harder. Getting enough safe liquid for the household was a question of economics, and much ingenuity had gone into making the results as good as possible within the constraints set by soil and climate. Which is not to say that people today would consider the drinks very tempting.

Whether or not people knew water was not safe to drink, it is nonetheless striking that they chose to produce drinks in ways that made them safer. Water could be made safe by boiling, but that consumed precious firewood. It could be made safe by alcohol, although that required sugar, an item that was very scarce, so there were limits to how much drink could be made this way. Or it could be made safe by acid, which was simpler. All three methods were used in different ways.

---

[*] This was known as ølost and was made in Denmark, Sweden, and Norway.

Table 8.1 Everyday Fermented Drinks that were Alcoholic and/or Acidic

Drink	Base	Alcoholic	Acidic
Bosa	Flour	Barely	Yes
Blande	Whey	No	Yes
Small beer	Malt	Yes	No
Rostdrikke	Spent grain and leftovers	No	Yes
Kvass	Bread/leftovers	Barely	Yes
Birch sap beer	Tree sap	Barely	Yes?
Juniper berry beer	Juniper berries	Yes	No?
Mead	Honey	Yes!	No
Sugar beer	Sugar/syrup	Yes	Yes

Table 8.2 Everyday Fermented Drinks with their Common Names by Local Language

Drinks discussed in this chapter	Norwegian	Swedish	Finnish	Estonian	Latvian	Lithuanian	Russian
Bosa	n/a	n/a?	Jauhokalja	Rokk	?	Raugala/gira	Kvass
Blande	Blande	?	n/a?	n/a?	?	Pasukos	n/a?
Small beer	Spissøl/tynnøl	Svagdricka	Kalja	Taherberi	Plānalus	Antrokas	Drugan
Rostdrikke	Rostdrikke	Spisöl?	Rapataari	Taar	Patakas/tapinš	Nakvoselis	Kvass
Kvass	Kvass	Bröddricka	Kalja/Vaassa	Kali	Kvass	Gira	Kvass
Birch sap beer	Bjørkevin	Björkdricka	Mahlakalja	Kasemah-la taar	?	Sulos	Berezovka
Juniper berry beer	Einebærøl	En-bärs-dricka	Kata-jan-mar-jaolut	Kada-ka-marja-jook	?	Gira	?
Mead	Mjød	Mjöd	Sima	Mõdu	Medus	Midus	Myod
Sugar beer	Sukkerøl	?	Sima	n/a?	?	Gira/nak-vosas	?

Notes: These are far from the only names for these drinks, just the most common. Many of them have five to ten different names in just a single language. Many of these names also cover multiple kinds of drinks in some languages.

Danish has been omitted because, basically, the Danes had no need for most of these drinks.

The Russian "myod" is a deliberate transliteration of "ë" as "yo," because it is pronounced that way. I have tried to stick to that transliteration throughout, even though "e" is a more common transliteration in English, but I feel that is unhelpful. (I did put Perm as Perm, since everyone writes it that way.)

Flour-Based Beverages

Skellefteå in northern Sweden is so far north that growing grain was difficult. While farmers there did grow grain, they never malted it. The light grain, together with some husks and straw, was dried in the bastu (smoke sauna, *see* p. 67) then ground and used to make the everyday bread, which was "a foul gray color." Note that this was not leavened bread, but flat, thin, wafer-like crispbread. That, presumably, used up all their grain. These farmers made a kind of drink by boiling hacked green straw in a kettle, then sieving off the liquid and mixing boiled, mashed potatoes and some rye flour into it. It was stirred well, left to cool, and then yeast was added. It fermented for three days before being stored in the cellar in wooden "bottles." For meals consisting of potato and salted fish, which made people thirsty, each member of the household got a cup of this drink.[10]

This type of sour flour-based drink was made in many parts of eastern Europe. It is particularly well documented in Finland.[11] In the Balkans, Turkey, and Central Asia, a similar drink called boza, often made from millet flour, is still very common.[12]

Figure 8.2. Blande vat. This usually stood on a small bench just inside the door, so anyone who was thirsty could grab a drink. From Maihaugen museum, Lillehammer, eastern Norway.

Blande

Another very common drink was based on milk. In Norway people drank what they called *blande* (literally "mix"). Norwegian farmers stored whey (the thin, milky liquid that is a by-product of cheesemaking) in huge wooden vats, where it soured. People who have tried blande say it was "terribly sour," and it was diluted with water to make it drinkable.[13] This drink was also common in Sweden, especially northern Sweden where the farmers had less grain.[14] In northern Scotland farmers drank a similar drink, known as "blaand."[15]

People in these poorer areas did not drink only blande or flour-based drinks. Beer was still drunk almost everywhere, even if people couldn't afford it every day. For the most part, people drank a weaker kind of beer called "small beer" if they were thirsty.

Small Beer

Small beer for work, beer for celebration.

—Finnish saying, quoted in the epigraph
of Matti Räsänen, *Vom Halm zum Fass*

During lautering, the wort is run off slowly from the mash, and, as this continues, more and more sugar is washed out of the grain and the wort becomes less and less sweet. As we saw with Carlo Aall (chapter 1), the brewer tasted the wort and stopped running off once most of the sweetness was gone, to make sure the beer had the right strength. This was how farmhouse brewers made sure the beer had the right strength. There would still be sugar left in the grain bed. Rather than wasting it by throwing the not-quite spent grain away, brewers would continue to lauter the wort. This lower-gravity wort was fermented separately, but was otherwise treated the same way as the higher-gravity wort, effectively creating a weaker version of the main beer. When made this way, people usually got about twice as much of the strong beer as they did of the small beer.[16]

Precise figures for the alcohol content of typical farmhouse small beer are very hard to find. Twice I have been able to measure the strength of small beer during brewing sessions and found them to be 2.2% and 3.8% ABV.[17] I do not know whether these values are typical, but I assume in the old days the small beer would usually be weaker than this, because farmers needing a safe drink would tend to make as much small beer as possible, and therefore they would probably make it weak. My guess is that traditionally small beer would have been around 1%–2%. Sjur Rørlien thinks that in 1970s Voss it was probably 2%–3%.[18]

Of course, small beer was made mainly because it was necessary to make the most out of the grain. People much preferred the strong beer. From Bornholm in Denmark:

> I was in the kitchen talking with the wife on the farm, when one of the dairy workers came in and asked for some small beer.
>
> "Oh, Munk, can't you go down in the cellar yourself and pour some? I'm busy."
>
> Munk, who was an older hired hand, and a quietly humorous man, said yes, and went down in the cellar. They had just brewed a couple of days before and also brewed good beer. Down in the cellar Munk went quickly over and tapped from the barrel of good beer into a small bucket that held four to five liters. The wife, who just passed by the cellar trap door, noticed that Munk was pouring from the good beer.
>
> "Stop, stop, Munk," she shouted, "take the rest from the big barrel."
>
> "Aaaee, there's no call for that. This here can surely be drunk as it is," replied Munk, "I don't think it needs to be watered down." (Højrup 1966, 60)

Later, once sugar became readily available, it was common to add sugar to the small beer, often to the extent that the small beer ended up stronger than the main beer.[19]

Small beer was drunk as an everyday beverage as long as it was available. In England, Denmark, southern Sweden (Skåne and Småland), and further south, this was not a problem. People had enough grain to make strong beer and also have small beer year-round. In central and northern Sweden, as well as Norway and Finland, there was not enough grain, so other solutions had to be found. The Swedes and the Norwegians approached this in different ways.

In Sweden, most farmers seem to have made only *svagdricka* (literally "weak drink", but in practice small beer), which means that, instead of making one strong and one weak beer from the same mash, they ran off as much wort as possible and produced only weak beer. This meant that they had a weak beer available all year, but it also meant that some farmers could not make strong beer. And in many places they had to use adjuncts to make the malt go further.

In Norway, strong beer was such an important part of farm life that it was inconceivable to go without it. This meant that there was no small beer (*spissøl*) to drink for much of the year, which is when people turned to blande.

There was no hard distinction between small beer from the second runnings and small beer made by just using less malt. And there may have been more than two runnings. In many places it was common to do a third running, so weak that it was just barely fermentable. In parts of Norway it was called *etterrensle* (after runs). The Lithuanians had a system in which the runnings were called *pirmokas* (first), *antrokas* (second), and *trečiokas* (third) or *nakvoselis*.[20]

Rostdrikke

Enterprising housekeepers long ago realized that there was still one more way to get a safe beverage out of the mash, even if there was not enough sugar left to make it alcoholic. After the last of the wort for the small beer had been collected, many farmers added fresh water to the mash, then let it stand overnight. Lactic acid bacteria got to work and turned the mix sour. The next day, the liquid could be collected as a sour beverage. It was not alcoholic but the acid protected it from harmful microbes—yet another way of making something that was safe to drink. Water could be added more than once and the mash would continue to produce sour liquid. In Estonia, this drink was called *taar*, in Norway *rostdrikke*, and in Latvia *patakas*.[21]

This drink was produced on the Estonian islands of Saaremaa and Hiiumaa up until recently. However, many have stopped making it because it requires a separate fermentor because the lactic acid bacteria settle into the wood.[22]

Quite a large volume of drink could be made this way, even if it might not look very tempting to modern eyes: "The lauter tun was often the best milk cow in the byre. It was perhaps not entirely impossible that in the tun some small creatures might develop, but these were less feared than today's microbes."[23]

The same problem was known in Finland. In 1780, Carl Niclas Hellenius wrote about how the Finns made beer. He says that in eastern Finland, which was the poorest part because of its poor soil, the farmers made something they called *rapataari*. They kept the mash for a long time, adding new water whenever they ran off some rapataari. The mash was kept until what came out of the vat no longer had any acid in it. Hellenius did not much like this habit, and went on:

> Who first sees this procedure cannot but feel disgust and horror for it, and will have difficulty convincing himself that here is prepared a drink for human beings. The vessel is left uncovered, presumably so that the contents are not to attract mold and uncleanliness, but therefore it is also besmirched with all the uncleanness which can be found in their dwellings, in which hundreds of larvae of Blatta, Silphae, and Tenebriones find their natural home. Onto this is now ladled the water which when it has run through this sinister mass is to be used for drink. (Hellenius 1780, 16)

This was most likely common practice over a large area. It was never common in areas where there was enough grain to supply the farm with strong and small beer all year round, since there would be no need for it and the small beer must have tasted better.

Of course, the wort coming out of the lauter tun would keep getting weaker as more water was added. Estonian has the expression "like seventh water on a taar" to describe something that is very weak or watery.[24] Housekeepers had found a way to make it last longer by "feeding" the tun. Schøning and Igsi[25] wrote, "One added water as the drink was run off, and also one added bran, potato peel, and so on." By adding suitable kitchen scraps, this acidic drink could be made to last longer. This was an enterprising use of leftovers, and echoes the approach used to make *kvass*, which may have developed from a beverage similar to rostdrikke.

Kvass

Kvass is far and away the most important of these beer-like drinks, but it is also the most confusing. Those who have heard of it generally think of it as "Russian beer from rye bread," but that is not quite right. For one thing, kvass is not beer. For another, kvass can be made from almost anything, such as flour, malt, dried rye bread, beets, fruit, or berries. The key thing is that the liquid sours and is made safe by acid, not alcohol.

To add to the confusion, it has many names. The most common (in Russian, Ukrainian, Belarussian, Polish, and Latvian) is *kvass*, but it is also known as *kisiel* (from "sour") in Slovakian and Polish. In Lithuanian, it is called *gira*, in Estonian *kali*, and in Finnish *kalja*. (Although in Finnish *kalja* can also mean "weak beer.") Historically, it had many more names in various local dialects, and recipes varied dramatically, so keeping track of the many varieties and permutations is very difficult.

There is no clear dividing line between beer and kvass. You can push your kvass recipe in the direction of beer until it is clearly beer, not kvass, but there is no consensus on exactly where the dividing line lies. There is a Russian GOST standard for kvass,[*] which defines kvass as drink with 1.2% ABV or less, "a result of incomplete alcohol and lactic fermentation of wort." When I asked Aleksandr Gromov, he set the limit at 2.0%. Simonova[26] sets the limit at 1.0%. In short, true kvass should be very low in alcohol.

Nobody knows who invented kvass, or when. The first written mention of it is in Nestor's *Primary Chronicle*, compiled in Kiev in the early twelfth century.[†] At that time there was no Russia as we understand it today, and whether it was a Slavic people or some other eastern European ethnicity that invented kvass will probably never be known.

Kvass was, and is, extremely popular in Russia and throughout much of eastern Europe. It was made in every peasant household but also on a larger scale for hospitals, monasteries, army camps, and so on. Today, it is less common for kvass to be made at home, but many people still do. Many large eastern European breweries also produce kvass on an industrial scale. These mass-produced kvass types are usually sweeter and less interesting, and do not follow the traditional processes. It is also quite common for cafés, restaurants, and brewpubs to make their own kvass, which tend to be more interesting and traditional.

During the Soviet period, street vendors selling kvass from tanks pulled by cars were a common sight in cities. The tanks usually had no brand name, just the word "kvass" in big letters. These vendors can still be seen in regional towns; unfortunately, they generally sell industrial kvass.

---

[*] GOST R 52409-2005: 2.3. This was translated for me by Aleksandr Gromov.
[†] The text only mentions kvass by name without saying how it was made, so, in reality, this could equally well be rostdrikke.

Figure 8.3. Industrial production of kvass. Kirov, Russia.

Figure 8.4. Street vendor selling kvass from a tank on a trailer. Yoshkar-Ola, Russia.

The most common form of kvass is made from rye bread, but rye malt, rye flour, wheat bread, potatoes, or really almost anything can be used to make kvass. The main thing is that there should be lactic fermentation, producing carbon dioxide, lactic acid, and a little alcohol. In fact, the very word "kvass" in Russian derives from the same root as the word for pickling, which indicates that acidity was a key part of the concept right from the beginning.[27]

It seems that, originally, the purpose of making kvass was to produce a safe, tasty, nutritious drink made safe by hot water, a little alcohol, and lactic acid. As for ingredients, lots of different types of kitchen leftovers could be used, so the ingredients depended on how well the household was doing. A rich household might use rye malt, honey, or sugar beets, while a poor one might have to rely on stale rye bread and potato peels.

Rostdrikke starts with the spent grains left over from brewing, but kvass is made from scratch. In both cases, kitchen leftovers are an important part of the ingredients. It seems likely that kvass developed from a drink similar to rostdrikke. One indication of this is that in some parts of Lithuania gira meant the same thing as rostdrikke, not kvass.[28] Similarly, in parts of Estonia kali also meant rostdrikke and not kvass.[29]

Classic bread-based kvass is nowadays made from dry rye bread; some will put the bread in the oven first to dry it out completely. The bread is then placed in a vessel and boiling water poured over it. The bread is left in the water for at least three hours but sometimes much longer. One recipe says you should wait until foam appears and the water turns pink. Then, the bread is strained off, some sugar is added, and yeast is pitched at typical farmhouse temperatures. The fermentation should happen somewhere warm. Hop tea is added in some cases. It is very common to bottle the kvass and add a raisin to each bottle. Drying the bread deliberately and adding sugar and raisins, are, of course, all modern innovations that people in the past would not have been able to afford.

Today, bread yeast is usually used to make kvass but, historically, in eastern Europe people maintained two yeast cultures, one for kvass and one for beer. They had to be separate because the kvass should be sour, and the beer should not. A good kvass-maker would have several kvass vessels going at the same time, each with its own culture. The slurry at the bottom would be used to start the next batch. If one of them started to develop bad flavors it would be thrown away. If they all went bad at the same time one could start over and let the kvass ferment spontaneously. Adding fruit could be useful for starting a new culture.[30]

Another approach, which shows up in many old recipe books, was to mix some malt with lots of flour from rye, barley, wheat, buckwheat, or oats. Usually, several types of grain were mixed, usually one type for the flour and another for the malt. The ground malt and flour mix was treated with boiling water to make a thick dough, which was placed in a korchaga (chap. 5, p. 161) and put in a very hot oven for about a day. Once finished in the oven, the korchaga was taken out and the contents mixed with boiling water and left for about four hours before the kvass yeast culture was pitched. It was also very common to add mint.[31]

Temperatures are not given in these old recipes for malt and flour, so it is hard to say exactly what is going on. However, it seems fair to assume that some form of mashing occurred, where the enzymes from the malt worked to some extent on the flour as well. The end result was very likely sour because the kvass culture was used.

The same anonymous source from 1865 cited above ends the kvass recipe by saying that it was possible to make a drink known as *braga* from the same wort. The difference is that hop tea was added to the wort and a beer yeast culture used instead. The result was presumably more alcoholic and less sour. Braga is a drink type that is even more confusing than kvass, but it seems to sit somewhere between kvass and beer. Braga should be about the same strength as beer, be hoppy and slightly acidic, but also sweeter than beer.[32]

The similarity of kvass to Russian farmhouse ales and keptinis should be obvious, but the differences are that kvass has a large proportion of flour or bread and it turns acidic instead of being alcoholic. Bread-based kvass really is based on normal, edible bread, while keptinis is based on the mash being baked in the oven. While kvass and oven-baked beers (chap. 5, p. 162) may seem similar, these really are very different beverages.

Many more variations exist. For example, potatoes can be used as the starch source instead; beetroots, apples, and other ingredients are also common. Even horseradish has been used. In industrial production, and also in some modern homebrewed versions, it is common to add lemon juice to provide acidity.

In Finland, it was very common to make a weak beverage from rye flour with a certain proportion of rye malt, which, in parts of eastern Finland, was heated in the oven. It was very similar to the Russian malt-flour kvass described above. This Finnish drink was usually known as *kalja*; in eastern Finland, the word was *vaasa*, clearly a Finnish version of the Russian word "kvass."[33] Today, this drink is generally known as *kotikalja* (lit. "home kalja") and is very common. Kotikalja kits can be bought in most shops, and kotikalja is often served in work canteens, at gas stations, and low-end restaurants. Kotikalja is very similar to bosa and the Swedish flour-based drink described earlier, which shows how these types of drink tend to overlap with one another.

Kvass was also made in Sweden, where it was known as *bröddricka* (lit. "bread drink"). It is not clear how widespread it was, but many farms on the island of Öland made bröddricka and were still doing so in 1935.[34] It was a way to make use of stale rye bread, and people thought it was the best drink one could get on a farm in terms of taste and nutrition. The recipe was very similar to the first kvass recipe given above.

Given how hard it was to make a large volume of something safe to drink, one has to wonder why kvass only existed in northeast of Europe. One plausible reason is that the rest of the rye bread area produced enough grain for beer to be the daily drink. Meanwhile, areas north of that and further west, like Norway and western Sweden, probably mostly did not have enough suitable kitchen leftovers because people there ate crispbread, which does not stale. Very likely bröddricka was limited to those parts of Sweden where rye bread was the standard form of bread. In Norway there was no tradition of rye bread, but in the northernmost parts of Norway people bought rye from the Russians or Finns and some made kvass from it. Unfortunately, no details survive.[35]

Figure 8.5. Finnish commercial kotikalja kit, enough for three three-liter batches of kalja.

Birch Sap Beer

In spring, in spring
The knight leads his darling home!
In spring there's birch sap
No need for beer.

—**Latvian folk song,** Bielenstein, *Die Holzbauten und Holzgeräte der Letten* (1918)

Drawing sap from birch, and to some extent from maple, was a traditional practice in most of northern and eastern Europe. In some areas it was used as an emergency source of food and drink, while in other places it was a fixed part of life's annual rhythm. Given how hard it was to produce safe beverages, it is not surprising that people used birch sap, which is so readily available. In this case, it is the tree's immune system that makes the drink safe.

The tradition has died out in northern Europe, where tree sap is now only used by a few enthusiasts. In eastern Europe this tradition was very strong, to the point where March or April in many countries was known as "the month of birches."

Figure 8.6. Tapping birch sap.

Bielenstein[36] called birch sap "the third national drink" in Latvia, after beer and mead. In the Baltic states, Russia, Belarus, and Ukraine the tradition is still very much alive, with tree sap widely used both privately and commercially. Belarussian authorities estimate that 25 million liters of birch sap were produced in 2011.[37] Spring, when the snow has melted but before the trees start budding, is the time to collect sap. In the north, people mostly used birch (*Betula pendula* and *Betula pubescens*) since birch trees are much more common there. Maple (*Acer platanoides* and *Acer pseudoplatanus*) has sweeter sap. In Lithuania, people tap the maples first and only tap the birches when the maples run out.[38]

In the old days, the most common method of drawing sap was to bore a hole about 50–90 cm above ground and 7–8 cm into the tree. An account from Kråksmåla, southern Sweden, describes how a stick with a groove carved along the top was stuck in the hole so that the sap ran along the groove and collected in a bucket under the tree.[39] In some places, more sophisticated wooden tubes were made by hollowing out the wood with a red-hot knitting needle.[40] Laying a cloth over the bucket prevented dirt from getting into it. Another method was to cut a slanted groove through the bark all the way into the wood and then set a furrow made from folded birch bark into the groove. The sap then ran along the furrow.[41] In eastern Europe today, it is common to use furrows made of thin sheet metal.[42]

It is best to choose big birches for tapping. In some places, people preferred trees with hanging crowns, some distance away from running water.[43] A birch can produce anything from 0.5 to 10 liters of sap a day, while well-chosen maples produce 3–5 liters. As long as only one hole is bored in each tree, the tree is not harmed, although it is necessary to close up the hole with a wooden plug when finished.

Fresh birch sap is lightly sweet (specific gravity 1.002 to 1.003) and pleasant tasting, but does not have very much flavor.[44] It was drunk immediately as a replacement for water and as a welcome rare source of sugar. Children especially liked to tap birch, although they were not always allowed to for fear of harming the trees.

Once collected, the sap goes sour within a few days, even in a refrigerator.[45] Traditional practice in Latvia was to collect the sap in wooden barrels and let it sour naturally there for at least eight days before drinking.[46] Raw sap could be botted with herbs or spices (stalks of blackcurrant, orange or lemon peel, and cloves) and a little sugar with some raisins. It was necessary to use strong bottles because it fermented spontaneously. When it was served, one could add a little sugar to make the drink foam up "like champagne."[47] These recipes were typically used by townspeople and the relatively wealthy.

Another method was to boil the sap. This reportedly brought out the resinous character and gave the sap more flavor. In Kråksmåla, older folk said it had to be boiled because "it has the winter cold in it, and will make us feel cold when we drink it." They boiled it with sweet gale, removing the foam, and then poured the liquid through a sieve to remove the sweet gale. Beer yeast was added, and the liquid lightly fermented for 24 hours. The result was said to be like third runnings beer, but better.[48] Some used hops instead of sweet gale.[49]

Instead of boiling it, the birch sap could be used as mash liquor in place of a juniper infusion. This added a little flavor to the beer and also some sugar. The beer would then be brewed in the normal way.[50] Used this way, the birch sap is said to add resin-like flavors, and often a light acidity, which I have also found from personal experience.[51]

A third way to use sap is to boil off most of the water, reducing it to a syrup. This syrup is very sweet and strong in flavor. In this form, it is much easier to store and add to beers or other drinks. About 80–90 liters of birch sap is needed to make 1 liter of syrup;[52] for maple sap about 40 liters is needed. Concentrating the syrup by boiling is very energy intensive. Nowadays, reverse osmosis can be a cheaper alternative.[53]

Several modern craft brewers have used birch sap, usually boiled down, in their beer. In Estonia, Tanker Brewery's Sauna Session has become very popular. The sap adds an herbal, spicy tang.

Juniper Berry Beer

At the very least, in Norway, Sweden, Denmark, Finland, Estonia and Poland, people have traditionally made a fermented beverage from juniper berries.[54] The same drink is called *smreka* in Bosnia and *hardic* in Albania. It is very likely that some form of juniper berry drink has also been made in the rest of northern and eastern Europe where there was enough juniper.

Juniper berry beer was a very common beverage in Sweden and Norway. In Sweden, it was even produced commercially, just like it is in Poland today. It was produced in large quantities in some areas of Sweden. Carl Wiking from Kråksmåla, Sweden reported that his father had the women workers pick 400 liters of juniper berries per year.[55] That sounds incredible, but Wiking said a skilled woman could pick over 70 liters a day, which means it is about six woman-days of work.

Juniper berry beer may sound like an awkward beverage to make given how labor-intensive it is to pick the berries, but compared with beer it actually did not require that much effort. One day of effort to pick enough berries to make hundreds of liters compared favorably with the effort to make the malt needed for the same volume of beer. The plowing and sowing of grain alone required terrible effort, and then there was the harvest, threshing, drying, and finally malting. It is not surprising that people made so much juniper berry beer.

Figure 8.7. A sprig of juniper with both mature (blue) and immature (green) berries.

It seems that, before sugar became readily available, the drink really was based on juniper berries as the sole fermentable. Mature berries contain 30%–40% sugar, mostly glucose and fructose, which makes it possible to produce a fermented beverage, if one is willing to go through the tedium of processing the berries.[56]

The berries were collected in autumn after they had matured. Juniper berries have a two-year cycle: the first year they are green, and the next year they mature and turn blue. Green berries were sometimes included in the harvest.[57] The berries were collected in a cloth or other container, either by beating them off the branch with a stick or putting on mittens or gloves and rubbing them off.[58] Either way, they had to be shaken in a coarse sieve so that the dirt would fall off. Any bits of branches that came along floated on top of the berries, where they could be removed by hand. Many people slowly dropped the berries onto a cloth on a windy day so that the debris blew away.

Most people dried the berries, using the oven after baking bread, for example, or in the sun or a warm, dry room such as a loft. The drying seems to have been necessary so that the berries would keep and could be ground with the same quern used for malt. The quern had to be adjusted so that the kernels of the berries were not broken, otherwise the beer would be bitter. People who used the berries right away, mashing them with a round stone or a pestle, did not need to dry them first.

Just as with the real farmhouse beer, there were several brewing processes. The simplest was to put the crushed berries in cold water and let them stand for a while; some even let it stand overnight. The resulting liquid was put through a sieve, with a few people adding hop tea. Finally, the liquid had to be heated to pitching temperature (probably body temperature) and the yeast pitched.[59] One source added: "There was enough sweetness in the berries that it fermented."[60]

How many berries were used to produce a certain volume of drink seems to have varied significantly, ranging from 0.05 liters of berries for 1 liter of beverage, up to 0.1 or even 0.19 liters of berries.[61] The source citing 0.19 liters said the infusion was reduced somewhat by boiling. One account even claimed they got the same number of liters of drink as there were liters of berries to begin with, which is hard to believe.[62] With all of these, it is very difficult to estimate the strength of the drink, but, in theory, any strength was possible simply by reducing the infusion through boiling.

Some people boiled the berries instead, then strained the mixture through a sieve before cooling the liquid and pitching the yeast.[63] Another variation was to soak the berries in cold water, strain, and then boil the liquid.[64] What effect this had on the flavor is impossible to say.

Later, when sugar became available, people found they could make much the same drink without having to go through all the trouble of picking, sieving, drying, and crushing the berries. Instead, they could use sugar or syrup as the main fermentable and use juniper branches, with or without the berries, for flavoring. Some people continued using berries but added sugar in order to get a greater volume of beverage from the same amount of berries. These methods are more recent, which means we have actual recipes to work with.

The basic approach with juniper branches seems to be to boil the branches, possibly letting them steep for a while, strain the liquid off, stir in the sugar, cool, and then pitch the yeast. Boiling can be stopped after 10 minutes "once it boils properly," or after an hour. If desired, the branches can then be steeped in the hot water for 20 minutes, or even overnight. The amount of juniper is either "two shopping bags" for 10 liters of water, or "like a big bouquet of flowers" for 30 liters; 50–100 grams of sugar is added per liter of water.[65]

Figure 8.8. Women harvesting juniper berries. Sweden, early twentieth century. Photo by Nils Keyland. Reproduced by permission of the Nordic Museum.

What juniper berry beer tastes like I don't know. Just as with birch sap, people would sometimes boil the extract from the berries to concentrate it and make a juniper syrup. This type of syrup is still produced commercially today in Estonia.

Figure 8.9. Bottled juniper syrup, Pihtla, Saaremaa, Estonia.

Mead

Humans have a long history of using honey, of which I can only give the briefest of summaries here. Much of this was taken from Eva Crane's *World History of Beekeeping and Honey Hunting.*[66]

Our hominid ancestors collected honey and chimpanzees still do. All over the world where there are honey-producing insects, humans have collected their honey. In Africa, this has been going on long enough that a species of bird has evolved, the greater honeyguide (*Indicator indicator*), that guides humans to beehives in return for eating the leftovers. In large parts of the world, collecting honey is celebrated in rock paintings, many of them very old.

In many parts of the world, people who scavenge honey simply eat the honey, wax, and the brood from the hive, but in Africa the main use of honey is for the production of mead. Since wild yeast is naturally found in honey, all that is strictly necessary to make mead is to dilute the honey with water. It follows that mead must be a very old drink and very likely the oldest alcoholic drink.

Figure 8.10. Male greater honeyguide (*Indicator indicator*). Illustration by Nicolas Huet the Younger, 1838.

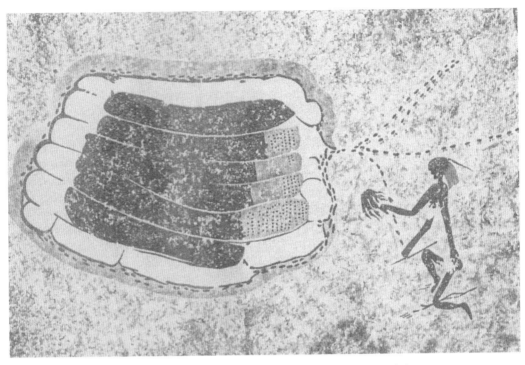

Figure 8.11. A rock painting of collecting honey with smoke from Toghwana Dam, Zimbabwe.

Honey was generally regarded as very important by traditional societies, and many had laws or customs that regulated the ownership and marking of and the right to honey from beehives. With the rise of agriculture, the human population density increased and deforestation reduced the number of suitable nesting sites, which caused people to start creating dedicated sites for beehives. Gradually, this developed into deliberate beekeeping.

The production of honey was always limited and, since it was one of very few available sources of sugar, honey was also very highly prized. Until the eighteenth century, beekeeping was only possible in the north up to a line that ran south of Norway and through southern Sweden. North of this line honey had to be imported and was therefore even more expensive, so much so that only the wealthiest could afford it.[67]

As a rule, only farmers who kept bees could afford to make mead, but some might collect honey from wild bees, and the wealthiest farmers might buy honey to make mead. The traditional way to keep bees was to maintain several hives and let them divide up as they wanted. Each autumn, the oldest and least productive hives were selected for "slaughter" and the honey taken.[68] The more modern type of beehive from which honey can be collected without killing the bees was introduced in Scandinavia in the late nineteenth century, but, even so, the older type seems to have persisted in the region for a long time.

Since honey was so valuable, it was generally sold. However, some honey remained on the wax combs and this was usually what was used to make mead. This approach was common in Norway, Sweden, Denmark, and Wales. Only very rich farmers could afford to use their own refined honey or buy honey for making mead. One way to get the honey out was to melt the wax combs in a kettle and then let them solidify. The wax would rise to form the top layer and could be removed. Another way was to dissolve the honey in hot water, remove the combs, and brew with the water.

The simplest way to make mead was to simply let the honey dissolve over a few days in cold water. The liquid was then moved into another vessel where it spontaneously fermented. Fourteen days later the mead was ready to drink.[69] The most common method, however, was to dissolve the honey of the combs in warm water as just described, then boil the honey and water while removing the foam. If herbal additives like hops were used, these would be in a bag during the boil. Finally, it was fermented.

Most farmers originally could not afford to use any herbs or spices in their honey, but in more recent times some could. Apart from hops, ginger and cinnamon were common, while cloves, cardamom, coriander, and sage were also used.

Figure 8.12. An old style of beehive in Rumšiskes museum, Lithuania.

Sugar Beer

By the early twentieth century, many farmers had switched from growing grain to feed their families to growing cash crops for sale. This meant there was little or no grain for brewing, but it did give them money to spend. At around the same time it became possible to buy sugar, which was a fermentable alternative to malt. This led people in many areas to switch from brewing beer to making a simple kind of fermented beverage from sugar, herbs, and spices. In Norway, Sweden, and Poland, the flavoring agent was usually juniper and sometimes hops. In Norway, it was often called "sugar beer" or "syrup beer." Spice and sugar mixes for this type of beer also came on the market around this time.

These brews are actually still quite common today and many families make them, especially for Christmas. It is quite common to serve it to children in the belief that it is alcohol-free. Discussing it with people who make it, I have several times been met with disbelief when I tell them that of course it contains alcohol. Usually they go silent when I ask them what they think happens when they add sugar and yeast and it starts bubbling.

Similar drinks are documented in early twentieth century Belgium and France.[70] It is very possible that these are also farmhouse ales that have degenerated into simple spiced "sugar beer."

9

STYLES AND HOW TO BREW THEM

"Well," says Saakvitne, "one thing is to brew good beer; quite another is to give a recipe for it. Such things cannot be taught in words. You have to take part in the brewing and see for yourself. And many will not learn even then. Some brew all their lives and never make good beer. But if one has the skill, and patience to keep trying, then there can be guidance in a recipe."

—**Hans Saakvitne**, 1898,
quoted in *Hardanger Sogelag Årsbok* (1984)

Brewing Like a Farmer

Farmhouse brewers have a different attitude compared to modern brewers. The recent buzz around farmhouse brewing has caused Stjørdalen brewer Jørund Geving to get to know some modern homebrewers and their way of thinking. As a result, he has taken to calling the most extreme of them "millimeter brewers," people who need to have every number exactly right.[1] That is an approach that puzzles him.

If you are brewing on an industrial scale obsessing over the numbers makes sense, but in home-brewing it definitely does not. And the figures are often less precise than you think anyway. As Norwegian brewer Gahr Smith Gahrsen says, "If you don't like the mash temperature, just move the thermometer a bit." And he is a commercial brewer! Because, as Gahr notes, the temperature varies somewhat throughout the mash.

It is fine to make measurements when brewing farmhouse ale, but do not obsess over hitting the exact numbers in these recipes. In Morgedal, I brewed with Halvor Bjåland and Terje Haugen. They are farmhouse brewers but follow modern brewing in that they keep a brewing log for every brew. When they were boiling the wort, I saw Terje take three handfuls of hops and drop them in the wort at roughly the prescribed time, then note in the log "13:15 added 25g hops." When I pointed out that he did not actually weigh the hops Terje just shrugged and laughed, saying it was "close enough." [2] And it probably was, because their beer is always excellent.

When brewing farmhouse ale, a good tip is to take a deep breath, lower your shoulders, and relax a bit. Try to forget all the things you think you know and instead let the tradition guide you. Feel free to take the numbers seriously, but allow yourself some latitude.

Before we start on the actual styles and recipes let's talk a little about how to approach the general differences between farmhouse brewing and modern brewing. The advice applies to most of the recipes that appear in this chapter.

Carbonation

All of the farmhouse beers we will describe have one thing in common: the carbonation level should be very low by modern standards. The carbonation in British cask ale is a very close equivalent. In fact, treating and serving these beers as though they were British cask ale is probably the best way to serve them in modern pubs.

Some breweries have tried to brew these beers with low carbonation and have found that bars and drinkers assume there is something wrong with the beer. Exactly how this plays out will vary with local expectations, but if the carbonation is as low as it ought to be, then the more the bar staff understands about the beer and the more opportunity they have for explaining the beer to the customer, the better the odds that the customer gets a good experience.

No guidelines for carbonation are given in the recipes that follow, because the normal approach of farmhouse brewers is to just rack the beer, store it in a cool place, and then serve it. The beer may be moved to a warm place before serving to build up a little carbonation, or it may be allowed to just start fermenting gently as it is being served (see the section on carbonation in chap. 6). Adding priming sugar or yeast to increase carbonation is completely alien to the tradition, although for commercial brewers it may be a necessary compromise in order to be able to sell the beer.

Working with Kveik

People who brew with kveik for the first time often treat it the same way they do any other yeast and are then disappointed when they do not get any unusual flavors. For best results, kveik should be treated in a way that would stress normal brewer's yeast. That said, kveik strains are quite different from one another even though they all belong to the same family, so it is important to know how to handle the specific yeast you are using. Also bear in mind that kveik is quite different from other farmhouse yeasts, so what works with kveik does not necessarily work with, say, Lithuanian yeast cultures. See the section on other farmhouse yeasts below.

It is perhaps best to think of kveik as a highly aromatic ale yeast that makes tropical fruit flavors. You can make use of those or, through careful use, you can dial down the kveik flavor to get a profile closer to that of normal ale yeast.

Many people think of kveik as a saison-like yeast because it is a farmhouse yeast, but the flavor profiles are very different. Kveik belongs to the Beer 1 group, along with normal top-fermenting yeast, whereas saison yeasts are in Beer 2 (this is discussed in more detail in chap. 4). The non-kveik farmhouse yeasts are a better fit for saison and Belgian-style beers because they are more often POF[+].

Kveik can be used in many different kinds of beer, but the main ways people tend to use them is either to recreate traditional farmhouse beer or to make well-known styles like porter or IPA. The point of using kveik to ferment ordinary beers is that it ferments more rapidly, plus, you do not need temperature control even in summer and you get a drinkable beer much more quickly. Plus, the beer has a different flavor profile and mouthfeel.

Kveik can work very well in both IPA and NEIPA because the tropical fruit flavors from the kveik complements the hop flavors. The kveik also tends to produce a softer and rounder mouthfeel, which can take some of the bite out of the hop profile.

If you are using kveik in a traditional beer, or in a beer where you want the yeast profile to be clearly discernible, do not use lots of modern, super aromatic hops. The hops will drown all other flavors and you will have a hard time picking out the flavor of the kveik through all the hoppiness.

Kveik is less sensitive to pitching temperature than most other yeasts, so the time required for fermentation and the aroma profile remain relatively unaffected even if the pitching temperature changes quite a lot. However, there does appear to be a threshold around 18–20°C below which many kveik strains produce a more subdued aroma.[3] Unlike other yeast, kveik do not produce fusels or other off-flavors at the high end of their temperature range. It is recommended to use the pitching temperature given in table 4.1 (p. 108).

For homebrewers who have no means to control the fermentation temperature, if the temperature in the room where fermentation takes place is low, it is common to cover the fermentor with a blanket or something like that to keep the temperature up. If you have a heated bathroom floor, placing the fermentor on it may work well.

The best way to adjust how much aroma you get from kveik is the size of the initial pitch. Norwegian brewers usually pitch very little yeast compared to the volume they ferment. Sigurd Johan Saure says his family would usually pitch 3–5 flakes of dried yeast for 120 liters of quite strong beer.[4] Other brewers seem to have been less extreme, but in general it seems that you should underpitch.

For a wort with an original gravity of 1.060–1.080, a good pitching rate is 1–2 million cells per milliliter.[5] That is equivalent to roughly a tablespoon of yeast slurry for 25 liters of beer at 7%–8% ABV. In dried form kveik has roughly 10–15 billion cells per gram, so 2–3 grams of dried kveik is enough for a 25 liter brew. Even though this rate would be considered massive underpitching for normal brewer's yeast, kveik does not produce off-flavors when treated this way. Instead, underpitching makes the yeast produce more aroma.

For pitching at these rates to work well, it is important to ensure the yeast has enough oxygen. Farmhouse brewers pour the cooled wort into the fermentor from waist height with lots of splashing, which is sufficient for aeration. In technical terms, this translates to roughly 5–8 ppm of oxygen. Most farmhouse brewers use open fermentors; in a closed fermentor 10–12 ppm of oxygen may be safer.[6]

When farmhouse brewers make yeast starters they usually use the first runnings, which is the strongest. And, in general, their beers are very strong. Probably because of this, kveik strains seem to need a lot of nutrients.[7] If you try to make a weaker beer, that is, with an OG below 1.050, you may find that the kveik ferments slowly and that you get low attenuation. With cider and mead you may find that it barely ferments at all. This can be solved by adding a good amount of yeast nutrient.

One practical benefit of kveik is that it ferments faster than other yeast strains. Exactly how fast varies both with the specific strain/culture and with yeast health, but complete fermentation of a 6%–8% ABV beer in 36 hours or less is not unusual. In Dyrvedalen in Voss, fermenting a 10%–12% beer in three to four days was, and still is, the norm. There have been cases of modern homebrewers posting on the internet that their kveik seems to be dead. Then, when they measure the FG of the starter it turns out the kveik started and finished propagating while they were asleep, so quick that they never saw the foam layer cover the surface at all.

Another benefit is that beer fermented with kveik has little need for maturation, so the beer really can be drunk 48 hours after pitching. Some brewers think the beer is at its best then, while others think it is best after a week or two. The reason seems to be that not much is produced in the way of off-flavors like diacetyl, so the yeast does not need much time to clean up afterward. It is perfectly possible to release a commercial kveik beer one week after pitching and some commercial breweries have done just that. Note that this also applies when fermenting cider. I have been able to make fine cider with kveik in 10 days.

While beers brewed with kveik can be cellared for years without producing off-flavors, the fruity flavors tend to disappear after some months. It is possible that the yeast is metabolizing the esters. Flavors produced by kveik that has been purified in a laboratory seem stronger and last longer, so probably the original cultures have contaminants that consume esters faster.

Commercial brewers are often wary of using kveik because they are worried about cross contamination from the kveik in their brewery. In practice, this is not a concern with kveik. Kveik is not phenolic, does not produce barnyard aromas, and is not diastatic. So if an infection does happen you are unlikely to notice, because kveik is so similar to normal yeast. If you do get a cross-infection with kveik, the main way you are likely to notice is that the supposedly non-kveik beer suddenly starts fermenting after just four hours.

Kveik, especially if an original mixed culture, tends to flocculate very rapidly and then stick to the bottom of the vessel. In many cases, the kveik will flocculate out of the liquid within a few minutes as you watch. This great propensity to flocculate is probably because kveik has been put under tremendous evolutionary pressure to flocculate. Yeasts that were not highly flocculant were not harvested and died out. This highly flocculant character is positive in the sense that it tends to produce a clear beer with no yeasty off-flavor, but the downside is that sometimes the kveik flocculates out of the beer before fermentation is complete. In these instances, rousing it again can be tricky. This behaviour can also make it difficult to carbonate the beer in secondary fermentation because the kveik just sticks to the bottom of the bottles or vessels and refuses to ferment. One way to solve this is to add additional yeast for conditioning, either kveik or your usual conditioning yeast.

Kveik can be propagated just like ordinary brewer's yeast. But, since it grows more rapidly, kveik usually benefits from shorter propagation times.

As for what kveik strain or culture to use, there is no lack of alternatives. The kveik yeasts sold by commercial labs are usually sold as single strains, but sometimes as mixed strains. Some labs try to keep all of the strains in the cultures they sell to stay as close to the original mixed culture as possible. The benefit of commercially sold kveik is that it is very unlikely to be infected, whereas you can never be sure with cultures shared by homebrewers. The downside is that commercial kveik cultures are not necessarily the same as the original ones and thus may produce different flavors.

How much the difference between single-strain cultures and the original farmhouse kveik matters varies. Sigmund's kveik contains strains that are so similar there is little difference between a single strain and the entire culture. Northern kveik cultures consist of a very complex set of strains, so here the situation may be more complicated, although no systematic research has been done on it.

If you brew with kveik, it is of course possible to keep reusing it in the same way the farmhouse brewers do. The problem is keeping the culture free of infections and unwanted mutations. As traditional kveik brewers have shown, this is definitely possible with careful management of the culture, even without any equipment more sophisticated than a piece of wood. Managing a mixed culture, however, is more challenging than a single strain. In a mixed culture, the exact composition of the culture matters. Even without infections and mutations, you may see unwanted effects if the relative proportions of each strain change over time. You may end up with a culture that contains less of your preferred strains and more of strains you are not so happy with.

For best results, it is recommended you harvest the kveik for reuse at the same time and from the same place as the original owner (see table 4.1, p. 108). Yeast that is used to top-cropping will usually form a thick creamy layer on the surface of the wort toward the end of fermentation. This layer tends to drop out before too long so it is important not to harvest too late. Similarly, bottom-cropping yeast tends to drop out of suspension and stick to the bottom of the vessel. For example, if you have a yeast that is usually harvested from the surface of the fermenting wort after 40 hours, whereas you collect it from the bottom two weeks later, you may change which strains are dominant in the culture. Within a batch or two you may have a culture that no longer flocculates well, because now the non-flocculant strains have become much more prevalent. When this happens, you also risk promoting strains that have poor attenuation, resulting in a yeast culture that takes much longer to attenuate the beer, if it attenuates at all.

Once the yeast has been harvested, there are two main ways to preserve it. The easiest is to simply keep the unwashed slurry in a glass in your fridge. Keep the container closed but not sealed, because the kveik may continue to ferment. The yeast will keep this way for one to two years without any problems.* However, it may continue to ferment in your fridge. Beware of bottles and glasses being forced open by the pressure. If the yeast is older than six months it is best to make a starter, otherwise you may get poor attenuation.

---

* This is my personal experience with #1 Sigmund, #7 Granvin, and "#16 Simonaitis" as listed in table 4.1, 108.

The best way to preserve farmhouse yeast, at least for kveik, is to dry it and then store it in the freezer. Smear the yeast slurry on baking parchment with some layers of tissue paper underneath to soak up moisture. Try to decant as much liquid as possible beforehand. Then, either leave it in a clean room for several days or put it in an oven set to 30°C overnight, with the oven blowing warm air and something placed in the door to hold it slightly ajar. Once the slurry has dried to a hard crust, simply crumple the paper so that the crust breaks up into flakes. Put the flakes into a resealable plastic bag and store in the freezer.

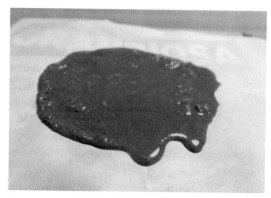

Figure 9.1. Kveik on baking parchment, ready to be dried. Rælingen, Norway.

Dried yeast will keep a long time when stored in the freezer. When the kveik buzz started in 2016, Sigurd Johan Saure retrieved dried yeast that was put in his freezer in 2001 and dropped it into a starter on his magnetic stirrer. The yeast grew with no problems at all.[8] An extreme example is Aave Nystein of Stathelle, Norway. He put kveik in the freezer in 1997 and retrieved it in 2017 to see if it could be revived. I was puzzled to receive an envelope containing what seemed to be a small balloon with yeast sludge. I asked Aave, who said he had taken out the frozen flakes from the freezer, vacuum-packed them in their original unopened bag, then stuffed it all in an envelope.[9] The envelope was flat when he mailed it but somehow the 20-year-old kveik found enough liquid and sugar to start fermenting while in the mail.

Dried and frozen kveik can be revived simply by thawing it then dropping it into wort at pitching temperature. Jarle Nupen[10] was taught that he should drop the kveik still frozen into the wort, but as far as I know he is the only one to do that.

If you want to keep using a specific kveik yeast for a long period it is important to keep backup cultures. That way, if you have an infection or the yeast changes, you can go back and begin again. This is basically a primitive version of Hansen's method described in chapter 4 (p. 93). It is also a good idea to label the different generations clearly with the batch they come from, and to reuse mostly the ones that give the best beer. This way you can "breed" the yeast to evolve in the direction you want. Since so little kveik is needed for pitching, yeast from a single batch can be enough for many brews. Because contamination generally develops slowly, this is also a way to keep the problem under control.

You can, of course, give the yeast to other people so that they will help you keep it alive, but this method is not foolproof. People often forget which yeast is which, so you do not necessarily know what it is you are getting back. And not everyone can be trusted to keep a yeast culture free from infection.

Working with Non-Kveik Farmhouse Yeast

To date, most of the interest in farmhouse yeast has focused on kveik. Because of this, we do not know nearly as much about the other farmhouse yeasts from Lithuania, Latvia, and Russia. These strains seem to be closer to Belgian yeast strains than kveik in terms of flavor, but they too seem to be quite unique.

As with kveik, it is a good idea to use these farmhouse yeasts the same way the original owner does (*see* table 4.1, p. 108). These farmhouse yeasts also tend to ferment more quickly and at higher temperatures than ordinary brewer's yeast.

The same rules about reusing that apply to kveik also apply here. The one exception is that many of these farmhouse yeasts cannot handle drying; refer to table 4.1 to see which strains can and cannot be dried. Therefore, if you want to freeze non-kveik farmhouse yeasts, you will probably need to freeze them in liquid form with about 15% glycerol. Be aware that glycerol acts as an antifreeze when mixed with water, so if you use too much glycerol you may find that your freezer is not cold enough to freeze the mix. Even if it does not freeze, however, cooling should still have a strong preservative effect.

Brewing with Juniper

Juniper is a bit tricky as an ingredient because it is far less standardized than hops, so knowing exactly what it will do in your beer is harder to judge. Still, it is possible to give some guidance. We will start with *Juniperus communis*, then discuss alternatives for people who do not have access to this species of juniper.

In many countries, juniper is easy to find in the forest. It likes sunlight and some protection from the wind, so it is often found on south-facing hillsides, and on little hillocks in forest clearings. It is best to pick green, healthy juniper branches. Beyond that, there are a few choices. The branches with berries are more aromatic than those without. There is also a clear difference in flavor between thin twigs and the wood of thicker branches. Many farmhouse brewers consider branches to be "thick" when they are thicker than a finger.

Once you have picked the juniper, you now get to choose how to treat it. Branches can be boiled, steeped in hot water, or used in the filter. The last option imparts less flavor than using a juniper infusion as brewing liquor.

Boiling juniper branches extracts more bitterness, and if you use too much juniper, especially thicker branches, you can get a sharp, solvent-like flavor that is quite unpleasant. It tastes somewhat similar to a cleaning agent—the first two times I brewed and got this flavor, I thought I had not rinsed off the cleaning solution properly. In my experience, if the infusion is boiled for an hour, 115 grams of branches per liter of water is enough to produce this flavor. This flavor seems to be much less of a problem when only green twigs are used.

Steeping juniper branches at 80–90°C for 2–3 hours seems to be best to get an infusion with a distinct, fresh juniper flavor. For quantities, 100 grams of branches per liter of infusion seems about right, but beware that the thicker wood is much denser than the thin twigs with needles, so weight is a less reliable guide than it might seem. If you boil the infusion it will extract more bitterness, so be careful when using thick branches; in this case, 50 grams per liter is probably more appropriate. The juniper infusion will get darker when boiled, turning first golden, then brown in color.

It has been said that North American *Juniperus communis* has less flavor than European versions.[11] I have not been able to compare them personally, so I do not know. However, many countries do not have *Juniperus communis* at all, which makes it harder to brew authentic versions of some farmhouse styles. According to Laitinen, the flavor extracted from juniper berries might serve as a possible substitute even though this flavor is somewhat different.[12] According to Pekka Kääriäinen, juniper wood chips are a good substitute, if you are able to get hold of them.

Figure 9.2. Making a juniper infusion with a modern homebrewing setup. Oslo, Norway.

There are also other plants in the genus *Juniperus* that can be used. In the US, by far the most common substitute seems to be eastern red cedar, *Juniperus virginiana*. I have had one beer made with it and it had a strong and very interesting flavor: floral, woody, and citrusy. It is not like common juniper but is still an interesting and useful ingredient. According to DeWayne Schaaf, branches have a stronger flavor the older they get. Schaaf recommends one to two older branches (50 cm in length) for 20 liters, or three younger branches (50 cm in length).[13] People have also reported success with *Juniperus scopulorum*, *Juniperus californica*, and *Juniperus oxycedrus*, but the use of these species seems to be less common.[14]

Making Your Own Malt

If you want to try making your own malt, an easy way to steep the grain is to put it into some kind of watertight tub and use a garden hose to fill it with water. Keep the water running into the tub for two to three days, or, if that is too extravagant, replace the water two to three times a day. Check the grain periodically to see how it is progressing. The kernels should be wet through but not completely or otherwise they will drown; there should be a small dry spot left in the middle. Split a few grains to keep an eye on this.

To germinate the moistened grain any level surface will do, but the grain needs to be kept somewhat warm. Several sources claim that it should not get too warm, which they say is above 20–21°C.[15] You can use an ordinary garden rake to turn the grain.

Once the shoot is two-thirds the length of the grain itself it is time to dry the malt. To make extremely pale malt at home, all you need is a cloth for sun-drying the malt so you can fold up the malt and take it indoors in the evening. If you want to be more advanced, a simple wooden frame to place the cloth on will make things easier. Alternatively, the floor of some well-heated and well-ventilated room can be used. Be sure to spread the green malt out thinly. The biggest problem is birds and mice, which will have to be kept away somehow. Another way to produce the same pale malt flavor is to make a wooden frame with a fine-mesh screen in the bottom and raise it off the floor. Then use a hot air fan underneath to blow the moisture away. This setup will also make it harder for vermin to get into the malt.

The easiest way to make heavily smoked malt is to build a Stjørdal-style såinn with concrete masonry units and a wooden frame on top (*see* chap. 3, p. 71). You need to be very careful to prevent it from catching fire, so you must include a stone spark catcher around the fireplace. Expect drying to take 15–28 hours, which can mean sleep will be a problem. Drying can be done faster with more heat but increases the risk of fire and of destroying the enzymes in the malt.

When using a såinn, it is necessary to have a relatively hot fire at the beginning in order to heat up the masonry and the malt, as well as to replace heat lost to evaporation while the malt is still very moist. The heat is also important in order to stop the grain from germinating further and consuming more of the sugars. Once everything has heated up, the kiln will maintain a relatively stable temperature for a long time even without a fire. This means the fire can be reduced later. Jørund

Geving reports the kiln he uses only loses 5°C of heat during the night,[16] which means you may be able to catch some sleep once the kiln is properly heated.

In Stjørdal, maltsters use well-dried alder that has been chopped into small pieces to make it easier to keep an even fire that is not too hot and has a good flow of air through it. The malt aroma will be affected not just by the species of wood you use, but also how well it has been dried, how it has been chopped, what kind of tree you choose, and how you control the fire itself.

For oven drying, you can use an ordinary kitchen stove set to, for example, 50°C and blowing warm air. This should be enough to dry the malt overnight, producing a very pale malt. It will not, however, give you something like the Chuvashian malt. For that, you will need a higher initial temperature, something closer to the mash temperature or perhaps even a little higher, but this requires care so that the malt enzymes are not damaged. How high you can go will depend on the grain variety, as different types of grain have different levels of heat tolerance. Note that evaporation from the moist grain will consume a good bit of heat, so the grain will be somewhat cooler than the air in the oven. A kitchen stove has limited capacity, so you need to take care not to try to malt too much grain in one go.

What is Farmhouse Ale?

Styles in Farmhouse Brewing

Farmhouse brewing does not really have defined styles in the way that commercial brewing does. For commercial beers, the style is a tag on the product that tells the customer what to expect. When someone comes across a beer they have never tried before, seeing "IPA," "Pilsner," or "porter" gives them enough of an idea to make a choice.

In farmhouse brewing, knowing the style was never an issue. If you visited a farm, they had one beer and it was their obligation as hosts to serve you that beer, and your obligation as a guest to drink it. There was no use for style names.

To the extent that these beers had names, it was to distinguish different kinds of beers made in the same area. But the term "beer" was used in quite a broad sense a century or two ago, as it included drinks made from ingredients other than malt, such as juniper berries, sugar, or birch sap, for instance (these are described in chap. 8). So, the true beer might have been called "grain beer" or "malt beer," or something similar. There were usually also terms for distinguishing the main beer from the small beer.

The one named historical farmhouse ale style I know of is the Norwegian *hardangerøl*, the farmhouse style of the Hardanger area in southwestern Norway. It was frequently mentioned in newspapers and books from about 1890 to 1920. The reason it was so well-known was that hardangerøl was produced by commercial breweries. As far as I know, it was the only farmhouse ale style that was made commercially so early, except for *saison* and *bière de garde*. Later on, Michael Jackson would go on to name a couple of styles: gotlandsdricke and sahti. *Dricka* was the word for beer over nearly all of Sweden, although in many places it referred to small beer. Thus, gotlandsdricke is just "beer from Gotland," in the same way as hardangerøl is "beer from Hardanger." Sahti, on the other hand, is one of many Finnish names for farmhouse ale.

At time of writing, there has been a move toward having one national term for farmhouse ale made in a particular country. While this mostly works for Finland, it does not work for other countries where farmhouse brewing is still alive because these countries have more than one style. So, although *maltøl*

Figure 9.3. Woman greeting guests in the farmyard with the traditional bowl of ale. Norsk Folkemuseum.

has been the traditional name for Norwegian farmhouse ale, it does not appear as a style in this book for the simple reason that the beers it describes are far too diverse to be described as a single style.

In this book, I have tried to use the already established names, only introducing new names where necessary. But this problem does not have a neat solution. Commercial beer styles are messy to the point where it could be argued that they do not actually exist. Farmhouse ale styles really never used to exist in any meaningful sense, but the extinction of the brewing in most of the brewing areas and later reintroduction in some areas has made these beers more homogenous and amenable to regional classification, which makes the task at least approachable.

Table 9.1 Farmhouse Styles Still Alive Today

Style/type	Mash	Wort	Juniper	Color	Smoked	Yeast
Gotlandsdricke	Variable	Variable	Yes	Variable	Usually	Bread
Heimabrygg	Infusion	Reduction boil	Yes	Brown	Today: rarely	Kveik
Kaimiškas	Infusion	Raw	No	Hazy yellow	No	Farmhouse/bread
Keptinis	Infusion + bake	Raw	No	Brown/black	No	Bread
Koduõlu	Infusion	Raw	Yes	Hazy yellow	No	Bread
Kornøl	Infusion	Raw	Yes	Hazy yellow	Today: rarely	Kveik
Landøl	Variable	Variable	No	Variable	Variable	Today: brewer's
Sahti	Complex	Raw	Yes	Hazy yellow	No	Bread
Stjørdalsøl	Complex	Mostly raw	Usually	Brown	Yes!	Bread
Stone beer	Variable + stone	Variable	Variable	Brown?	Variable	Variable

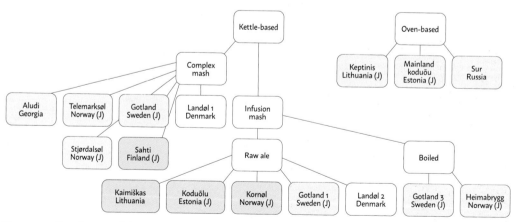

Figure 9.4. Classification of the main farmhouse ale styles and their countries of origin. The stone beers are omitted because they are so few that it makes little sense to talk about styles.

Defining Farmhouse Ale

Breweries today may decide to call their beer a farmhouse ale because they either use saison yeast, brew on a farm, pick some ingredient themselves, or simply because they feel like it. This chapter tries to give an exhaustive overview of European farmhouse ale, so it is worth trying to explain what criteria were used.

Originally, the definition of farmhouse ale was simple: it was beer made on the farm for the household, from the farm's own grain. Then, in the late nineteenth century, many farmers started buying grain, hops, or yeast, or a combination of these ingredients. But they were still trying to brew the same beer as they had before. The following century saw many changes, not least of which was a dramatic drop in the number of farmers. Today, few people in the traditional heartlands of farmhouse brewing are farmers. Present-day brewers still make descendants of the same farmhouse beer but most of these people are no longer farmers.

Thus, if today the original definition only fits a very small number of brewers, the most important characteristic for classifying beer is the flavor, and what makes these beers different is that they come out of a tradition of brewing that was completely different from commercial brewing. Farmhouse brewing and commercial brewing traditions have evolved separately, drifting apart over many centuries.

The key to farmhouse brewing is really the tradition, the unbroken chain of unwritten brewing lore passed on from brewer to brewer by direct instruction. This tradition is also what creates farmhouse styles, to the extent that such styles exist at all. So, in this book, any beer brewed within a farmhouse brewing tradition, or brewed to imitate beers from one of the traditions, is a farmhouse ale.

When Pekka Kääriäinen buys commercial malt and baking yeast to brew a batch of 1,300 liters in stainless steel equipment, then sells it via bars and shops, I consider that to be farmhouse ale. Not because Pekka picks the juniper branches himself, but because he is trying to brew the farmhouse ale as it was brewed in his village of Lammi in Finland back in the days when the farmers brewed from their own grain.

A truly traditional beer always comes out of a specific tradition. That is, the tradition as it is or was in some specific place. If you claim to brew a traditional farmhouse ale but you cannot say exactly where that tradition comes from, then, inevitably, your farmhouse ale loses some authenticity. Today, some breweries have started making, for example, IPAs where they add some element from the farmhouse brewing tradition, such as not boiling the wort, a juniper infusion, or kveik. To me, those beers are still IPAs, since most of the beer still comes out of the commercial IPA brewing tradition.

Exactly how close you need to be to the tradition and how precise you need to be about which tradition you mean will always be a matter of individual judgment. But the basic principle should at least be clear.

A Note About the Recipes

As the epigraph for this chapter implies, a written recipe is basically counter to the entire ethos of farmhouse brewing. When people produced malt, gathered hops and juniper, and cultivated yeast all by themselves, the ingredients varied from year to year. Without measuring instruments, the only available guides were sight, smell, taste, and experience. Even today, that is how most farmhouse brewers work.

With this in mind, you can appreciate that putting down the recipes of these brewers in words and numbers can be very difficult. I was quizzing Jørund Geving about his brewing to fill out his recipe, but when I asked him how he knew the beer had finished fermenting he had difficulty answering. "You want everything in words," he complained, before explaining that he did it by taste and looking at the activity.

Coming up with a good rule for how much foam there should be in the fermentor when the beer is ready can be difficult. One of the more creative solutions was from Ole Sivert Schiefloe, also in Stjørdal. Ole said his father told him the beer had fermented enough when the foam on top of the beer looked "like a map of Europe." He did not mean in shape, but the same proportion of foam and beer as a map of Europe has land and sea.

With all this in mind, I have tried my best with the recipes in this chapter, but know that some are incomplete, and some of the ingredients can be very hard to get hold of. A more detailed description of the various malting methods is given in chapter 3, while chapter 5 details many of the brewing processes. Refer to table 4.1 on p. 108-09 for information about the yeast strains.

Raw Ales

The raw ale styles all have a family resemblance, but they are still quite different from one another. The resemblance comes mostly from all of them using pale malt, very few hops, and not boiling the wort. Whether these similarities are accidental, or whether there is some deeper reason for them, it is hard to say. The important thing is that there is a group of beer styles, all with unboiled wort, which have sufficiently clear similarities that it makes sense to treat them as a group. Note that there are other beers with unboiled wort that are not included here because the flavors are just too different.

To summarize: kornøl and kaimiškas are made with farmhouse yeast, koduõlu and sahti with baking yeast. All except kaimiškas are made with juniper. The kaimiškas also stand out because of the use of Lithuanian malt, which has a unique character. Sahti is quite different from the others due to the mashing process and the use of rye in various forms. Note that Seto koduõlu is a specific type of farmhouse ale that involves baking the wet grist into a "bread" and is included in the section on oven beers (p. 320).

Brewing Raw Ales

There is a clear and definite flavor profile unique to raw ales, but it is not a powerful flavor like you might expect from roasted malt or lots of hops. If you want to be able to taste the raw ale flavor, it is important not to use very aromatic hops or a very dark malt bill. The recipes in this section will give you the raw ale flavor.

Some craft breweries in Norway have begun experimenting with raw ale. The first ones to try it did not really manage to make much use of the distinctive raw ale flavors, since no one had ever tasted the original beers and therefore they did not know how to put together an authentic recipe. Some simply drowned the raw ale flavor in US West Coast hops. The first brewery to really succeed with this method, Nøgne Ø, composed the recipe after visiting the Norwegian farmhouse ale festival and tasting a whole range of local raw farmhouse ales.

So, beware that making good raw ale is not trivial. A good approach on your first try may be to take a saison recipe and dial the hops down, then not boil it. Or you can brew a traditional style using the recipes in this book. However, in both cases, the problem is that you do not really know the flavor you are trying to produce. The best solution is to find a traditional raw ale and taste that. Of course, that is hard to do outside of rural northern Europe.

In raw ale brewing, be aware that you have to sanitize equipment that you would normally not sanitize if you were going to boil the wort. Farmhouse brewers making raw ale take care to sanitize their lauter tuns, especially the false bottom, because not all parts of the lautering equipment will become hot enough to kill any microbes present. Since there is no boil, it is also important to mash long enough and/or hot enough to properly pasteurize the wort. The hotter the mash, the shorter it can be, but it is difficult to be precise about the exact relationship. Adding either hot sparge water or hot juniper infusion at the end of the mash also helps.

Some modern brewers making raw ale find that the beer ferments out completely, leaving almost no sugar at all. It is possible that these brewers have infections with diastatic yeast, but another possibility is that the enzymes in the malt survive the mash and continue to work in the fermentor. This is another reason to sparge with boiling water or a juniper infusion.

Well-made raw ale will keep for years without going sour, but the protein in the beer will break down over time and cause the flavors to change. I have had raw ales that were one and two years old, both of which were very good but somewhat different from the original beer.

Kornøl

Kornøl is a style brewed north of the Jostedalen glacier, western Norway, in the three traditional districts of Sunnfjord, Nordfjord, and Sunnmøre. Terje Raftevold, whom we met in chapter 5, brews

Figure 9.5. Hjørundfjorden in Sunnmøre, western Norway. Mount Slogen is on the left.

a classic example of this style. The name literally means "grain-beer," because this was the beer that was made from grain as opposed to the "beers" that were made from syrup, juniper berries, and so on (*see* chap. 8).

Historically, these beers were brewed from barley, although on the coast the poor mixed in oats when necessary. The malt was dried either in the sun, in a badstu-type kiln, or in something closer to a small såinn. Today, most people use a mix of 50% pale malt and 50% Pilsner malt, but there are still a few brewers who make their own malt in the traditional way. Gunnar Skare in Ørsta makes a fantastic kornøl from traditionally kilned malt. The malt can range from strongly smoked to not smoked at all, although today it is rare to find smoked versions. The malt should be smoked with birch or alder.

Kornøl is always made with a boiled juniper infusion and lautered through juniper. The hops can be boiled in a little wort (humlebeit), or the hot wort can just run through the hop bag. In either case, the hop character should be very low, usually not detectable at all. The beer's profile is balanced by the juniper and the raw ale character. Making the juniper aroma very prominent is not necessary but can really improve these beers.

In the glass, kornøl looks like a hefeweizen with little carbonation: yellow, hazy opaque, with a small, coarse head. The aromas are variable, but should include boiled juniper, raw ale aromas, strong straw/grain flavors from the malt, and tropical fruitiness from the kveik. Hornindal beers tend to have a recognizable soft, smooth milky caramel aroma, often with mushroomy notes, that comes from the kveik. Very likely it's the lactic acid bacteria in these kveiks that make this flavor. In flavor, a kornøl should be sweetish, with very little hop character. The mouthfeel should be full, both from the sugar and protein from the raw ale, and also from the kveik yeast. It should also be somewhat mealy, from the lack of filtration and the raw character. Carbonation should be low, like British cask ale.

A kornøl normally ferments for two days, three if necessary, after which the beer is racked and then stored cool. The strength of the final beer is usually 5.3% to 7.6% ABV, and the final gravity ranges from 1.013 to 1.024, with attenuation in the 65% to 80% range.[*]

From the 1990s onward, quite a few of the local brewers have started boiling the wort. Some boil for an hour, but others boil just 10–15 minutes to sterilize the wort.

---

[*] Ken Robin Ruud and Gustav Foseid, from the Norwegian project "Vit hva du drikker," used an Anton Paar Alex 500 alcohol and extract meter to analyze the kornøl entries at the farmhouse ale festival in Hornindal in 2016 and 2017. These figures are based on their results.

Terje Raftevold's Kornøl

Batch volume: 25 liters (6.6 US gal.)
Original gravity: 1.075 (18.2°P)
Final gravity: 1.018 (4.6°P)

Color: 5.5 SRM
Bitterness: 0 IBU
ABV: 7.5%

Malts
- 5.2 kg (11.5 lb.) pale malt
- 5.2 kg (11.5 lb.) Pilsner malt

Additional Items
- 1 juniper branch for infusion
- additional juniper branches for lauter tun

Hops
- 60 g (2 oz.) Saaz @ lauter

Yeast
- Kveik #5 Hornindal

Brewing Notes

The juniper infusion will be your hot liquor for mashing and lautering. Use only the outermost tips (30–40 cm; 12–15″) of the juniper for the infusion. Do not use thick branches. Put the juniper branches in the kettle with cold water, slowly heat it to boiling, then let it boil boil for about 5 to 15 minutes, but do not worry too much about the exact timing. Beware of using too much of the thicker juniper wood, because boiling this can result in a sharp, solvent-like flavor.

Take off a portion of the boiling juniper infusion and let it cool sufficiently for use in the mash. Mash in, using the infusion liquor, for an initial mash temperature of 74°C (165°F). Mash for at least an hour and try to keep the temperature at 74°C.

The lauter tun filter should be juniper branches. Run off the first runnings through a bag containing the hops, then cool to pitching temperature and transfer to the fermentor. Traditionally, one should start the dry yeast with the first runnings (which is also the strongest) and pitch the starter after a few hours. With modern, rapid lautering this can be difficult, in which case making a yeast starter using DME is a good alternative.

Meanwhile, continue lautering by adding the hot juniper infusion as necessary and draining through the hops bag. Ideally, lautering should be very slow. If it is not you may want to extend the mashing by an hour.

Cool all of the collected wort to 30°C (86°F), then pitch the yeast. Screaming is traditional, but optional. Insulate the fermentor so that the fermentation temperature will be high. If it goes up to 35°C (95°F) that is fine.

Harvest the yeast by top-cropping after 40 hours.

The FG after 40 hours should be 1.018. Rack the beer after 48 hours and cellar cold to stop fermentation.

Reidar Hovelsen's Kornøl

This recipe comes from Geiranger, a little north of Hornindal. I have assumed 75% mash efficiency and 75% attenuation for this recipe.

Batch volume: 25 liters (6.6 US gal.)
Original gravity: 1.063 (15.4°P) estimated
Final gravity: 1.015 (3.8°P) estimated

Bitterness: 0 IBU
ABV: 6.3% estimated

Malts
- 6.5 kg (14.3 lb.) Munich malt
- 0.5 kg (1.1 lb.) Caramunich® malt

Hops
- 25 g (0.9 oz.) bittering hops
- 50 g (1.8 oz.) aroma hops (noble hops)

Additional Items
- Thick alder sticks with the bark peeled off, in the filter
- Thin juniper branches in the filter

Yeast
- Kveik #13 Årset

Brewing Notes

Mix the grist with hot water at around 80–90°C (176–194°F) for a mash temperature of 70°C (158°F). Insulate the mash tun well, then let stand for 3 to 4 hours. The temperature should stay as close to 70°C as possible the entire time.

In the lauter tun, put alder sticks at the bottom, then add thin juniper branches, and, over that, a metal mesh.

Transfer the mash to the lauter tun, and run off wort slowly (1 liter [1 qt.] per minute is ideal) while sparging with water at 80–90°C (176–194°F). Let the wort run through a bag of hops.

Cool the wort to 28°C (82°F) and pitch the yeast. Ferment 1–2 days until the foam has disappeared.

Sahti

Originally, farmhouse ale was brewed in all of Finland where people grew grain, which was roughly as far north as Oulu. Historically, there seem to have been three main groups of Finnish farmhouse ale: the nameless small beer brewed from rye by the Swedes on the coast, the Finnish strong barley ale inland in western Finland (sahti), and the weaker rye oven-based and mash-fermented farmhouse ales of eastern Finland (taari).

Sahti was one of the many names for traditional western Finnish farmhouse ale, but has gradually come to be the only name for it. Taari and the Swedish rye beer seem to have died out. Today, sahti is brewed in a region stretching from Isojoki in the west to Mäntyharju in the east, and from Orimattila in the south to Jämsä in the north.

Figure 9.6. A lakeside glass of sahti near Isojoki in western Finland.

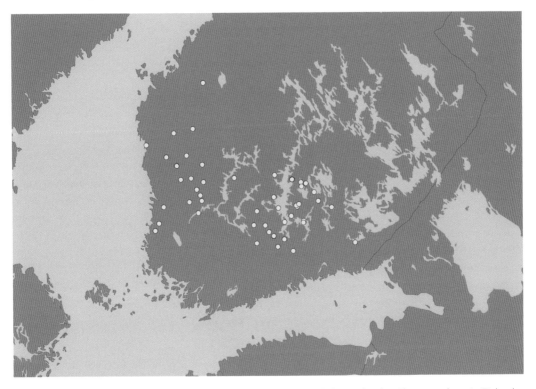

Figure 9.7. Each dot represents one place where I know sahti is actively brewed today. There are places in Finland where it is brewed for which I have no documentation.

Traditionally, sahti was brewed mostly from barley, sometimes with rye included. In the west of the country, traditional practice was to dry the malt in smoke saunas using mostly alder but also sometimes birch wood. In the east, the riihi (ria in Swedish) was the most common type of kiln.

Today, sahti is nearly universally made from Viking Sahti Malt (a commercial malt blend) and often, but not always, in combination with rye in some form. The rye can be roasted rye malt, normal rye malt, or even rye flour. The composition of the commercial sahti malt is a secret, but the product sheet implies the main part is Pilsner malt with darker malt added. It specifies a color of EBC 7.5 (3.4°L) with a diastatic power of at least 200°WK (62 Lintner degrees). Mika Laitinen[17] has done experiments and found that a mix of 80–90% Pilsner malt and 10–20% Munich malt is a good substitute. Many brewers use the so-called *tuoppi* malt, a roasted rye malt, to darken the beer and make it taste maltier. The use of this malt has been spreading in recent years, probably because more brewers want a darker sahti. If too much of this malt is used, say more than 10%, it tends to become dominant and starts obscuring the fruity yeast flavor.[18]

Sahti has a very unique flavor profile and viscous texture. These characteristics are clearly different from other raw ales, and it seems to be the result of using rye along with the particular brewing process, which involves very long step mashes and kettle mashing.

Most sahti brewers today use a commercial baker's yeast called Suomen Hiiva, which has a very characteristic fruity yeast profile dominated by banana flavors. This yeast is very aggressive and can be difficult to manage. It also contains a small amount of lactic acid bacteria, which makes it difficult to prevent sahti from going sour. This combination has forced sahti brewers to adopt very unusual approaches to fermentation. A few brewers use Sunnuntai bread yeast instead.

Historically, Finnish brewers had their own yeast just like everywhere else. The pitching temperature then was described as "milk-warm," and fermentation was basically the same as for the brewers who use kveik today. A few brewers can still remember homegrown yeast from their childhoods, but it seems to have disappeared in the 1960s.

Hop usage in Finland has historically been very low, and even today many sahti brewers do not use any at all. Hops generally cannot be tasted in the finished beer. Juniper is very widely used. A juniper infusion is relatively rare, but lautering through juniper branches is very common.

The thick, viscous sahti mashes can be difficult to lauter on modern brewing equipment. The long and shallow shape of the kuurna makes lautering these mashes easier because of the relatively thin layer of mash on top of the branches. This may be why the Finns have consistently stuck to using kuurnas for their lautering.

Brian Gibson's group analyzed 12 samples of Finnish homebrewed sahti and found that ABV was on average 7.9%, with most samples in the range 7.5% to 9%.[19] The average FG was 1.038 (9.5°P), which means the average OG must have been 1.092 (22°P). The bitterness level was mostly around 10 IBU.

On our expedition in Finland in 2018, Mika Laitinen measured the final gravities of the beers with a hydrometer while I measured them with a refractometer. Based on this, we computed the theoretical original gravities and strengths. Measuring 16 beers we found strengths from 6% to 13% ABV, with an average of 10.5%.

The main commercial examples are Lammin Sahti and Finlandia Sahti. Others are Pihamaan Sahti, Olut Pryki Raum, and Hollolan Hirvi Sahti. The United Gypsies and Pyynikin craft breweries sometimes also brew genuine sahti. All of these are brewed in Finland. Lammin Sahti is exported to the US in small amounts.

The best overview of the sahti tradition and how to brew sahti in English is Laitinen.[20] Räsänen gives a very thorough treatment of the ethnographic tradition,[21] but it is out of print and only available in Finnish and German.

Figure 9.8. Finlandia Sahti bottles, at the brewery in Sastamala, Finland.

Sahti in the European Union

In 2001, the European Union granted sahti the status of Traditional Speciality Guaranteed (TSG), which means that within the EU only products conforming to that specification can be sold as sahti. The TSG rules only limit how sahti can be made, so it is perfectly legal to brew sahti in other EU countries as long as the TSG rules are followed.

The TSG for sahti is quite broad in scope, but says sahti is not pasteurized, not filtered, has an OG of at least 19°P (1.079), 6%–12% ABV, and has a pH below 5. The color should be yellow to dark brown, and the taste slightly sweet. The yeast should either be baker's yeast or "harvested yeast." The second point is somewhat open to interpretation but, in Finland, beers brewed with ordinary brewer's yeast are considered to be in violation of the TSG terms.[22]

The main driver behind the TSG appellation was Pekka Kääriäinen. According to Laitinen,[23] Pekka says that deviations from the TSG are acceptable, so long as the deviations can be justified by referencing the sahti tradition. The purpose is mainly to prevent brewers from selling completely different beers as sahti.

2001 O.J. (C. 125) 5–6.

Olavi Viheroja's Sahti

Olavi Viheroja lives in Häämenkyrö in western Finland. He learned to brew from his father and a neighbor in nearby Jämijärvi, but has incorporated some tricks from his neighbors in Häämenkyrö. "You can steal knowledge," as he puts it.

Batch volume: 25 liters (6.6 US gal.)
Original gravity: 1.095 (22.7°P)

Final gravity: 1.018 (4.6°P)
ABV: 8.9%

Malts
- 11 kg (24.3 lb.) sahti malt
- 0.6 kg (1.3 lb.) roasted rye malt

Hops
- 1 handful of noble hops

Additional Items
- Juniper branches for the filter
- Straw for the filter
  (optional, used historically)

Yeast
- 1 cube of Suomen Hiiva yeast

Brewing Notes

The mash program is quite complex and best reproduced as the timetable Olavi uses on the day.

6:00 a.m.: Mix grist with lukewarm water but not too much.

7:30 a.m.: Add slightly warmer water to the mash.

12:00 p.m.: Add more hot water, this time bringing the mash to 58°C (136°F).

2:00 p.m.: Transfer mash to kettle and start heating it by fire, while stirring constantly.

2:50 p.m.: Stop heating when the surface of the mash is covered in foam and grains start rising to the surface in little spurts. The temperature at the center should be 80°C (176°F).

Originally, Olavi used juniper and straw as the filter bed support for the lauter tun but nowadays he uses only a fine steel mesh.

Transfer the hot mash to the lauter tun. Start running off and, as long as the wort is not clear, pour it back on top to be filtered again. Add hot liquid as necessary to get enough wort.

Cool the collected wort to 22°C (72°F), then pitch yeast together with the handful of hops. Ferment for 3 days. Ferment to the point where you can make a furrow through the foam on the fermenting beer and the furrow does not close again quickly.

Olavi also makes small beer by running off more wort after he's lautered the main beer. For 25 liters (6.6 gal.) of main beer, you would get about 3 liters (3.2 qt.) of small beer.

Eila Tuominen's Sahti

Eila Tuominen lives on a farm in Pertunmaa, on the east side of Lake Päijänne, about 200 km due east of Olavi Viheroja.

Batch volume: 25 liters (6.6 US gal.)
Original gravity: 1.105 (25°P)
Final gravity: 1.038 (9.5°P)

Bitterness: 0 IBU
ABV: 10%

Malts
- 8.5 kg (18.7 lb.) sahti malt
- 2 kg (4.4 lb.) unmalted whole rye grain

Hops
- None used, bitterness comes from the juniper

Additional Items
- 1 small juniper branch for infusion

Yeast
- 25 grams of Suomen Hiiva yeast

Brewing Notes

First make the juniper infusion from the branch, then set the branch aside in case you need to make more of the infusion later. As with Olavi Viheroja's recipe, the mash regime is complicated and best given as a timetable.

6:00 a.m.: Mix juniper infusion and the grist in the kettle. The infusion should be so hot that you can just bear to make a large circle in it with your finger. Start the fire underneath and let it burn out while stirring the mash.

8:00 a.m.: The mash temperature should now be 49°C (120°F). Start the fire again, stirring all the time. Let the fire burn for roughly an hour. The temperature should then have reached 53°C (127°F).

11:30 a.m.: Start the fire again, this time using more firewood. Keep stirring and keep adding wood so that, after about an hour, the mash is visibly boiling, with clumps of mash sputtering and jumping out of the kettle. Put out the fire, cover well, and let the mash simmer for another hour.

Transfer the mash to the lauter tun and run off through a fine steel mesh. Cool the collected wort to 4°C (39°F), then pour into the fermentor. Pitch the yeast and let the temperature slowly rise to room temperature.

After 3 days, rack the beer, then cold mature for 10 days. The finished beer will be very sweet, so it may be best to serve it cold. In practice, however, the raw ale flavor makes it taste far more balanced than you would expect from the recipe.

Island Koduõlu

Koduõlu, which literally means "home beer," is brewed on the Estonian islands of Saaremaa, Hiiumaa, and Muhu.* Traditionally, it was made from home-malted barley, which was either dried in the sun or on a heated floor, and the resulting malt would be very pale and not smoky. A few maltsters chose to further dry the sun-dried malt in an oven. Today, most koduõlu brewers buy Pilsner malt, but some, like Meelis Sepp, still make their own malt in the traditional way. Some of these brewers make beer that is darkened by boiling the juniper infusion.

Visually, koduõlu usually looks exactly like kornøl, although sometimes it is darker. The aroma should be juniper and fruit, typically banana, and also include the classic raw ale aromas. The flavor can be yeasty. Often, the mouthfeel is light, fluffy, rounded, and delicate. Carbonation should be low.

Some brewers use a juniper infusion, but most use the juniper only in the filter. Nearly all brewers seem to use juniper. Historically, quite a few brewers have also used sweet gale and marsh tea; some present-day brewers still use sweet gale.

The yeast is usually one of two local baker's yeasts: Nordic Pärm, produced in Viljandi, Estonia, and Pärm Euroferm, made by Salutaguse. The second is the Finnish Suomen Hiiva baker's yeast, sold under a different brand name in Estonia, which explains why many of the beers have a yeast profile very similar to sahti.†

Figure 9.9. Pihtla brewery (formally Taako OÜ). Pihtla village, Saaremaa, Estonia.

---

* This section is based on interviews and a brewing session in the summer of 2016, plus Jakovlev (1997) and Estonian National Museum (ERM) archive materials.
† Phone interview with Erkki Varonen of Suomen Hiiva Oy, conducted by Ilkka Miettinen, February 7, 2018.

Historically, Estonian farmhouse brewers had their own yeast, but these seem to have died out gradually. One brewer says he stopped using it in the 1970s or 80s, another that he stopped in the 1990s. Repeated attempts to find brewers who still have their own yeast have led to nothing, so the yeast seems to be gone.

Some brewers do a two-step infusion mash before running off, but the most common method is a single infusion mash. Some add the hops in the mash, but others boil hop tea and add it to taste after or before fermentation. Some pour the tea through the lauter tun, leaving the hops in the mash. In any case, the hop character in koduõlu is very weak. Most brewers use 0.5–4.0 grams of hops per liter. They use continental European hops with a low aroma and a low alpha acid content, so the beers are probably 5–10 IBU for the most part.

The alcohol content seems to be 6.5%–7.5% ABV, with a final gravity of about 1.008 to 1.019 (2.1–4.8°P). The original gravity is somewhere between 1.060 and 1.066 (14.7–16.1°P).*

Only two commercial examples are distributed outside the island. Taako Pihtla Õlu, at 7.6% ABV, is the best-

Figure 9.10. Koduõlu is traditionally served with smoked fish. Several islanders told us, "Koduõlu and smoked fish, that's the Saaremaa way of life!" Nasva, Saaremaa, Estonia.

known and brewed by Pihtla Õlleköök. The other beer is also named Pihtla Õlu, but is 8.8% ABV and made by Pihtla Pruulikoda. Both are brewed in the village of Pihtla on Saaremaa.

The beer on the mainland seems to have been very different from that on the islands. On the mainland, oven-dried caramel malt was commonly used, although some people made very pale malt too. By far the most common brewing process on the mainland was oven-baking malt loaves à la keptinis, usually without mashing before baking. Farmhouse brewing was alive across most of the mainland in 1940, especially in the southern and eastern parts (based on a summary of 53 responses to ERM KK-X). Today it appears to be completely dead.

---

* These figures come from the brewing session with Paavo Pruul in August of 2016, as well as measuring the wort of many of the beers with a refractometer and then making estimates based on the recipes.

Paavo Pruul's Koduõlu

Batch volume: 25 liters (6.6 US gal.)
Original gravity: 1.066 (16.1°P)

Final gravity: 1.016 (4.1°P) estimated
ABV: 6.6% estimated

Malts
- 7 kg (15.4 lb.) Weyermann Vienna malt

Hops
- 1 handful noble hops hop tea added to mash

Additional Items
- 3–4 juniper branches (one for the infusion and 2–3 for filtration)
- several sprigs of sweet gale (*Myrica gale*)
- 2–3 blackberry leaves

Yeast
- Fermentis S-04

Brewing Notes

Boil water and mash in for 71°C (160°F) initial mash temperature. Wait two hours while the temperature of the mash drops somewhat. Meanwhile, boil the hops and the sweet gale in water.

Pour the hops and sweet gale tea on the mash. Wait another hour while the temperature drops again. Meanwhile, fill the kettle with water and a juniper branch and let that boil. Add the juniper infusion to the mash at the end of the hour. The mash temperature should be 67°C (153°F) and the mash pH 5.8.

Filter the mash slowly through the remaining juniper branches. While the mash is filtering, make a yeast starter with blackcurrant leaves crushed with mortar and pestle and some of the first wort.

Cool the collected wort to 20°C (68°F), then pitch the yeast starter, including the blackcurrant leaves, while saying the names of all the angry dogs in your village. Ferment three days, then keg.

Kaimiškas

Kaimiškas literally means "from the village," so the full name of the beer is *kaimiškas alus*. This is the general the name for Lithuanian farmhouse ale, regardless of how it is made. The particular style of kaimiškas in the recipe that follows is from Biržai in northern Lithuania and the area around Pakruojis, to the southwest of Biržai. What makes this type of kaimiškas stand out from the other raw ales is that there is no tradition of using juniper and the farmhouse yeast is quite different.

Traditionally, these Lithuanian beers were made using barley malt from six-row barley, which was home-malted and dried either in the sun, in a heated loft, or on top of or inside the great stove. The resulting malt was very pale. Today, most brewers buy malt, but they still make very pale beer as a rule. The brewing process is usually a simple infusion mash, followed by lautering, cooling, mixing in of the hop tea, and then fermentation.

Commercial examples of kaimiškas are usually sweet, lightly hopped, and

Figure 9.11. Jovaru Alus, at the brewery in Jovarai, northern Lithuania.

taste of Lithuanian malt and raw ale flavor, and have a distinct yeast profile. Many of the brewers have their own family yeast, but not much is known about these yeasts yet. Some brewers do use baker's yeast. Of the Lithuanian farmhouse yeasts that have been analyzed, one was found to be *Nakazawaea holstii*, one to be *Brettanomyces*, and four to be *Saccharomyces cerevisiae*. Most of the yeasts seem to be phenolic and ferment at very warm temperatures.

Carbonation tends to be very low when kaimiškas is consumed even though the beer is usually stored in casks under very high pressure. When tapped, the beer looks more like porridge than beer until the foam subsides.

There is a whole range of these beers on the market in Lithuania. Important examples are the beers from the breweries Jovaru Alus, Su Puta, Piniavos, A. Grigonio, and Apynys. Commercial kaimiškas tends to be carbonated closer to what is normal for other commercial beers.

Julius Simonaitis's Kaimiškas

In Joniškelis in northern Lithuania, farmhouse brewing is still going strong, and the best-known of the local brewers is Julius Simonaitis. He grows his own hops, makes his own barley malt, which is dried in the loft, and gets yeast from his neighbors, who keep it in the well.

This recipe is based mainly on information from Simonas Gutautas, but also from Kølster.[24] Julius Simonaitis's beer stands out because it tastes very hoppy, with a hop character not too unlike a hoppier version of Brouwerij De Ranke's XX Bitter. Since his hops are a Lithuanian land-race, we do not know the alpha acid content, but Lithuanian hops seem generally to have 1.0%–2.5% alpha acid.[25] Simonas Gutautas estimates Julius's hops contain perhaps 3.5% alpha acids.[26]

The taste of Julius's beer is dominated by a massive earthy, floral hop aroma, and it is powerfully bitter, with low carbonation. Julius's yeast is phenolic and very aromatic, but in his beer the yeast character is dominated by the hops.

Batch volume: 25 liters (6.6 US gal.)   **ABV:** 5%–6%
Bitterness: (see description of flavor above)

Malts
- 7 kg (15.4 lb.) Pilsner malt

Hops
- 200 g noble hops (ideally Czech or Polish, roughly 3.5% AA), use as hop tea

Additional Items
- Lime/basswood wood for the filter
- Straw for the filter

Yeast
- Farmhouse yeast #16 Simonaitis

Brewing Notes

Prior to mashing, boil the water, then remove the fire and let the water cool to 72–75°C (162–167°F) before decanting it. Simonaitis does this step in order to get the right softness in his water for brewing. Whether it matters or not will depend on your water profile.

Pour the decanted hot water over the grist and aim for a mash temperature of 64–66°C (147–151°F).

While the mash is resting, make the hop tea. Boil half the hops in 1 liter of water for 60 minutes, and boil the other half of the hops in another liter of water for 15 minutes. When the hop tea is done, the mash is also finished.

In the lauter tun put first chopped lime tree wood, then add barley straw on top. Pour the two hop teas through the filter, so that the hops remain but the tea goes through. Set aside the tea for use later.

Transfer the mash into the lauter tun on top of the hops. Run off the wort and lauter the mash with almost boiling water.

Cool the collected wort to 35°C (95°F), then pitch the yeast. Add ⅕ of the hop tea, roughly 0.4 liters (14 fl. oz.).

Ferment 12–16 hours, depending on activity (#16 Simonaitis is a very, very rapid fermenter). Make a hole in the foam with a ladle; if the hole closes again the beer is still fermenting.

After the 12–16 hour fermentation, the beer should be racked. The goal of this short fermentation is to allow the beer to build up high pressure in the cask, so that when served it comes out as pure foam.

Once fermentation is done, add the remaining hop tea to taste. Julius Simonaitis actually racks first, then pours different amounts of hop tea into different casks, so that when he serves the beer people can get the amount of bitterness they want.

Šimonys-Style Kaimiškas

This recipe is based on information in Kavaliuskaitė and Sutkaitis, which relies on a long series of interviews the two authors did in 2003 in the Šimonys area near Kupiškis, north Lithuania.[27] Šimonys is really a keptinis brewing area, but the locals also make what they call mieštinis, which is not baked in the oven. Mieštinis was typically made when one needed a batch size larger than what the oven could handle.

The locals used homemade barley dried in the oven, which would produce caramel malt. Sometimes one-third of the grist would be wheat malt. The hops were usually local.

Batch volume: 25 liters (6.6 US gal.)

Malts
- 35 kg (77 lb.) caramel malt

Hops
- 350 g (12 oz.) noble hops (ideally Czech or Polish, 2.5% AA) added after lauter

Additional Items
- Aspen branches for the filter
- Straw for the filter

Yeast
- Bread yeast (or #16 Simonaitis)

Brewing Notes

The brewers said the water should be soft, without being more specific.

Pour some cold water in the bottom of the mash tun, then add the grist. Pour boiling water on until the thickness is like porridge. Leave the mash for 4–8 hours.

Put the aspen branches in the bottom of the lauter tun, with the straw on top. Sometimes brewers would use raspberry canes or red clover in between, for color and flavor. Some also placed hops on top to help protect the beer from microbial contamination.

Boil the hops in a bag in water to make hop tea. Transfer the mash to the lauter tun, then add the boiling hop tea and allow the mash to rest for about two hours. Once you start lautering, the wort should be nicely brown. Cool the collected wort to 20–22°C (68–72°F) if using bread yeast; #16 Simonaitis can be pitched at 35°C (95°F).

Make a yeast starter in a small glass, then sink the glass in the wort so that the lip of the glass is at the level of the wort. The yeast should then start and "climb" out of the glass and into the wort. If using bread yeast, make sure the wort remains cool during fermentation. Once the yeast has started, add the sugar or honey. Ferment 24 hours, then test the foam: make a hole in the foam with a ladle, if the hole closes again the beer is still fermenting.

Danish Landøl

Farmhouse ale was brewed all over Denmark. While the most common kind was heavily smoked raw ale, there was considerable variation across the country. Danish farmhouse ale never seems to have had a clear name, but the name *landøl* (lit. "country beer") pops up in a few places. Given how varied the brewing was, it does not really make sense to speak of landøl as a style, but more as the Danish name for farmhouse ale.

Landøl is still alive on eastern Møn and in northern Funen. Brewing as it exists today is not well documented. I visited Lotte Vinge, who still carries on the brewing tradition on Møn, but she is about to start brewing commercially and wanted to keep the recipe a family secret.

Figure 9.12. Nøddebjerggaard farm, where Lotte Vinge lives on the island of Møn, Denmark.

Gammeltøl

In Denmark, it was very common to brew a beer called *gammeltøl*, literally "old ale." Again, this was not a style but a variant on the common farmhouse ale: extra strong beer brewed in March/April and saved for the hard harvest work in autumn. Gammeltøl was generally brewed exactly the same way as the ordinary beer, just stronger and with more hops.

A similar custom was practiced in Lithuania.[28] The link with German Märzen seems obvious, particularly as the Lithuanian version was even called *morcenas*, but since German farmhouse ale is so far largely undocumented it is too early to say much more on the subject.

Jensgård i Tiufkjær

This recipe is based on two YouTube videos, one made by Sigvald Ellkier-Pedersen in 1975 and one by his son, Stig Ellkier-Pedersen, in 2015. It is also based on a December 1992 article in *Vejle Amts Folkeblad*.[29] All three sources describe how Aase and Børge Pedersen at the Jensgård farm in Tiufkjær, south of Vejle in central Jutland, made their gammeltøl in March every year. Although they brewed only once a year, they brewed 460 liters. There is no indication in the video of what malt they used, but the beer is visibly very pale. I have assumed 75% efficiency and 75% attenuation for this recipe.

Batch volume: 25 liters (6.6 US gal.)
Original gravity: 1.078 (18.9°P)
Final gravity: 1.019 (4.8°P)

Bitterness: 87 IBU, estimated based on 2.5% AA content
ABV: 7.7%

Malts
- 8.7 kg (19.2 lb.) Pilsner malt

Hops
- 250 g (9 oz.) noble hops added during mash as hop tea

Additional Items
- Oat straw for the filter
- 1 raw egg, unbroken, added in secondary

Yeast
- Danish farmhouse yeast; substitute #16 Simonaitis or kveik

Brewing Notes
Boil hop tea; it should boil for a couple of hours.
Pour hot water into the mash tun, then the grist on top. Stir well and wait a while.
Twist the oat straw into fan-like shapes, put them in the lauter tun, then pour the hop tea on top. Add the mash on top, add more hot water, and leave for "several hours."
Run off the wort, cool to appropriate temperature, then pitch the yeast. Let it ferment 2–4 days before racking the beer into a cask.
Allow 5–6 days further fermentation in secondary, after which add one raw egg—unbroken—to the cask so that the beer will clear. Wait 3–4 months before serving.

Landøl from North Jutland

This recipe is adapted from NEU 3404, from the village of Vigsø on the northwest coast of Jutland. The account was recorded by an elderly woman in 1945 describing her youth on a farm in Vigsø between 1870 and 1880.

This recipe is for their Christmas beer. With 19 kg of malt and 250 g of hops, it was much stronger than the everyday beer. The gammeltøl was stronger still, using 26 kg of malt and the same amount of hops. For comparison, the everyday beer would have 5 kg of malt and 60 grams of hops for the same batch size.

The malt was homemade from local six-row barley, dried in a drawer underneath the oven. At a guess, this must have produced pale unsmoked malt. This was the normal type of malt in northern Jutland. They sometimes toasted some of the malt to give the beer a darker color.

The hops were bought from travelling hop traders from Funen. At a guess, I would say that the hops must have been rather like German noble hops. Some farms in the area that could not afford to buy the full annual supply of hops used wormwood to save on the hops. The woman in NEU 3404 says this was "not as good" because the wormwood had a rather sharp bitterness.

The farm had its own yeast, which was stored in a jar between brews. You will have to substitute another type of farmhouse yeast. Since the yeast was stored wet, a Baltic farmhouse yeast may be the closest approximation.

Batch volume: 25 liters (6.6 US gal.)

Malts
- 19 kg (41.9 lb.) pale malt

Hops
- 250 g (9 oz.) Danish Funen hops (German noble hops probably closest substitute)

Additional Items
- Straw, braided and loose

Yeast
- Danish farmhouse yeast; a Baltic farmhouse yeast is probably the best substitute

Brewing Notes

Some fans made of braided straw were laid on the floor of the lauter tun, followed by a wooden grating, and then loose straw. Some stones were brought in to weigh everything down. The hop tea was boiled in an ordinary pot and then poured through the lauter tun and stored in a jar, to be added to the fermentor later.

The grist was placed in another vessel. Boiling water was poured over it, and the mash was stirred well. The mash temperature is not known, but she says all the water was added in one go, and that the result looked like "liquid gruel". It sounds like the mash was stirred a little less than an hour. Then it was transferred to the lauter tun and allowed to stand for an hour and a half.

Finally, the wort was run off, mixed with the hop tea, and set to cool 3–4 hours in the fermentor before the yeast was pitched. She does not give any pitching temperature, but it sounds warm. Since the yeast was stored wet, a Baltic farmhouse yeast may be the closest approximation. She does not say how long it fermented.

Dark, Smoky Ales

In some regions, the malt was dried with methods that produced dark, highly smoked beers. This was common in southeastern Norway, southern Sweden, all of Denmark except western Jutland, and on the island of Gotland. Most of these beers are no longer made, but two styles still exist.

Stjørdalsøl

No area in Europe has more farmhouse brewers per capita than Stjørdal, and there is definitely no other place where more people make their own malt (*see* "Stjørdal: Malt-Making Hotspot" in chap. 3). Not so long ago, however, there was nothing special about Stjørdal. The 1950s survey of farmhouse brewing in Norway does not mention Stjørdal at all. The low point for farmhouse brewing was probably in the 1960s, but then brewing picked up again. Very few people made malt, because this requires a separate building for the kiln, but there were people who made malt privately and sold it to local brewers, even though this was technically illegal under Norwegian law at the time.

Then, in 1986, a group of local brewers started Hognesaunet Såinnhuslag, an association of brewers that built and owned a malt kiln together. This was revolutionary. The cost of building and maintaining a malt kiln made little sense for a single person using it perhaps once or twice per year, but now the costs could be shared between 10–20 people. The concept of a *såinnhuslag* caught on, and today there are around 50 actively used såinnhus in the area. On average, an association has about 10 members.[30]

The local brewers themselves refer to the beer as maltøl, and the name *stjørdalsøl* is usually only used when speaking to outsiders. Maltøl was the traditional word for farmhouse ale in most of Norway, and so today, outside of Stjørdal, it is mostly used as an umbrella term for Norwegian farmhouse ale in general.

The malt is invariably made from local barley of many different varieties. The maltsters do not seem to care very much what variety they use, although several have noted that Saana dries faster and makes darker beer. And, as noted in chapter 3 (p. 42), Maskin was a very popular variety that still has die-hard fans today. Those brewers who are farmers use some of their own harvest for malting, while the rest buy seed grain from local suppliers or farmers.

The soaking and sprouting process is fairly straightforward, and everyone dries the malts on the såinn kiln, which seems to be roughly the same everywhere. Measuring the temperature during drying seems to be very rare. The maltsters instead check the temperature by feeling with their hands under the drying malt, and listening for popping sounds from the malt and the wooden boards under the malt. Everyone uses alder wood to dry their malt, giving stjørdalsøl its characteristic intense smoke aroma. A common saying in the area is, "If you have good malt, you can hardly fail to have good beer." That is, the emphasis is on the malting process much more than on the brewing, which is considered a fairly simple process by comparison.

The most common brewing process is to put the grist in cold water overnight, then do a rotating continuous mash where wort is run off, heated in the kettle, poured back, and run off again. This process continues until some temperature in the low, or sometimes even high, 70s (°C) is reached. The wort may then be boiled or not. The flavor of the malt is so powerful that the boil does not affect the flavor that much.

Everyone used to use both juniper and hops in their stjørdalsøl, but some brewers have stopped using one or the other or both, in order to let the flavor of the malt really stand out. Thus, the juniper flavor tends to be quite subdued and the hop flavor usually very discreet.

The most common yeast by far is Idun Blå, the standard Norwegian bread yeast. The local lager brewery in Trondheim used to give away lager yeast for free to homebrewers, which some brewers would use, and a few brewers have switched to buying conventional homebrewer yeast strains. The local farmhouse yeast seems to have died out in the 1970s, and so people switched to bread yeast. Older sources say the flavor is not the same as it was with the traditional yeast.[31] Interestingly, experiments using kveik to ferment stjørdalsøl have been highly successful.[*]

Local brewers seem to use 300–450 grams of malt per liter of beer. For sugar, anything from zero to 90 grams of sugar per liter of beer is used, although 80–90 grams seems to be most common. If we assume a 50% mash efficiency (which is what Roar Sandodden reports he had when he started malting) then the beer usually has an ABV of 8%–10.5%. Some beers are weaker, and some brewers still make small beer after the main wort has been run off.

Stjørdalsøl can range from deep reddish brown to pale brown, with low carbonation and a powerful alder smoke aroma. The beers tend to be sweetish, with little juniper and hardly any hop character, but other than that they vary dramatically.[†]

Jørund Geving's Stjørdalsøl

Jørund's stjørdalsøl won the Norwegian farmhouse ale brewing championship in 2017 and placed second in 2018. It is not really possible to emulate this beer with commercial malt because it will not taste like the original. If you are serious about brewing this beer you will need to make your own Stjørdal-style malt (see p. 43).

The specifications for this beer are based on measurements taken by Øyvind Arnesen from the Norwegian project "Vit hva du drikker." Øyvind took readings of the beer at the farmhouse ale festival in Hornindal in 2018 using an Anton Paar Alex 500 alcohol and extract meter.

Batch volume: 25 liters (6.6 US gal.)
Original gravity: 1.084 (20.2°P)
Final gravity: 1.040 (10°P)

Bitterness: 0 IBU
(no hops are boiled—see notes)
ABV: 5.7%

Malts
- 11 kg (24.3 lb.) Stjørdal-style malt
- 2 kg (4.4 lb.) white sugar (may replace ⅓ of it with dark syrup or rock candy)

Hops
- 15 g (0.5 oz.) Hersbrucker hops (2.3% AA) @ mash

Additional Items
- 4 liters of juniper (not compressed)

Yeast
- ¼ cube of Idun Blå bread yeast (but see variations)

Brewing Notes
The traditional method for making this stjørdalsøl was to have the mash in the lauter tun, run off the wort, heat it in the kettle, then pour it back. The wort would be recirculated like this until the mash was hot enough. Today, Jørund uses a relatively modern setup with a kettle that has a built-in electric heater. He runs off and pours the wort back just to recirculate the mash. The two methods should yield similar results.

---

[*]   By Jørund Geving; Morten Granås; Jogeir Halland; Klostergården bryggeri; and Roar Sandodden.
[†]   Based on many conversations with Roar Sandodden and Jørund Geving, as well as interviews at eight såinnhus, and three major tasting sessions.

Place the hops, juniper, and grist in the kettle and pour cold water over it all. Leave the mix overnight. It is important that the temperature stays below 10°C (50°F) all the time. The next morning, start heating and circulating the wort until it reaches 50°C (122°F), which should take about 2.5 hours. Pause there for 20 minutes, then keep heating for a couple of hours until the temperature goes a little above 70°C (158°F). Keep it there for about two hours.

Run off the wort. Following Jørund's method, taste the wort to judge how sweet it is, which, if using traditional Stjørdal-style malt, will vary with the quality of the grain and the malting process. Adjust the amount of sugar accordingly. Stir the sugar in while the wort is still hot so that the sugar dissolves easily.

Cool the wort to the appropriate pitching temperature, which depends on the yeast, then pitch while screaming as loud as you can. "The yeast scream is very important," says Jørund with a smile.

Jørund usually uses Norwegian baker's yeast (Idun Blå), pitching a ¼ cube at 22°C (72°F).

Ferment 4–8 days. Jørund decided whether the beer has finished fermenting by tasting it and judging the activity in the fermentor. Based on the specifications above, expect an extract efficiency of 46% with an apparent attenuation of 50%.

In practice, this beer has zero IBU from the hops, since the hops are never boiled. This may sound unbalanced, but the smoke, juniper, and raw ale character make it work better than one might expect. Serve with very low carbonation.

Variations

Jørund has used Safale US-05 at 22–24°C (72–75°F), fermented for about a week. Personally, I thought his version with this yeast was not as good as the others: thinner, with more prominent ashy smoke, but otherwise more neutral.

Jørund has also successfully used the #11 Lida kveik (see table 4.1, p. 108). He mixes several generations of kveik by dropping them dry into 33°C (91°F) wort and fermenting for 4–5 days. This was the version that won in 2017 and it was highly acclaimed by many tasters.

Figure 9.13. Roar Sandodden's såinnhus. Skatval, Stjørdal, Norway.

Roar Sandodden's Christmas Beer

Roar started out as a pure farmhouse brewer, then taught himself modern brewing and updated his recipe. In later years, he has returned to using more traditional ingredients and methods. As with Jørund Geving's Stjørdalsøl recipe, it is really the Stjørdal-style malt that makes this beer. This beer is powerfully smoked.

Batch volume: 25 liters (6.6 US gal.)
Original gravity: 1.075 ±.005 (18.2°P ±1.1°P)
Final gravity: 1.016 ±.002 (4.1°P ±0.5°P)

Bitterness: 10 IBU
ABV: 7.5%

Malts
- 6.2 kg (13.7 lb.) Stjørdal-style malt
- 0.7 kg (1.5 lb.) crystal malt
- 1.8 kg (4 lb.) pale malt
- 0.18 kg (0.4 lb.) dark syrup

Hops
- 50 g (2 oz.) Saaz hops (2.8% AA) @ 60 min.

Additional Items
- Juniper branches for the filter (see notes)

Yeast
- Kveik #1 Sigmund (see variations)

Brewing Notes
Roar's brew water is 14 dGH (250 ppm $CaCO_3$).

For the juniper branches, Roar selects the juniper from around his house, looking for branches with few berries and a lot of needles compared to wood. The branches are cut at the point where they narrow to the thickness of a finger, and only the outermost parts are used.

Prepare the lauter tun with the juniper branches and then pour the grist on top. Add a little juniper to the grist as well. Pour warm water over the grist to get a mash temperature of roughly 50°C (122°F).

Run off the wort, heat it in the kettle, and pour it back into the lauter tun. Spend a little more than an hour doing this until the temperature rises to 66–67°C (151–153°F). The temperature at the top of the lauter tun should then be roughly the same as the temperature of the wort coming out. Leave it for an hour.

Run off the wort, then boil it for an hour with the hops. Cool to pitching temperature (see below), then pitch the yeast while shouting "Hoi, hoi, hoosh, get lost!"

Ferment according to which yeast you use (see below). Roar's experience has been that he gets roughly 60% efficiency and 75% attenuation with this much homemade malt.

Serve the final beer with low carbonation.

Variations
Roar has used three different yeasts:

#1 Sigmund kveik: I preferred his beer with this yeast. Pitch at 39°C (102°F), keep it warm, ferment 4 days.

Wyeast 1318 London Ale III: Pitch at 18°C (64°F), ferment 14 days.

Norwegian baker's yeast (Idun Blå): Pitch at 22–24°C (72–75°F) and try to maintain that temperature; ferment 5–7 days.

Gotlandsdricke

Gotland is the largest island in the Baltic, about three hours east of mainland Sweden by ferry. For millennia, Gotland was a major regional trading hub, and hoards of ancient silver coins are regularly dug up on the island. It only became part of Sweden in the fifteenth century, and is famous for having preserved more of its traditional culture than other parts of Sweden. The island's farmhouse ale is a well-known part of that heritage.

The name of the style derives from the traditional Swedish dialect word for farmhouse ale: *dricka*. It literally means "drink"—historically, people in Sweden commonly brewed weak beer as their everyday drink, only brewing strong beer for special occasions, if at all. So *Gotlandsdricke* is "drink from the island of Gotland." The name ends in *e* because that is how people say it in Gotland, while in mainland Swedish it would end in *a*. In Swedish, one will sometimes see *dricku* as well. This is the definite form (*the* drink) in the Gotland dialect.[32]

Every household in Sweden that grew grain also brewed farmhouse ale if they could afford it, but the custom died out in mainland Sweden. Exactly when it died out is hard to say, as most of my data is from the 1930s. At that point, farmhouse brewing was alive around Hanö Bay in southern Sweden and in northern Dalarna but seemed to have mostly died out elsewhere. In Gotland, brewing did die out for a while in the northern part of the island, but in the southern part it has survived into the present day. Brewing has also been reintroduced in the northern part of the island, and on the island of Fårö, just north of Gotland.

Figure 9.14. Farmhouse on Gotland, near Värsände.

Gotland is rich in agriculture, particularly so in the south. Historically, the island's brewers mostly brewed from barley. On the east coast and on Fårö, they also used rye. In the southeast, some brewers used oats, and on the southern tip of the island some brewers used wheat.[33]

Traditionally, the most common way to dry malt on Gotland was using a loft kiln.[34] Some brewers used a kiln that looks very like the såinn kilns of Stjørdal, while others used a two-storey kiln. All of the methods seem to have produced heavily smoked malt. Far and away the most common wood for smoking the malt was birch (six out of eight accounts), but there is one report that mentions alder and another, incredibly, claims that spruce was used.[35] In the international literature, there have been claims that gotlandsdricke was smoked with beech but I have found no trace of that in any reliable source. In any case, beech does not grow on Gotland.

Today very few of the brewers make their own malts, but most appear to use locally made, traditional smoked malt from a few farmhouse maltsters.

Many different brewing processes have been used on Gotland. The two most common were ordinary raw ale or the normal infusion mash and boil process. Boiling the mash was also done, with and without boiling the wort afterwards. Given this, it is not clear whether it is correct to speak about gotlandsdricke as a single style.

Just about everyone seems to have used juniper in their beer, the most common method being a juniper infusion and juniper in the filter. On the east coast and on Fårö, people seem to have skipped the juniper infusion.

As for the hops, archival sources are in wild disagreement. People seem to have used everything from 0.05 grams per liter to 5 grams per liter. Around 1 gram per liter seems to be the most common. People grew their own hops, and it is only recently that they have started buying the hops; some farmhouse brewers still use their own.

Historically, the brewers of Gotland had their own yeast, as was the case everywhere else. Salomonsson (1979, 79) writes that the last time he heard about *hemjäst* (lit. "home yeast") was in the early 1970s, so the yeast probably died out around that time. Today, everyone seems to use bread yeast, specifically the brand Kronjäst.[37] Gotlandsdricke is still usually made with smoked homemade malt, and nowadays the use of sugar and honey is common.

I have only tasted small sips of a single sample of gotlandsdricke, so I cannot describe the flavor properly.

Anders Mattson's Gotlandsdricke

Anders Mattsson lives on a farm in Hablingbo in the south of Gotland. He learned to brew from his uncle, and today he gives brewing courses in the summer. As with stjørdalsøl, the key to gotlandsdricke is in the malt, so anything other than homemade malt is not going to impart the same flavor to the beer.

Anders himself does not take measurements. Because I was not able to brew with Anders and take my own measurements, the values for OG, FG, IBU, and ABV are theoretical. I have assumed 60% extract efficiency and 75% apparent attenuation.

Batch volume: 25 liters (6.6 US gal.)
Original gravity: 1.073 (17.7°P) theoretically
Final gravity: 1.018 (4.6°P) theoretically

Bitterness: 33 IBU theoretically
ABV: 7.2%

Malts
- 7 kg (15.4 lb.) alder-smoked malt
- 1.25 kg (2.75 lb.) white sugar

Hops
- 100 g (3.5 oz.) noble hops

Additional Items
- juniper branches for infusion
- additional juniper branches for lauter tun

Yeast
- 1 thumbnail of Swedish Kronjäst baking yeast

Brewing Notes

Put the juniper branches for the infusion in water and boil them. Pour about 2.5 liters (just over 2½ qt.) of the juniper infusion into the mash tun, then add the grist and stir thoroughly. Add more of the juniper infusion if necessary. Leave it for at least an hour. Anders does not specify the mash temperature, relying on the fixed temperature of the infusion (100°C, or 212°F) and the fixed malt/infusion ratio to hit the right temperature.

Put fresh juniper branches at the bottom of the lauter tun. It is a good idea to dip these branches in the boiling juniper infusion first. Pour the mash into the lauter tun over the top of the juniper branches. Run off about 5 liters (just over 5¼ qt.) of wort, and then pour it back on top to filter it again. Now run off the wort very, very slowly. (At this point Anders recommends celebrating with a cup of hot wort mixed with some hard liquor.) Add more of the juniper infusion on top as needed.

Take 2–3 liters (roughly 2–3 qt.) of wort and boil the hops with those for an hour.

Once everything has been run off, you can stir in the sugar and add back the wort that was boiled with hops. Cool the wort to 23°C (73°F) and pitch the yeast.

Let ferment for a week before transferring to a cool place, somewhere around 10–15°C (50–59°F). It will keep about 2–3 months.

Gotlandsdricke from Fide

This recipe is taken from KU 2364, a compilation of oral evidence collected from three farms on Gotland in preparation for a movie about Gotlandsdricke made by the Nordic Museum. It was recorded in 1959.

The malt was homemade, dried on a Gotland-style loft kiln, and smoked with birch wood. The malt would have been quite heavily smoked. The hops were homegrown, probably best emulated with noble hops.

The farmhouse yeast was mostly kept in a jar, but could also be dried on juniper branches. Therefore, the original yeast is probably best emulated with kveik, but Baltic farmhouse yeast could also work. I have assumed 50% extract efficiency and 75% apparent attenuation.

Batch volume: 25 liters (6.6 US gal.)
Original gravity: 1.026
Final gravity: 1.006

Bitterness: 0 IBU
ABV: 2.6%

Malts
- 4 kg (8.8 lb.) birch-smoked malt

Hops
- 150 g (5.3 oz.) hops

Additional Items
- 4–5 juniper sticks, 3 cm ($1\frac{3}{16}$ in.) thick
- 1 juniper branch
- rye straw

Yeast
- 1 tablespoon of farmhouse yeast (kveik or Baltic farmhouse culture)

Brewing Notes

Prepare the lauter tun first with juniper sticks, adding next a juniper branch, and then a "pillow" of straw. The straw should be scalded in hot water first. Pour the grist on, then add a little hot juniper infusion. Leave it "a short while," then add hot juniper infusion again. "Let it stand." Start running off, but pour the first bucket of wort back on top. Then run off the rest, cool, and pitch. No pitching temperature is given. The hops could be added either to the cooling wort or directly in the fermentor.

Landøl from South Funen

The other two landøl recipes are from brewers that happened to use pale malt, but this recipe has a more typical grain bill. It comes from archival source AFD Frederik Dahlkild, from Svanninge on south Funen, written in 1969.

The account says nothing about what kind of malt was used, but all the accounts from south Funen that describe malting say the malt was dried inside the chimney of the oven using alder wood. For the specifications, I have assumed 75% efficiency and 75% attenuation. If we assume the Bavarian hops had an alpha acid content of 3.5%, this beer should be about 53 IBU.

Batch volume: 25 liters (6.6 US gal.)
Original gravity: 1.049 (12.2°P)
Final gravity: 1.012 (3.1°P)

Bitterness: 53 IBU
ABV: 4.8%

Malts
- 5.5 kg (12.1 lb.) alder-smoked malt

Additional Items
- rye straw

Hops
- 110 g (4 oz.) Bavarian noble hops (or 165 g [6 oz.] Funen hops) @ hop tea

Yeast
- Farmhouse yeast or bread yeast

Brewing Notes

Soak the grist in 60°C (140°F) water (yes, that is what the account says!) for two hours. Meanwhile, the hops are boiled in 2 liters (just over 2 qt.) of water in a kettle to make a hop tea.

Put a wooden grating at the bottom of the lauter tun, then place the rye straw twisted into fan shapes on top. Pour the hop tea through the support for the filter bed into a bucket, leaving the hops behind. Move the mash into the kettle and boil it. Note that the original batch size was 230 liters and used 50 kg of malt (roughly 60 gal. and 110 lb.), so reaching the boiling point would have taken a long time, probably taking the mash through the entire range of rest temperatures relatively slowly.

Transfer the mash to the lauter tun and start running off while adding hot water at regular intervals. The wort that is run off is poured into the fermentor and left to cool to 18–22°C (64–72°F). Add 0.2 liters (7 fl. oz.) of the hop tea. Let it ferment overnight. The yeast often fermented so strongly that the foam had to be removed by hand so the fermentor would not overflow.

After 24 hours, rack the beer. Wait a couple more days, then close the cask. The account never says anything about what to do with the remaining 90% of the hop tea, but most likely it was added to the beer to taste after fermentation.

Brown Boiled Beers

There are a few of these, made in a few different ways. The main difference lies in the mash program.

Heimabrygg: Western Norwegian Beers

The three traditional western Norwegian districts of Hardanger, Voss, and Sogn have very similar brewing traditions. The farmhouse ale in these regions is usually referred to by the brewers themselves as *heimabrygg*, so here we treat them as one style under that name.

The kornøl and heimabrygg regions are both on the west coast, but the brewing traditions are quite different. The reason for this is the large mountain range capped by the Jostedalen glacier, the biggest glacier in mainland Europe, that separates the two regions. A major dialect border runs along the exact same divide.

In Voss, the low point for farmhouse brewing was probably the 1970s, after which it has recovered. The Dyrvedalen valley seems to have been a particularly strong area for brewing, and several of the kveiks collected from the Sogn and Voss areas come from that little valley. Kornøl brewers to the north traditionally mixed their kveiks, but in the heimabrygg region that was relatively rare. Thus, kveik cultures collected from the southern region tend to have fewer strains than the northern ones.

Figure 9.15. The brothers Jarand and Reidar Eitrheim chopping juniper for the infusion. Aga, Hardanger, western Norway.

In the late 1980s, a manager for the national farm supply retail chain Felleskjøpet visited Voss and was astonished not to see a single field of grain. According to his statistics for the sale of seed grain, the county of Voss should be the biggest producer of grain in all of Norway. But the seed grain was, of course, all going toward malting, not farming.[38]

Historically, malt was made from barley grown in Voss. The malt was dried in several very different ways:

- Sigmund Gjernes (introduced in chap. 4, p. 81) says his family sun-dried their malt, a method also mentioned by Nordland.[39]
- Sjur Rørlien says in Dyrvedalen people mostly dried the malt on a heated shelf next to the fireplace.[40]
- Sjur Rørlien and the Voss Museum both mention that some farmhouse brewers dried their malt in iron pots (*see* chap. 3, p. 77).
- Nordland[41] and the Voss Museum both mention farmers drying their malt on rough mats woven from horsehair over a fire.In Hardanger and Sogn, it seems that badstu-kilned malt was the norm (*see* chap. 3, p. 67).

Importing malt seems to have begun in western Norway in the 1980s, which caused traditional malting to decline. Today, there are very few brewers who still make their own malt, but Sigmund Gjernes's brother Gunleiv Gjernes still does. There are also a handful of people doing it in Hardanger.

The process begins by heating a juniper infusion—but usually not boiling it—and using it for an infusion mash for three to four hours. This was followed by a slow run-off through juniper branches and then boiling with hops. The boil can last just an hour or it can be longer. A reduction boil of 2–4 hours is the normal. Pitching temperatures tend to be high, in the 37–40°C range (99–104°F). Fermentation is usually three to four days.

In Voss, the classic recipe is 50 kilograms of malt for 150 liters of beer. Sigmund Gjernes aims for an OG of 1.080, which seems to be on the low end of the typical range. Sogn and Hardanger beers are in the same range, and they typically seem to be about 8%–12% ABV.

Hop usage varies dramatically from very low to very high. Some beers can be as low as 7–10 IBU. Sigmund Gjernes's seems to be about 38 IBU, but the Eitrheim family in Hardanger goes as high as 80 IBU. From historic documentation, it seems hop rates have been as high as 10–13 grams per liter; given the normal alpha acid content of Norwegian landrace hops is 4.5%–7%, that theoretically gives an IBU in the 213–331 range. Exactly what these beers tasted like is hard to say, but there have been recent anecdotal reports of unbearably bitter beers from this area.

The beers are generally reddish brown to dark brown, sweet and fruity, full-bodied and malty, with a clear juniper character. The Voss beers tend to have an orangey flavor from the kveik, while in other areas the yeast can impart a different flavor profile. In the beers I have tried, hop bitterness has varied from not noticeable to moderate, with very little hop aroma.

These beers are served with low carbonation. In Dyrvedalen, the beer should be completely flat.

Hardangerøl

This recipe comes from the brothers Jarand and Reidar Eitrheim, who live in Bleie in Hardanger, western Norway, a little south of Voss. The brothers learned to brew from their grandfather Jakob Eitrheim, who brewed his first beer in 1937 at the age of 17.

Originally, the family had a badstu-type malt kiln, but their farm was razed to make room for the zinc works in Odda. After this, Jakob dried his malt in the sun on the roof of an outbuilding, then smoked them by hanging a bag in the fireplace when heating the juniper infusion. Today, the brothers do not use any smoked malt at all. I have no measurements, but the final beer is very strong, very sweet, and very bitter.

Batch volume: 25 liters (6.6 US gal.)   **Original gravity:** 1.125 (29.1°P)

Malts
- 5.7 kg (12.6 lb.) pale malt
- 5.7 kg (12.6 lb.) Munich malt

Hops
- 130 g (4.5 oz.) Magnum hops (15% AA) @ FWH
- 45 g (1.5 oz.) noble hops (4% AA) @ 20 min.

Additional Items
- 1 small juniper branch for infusion
- additional juniper branches for lauter tun
- alder sticks without bark for lauter tun
- 70 g (2.5 oz.) rock candy for fermentor

Yeast
- #14 Eitrheim kveik

Brewing Notes

Put one small branch of juniper in the kettle with water and heat to make an infusion. Do not boil. Use the infusion liquor to mash in at a mash temperature of 72°C (162°F). The initial mash pH should be 4.5. Leave mash for an hour; at the end the temperature should be around 70°C (158°F).

Run off the wort through a layer of alder sticks and juniper branches. Transfer the collected wort to the kettle and boil it for 2–3 hours. Add the bittering hops at the beginning and the aroma hops 20 minutes before the end.

Pour the boiled wort into the fermentor, filtering out the hops, and add the rock candy. Pitch the kveik at 37°C (99°F) and ferment 3–4 days before racking.

Sigmund Gjernes's Vossaøl

Batch volume: 25 liters (6.6 US gal.)
Original gravity: 1.080 (19.3°P)

Final gravity: 1.014 (3.6°P)
ABV: 8.8%

Malts
- 4.2 kg (9.3 lb.) Pilsner malt.
- 4.2 kg (9.3 lb.) pale malt.

Additional Items
- 10 liters (2.6 gal.) of juniper branches in kettle (do not compress)
- additional juniper branches for lauter tun

Hops
- 40 g (1.5 oz.) Saaz @ mash
- 40 g (1.5 oz.) Saaz @ FWH

Yeast
- Voss kveik #1 Sigmund

Brewing Notes
The juniper should be green and preferably have no berries. Use the outermost thin tips, no thicker than your finger. Fill the kettle with juniper to the stated volume but do not compress the branches. Heat the juniper slowly in the brewing liquor to 90°C (194°F), then pour it over the grist.

Add 40 g (1.5 oz.) of hop cones to the mash and stir well.

Prepare the lauter tun with juniper branches on the bottom and a thin wire mesh on top. Pour the mash, including the hops, on top. The mash temperature should be 69°C (156°F). Leave the mash for at least 3 hours in the lauter tun and ensure the temperature does not drop below 50°C (122°F); insulate the tun if necessary.

Run off the wort slowly. Pour back the first wort to filter it again. Run off all of the wort into the kettle after recirculating.

Boil the wort powerfully for four hours with the remaining 40 g (1.5 oz.) of hops. Use a kitchen sieve to remove the foam ("the headache").

Cool the wort to 39°C (102°F), then pitch the yeast. Insulate the fermentor to ensure it stays warm.

Ferment for four days before racking. The beer can be drunk right away.

Vossaøl à la Vossestrand

Vossestrand is a remote part of Voss, higher up the valley, just before the mountain crossings into Sogn. The brewing in this area was slightly different, as described below. This recipe comes from Ivar Geithung, who learned it from his father-in-law Olav Selland.

Batch volume: 25 liters (6.6 US gal.)
Original gravity: 1.082 (19.8°P)

Final gravity: 1.017 (4.3°P)
ABV: 8.4%

Malts
- 9 kg (19.8 lb.) pale malt.

Hops
- 93 g (3.25 oz.) Saaz @ mash
- 93 g (3.25 oz.) Saaz @ FWH

Additional Items
- juniper branches, for infusion and filter
- handful of meadowsweet, flowers and stalks

Yeast
- Voss kveik #1 Sigmund or Idun Blå baker's yeast

Brewing Notes

Before brewing, take 900 grams (2 lb.) of the malt and toast it in a pot. The meadowsweet is rubbed on the inside of the fermentor before use.

The juniper should be green and preferably have no berries. Use the outermost thin tips, no thicker than your finger. Fill the kettle with juniper to the stated volume but do not compress the branches. Heat the juniper slowly in the brewing liquor to 90°C (194°F), then pour it over the grist.

Add 93 g (3.25 oz.) of hop cones to the mash and stir well

Prepare the lauter tun with juniper branches on the bottom and a thin wire mesh on top. Pour the mash, including the hops, on top. The mash temperature should be 69°C (156°F). Leave the mash for at least 3 hours in the lauter tun and ensure the temperature does not drop below 50°C (122°F); insulate the tun if necessary.

Run off the wort slowly. Pour back the first wort to filter it again. Run off all of the wort into the kettle after recirculating.

Boil the wort powerfully for four hours with the remaining 93 g (3.25 oz.) of hops. Use a kitchen sieve to remove the foam.

If using kveik, cool the wort to 39°C (102°F) before pitching.

If using Idun Blå, cool the wort to 30–35°C (86–95°F) before pitching.

Insulate the fermentor to ensure it stays warm. Ferment for four days before racking. The beer can be drunk right away.

Dyrvedal-Style Vossaøl

The brewers in the Dyrvedalen valley do not all brew exactly the same way, so this is Bjørne Røthe's recipe.

Batch volume: 25 liters (6.6 US gal.)

ABV: 10%–11%

Malts
- 5.2 kg (11.5 lb.) Pilsner malt
- 5.2 kg (11.5 lb.) pale malt

Hops
- 100 g (3.5 oz.) East Kent Goldings or Northern Brewer @ FWH

Additional Items
- juniper branches for infusion
- additional juniper branches for lauter tun

Yeast
- #2 Rivenes kveik
  (#1 Sigmund kveik is similar)

Brewing Notes

The juniper branches should be the tips only, no thick branches because those yield tannins. Avoid branches with many berries.

Put the juniper branches in water and heat the water to 72°C (162°F), then start ladling this infusion onto the grist. The mash temperature should be in the 66–68°C range (151–154°F), although none of the local brewers know for sure. Leave the mash for one hour. In summer, put a small handful of extra hops in the mash to prevent it going sour.

Run off the wort through juniper branches in the lauter tun, transfer to the kettle, then boil for 6–7 hours. Leave the hops in for the entire boil. The boil should reduce the wort volume quite substantially.

Cool the wort to 37°C (99°F), then pitch the yeast. Insulate the fermentor so it will keep warm during fermentation.

Let it ferment 3 days. The beer should not be carbonated.

Sogneøl

Sogn is the region north of Voss, along the Sognefjord. The entire fjord is 180 km long and has several arms, so Sogn is a fairly large region, and brewing methods differ over the entire area. Kveik seems to have completely disappeared in this area, except for in Lærdal. This is Carlo Aall's recipe for his Christmas ale. It is from a brew session before I had bought measuring equipment, so the gravity readings and ABV are estimates.

Batch volume: 25 liters (6.6 US gal.)
Original gravity: 1.100 (23.8°P) estimated

Final gravity: 1.025 (6.3°P) estimated
ABV: 10% estimated

Malts
- 8.3 kg (18.3 lb.) Munich malt
- 3.3 kg (7.3 lb.) pale ale malt
- 0.67 kg (1.5 lb.) crystal malt
- 50 g (2 oz.) chocolate malt

Hops
- 50 g (2 oz.) noble hops @ FWH

Additional Items
- thin juniper branches for infusion
- additional juniper branches for lauter tun

Yeast
- 1 pk Safale S-04 (11.5 g) or Voss/Lærdal kveik

Brewing Notes

The juniper branches for the infusion should not be thick and should not have too many berries. Split at least one branch lengthwise to get the sap from the wood. Use enough to fill the kettle without compressing the juniper. Add cold water, then heat to 80°C (176°F).

Pour the hot juniper infusion over the grist and stir. The initial mash temperature should be 72°C (162°F). Let it stand for two hours while the temperature falls slowly.

Place a layer of juniper branches in the lauter tun, move the mash over, and run off the wort slowly. Add one bucket of the hot infusion for every bucket of wort taken off.

Boil the wort for an hour, adding all the hops at the beginning. OG is estimated to be 1.100, and FG around 1.025, for a strength of around 10% ABV.

If using S-04 ale yeast: cool the wort to 20°C (68°F), pitch the yeast, and let it ferment for 2–4 days. Once the fermentation calms down and the foam collapses, transfer the beer to kegs and store cool.

If using kveik: use the appropriate pitching temperature for the kveik culture. For the fermentation, follow the same procedure as for S-04.

Eastern Norway

The next two recipes are from eastern Norway, where the brewing process is quite different from western Norway. The southern third of Norway is divided by a large, nameless mountain range that runs roughly down the middle. As a result, the west coast and the eastern inland regions have developed somewhat different beer cultures.

Telemark

Telemark is a rugged, mountainous region on the eastern side of the mountains in Norway, long famous for its traditional culture. High up in the valleys, toward the edge of the central mountain plateau, is the village of Morgedal, best known as the cradle of modern skiing. Farmhouse brewing here died out in the 1970s but was revived by Aslak Slettemeås. I visited Halvor Bjåland and Terje Haugen in Morgedal, and they showed me the local style of brewing. This is their recipe.

Batch volume: 25 liters (6.6 US gal.)
Original gravity: 1.074 (18°P)
Final gravity: 1.018 (4.6°P)

Bitterness: 11 IBU
ABV: 7.3%

Malts
- 5.5 kg (12.1 lb.) Pilsner malt
- 2.7 kg (6 lb.) Munich malt
- 220 g (8 oz.) Carahell® malt
- 220 g (8 oz.) smoked malt

Hops
- 30 g Saaz @ 60 min.

Additional Items
- juniper branches for infusion
- additional juniper branches for lauter tun

Yeast
- 1 pk Safale S-04 (11.5 g) or #1 Sigmund Voss kveik

Brewing Notes

Pour cold water over the grist in the kettle, but not too much, just barely enough to wet the grain. Leave overnight. Make sure the mash stays below 10°C (50°F) the whole time.

Add hot water from the tap the next morning to get what you consider a good consistency for mashing. Start the fire under the kettle and heat the mash slowly to 62°C (144°F). Leave it there for two hours. Then heat to 70°C (158°F) and leave for another hour. Mash out by heating to 78°C (172°F) and then you are ready for lautering.

While heating the mash, the juniper infusion is boiled in another kettle. The kettle should be very full of juniper branches. The infusion should boil 60–90 minutes until it turns golden brown.

Place the additional juniper branches on the bottom of the lauter tun and put stones on them so the branches do not float. Ladle the mash on top of the branches and start running off the wort slowly. As wort is run off, add the juniper infusion on top.

Boil the wort with the hops for an hour. Cool the wort to the temperature suitable for the yeast you are using, then pitch the yeast.

If using S-04, let the beer ferment for a week; if using kveik, 3–4 days is enough.

Figure 9.16. Terje Haugen measuring the temperature of the mash in the kettle. Morgedal, Telemark, Norway.

Hallingdal

This recipe comes from Sverre Skrindo in Ål in Hallingdal, eastern Norway. He learned to brew from his father and grew up in the brewing tradition. He calls his yeast "gong," and he inherited it from his father. This yeast is not generally available, so the recipe suggests a substitute.

The amount of malt is a bit tricky: Sverre measures it in "settung," which is a local measure that has varied from place to place. In any case, Sverre's definition of a settung is a wooden container on his farm. So, the malt amounts below are a combination of guesswork based on the size of the container and theoretical calculations. I brewed with Sverre in November of 2017 and was able to take some measurements.

Batch volume: 25 liters (6.6 US gal.)
Original gravity: 1.105 (24.9°P)
Final gravity: 1.026 (6.6°P), but see "Attenuation" below

ABV: 10.5%, but see "Attenuation" below

Malts
- 6.5 kg (14.3 lb.) pale malt
- 6.5 kg (14.3 lb.) Pilsner malt
- 1.1 kg (2.4 lb.) caramel malt

Additional Items
- juniper branch tips for infusion and lauter tun
- alder wood thick branches for lauter tun

Hops
- Hops not specified

Yeast
- "Gong" #23 Skrindo (possible substitutes: #41 Skare kveik; a Voss kveik)

Brewing Notes
Pour the grist into the kettle, then add cold water and stir it in. The resulting mix should be just barely wet. Leave overnight, and make sure it stays below 10°C (50°F).

The next morning, add cold water until the mash is like a soup. Start the fire under the mash and stir while it heats up. It should take about three hours for the mash to get to 67°C (153°F), stirring all the while. Stirring is necessary so the mash doesn't burn. Try not to go above 67°C. If the temperature gets too high, add cold water. When brewing with Sverre, I measured the mash pH toward the end (at 62°C [144°F]) as 6.0. The mash liquor had a pH of 6.7.

Cut little marks in the bark of the alder branches to let the sap out and place in the lauter tun. Then pile a thick layer of juniper branches on top. Sverre did not care if there were berries or not, but he used only thin juniper tips.

Once the mash has reached 67°C (153°F), transfer it to the lauter tun. Close the lid, and let it sit for 2.5 hours. While the mash sits, rinse the kettle and start boiling the juniper infusion in it. Once mashing has finished, start lautering the wort slowly. Sparge with boiled juniper infusion toward the end. Then lightly boil the wort and hops for 2 hours, with the hops in a bag.

Cool the wort to 35°C (95°F), transfer to the fermentor, and pitch the yeast. Ferment for three days, then move to the secondary. Leave it there two days, then bottle.

Attenuation: Sverre's yeast created highly unique flavors, but the attenuation was very low. While the OG was 1.105, the FG was still 1.084. It tasted that way, too, but the final beer was acidic and had many flavors balancing it, so it was still drinkable. However, getting this result with a different yeast will likely be very difficult. Evidence from some older residents also indicates that farmhouse ale in Ål used to be very strong, maybe 10%–12% ABV, at least higher than 3.2%. So, the attenuation was probably higher in the old days. I recommend using kveik, for example, a Voss kveik or #41 Skare, which should be able to achieve 75% attenuation that yields 10.5% ABV and an FG of 1.026.

Figure 9.17. Kolbjørn Sando cooling the wort in the snow. Ål, Hallingdal, eastern Norway.

Swedish Farmhouse Ale: Öxabäck

Farmhouse brewing has died out completely on the Swedish mainland, so there are no living brewers to learn from. This recipe is taken from EU 8761 from Öxabäck, southeast of Gothenburg in western Sweden. It was written in 1935, and it gives the impression brewing had already died out by that time.

In the Öxabäck area, people used their own barley and dried it in a badstu-type kiln, smoking it with juniper wood. The result would have been brownish, lightly smoked malt. They had their own yeast, but what type of yeast is not clear. It might have been like kveik (or it might even have *been* kveik), or it might have been like the Baltic farmhouse yeasts. However, the yeast was dried, just as with kveik.

Öxabäck Ale

Lucy Clarke and Marcus Brand tested the recipe with 40% Gotland malt (smoked), 60% Belgian ale malt, and 10% mashed potato, fermenting it with #1 Sigmund kveik. The beer was good and very easy-drinking, being darkish brown, with a clear fruity banana aroma and herbal, woody notes (probably from the alder). It was lightly smoked, and had a very light, faint acidity, probably from the long mash.

Batch volume: 25 liters (6.6 US gal.)

Fermentables
- 8.5 kg (18.7 lb.) lightly juniper-smoked malt
- 800 g (1.8 lb.) potatoes, boiled and crushed

Hops
- 115 g (4 oz.) noble hops for hop tea

Additional Items
- alder sticks for the lauter tun
- rye straw for the lauter tun

Yeast
- #1 Sigmund kveik has been shown to work well

Brewing Notes
The brewing process is decidedly unusual:
Pour cold water over the milled malt, stir it in, then leave overnight. The mash should be fairly dry at this point because you will add more water the next day. It is important to ensure the mash stays below 10°C (<50°F) the entire time.
The next day, boil the potatoes and crush them.
Prepare the lauter tun by placing alder sticks in the bottom, then rye straw, then a cloth filter. Add the mash and the potatoes, then pour hot water over the mash and leave it for 24 hours. Try to keep the temperature above 50°C (122°F) the whole time. The source mentioned that hot water might be added a second time, presumably if it was necessary to keep the temperature up.
Run off the wort slowly, then boil it for an hour. During the boil, add water to adjust the volume so that you end up with 25 liters (6.6 gal.) of beer.
While the wort is run off, boil the hops in a little water for about two hours to make hop tea.
Cool the boiled wort (the original account says "to body temperature"), then transfer it to the fermentor. Add the hop tea, sieving off the hop cones. Pitch yeast, put the lid on the fermentor and cover with a blanket so it will stay warm. Put the fermentor somewhere warm.
Let it ferment 12–15 hours. That time is according to the original account, but obviously this depends on the yeast.

Oven Beers

Oven-based brewing is one of the main branches of farmhouse ale, so it includes a rather large selection of styles. This section only documents a few of those styles.

Seto Koduõlu

In the southeastern corner of Estonia is the traditional region of Setomaa, which stretches over the border into Russia. This is the homeland of the Seto people, who speak a language closely related to Estonian. The Seto are famous for having kept many of their traditional customs, even including their traditional folk religion. Their farmhouse brewing is also, just barely, alive.

Historically, the Seto made their own malt from barley or rye. The wet mash was shaped into a "bread" that looked like a thick pizza base and was baked in a pre-heated oven on rhubarb leaves. It was baked so hard that it turned black on the outside. Afterwards, it was broken up into the lauter tun, which had straw and juniper twigs in the bottom. The wort was run off, heated, and poured back through the grain bed many times.[42]

Today the Seto use malt "bread" made entirely from rye already pre-baked and sold in shops. The bread is too dense and dry to really be edible, so they are only used for brewing. The bread is extremely aromatic.

Seto Koduõlu "Bread"

Martin Thibault decided to recreate the Seto beer and bread in Canada and enlisted Mathieu Lhomelet, a *boulanger* in Montréal, to help him. Together they came up with a recipe for the "bread." Here are the ingredients for one "loaf" of slightly more than 1 kilogram (2.2 lb.):

- 150 g (5.3 oz.) kvass concentrate
- 550 g (1.2 lb.) dark rye malt
- 270 g (9.5 oz.) rye flour
- pinch of cumin, ground cocoa, and coffee

Notes on Brewing Koduõlu

Brewing this form of koduõlu generally happens in the kitchen, where a single one-kilogram (2.2 lb.) loaf is broken up and added to 10 liters (2.6 gal.) of water along with 0.5–1.0 kilograms (1.1–2.2 lb.) of sugar. After an hour the wort is run off through a sieve, cooled to 37°C (99°F), and fermented with baking yeast. Some brewers flavor the wort with juniper.

I tried this myself at home with malt bread from a shop in Obinitsa, Estonia. The bread itself yielded an OG of only 1.009, but the wort was dark and very aromatic. Adding one kilogram of sugar took the OG to 1.052. I fermented it with kveik to 1.016 FG and 4.9% ABV. No hops were added.

The resulting beer was very similar to the ones I tasted in Setomaa: a raisiny, prune-like aroma with a massive rye character. It had a sweetish taste with a lingering, fruity, rye-like flavor with no real aftertaste and no bitterness. The beer was both spicy and dry enough from the rye to be balanced without the bitterness.

Oven-Mashed Russian Farmhouse Ale

Oven-mashed Russian farmhouse ale is not really a style but more a kind of beer that has been brewed over a large area of Russia. Not all Russian farmhouse ale is brewed from rye, and not all of it is oven-mashed. Russians do not seem to have a generally agreed name for farmhouse ale, but some sources refer to *derevenskoye pivo*, or "village beer."

Dmitriy Zhezlov's Farmhouse Ale

This recipe comes from a brewing session with Dmitriy Zhezlov outside Kirov in Kirov oblast, Russia in the summer of 2017 (chap. 5, p. 159). Dmitriy learned to brew from a local old man when Dmitriy was living in the village of Vsekhsvyatskoye, about two hours' drive from Kirov, in the 1990s.

Dmitriy buys rye grain and malts it himself. He soaks the rye for 6 hours, then sprouts it 3 days until the shoot is 7–8 mm (¼–$^5\!/_{16}$ in.) long. He does not dry the malt at all. Instead, he makes a new batch of malt for each brew and uses a meat grinder to mill it (chap. 3, p. 78). The recipe that follows does not include instructions per se, but is a record of what Dmitriy did during the brewing session.

Batch volume: 10 liters (2.64 US gal.)

Original gravity: 1.045 (11.2°P)

Malts
- 2–3 kg (4.4–6.6 lb.) homemade undried rye malt

Hops
- few handfuls of wild Russian hops

Additional Items
- juniper branch tips, young (optional)
- rye straw
- two slices of bread
- one small stone

Yeast
- Baker's yeast

Brewing Notes

The mashing happens in the *korchaga*, a ceramic vessel with a small hole near the bottom. The hole was closed with a small wooden plug. Rye straw was cut to length and placed in the bottom of the korchaga to serve as the support for the filter bed, taking care to cover the hole with straw. The grist was placed on top and about 10 liters (2.64 gal.) of cold water added.

Meanwhile, a fire was lit in the great Russian stove and left to burn itself out so only a few embers remained. Dmitriy thought the oven temperature was around 150–180°C (300–350°F). The korchaga was placed inside the hot oven in the evening. After an hour I measured the mash temperature at 80°C (176°F). By the end, after 15 hours, the mash was at 63°C (145°F) and pH 5.7. The contents probably did not boil.

The korchaga was taken out of the oven and the wort was run off into a kettle. A couple of liters (a couple of quarts) of hot water was poured over the bed to sparge. When I visited Dmitriy something went wrong and the wort ran off too fast, taking too little sugar with it. The OG was only 1.030, but if we assume 60% extract efficiency he should have gotten something like 1.045.

Finally, the wort was boiled with hops. Dmitriy used wild Russian hops. (Some brewers add the tips of young juniper branches to the boiling wort near the end of the boil; they say this was to get juniper aroma and bitterness.) The hops were filtered out of the wort at the end of the boil.

The yeast was baker's yeast, which was started in some wort. A piece of bread was placed in a bowl and the yeast starter poured on. Together with a small stone and a handful of hop cones, the bread was placed in a cloth bag and then pitched into the wort. While preparing this, Dmitriy looked at me and said, "I am not understand why this method. I could just . . ." and he mimed pitching the starter directly in the wort. I have no idea either.

Dmitriy did not know the pitching temperature but said it should be "the same as when one bathes a small child." He measured it with his elbow, and when he declared the temperature correct I measured it with a thermometer to be 37°C (99°F).

Dmitriy usually lets the beer ferment for 7–10 days until the foam no longer covers the surface, then bottles the beer; the beer has low carbonation. The cloth bag is removed after a couple of days.

Dmitriy's beer is hazy dark brown. The head varies from none at all to big and off-white. The aroma is straw-like, fruity, and vaguely foresty, with rich, juicy rye notes. There are some grainy, herbal notes in the background too. The beer is clean, fresh, and easy to drink in large amounts. The finish is quite dry and astringent but in a pleasant way, and the dryness goes well with the rye flavor.

Chuvashian Farmhouse Ale

The region of Chuvashia in central Russia, along the Volga river between Kazan and Nizhniy Novgorod, is home to the Chuvash people, who speak a Turkic language. They are farmers, and famous for their farmhouse ale. Chuvashia was also chosen to be the center of Soviet hop growing, so most Soviet hops came from this area. Serebryanka, the hop variety that is one of the parents of Cascade, comes from Chuvashia.

Figure 9.18. Three Chuvash women cleaning the malt. Kshaushi, Chuvash Republic, Russia.

It is clear that Chuvashian farmhouse ale, known as *saura* locally, varies considerably. I attended a brew session with Marina Fyodorovna and two other Chuvash women at the Yasna ecovillage near the village of Kshaushi, and they made their own rye malt and brewed in a way very similar to Dmitriy Zhezlov (p. 78). One difference was that the Chuvashian brewers dried the malt in a preheated oven, thus, effectively making rye caramel malt.

However, Naumov[43] says Chuvashian farmhouse ale is generally made from homegrown barley, although rye, wheat, and millet may also be used. He describes a brewing process very similar to that of Zhezlov's, but the wort is not boiled, and hop tea is boiled separately then mixed in.

The Fyodorov family in Kshaushi described a different brewing process, where the mash is heated in a kettle over the fire and eventually boiled. No doubt there are more process variations than these. Everyone seems to use hops, while juniper is only used to clean the brewing vessels.

The brewing seems to be very widespread. I was told that every family with an old grandmother will be brewing. And it seems most of them have their own yeast. Marina Fyodorovna had her own yeast that she had inherited from her mother (#39 Marina). From the same village, I also collected #40 Rima (both strains are listed in table 4.1, p. 109).

The Fyodorov beer is not very strong, as they seem to use 1.0–1.5 kilograms of malt per 10 liters of water added (13–20 oz. per gallon). Before pitching the yeast, a starter is made with the semi-dry culture and a little wort, sugar, and rye flour. Once the starter is visibly fermenting, it is pitched. None of the brewers seem to know their pitching temperature, but I measured the temperature when Marina Fyodorovna said it was right and found it to be 39°C (102°F). The beer ferments for five to seven days.

The two yeast cultures that were collected both contained bacteria and non-*Saccharomyces* yeast, as well as several strains of *Saccharomyces*. The *Saccharomyces* strains seem to be genetically unique. Unfortunately, not much more is known about these yeasts at time of writing. It is possible that the non-*Saccharomyces* yeast comes from the rye flour that is stirred into the starter culture.

Figure 9.19. Marina Fyodorovna brewing in Kshaushi, Chuvash Republic, Russia.

Marina Fyodorovna's Farmhouse Ale

This recipe is based on the brew session I attended at Yasna. When Marina demonstrated her brewing process for us, the malt had not sprouted as fast as she had expected because the summer was too cold. The demonstration was done with this malt, and so all the measurements were off. The brewing process used a *kuurna*-like lauter tun, which is described in chapter 6 (p. 192).

Brewing liquor: 10 liters (2.64 US gal.) total added

Malts
• 1.5 kg (3.3 lb.) homemade rye caramel malt

Hops
• 1 or 2 handfuls of Chuvashian hops

Additional Items
• stones suitable for heating
• linden branches
• oat straw

Yeast
• #39 Marina

Brewing Notes

Heat the water until you can barely hold your hand in it. (Marina measured the temperature with a thermometer once and got 45°C [113°F].) Mix the water and grist in a ceramic or metal pot. Put it in an oven that has been heated over a fire with the embers and ashes removed (see chap. 3, p. 76). The oven should not be too hot, you should be able to hold your uncovered hand inside it. Leave the pot in the oven for 12–20 hours. The contents should not boil.

Take the pot out of the oven and transfer the contents to a pot suitable for boiling. Boil the mash strongly for 2–3 hours. It is ready when a (cooled) drop of liquid from the mash will sit on your fingernail without running off. While the mash is boiling, steep hop cones in hot water for 2–3 hours until the liquid turns brown and the hops sink to the bottom. It should not boil. This hop tea is added to the wort to taste once the wort has cooled.

Filter the mash in a kuurna-like trough with a hole in the middle and a rod for opening and closing the aperture. Place linden branches on the bottom, then oat straw on top. Run off the wort, then bring it briefly to a boil with hot stones. Leave it to cool to pitching temperature. (Marina judges the pitching temperature by tasting the wort—when she pronounced that it was right I measured it with a thermometer to be 39°C [102°F].)

Once the wort has been set aside to cool, begin the yeast starter. Marina's own yeast (#39 Marina) was mixed with rye flour and sugar, and was covered in foam and clearly fermenting after just three hours. Once you are satisfied the wort temperature is right and the yeast has gotten properly started, pitch the yeast. Ferment the beer for 5–7 days.

Sur

The Komi peoples live in northeastern European Russia, speaking a Uralic language remotely related to Finnish and Hungarian. Of these peoples, the southernmost are the Komi-Permyak, living in the area around the town of Kudymkar, just west of the Urals. I met Marina Ivanovna in a small village outside Kudymkar, and she gave us a brewing demonstration.

Marina says as recently as 2005 very few people in the area were brewing, but that brewing has picked up in recent years. Today there is even a festival for the local beer, known as *sur*, which Marina organizes. In the center of Kudymkar the Cafe Permyak serves sur.

Figure 9.20. Café Permyak in Kudymkar, Komi Republic, Russia.

Marina Ivanovna's Sur

Marina makes her own malt from rye, which she dries in a wooden trough on top of a Russian stove, so it is very gently dried. The recipe that follows does not include instructions per se, but is a record of what Marina did during the brewing session.

Batch volume: 25 liters (6.6 US gal.)

Malts
- 11.25 kg (24.8 lb.) rye malt

Additional Items
- straw

Hops
- optional, added to first runnings

Yeast
- #39 Marina farmhouse yeast, #40 Rima farmhouse yeast, or baker's yeast

Brewing Notes

The malt was milled, then put into a metal pot and hot water added. I measured the temperature to be 61°C (142°F). The pot was then placed in a hot oven and left for 24 hours. At the end, I measured the mash pH to 4.9.

The next morning, the contents were ladled into a low wooden trough with a hole in the bottom, very similar to the Finnish kuurna. The mash was filtered through straw and cloth resting on top of wooden spiles along the bottom of the trough.

The first wort was the sweetest. I measured the gravity to be 1.035, but Marina said something went wrong with this brew and that it should be sweeter. Assuming a 50% mash efficiency, we should have gotten 1.068, so I assume this is closer to the usual strength. The first wort may have hops added.

The wort was cooled to pitching temperature. Marina used Russian baking yeast:, taking 6–7 grams (0.20–0.25 oz.), she mixed it with wort and wheat flour, then waited until it started showing visible activity, which took about 30 minutes when we visited her. The starter was pitched into the wort at 31°C (88°F).

Marina said the beer can be drunk after 5 hours, but that it is best after 24 hours.

Keptinis

Today, keptinis seems only to be brewed in northeastern Lithuania, east of a line from Panevežys to Papilys. There are several commercial versions of it from Lithuanian breweries, but most of these do not have much of the style's characteristic caramel flavor, probably because the breweries are not able find ovens large enough to bake the entire mash for each batch. Perhaps it is also because producing that flavor in an oven is not as easy as it may seem.

Historically, there were brewers baking the mash in mainland Estonia and eastern Finland as well, but the brewing in these areas seems to have died out, leaving only the Seto people in Estonia brewing from malt "bread" bought in the shops (*see* "Seto Koduõlu" above).

The characteristic flavors in keptinis come from both Maillard reactions and caramelization of the sugars in the mash during oven baking. As you can see from table 9.2, the temperatures needed for caramelization lie above 100°C. This means that during the baking everything revolves around the water content in the mash. Under normal conditions, water cannot be heated to more than 100°C, because at that temperature it turns to steam. This means that during boiling of the wort to make vossaøl there is essentially no caramelization happening. Keptinis, however, is different, because the oven allows us to get rid of the water and reach temperatures higher than 100°C. This is a much more complicated issue than it might seem at first, however.

Table 9.2 Common Sugars in Wort by Caramelization Temperature

Sugar	Caramelization temp.	Typical percentage of total sugar in wort	Percentage of total sugar caramelized
Fructose	110°C (230°F)	3%	3%
Glucose	160°C (320°F)	22%	30%
Sucrose	160°C (320°F)	5%	30%
Maltotriose	170°C (338°F)	21%	51%
Maltose	180°C (356°F)	46%	97%
Maltotetraose	no data	5%	100%

On my first attempt to make keptinis, I set the electric kitchen oven at home to 180°C and baked the mash for three hours. The water in the mash visibly boiled for about two and a half hours—the top crust first turned brown, then dark brown, and finally almost black. After three hours I took the mash out and was astonished to find that the center temperature was just below 100°C. When I tasted the beer I was even more astonished to discover that it tasted very much like vossaøl. The boiling mash had behaved rather like a long wort boil and created similar flavors. This made me realize that to get a different flavor it was necessary to raise the temperature.

Armed with this experience, I decided to try again, this time with the oven at 250°C. I inserted a meat thermometer in the center of the middle box in order to track the temperature development. As can be seen in figure 9.21, the temperature first dropped gently, then rapidly rose until it hit 100°C, when it suddenly stopped.˙ I left the boxes in for over three hours, but the temperature simply refused to budge above 100°C.

What was going on? The heat was making the water in the mash evaporate, a process that carries away large amounts of heat energy. This is why sweating works for cooling down the human body: the evaporation of sweat consumes heat energy, carrying this heat away and so reducing the body's temperature. In southern Europe, a well-known trick for cooling the bedroom at night is to hang up wet laundry there, so that the drying will lower the temperature. While the center temperature of the mash was only 100°C, it was clearly very much higher at the edges because this time I burned the top crust black. Along the bottom and sides of the boxes the contents were also blackish. The flavor from this beer was completely different: toasty, mineral, and licorice-like, with very little caramel flavor. Surprisingly, it did not taste overly burned and was actually quite drinkable.

˙ The thermometer showed 101°C during the first attempt, 100°C during the second. It is not clear to me whether the difference is real or just measurement error.

What I learned from these two attempts was that 180°C was probably too low and 250°C was definitely too high. It was clear that if I wanted more caramelization without burning the sugars I would need to get rid of the water. So, for the third attempt I chose 190°C, with the oven fan on in order to blow away as much of the moisture as possible. A Lithuanian *duonkepis*, or bread-baking oven, is designed for burning a fire in the baking space, so it has a chimney for letting the smoke out. This means it probably also vents the steam from the mash, much like an electric oven with the fan on.

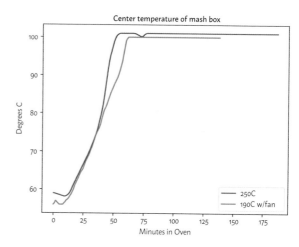

Figure 9.21. Temperatures in the center of mash boxes during oven baking, from two separate attempts.

The third attempt, at 190°C, came much closer. The boxes boiled quite violently for about an hour and twenty minutes, then stopped because there was no longer enough water for visible boiling. The top of the crust burned blackish during the last 45 minutes, but the sides and bottoms of the boxes had soft, gooey, caramel-tasting mash. The center temperature never went above 100°C, but that probably is not achievable anyway without causing far too much burning.

The reactions that cause the keptinis flavor are happening in the crust on top, but even more along the sides and bottoms of the boxes. Geoff Latham of Pope's Yard Brewery in the UK tried brewing keptinis both with an electric oven and a brick oven. He found there was much more caramelization in the brick oven because the boxes are placed directly on the hot bricks. This suggests that with an electric oven you probably want to preheat the oven with a pizza stone (or quarry tile) inserted for best effects.

All of these brews required a good bit of work to clean the kitchen and the bread pans afterward, but the 250°C brew was far worse than the other two. At those temperatures sugar burns into a black substance rather like concrete, which is very difficult to remove even from non-stick pans. It is hard enough that it could probably be used as a substitute for concrete in building projects. One of the pans had so much of this that, even after days of soaking in water and using far too much brewer's cleaning agents, I had to give up and throw the thing away.* So beware of the high temperatures!

When planning your brew, start with the bread pans. You want pans that have a large surface to volume ratio, since the reactions you are trying to create will happen at the edges. Also, the size of your pans will probably constrain the size of your batch. In general, dry malts fill about the same volume as the wet mash does (before the wet mash swells). I found 1 liter of milled malts weighed about half a kilogram. Beware of expansion—when the center temperature reaches about 70°C the mash will swell up. Do not fill the boxes to the rim, leave at least 1 cm of headroom. What spills will be burned black and lost, and it will also cause a mess that is difficult to clean.

It is clear that baking the mash in the oven can create a wide range of flavors, but exactly how is not yet understood. According to Simonas Gutautas,[44] keptinis brewers do not produce a consistent

---

* Warm thanks to my wife for being understanding about this.

flavor from batch to batch, so the details are probably quite involved. From seeing keptinis brewed a few times, many online reports, and some trials by myself, I get the clear impression that you get interesting flavors almost no matter what you do, and that burning the mash so much that the beer is undrinkable is quite hard. Do not panic just because the top layer burns! The layers below will be much paler. A little burning does no harm, and you can scrape off the burnt part if you overdo the baking. But you will still have to deal with the cleanup.

Vytautas Jančys's Keptinis

I do not have definite numbers for OG, FG, and ABV, unfortunately. Theoretically, the bitterness should be 28. However, I have brewed this myself with around 50 IBUs and found that to work well for balancing the sweet-tasting toffee and caramel flavors.

Batch volume: 25 liters (6.6 US gal.)

Bitterness: 28 IBU (theoretical)

Malts
- 10 kg (22 lb.) pale malt

Hops
- 25 g (0.9 oz.) bittering hops (14% AA) hop tea @ lauter
- 10 g (0.35 oz.) aroma hops (5%–6% AA) hop tea @ lauter

Yeast
- Safale S-04 or #16 Simonaitis farmhouse yeast

Brewing Notes

Boil water, then use the nearly boiling water to mash in for a temperature of 65°C (149°F). The mash should be relatively dry. Leave for an hour. At the end of the hour, the mash temperature should be around 58°C (136°F) and the pH 6.1.

Put the mash into baking trays, leaving a centimeter (⅜ in.) of headspace to allow the mash to swell. Insert the trays in the oven, which should be preheated to 180°C (356°F) and the oven fan on. Leave the entire mash in the oven for three hours. The purpose is to brown the mash, not to burn it. Once the top crust starts turning dark brown, reduce the temperature to avoid burning. While the mash bakes, make hop tea and prepare the lauter tun.

Make the hop tea by boiling the hops for 30 minutes in 2 liters of water (just over 2 qt.).

Prepare the lauter tun by lining it with straw to serve as filter. Once the trays are out of the oven, use a wooden spoon to break up the mash and scoop the contents into the lauter tun. Pour on the hop tea, then lauter with near-boiling water. The wort coming out should be dark brown or black. Cool, and pitch the yeast.

If Safale S-04 is used, pitch at 19–25°C (66–77°F) and ferment 2–4 days. If #16 Simonaitis is used, pitch at 35°C (95°F) and ferment for 24 hours.

Žiobiškis-Style Keptinis

Žiobiškis is in northeastern Lithuania, well north of Vikonys and almost on the border with Latvia. The recipe is taken from Dagys,[45] an ethnographic article based on interviews with eight older people in the village and published in a Lithuanian journal.

The malt was homemade and dried outside in the shade in summer. The hops were home-grown Lithuanian hops, so probably Polish or Czech noble hops would be the best substitute. I have assumed an extract efficiency of 55% from the homemade malt for the specifications.

Batch volume: 25 liters (6.6 US gal.)
Original gravity: 1.067 (16.4°P)
Final gravity: 1.016 (4.1°P)

Bitterness: 75 IBU
ABV: 6.7%

Malts/Fermentables
• 8.7 kg (19.1 lb.) Pilsner malt
• 550 g (1.2 lb.) sugar

Additional Items
• rye straw
• alder wood

Hops
• 175 g (6.2 oz.) noble hops for hop tea @ lauter

Yeast
• Baker's yeast or #16 Simonaitis farmhouse yeast

Brewing Notes
Pour the grist into the mash tun, then add boiling water and stir well. The mash should not be too watery. Leave the mash for 3–4 hours. Next, form the mash into loaf-like shapes, place them on a metal plate, and insert them into the oven. (Some brewers use metal containers.) The mash will bake overnight.

The next day, boil the hops in a relatively large volume of water in comparison to the cones for two hours while stirring continuously.

Prepare the lauter tun by placing a layer of rye straw on the bottom and then the alder wood; another top layer of rye straw is optional. Pour the hop tea through the filter, leaving only the hop cones behind. Set aside the filtered hop tea. Break up the malt loaves and drop them on top of the hops. Pour boiling water over the bed and wait three hours.

Run off the wort and cool it to 18–22°C if using baker's yeast, then add the hop tea. If using #16 Simonaitis, the wort only needs to be cooled to 35°C. When the foam turns brown and starts to fall, fermentation is done.

Mainland Estonian Oven-Based Beer

Today, people on the Estonian islands brew koduõlu, a raw ale style, but, historically, oven beers very similar to keptinis dominated on the Estonian mainland. However, farmhouse brewing on the mainland appears to have died out (except among the Seto people), so this recipe for oven-based beer is taken from an archival record, which was translated for me by Hans Üürike.[46] The record comes from the village of Meeksi, on the western shore of Lake Peipus.

The farmers made malt from barley, which was dried on steel plates over the oven. The drying was probably gentle, so Pilsner malt sounds like a good substitute. Of course, the specifications are unknown.

Batch volume: 25 liters (6.6 US gal.)

Malts
- 4.2 kg (9.3 lb.) Pilsner malt
- 2.1 kg (4.6 lb.) rye flour with hulls

Hops
- unknown amount, used for hop tea; noble hops are probably best

Yeast
- (no indication what kind)

Brewing Notes

Mix the grist and flour with cold water (I have presumed from the record that it was cold) to a thick dough. Place the dough in baking trays and bake the mash in a warm oven for 3–4 hours. Take care that the temperature in the mash does not rise so quickly that you destroy the enzymes before the sugar has formed.

Prepare a hop tea by boiling the hops for 4–6 hours.

Take the mash out of the oven and empty it into the lauter tun. Add hot water. Allow the mash to stand a few minutes, then lauter.

Add the hop tea to the collected wort, let cool, and pitch your yeast.

Fermented Mash

I can give no guidance on how best to brew this type of beer, because I have never seen it brewed and have no idea what it is supposed to taste like. I am adding the recipes anyway to document this type of beer for anyone who wants to try it. Ivar Husdal brought a fermented mash beer to the Norwegian farmhouse ale festival in 2019. That beer had a powerful taste of butyric acid, so I recommend mashing hot and long, and sparging hot to get rid of as much of the microbiology in the grain as possible.

Luumäki-Style

This recipe is adapted from an account I got from a Finnish brewer who claims to still brew this type of beer. It was quite detailed, but the grain bill is near-impossible to reproduce outside of eastern Finland. The barley and oats are nameless Finnish landraces, but not the rye, which is called Sarkalahti. Up to 10% of the grist can be oats from a black-colored landrace. Incredible as it sounds, the brewer claims the rye is enough to convert the unmalted barley in the mash, which does match up with some other sources. There really are no hops.

For the yeast, I recommend #39 Marina or #40 Rima, since they are the closest to this type of brewing, being usually mixed with rye flour in the yeast starter.

Batch volume: 25 liters (6.6 US gal.)

Grain bill
- 9.4 kg (20.7 lb.) unmalted barley
- 3.1 kg (6.8 lb.) unmalted rye

Yeast
- Unknown, but try substituting #39 Marina or #40 Rima

Additional Items
- straw for lauter tun
- juniper branches for lauter tun

Brewing Notes
Lay the straw on the bottom of the lauter tun, then the juniper branches on top. Pour the grist over the top of the bed, then add water at 80°C (176°F) and tightly cover the lauter tun. The mash should now stay like this until the temperature is down to 30–40°C (86–104°F), which in summer can take as long as 30 hours. If brewing in colder conditions, you may need to insulate to make sure it stays warm this long.

Once the temperature is low enough, pitch the yeast. The brewer who gave me this recipe says his own yeast can take "from a couple of days to a week."

Once fermentation is done, run off the beer, and cellar condition it for a couple of days.

Vanylven-Style

This recipe is adapted from the account in NEG 7329, from Vanylven in western Norway. The malt was dried on a kiln very like a såinn, using birch wood.

Batch volume: 25 liters (6.6 US gal.)

Malts
- 13.5 kg (29.8 lb.) birch-smoked barley malt

Hops
- no amounts given

Additional Items
- juniper branches with berries, for infusion
- straw
- alder branches

Yeast
- Kveik

Brewing Notes

Use juniper branches with as many berries as possible, and knock the branches so older needles fall off. Put the branches in the kettle, then boil to make a juniper infusion.

Use the alder branches and straw to line the bottom of the lauter tun. Pour the grist and hops into the lauter tun and add the boiling hot juniper infusion. Stir well.

Wait until the mash has cooled to a milk-warm temperature, 35–37°C (95–99°F). Pitch yeast and stir a little.

Once the fermentation has died down after 1 to 1.5 days, run off the beer.

Stone Beer

Styles of stone beer do not seem to exist, so these are just some of the stone beer recipes I have been able to find.

Nössemark Stone Beer

There is one account remarkable for being the only documentary record of stone brewing in Sweden, on which the recipe below is based.[47] It was written by Edith Råström in 1935 in Nössemark, western Sweden, very close to the Norwegian border.[48] The malt was mainly made from barley and oats, but rye and wheat were occasionally used. Normally, the malt bill comprised an even mix of barley and oat malt, but for the best beer only barley was used. The malt was homemade and dried in a kiln (see chap. 3, p. 70), but with the boards sloping down on each side instead. There is no record of what fuel was used. The beer would be made a little stronger for celebrations.

Batch volume: 25 liters (6.6 US gal.)

Fermentables
- 3 kg (6.6 lb.) homemade smoked malt
- rye bran (unknown quantity)

Hops
- unknown quantity

Additional Items
- syrup (optional)
- bitter orange peel (optional)
- alder branches, juniper branches, and rye straw for the filter

Yeast
- Unknown Swedish farmhouse yeast, kveik would be a good substitute

Brewing Notes

The lauter tun was prepared with alder sticks on the bottom, then juniper twigs, and finally covered with rye straw. Boiling water was poured into the lauter tun, left to stand for a while, and then run off to remove any impurities.

Cold water was poured over the grist, and the rye bran was mixed in. The vessel was covered up and left for a while. Water was boiled and then poured over the cold mash, which was stirred. Eventually, the mash was transferred to a kettle and boiled "until it separated." Some would skip adding the hot water and instead put the cold mash in a kettle to be boiled. Hot stones or iron weights could be added to keep the mash boiling longer.

The wort was then run off and boiled in the kettle. The longer it was boiled, the stronger the beer would be.

The hops were boiled separately in water. Syrup and bitter orange peel could be added to the hop tea.

The hop tea and wort were mixed and cooled to a temperature that was described as the same as for dough mixed with yeast, or lukewarm; that is probably roughly body temperature.

Then the yeast was pitched. This was farmhouse yeast, stored on a yeast log. There is no indication of how long the beer should ferment.

Rågö Stone Beer

The two Pakri islands just off the coast of north-western Estonia had a Swedish population until World War II. In 1940, Per Söderbäck published an ethnographic study of the islands, in which he included an account of the local brewing methods.[49] The malt was made from local barley dried in a *ria*, so presumably it would likely resemble rather lightly smoked Pilsner malt.

A local expression for the Christmas beer was "heads in the floor straw." The floors were covered in straw and this implied the Christmas beer should be strong enough that people would fall asleep on the floor. Söderbäck dryly adds: "Now the beer here is ordinarily quite strong, so no great quantities are required for it to have that effect."

Batch volume: 25 liters (6.6 US gal.)

Malts
- 9 kg (19.8 lb.) lightly smoked Pilsner malt

Hops
- 80 g (3 oz.) local hops, for hop tea

Additional Items
- Wooden sticks and straw, for the filter

Yeast
- Farmhouse yeast, probably like a Baltic farmhouse culture, prepared with a starter

Brewing Notes

Put the grist in the mash tun and pour boiling water over it. There should not be so much water that the mash paddle cannot stand upright in the mash. Add glowing hot iron balls or stones to the mash to boil it. The account does not say when the balls or stones were added, but waiting an hour or so to ensure saccharification sounds like a good idea.

Make the hop tea by boiling the hops in water.

Lay some wooden sticks across the bottom of the lauter tun, then put straw on top of that. Pour the hop tea onto the sticks and straw, making sure the lauter tun tap is closed.

Pour the mash into the lauter tun on top of everything. Run off the wort and transfer to the fermentor. Use hot water to sparge the filter bed until sufficient wort has been run off.

Allow the wort to cool until "lukewarm" and pitch the ready-prepared yeast starter.

Ferment the beer fermented for 12 hours, before transferring it to casks.

Solvychegodsk Stone Beer

The recipe below is taken from a paper written by the famous Russian ethnographer, Vladimir Ivanovich Lamanskiy, published in a Russian ethnographic journal in 1898. The paper covers the life and work of farmers in Solvychegodsk, near Kotlas in northern Russia. This area is about 300 km north of Kirov, where Dmitriy Zhezlov lives (see recipe on p. 321), and 800 km northeast of Moscow. In the district immediately to the south, at the eastern end of Vologda Oblast, stone brewing is still alive today.

There is no indication of how the malt was made, or what grain was used for this purpose. However, in this region, people generally seemed to use rye and to dry their malt on top of the oven. So, very likely, the malt would have been pale, homemade rye malt.

The hops amount seems incredible, I know, but it reflects what was recorded. The paper says for 10 buckets (each 12.29 liters) of beer, 15 funts (Russian pound) of hops are needed. Forty funts is one pood, which is 16.38 kilograms (36.1 lb.). The hops would have been Russian hops grown at latitude 61° north, so the aroma and alpha acid content are difficult to estimate. They would not be like modern craft hops.

Batch volume: 25 liters (6.6 US gal.):

Fermentables
- 3.33 kg (7.3 lb.) pale rye malt
- 3.33 kg (7.3 lb.) rye flour

Additional Items
- rye straw in lauter tun
- stones

Hops
- 1.1 kg (2.4 lb.) hops (see introductory notes) @ FWH
- 150 g (5.3 oz.) hops @ fermentor

Yeast
- Wild yeast, most likely what existed on the rye flour used for the starter

Brewing Notes
Place rye straw in the bottom of the lauter tun, then add the grist and flour on top. Boil the water and pour it over the grist. Start a fire that has a pyramid of cobblestones (i.e., large stones) on top. Once the stones are hot, use tongs (the account says wooden tongs) to lower them into the mash, making it boil. Wait half a day.

To judge whether the mash is ready, take a piece of straw and form a triangle. Dip the triangle in the liquid part of the mash and lift it up. If a film forms inside the triangle, the mash is ready.

Run off the wort and boil it in a cauldron with 1.1 kg (2.4 lb.) of the hops.

Cool the wort and pitch the yeast from a starter together with 150 g (5.3 oz.) of hops.

Make the yeast starter from rye flour mixed with water, hops, and some vodka. This seems to be the same method as the midsummer yeast (see chap. 4, p. 101) but without any attached superstition. The purpose of the vodka is probably to suppress microbes that have a low alcohol tolerance.

Farmhouse Beer from Other Regions

Below is a selection of beers that do not fit any of the other categories. Not all of the styles have sufficient documentation to allow me to create recipes for them.

Corn Ale

Farmhouse brewing was very common in Orkney up until World War II, and the brewing tradition is still alive today. It is not clear how many brewers there are, but at least one makes his own malt from the local *bere*, the Orkney landrace of barley, and brews it in the traditional way he learned from his mother.

Historically, the Orkney brewers used the traditional type of kiln found in the Northern Isles (see fig. 3.29). The fuel used was peat, giving the malt a familiar peat-smoke flavor.

The mash was either a single infusion mash or a three-step infusion mash. The mash was then filtered through oat straw and/or heather, and the wort boiled with hops. If people did not have enough hops, they sometimes used bogbean (*Menyanthes trifoliata*) to flavor and bitter the beer. The yeast, known locally as "barm," was pitched at the temperature of blood. The yeast was stored in a jar between brews.

There was a brewing tradition in nearby Shetland too.[50]

English Farmhouse Ale

Farmhouse brewing was very common in England until the introduction of a tax on malt caused a drastic decline in farmhouse brewing, but it clearly survived in some areas until quite recently. Unfortunately, there seems to be very little overall documentation on English farmhouse brewing, with the lucky exception of brewing in Blaxhall, Suffolk.[51] The author ends his account by noting that in the Capel St. Mary and Little Wenham parish "half a dozen families" still brew. What happened after 1956 is unknown.

Suffolk Farmhouse Ale

This recipe is taken from George Evans's 1956 classic, *Ask the Fellows who Cut the Hay*, which includes a description of brewing in the Suffolk village of Blaxhall. Unfortunately, there is no indication what kind of malt was used, but the malt was definitely bought. Very likely this was English pale malt from small producers in the area.

The yeast is a bit of a problem: it was clearly English ale yeast, but equally clearly not of a kind available today. Probably the closest equivalent would be kveik, but it is possible saison yeast would be just as close.

Batch volume: 25 liters (6.6 US gal.)

Malts
- 4.2 kg (9.3 lb.) malt

Hops
- 125 g (3.4 oz.) English hops (split between boils, see notes below)

Yeast
- English farmhouse yeast (now extinct); substitute a kveik or saison yeast

Account of Brewing Process

The grist was placed in the mash tun and two buckets of cold water were poured over it along with one bucket of boiling water. The malt was then thoroughly mixed by hand until all of the grist was wet. It was left for 15 minutes before five buckets of boiling water were poured over it. Then it mashed for four hours.

The wort was run off and another four buckets of boiling water added. Again, the mash was left for four hours. Meanwhile, the first wort was boiled with 95 g (3.4 oz.) of hops, also for four hours. Afterwards, the second wort was boiled, also for four hours, with the same hops used for the first wort and the remaining 30 g (1 oz.) of hops as well.

If they were kept separate, the beer from the first wort was known as strong beer, while that from the second was mild or small beer. However, the two were usually combined.

The wort was cooled until milk-warm, roughly 35°C (95°F), and the yeast was pitched. The village had a yeast chain, because every wife knew who had brewed last and would have the freshest yeast.

The beer would ferment overnight, then the yeast was skimmed off for the next brew and the beer was casked.

Welsh Farmhouse Ale

Farmhouse brewing was widespread in Wales into the late nineteenth century. Farmhouse ale was more or less a customary requirement for Christmas, the harvest, and social events like weddings. In parts of Monmouthshire, Brecknockshire, and Radnorshire, the farmers mostly made cider instead. The great religious revival of the late nineteenth century brought with it a strong temperance movement, which did much to reduce brewing. Government regulations were introduced in the nineteenth century to stop, or at least reduce, farmhouse brewing. Even so, farmhouse brewing still continued in parts of north Pembrokeshire and west Carmarthenshire into the 1970s.[52] One source claims it was still alive in the Gwaun valley in 1993, while another claims it was alive as late as 2009.[53]

Welsh Farmhouse Ale

The recipe is based on the account in Scourfield. Most market towns seem to have had commercial maltsters, and the farmers brought their barley there to have it malted. Unfortunately, I have no information on what malt was used, but pale malt seems a likely guess.

Batch volume: 25 liters (6.6 US gal.)

Fermentables
- 6.5 kg (14.3 lb.) malt
- 1.15 kg (2.5 lb.) sugar

Hops
- 10 g (0.4 oz.) English hops

Additional Items
- gorse branch or wheat straw

Yeast
- English ale yeast

Account of Brewing Process

First, the mash tun (known as *cerwyn*) was prepared by placing a furze branch or wheat straw on the bottom. Near-boiling water was poured into the mash tun and the grist added. The mash was then left to rest for three hours, after which more hot water was poured over the mash for another 30-minute rest.

The wort was run off and brought to a boil while the hops and sugar were stirred in. After the boil was finished, the wort was strained to remove the hops and poured into the fermentor (i.e., the mash tun, which had been cleaned in the meantime). The wort was left to cool overnight, then "brewer's yeast" was added.

The beer was left to ferment for 8 days, with the yeast being skimmed off daily. That yeast was stored in jars that were kept cool for use in the next beer. The beer was then left for further 7–10 days before it was ready to drink.

Westphalian Farmhouse Ale

Farmhouse brewing for the harvest months was widespread in several places around northern Germany up until World War I.[54] However, the only area I have proper documentation for is Westphalia, specifically the area northwest of Münster. In order to brew, the farm had to purchase a brewing concession at the local customs office. Under Hitler, it was raised to 4 Reichsmarks.

The farmhouse beer in this region seems to have been brewed in spring and was intended for field workers, especially during harvest. The farmers made their own malt from barley, drying the green malt either over the oven on a stone shelf known as an *est*, or inside the baking oven.

The brewing equipment seems to have been mostly wooden, but with copper kettles, often square in shape. Some lauter tuns had quite sophisticated false bottoms, while others used straw. In many cases, the wooden vessels were cleaned with a juniper infusion.

Brewing processes varied widely. I have come across three different ones described in the Westphalia Folklore Commission archives:

- A boiled mash, with hops and juniper berries in the mash and a raw (unboiled) wort. The mash had to boil a certain time to get the right flavor, the account says.[55]
- An infusion mash followed by boiling with hops for 1–3 hours.[56]
- The fermented mash process: mix hot water, grist, and hops, let it cool, then pitch yeast. Run off after fermentation.[57]

One account claims the beer was similar to *altbier* in flavor and strength.[58] That account describes the ordinary process with no special ingredients. All the farmers used hops, either wild varieties or ones they had cultivated themselves, and some also boiled juniper branches or juniper berries in their wort. One account added salt to the beer.[59]

Only a single account, in archive VOKO 313 (see n. 59), gives anything like a recipe. This account describes a normal brewing process, except that the boil lasted four hours. The recipe was for 200 liters (52.8 gal.) of beer and used 30 kg (66 lb.) of malt and 2 kg (4.4 lb.) of hops.

What kind of yeast the farmers used is not clear. One account from the same archive record says they obtained top-fermenting yeast from a nearby brewery and pitched it at 25–30°C (77–86°F), while two other accounts describe pitching temperatures of 8–10°C (46–50°F).

One account from 1953, again from VOKO 313, says the information was collected by visiting a certain farm in the village of Welbergen because he knew they had brewed on this farm. The farmer was not home, so he spoke to a neighbor instead and was greatly surprised to be told that this farm still brewed. He was shown customs papers that granted the farm the right to brew 2000 liters per year (roughly 17 bbl.). Siuts and Bartelt say that in some places farmers were brewing up until 1970.[60]

Aludi

Georgia, on the south side of the Caucasus mountains, is really a wine country. But, high up in the mountains where the climate is too cold for wine grapes, the highlanders brew beer. The information in this section is mostly based on Nadiradze.[61]

Today, two remote regions high up in the mountains have kept the brewing tradition alive, Khevsureti and, especially, Tusheti. In both regions, beer brewing is very closely bound up with local religious beliefs and the drinking of beer is seen as a religious act. Barley used for the beer is grown on lands that the entire village owns together, called *khati* lands. Brewing is also communal, led by the village elder, and the beer is drunk at religious rituals. The beer is called *aludi*.

The malt is homemade. This is done by throwing a sack of barley in a brook to soak it, before letting it sprout on an attic floor. The malt is then sun-dried and the rootlets removed by sifting.

Very large, tall copper kettles, shaped rather like vases, are used for brewing. These kettles can be 300–700 liters in size and are heated over a fire. The cauldron is filled with grist and water at a ratio of 1:1 and stirred while being heated. The mash is slowly heated until it boils. The mash is left to settle and the resulting clear part is removed by ladle. The sludge is filtered through goat-wool sacks.

The villagers use hops in the beer, even though hops do not grow this high up in the mountains. The villagers have to trade for hops or travel to pick them wild. Once the wort is filtered, it is boiled with hops to concentrate the wort.

The yeast can only be pitched by the village elder. This entire process is cast in mystery, because it is handled by the village elder, who is the mediator between the people and the gods. The villages have their own yeast, collected from the foam of the previous brew and mixed with flour. When the yeast is pitched a prayer is spoken.

The beer is left to ferment for 5–6 days. Several sources say the beer is completely black in color, although photos show beer the color of tea.[62]

Oat Beer

In areas that grew only oats, people were forced to brew from oats alone if they could not afford to buy or barter for barley. There are very few descriptions of pure oat beer, but one comes from Jølster in Sunnfjord, western Norway, just north of the great glacier.[63]

The oats were laid in a sack in a stream until "it was wet enough." The sack was taken up and laid on the bank to germinate, and turned now and again, until the rootlets started poking out of the bag. Then it was spread out in a malting frame or on a flat rock to keep sprouting, covered in wet sacks or straw. This was known as "turf malting," because the germinated grain would stick together like turf.

Another approach was to "loose malt," where the germinating grain was piled in small heaps and stirred by hand once a day. The benefit of this approach was that it avoided having to tear loose the "turf," which was hard work.

Oats are slower to germinate than barley, so germination usually took eight days. The sign that one should stop was either that the shoot turned green or that it was 1 cm long. The shoot and rootlets were then rubbed off by hand. Not removing the rootlets resulted in murky beer.

Finally, the green malt was dried on a shelf next to the fireplace. The stone shelf was not to be warmer than the hand could tolerate. Malt could also be floor dried in a heated loft. Either way, the drying was very gentle.

Figure 9.22. The painting *Buttercup Night* by Nikolai Astrup. Astrup was a farmhouse brewer in Jølster, western Norway.

Oat Beer

This basic recipe is based on an account (NEG 7398) from Jølster, a municipality in the district of Sunnfjord in western Norway.

Batch volume: 25 liters (6.6 US gal.):

Malts
- 7.8 kg (17.2 lb.) pale oat malt

Hops
- Noble hops, quantity unknown

Additional Items
- juniper branches for infusion, older specimens with berries
- additional juniper branches, or straw, for lauter tun

Yeast
- Kveik

Brewing Notes

The juniper for the infusion needed to be old, with cloven branches and many berries. The hot juniper infusion was poured over the grist and the mash stirred the whole time. The mash temperature was judged by observing how the mash ran off the mash paddle. Unfortunately, that means we have no idea what the temperature was. The mash was left until it had settled, which probably means the grist and the liquor had separated.

Lautering was done through straw or juniper branches. A small part of the wort was set aside and boiled with the hops. The collected wort was cooled to pitch temperature, which was 30°C (86°F). After pitching the yeast, the beer was fermented at least 24 hours.

10

TODAY AND TOMORROW

From the mid-nineteenth century onward, farmhouse brewing declined all over northern Europe. Major economic changes caused a dramatic restructuring of life in the countryside. Improved transportation made farmers part of the money economy, while increased efficiency in farming dramatically reduced the need for workers.

This economic restructuring profoundly changed the fabric of rural society. Sjur Rørlien, a farmhouse brewer in Voss, says he feels lucky to have grown up at a time when Dyrvedalen was an active farming society where everyone worked closely together on the many farms in that tiny valley. "Now," he says, "people have jobs elsewhere and spend most of their time out of the valley." Only a few of the farms in the valley have people living there full-time; the rest are now summer houses.

This process began in the mid-nineteenth century, and proceeded at different rates and at different times around Europe. For almost a century farmhouse brewing experienced a period of unbroken decline, until something totally unexpected happened in a totally unexpected region.

Baltic Time Capsule

The rise and fall of the Soviet Union may seem like an unlikely development to have influenced the history of farmhouse ale, but the fact is that it did. Toward the end of World War II, the Red Army pushed the Nazi forces out of the Soviet Union and all the way to Berlin. At the same time, the Soviet Union occupied the three Baltic states of Estonia, Latvia, and Lithuania and incorporated them into the Soviet Union. The Soviets dramatically restructured agriculture according to communist ideology by nationalizing most of the land and setting up collective farms. The collective farms were large state-owned enterprises where local farmers, who had previously been independent, now worked as employees. This broke up many of the traditional structures in the countryside, and meant the farmers no longer grew their own grain. However, in many places, collective farm employees were paid in grain, which meant they still had access to the necessary raw material for brewing.

The Soviet Union was isolated from outside influences, and, because of the slow pace of economic development under communism, the countryside remained even more isolated and backward. In addition, the locals had an incentive to preserve local brewing methods. Under communism, private enterprise was largely forbidden, so all the commercial breweries were nationalized. Their individual brands were wiped out and, instead of brewing their own beers, the government centrally devised a few recipes, which the breweries brewed in rotation.

The Soviet communist state was a centrally planned economy where the state planning bureau, Gosplan, set production quotas for the entire economy. This included how much beer the breweries should make, how much grain should be grown, how much malt should be made from the grain, and so on. Under this system, breweries no longer had any incentive to make good beer. The disappearance of brands meant quality had little influence on sales, and, in any case, the brewery would not benefit from selling more. All that was necessary was to meet the quota, which said nothing about quality. The ingredients were produced according to the same system, which meant getting good ingredients, and enough of them, could be a challenge. As a result, the commercial beer in this period was not very good.

At the same time, the countryside was full of people who knew how to brew, and who had every incentive to brew good beer. Since they malted the grain themselves, they had full control over the entire process. Those who were good maltsters and brewers could produce very high-quality beer.

In a society like the Soviet Union, where the alternatives were low-quality and where people had some money but little to spend it on, privately brewed beer was highly attractive. In both Lithuania and Estonia, collective farms started having local farmhouse brewers make farmhouse ale semi-officially. In Lithuania, even Communist Party officials started ordering farmhouse ale for their celebrations. People in southern Latvia started traveling south into Lithuania to order beer for weddings and other major celebrations. On the Estonian islands, the collective farms even held brewing competitions.

All this ensured that farmhouse brewing traditions lived on in the isolated bubbles of the Estonian islands and farmlands of northern Lithuania. And then, in 1990/91, the bubble burst. The Soviet Union fell apart and the Baltic states took their independence and set up market economies where private enterprise was once again allowed. In the countryside were large numbers of farmers skilled at malting and brewing, many of whom already had an existing customer base. They saw their chance and they took it. In Lithuania, this caused an explosion: literally hundreds of farmhouse breweries were established in the early 1990s.

Figure 10.1. Jovaru Alus brewery housed in what used to be the barn. The family home was immediately to the right. Jovarai, north Lithuania.

Beer enthusiast and journalist Vidmantas Laurinavičius drove through northern Lithuania in the late 1990s and was flabbergasted to discover a profusion of little breweries making farmhouse ales. Coming back to Vilnius, he tried to tell his friends about it but was met with flat disbelief. In July 2004, Josh Oakes (editor of RateBeer.com) and Per Samuelsson, both early pioneers of beer hunting, had heard rumors of interesting beers in Lithuania and did some exploring. They walked into a bar in Pasvalys, a small town in northern Lithuania, and were floored to find 11 farmhouse ales completely unlike any beers they had ever tasted. As Oakes put it, "Words in the English beer lexicon had not yet been developed to describe them."[1]

Unfortunately, the Lithuanian government subsequently tightened regulations, driving many of these breweries out of business. Tougher competition from the bigger commercial breweries and migration away from the countryside did not help either. Today, Lithuania has just a handful of farmhouse breweries left.

The Baltic States Today

It was in Lithuania that I first discovered farmhouse ale, simply because nowhere else in Europe is it so easy to buy true farmhouse ale over the bar. But it took me years to work out that it was farmhouse ale I was drinking, and it was only by actually visiting the breweries and talking to the brewers that I was able to figure it out.

In the summer of 2015, I visited the Piniavos brewery on the outskirts of Panevėžys in northern Lithuania. I had long been a fan of their unusual beers, and had puzzled over the one named

Figure 10.2. Laukinių Aviečių from a bottle. Bambalynė, Vilnius.

Figure 10.3. The brew kit at the Piniavos brewery. Mash tun on the right, lauter tun to its left.

Laukinių Aviečių, which advertises the use of raspberry canes on the label. Raspberry beer I knew of, but raspberry canes? What was the point of that?

The brewer, Vidmantas Perevičius, met us outside the brewery. He was a big, powerfully built man with close-cropped white hair and a broken nose, looking most of all like a friendly rhinoceros. I discovered later he was an amateur boxer, which made sense. Vidmantas showed us around what appeared to be a small modern brewery, until I started asking questions. The first big steel vat was the mash tun. The second one, next to it, was the lauter tun. "So, there's no copper, huh? You're making real raw ale," I asked. Of course, was the answer. Real Lithuanian farmhouse ale is unboiled, and that is that. Then I noticed that there was a third, much smaller, tank hidden behind the first two. "What's that," I asked. It turned out to be the hop tea cooker. That startled me. They could not have bought this brewing equipment off the shelf, because nobody sells hop tea cookers. I asked where it came from. "We made the drawings, and local masters came here and welded everything," Vidmantas said.

Clearly they had actually designed the brewery around the traditional brewing process. That made sense. It was at this point that a lightbulb went off in my head. If this was a traditional brewery, of course *that* is what the raspberry canes were for! I asked Vidmantas, and, sure enough, that was it—while most people used straw in the filter, in the Perevičius family, it was tradition to use raspberry canes. Hence that strange beer.

I asked Vidmantas were his family came from, and he said the Kupiškis region. "So why don't you brew keptinis," I asked, because that area is known for its keptinis. It turned out Vidmantas's family was from the far northwest in the region, where people make normal raw ale. Notice how everything about this brewery, its ingredients, brewing process, and physical design, is determined by the family and regional tradition. A farmhouse brewer cannot really choose what beer to brew.

In fact, the brick building I thought was a brewery was originally the farm's barn. As the brewery grew, it pushed more and more of the farming activities out of the barn. The brewery had come to fill the whole building and there was no longer time or room for farming. The building had been renovated and adapted to the point that I had not recognized it as a barn. This was a farmhouse brewery in the most literal sense.

Later, I discovered that the Su Puta, Jovaru Alus, and Ramunas Čižas breweries had all gone through the exact same evolution. And all of them still make traditional raw ale. While those three breweries still have the family yeast, Piniavos lost its yeast culture when it went bad. The Apynys brewery in Kaunas also brews traditional farmhouse ale with family yeast, and even uses wild hops.

I visited the Pihtla brewery on Saaremaa in Estonia, which makes a traditional koduõlu.˙ The brewery was built using gear taken from a Soviet soap factory, to be used for the same brewing process that Piniavos uses. The hop tea was boiled in a normal kitchen saucepan on a stove. Later, the brewery owner had taken on a young business partner who wanted to make craft beer. Craft beer was tricky to do with the brewery's raw ale brewing line, but they figured out a solution using garden hoses to transfer the wort back to the kettle for the strike water, boiling the wort there, and then hosing the wort back into the fermentor.

˙ There are now two breweries in the village of Pihtla, both using the Pihtla brand. This is the company named Taako OÜ.

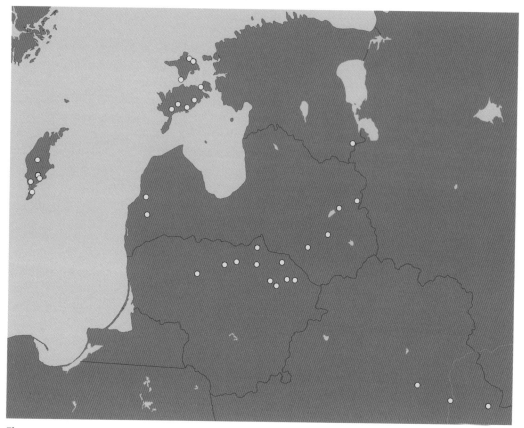

Figure 10.4. Map showing where there is definitely still farmhouse brewing in the Baltic states as of 2019.

Today, there are non-commercial Lithuanian farmhouse brewers in the countryside in the north, but exactly how many is hard to say. Part of the problem is that they are very suspicious of strangers. In Biržai, at least, there are enough farmhouse brewers to keep a homebrew supply store in business. Simonas Gutautas managed to visit a group of farmhouse brewers in this area (and get a sample of their yeast) by teaming up with the local doctor, who is very highly respected in the community.

In Estonia, farmhouse brewing is very active on the three big islands: Saaremaa, Hiiumaa, and Muhu. In the rest of the country, it seems to have mostly died out.

In Latvia, there is still active farmhouse brewing in the easternmost region, Latgale. Some brewers make their own malt, and some have their own yeast. How many they number is impossible to tell. The Suiti people, a Latvian Catholic minority in western Latvia, still brew raw ale from sun-dried barley malt.

Russia still has active farmhouse brewing in several regions. The areas with the most brewers are probably Chuvashia and the eastern part of Vologda Oblast, but there must be many more. Even in Siberia there is still active farmhouse brewing.

Belarus also has farmhouse brewing, but how much is not known. There are also indications that the brewing tradition is still alive in Ukraine.

Status in the West

In western Europe, the decline of farmhouse brewing continued for a little longer than in the east. The low point seems to have been some time around 1970. Around that time perceptions changed and locals started seeing farmhouse ale as a tradition worth preserving, rather than an embarrassing relic of the primitive past. At this point, so much of the tradition had died out that what was left was in a fairly precarious position. The outside world had little knowledge of this brewing tradition, and even less understanding for it.

Still, in the 1990s, Michael Jackson ensured that at least gotlandsdricke and sahti got some level of recognition, and farmhouse ale began to be brewed commercially in Finland. Farmhouse brewing expanded a little bit over the decade that followed. In the last decade, however, traditional brewing has come under pressure from modern homebrewing, with many young homebrewers seeming to prefer modern homebrewing methods over the traditional ones.

Today, farmhouse brewing is alive in western Norway deep in the fjords, from Hardanger in the south to Sunnmøre in the north. Voss is the strongest brewing region in this part of the country, with Hornindal in second place, and perhaps Ørsta as the third. Other areas in western Norway seem to have a fairly thin scattering of brewers. Oppdal in central Norway, upper Telemark, and Ål in Hallingdal also have a few brewers. The strongest farmhouse brewing region in Europe, however, is Stjørdal in central Norway.

Denmark still has one brewer on the eastern tip of Møn, and a few in northern Funen.

Sweden has a few dozen brewers on Gotland, but apparently nowhere else. Many parts of Sweden have historically been at least as isolated as western Norway, so this is somewhat surprising. It may be that because Swedish beer was mostly small beer people were less motivated to preserve it.

Finland is in a unique position in that it has a very large number of farmhouse brewers spread throughout the central parts of the country, and these brewers are well organized. They have a measure of government support and national recognition, and there is a handful of commercial breweries. Lammi, Finlandia, Pihanmaa, Olut Pryki Raum, Hollolan Hirvi, and Sahtikrouvin are commercial sahti breweries. The Pyynikin and United Gypsies craft breweries also sometimes make sahti.

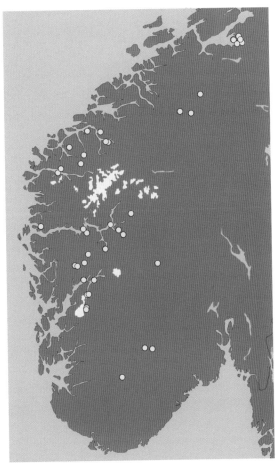

Figure 10.5. Locations in Norway where farmhouse brewing is definitely still alive as of 2019. The white areas are glaciers.

Figure 10.6. Locations in Europe where farmhouse brewing is definitely still alive today.

Remarkably, the United Kingdom also has two regions where farmhouse brewing has survived, although this seems to be just about completely unknown to outsiders. One cluster of brewers is in Orkney off the north coast of Scotland. The other is in the Gwaun Valley in southern Wales. How many brewers there are in these two areas is not known.

Farmhouse Ale in the Twenty-First Century

There are three main paradigms within modern brewing, each with their own ways of thinking: industrial lager brewing, old-school ale brewing, and craft brewing. These three paradigms, or mindsets, are relatively close to one another compared with the fourth, which is farmhouse brewing. The differences are so stark that probably the world of beer should be divided in two: modern brewing and farmhouse brewing. And farmhouse brewing is in many ways the larger half, since it has far greater diversity, a much longer history, and many, many more brewers.

Craft beer has taken off dramatically over the past couple of decades, and while craft beer is theoretically all about innovation and coming up with new flavors, farmhouse ale seems to be a little too innovative and different for most drinkers and brewers. When craft beer adopts a new method or ingredient, the resulting beer still tastes recognizably like craft beer. Farmhouse ale, by contrast, tastes nothing like craft beer, and the leap can be a bit too much for many craft beer drinkers.

Tuomas Pere grew up in the sahti brewing tradition but brews for a craft brewery in Tampere, Finland.[2] He makes both craft beer and sahti. Selling the sahti is not so easy, with the main customers for it being high-end restaurants. "They understand flavor," says Tuomas with a sigh.

Part of the challenge for farmhouse ale is that it does not fit naturally into the world of craft brewing. The carbonation is all wrong, the focus is on drinkability, not extreme flavors, and the thinking about what counts as off-flavors is completely different. Furthermore, in craft brewing there should be new beers and new flavors all the time. In farmhouse brewing, the tradition serves as a straight-jacket, so that any change takes many decades.

One commercial farmhouse brewer I met served me their commercial beer in the tasting pavilion in the garden. Later on it got too cold and dark to be outside and we went inside the house, where, suddenly, homemade berry wines were brought to the table instead. I was startled by how the focus shifted from the commercial product to this private homemade drink. Should the brewery not be promoting its commercial product? Eventually, I realized what was going on: the brewer had described everything about the commercial beer with reference to grandfather. The beer was cast in a fixed form dictated by tradition—it was not really a personal product because there was no room to play around. The berry wines were cherished because with them the brewer could actually develop something expressing their own personality and preferences.

The question of whether beer has terroir is often discussed, and to some extent, beer does, in the sense that Belgian-style beer tastes noticeably different from English-style beer. Historical farmhouse brewing was, in a way, all terroir. The grain varieties themselves, the malting methods, the yeast, the hops, the herbs, the brewing process, and the serving methods were all hyper-local, shaped by local conditions and developments over many centuries, even millennia. Once farmhouse brewers started buying malt, the connection to local conditions was weakened, but it is still there in the sense that farmhouse styles are still very local. And, in most cases, some of the ingredients are still local.

Figure 10.7. Matti Punakallio by the control panel for his automated sahti brewery, built from his old kuurna. Hartola, Finland.

Modern brewers trying to recreate these beers will nearly all be working blind, trying to emulate a beer very different from anything they have ever tasted based on nothing more than a recipe. In so doing, they will inevitably be making a fusion of traditions rather than reproducing the original. Belgian-style beer brewed in the United States tastes quite different from that made in Belgium. The ingredients, processes, and mindset are just not the same, and that affects the taste.

Some have questioned whether brewing vossaøl in another country is "cultural appropriation," disrespectful of the original tradition. This is a complicated question. If someone spends time, money, and resources to make a beer inspired by vossaøl, they must have seen something in the original tradition that seemed valuable enough for them to pay this cost. In this sense, the recreation should probably be seen as an homage, a paying of respect rather than as a form of theft.

Over the years, several commercial breweries have brewed beers that they *call* gotlandsdricke or sahti, without really taking the trouble to learn anything much about the style whose name they have borrowed. The results have generally been modern craft beer with a couple of novel ingredients borrowed from the tradition (or from an imagined tradition), often with elements added that have nothing to do with the tradition. This is clearly more problematic. It is difficult to consider a beer like that an homage when so little was done to actually understand the tradition it came from. At the same time, it does not seem that any actual disrespect was intended. It is, perhaps, more a question of not taking the beer seriously. For people working in a relatively mainstream tradition like craft brewing, to treat a tradition so marginalized and misunderstood as farmhouse brewing this way does not seem right to me.

Another problem with these misleading beers is that serving people who have never tried farmhouse ale a beer and describing it as, say, sahti, when in fact it tastes nothing like sahti and is not actually a serious attempt to brew sahti, has consequences. Many drinkers believe what they are told, so become misled into thinking that they have tried sahti and that they have some idea what it tastes like.

Developments like this could do real harm to the culture of brewing, because the main thing that makes sahti and the other farmhouse ales valuable is that they taste radically different from modern beers. When brewers and drinkers are misled into believing that, actually, farmhouse ale just tastes like craft beer with juniper in it, then inevitably that will make farmhouse ale seem much less important than it is.

Farmhouse ale already has one foot in the grave. In Norway, prospects for farmhouse brewing a few years ago seemed bleak, to put it mildly.

Over the last few years, there has been a surge of interest in farmhouse brewing in Norway, but whether this will lead to traditional brewing becoming more popular is not yet clear. So far, the main effect has been modern brewers borrowing ingredients and methods from traditional brewing and adopting them for modern brewing, rather than any clear expansion of the brewing tradition itself.

With this book I hope to introduce brewers around the world to the methods, techniques, and mindset of traditional farmhouse brewing. My wish is that people around the world will develop a new respect and understanding for these styles, and perhaps brew and drink them too. However, the future story of koduõlu and kornøl cannot really be told anywhere else than on the island of Saaremaa and in the fjord country.

My hope is that renewed interest from the major beer nations for these beers will help people in the Nordic and Baltic regions, as well as in Russia, see that these traditions are important and must be preserved. But, again, it is really the locals in the farmhouse brewing regions that have to preserve the tradition by taking it up and keeping it alive. Farmhouse brewing is a *tradition*. It is not communicated through reading books, but through direct learning from an experienced brewmaster already living in the tradition, and direct contact with other brewers in the same tradition as yourself.

When modern brewers around the world show interest in and pay homage to traditional beers, this is of course picked up by the locals. Most of the people who already brew will probably continue no matter what happens, but the people around them will, I hope, notice and their estimation of traditional brewing will go up. I am hoping increased interest, respect, and understanding for traditional farmhouse brewing will make more people brew and drink locally, since that is the only thing that can keep it alive.

Into the Future

Farmhouse ale is still alive in many parts of Europe, but seems under threat in nearly all of these places. Modern homebrewing, the craft beer trend, and the general decline of rural populations all threaten to drive it out of existence. The general lack of understanding for these beers makes a revival hard. At the moment, farmhouse brewing is in a position so weak that almost any attention and appreciation is valuable.

So, what future does farmhouse brewing have?

Every time the last traditional brewer in some region puts away their equipment for the last time, a unique part of the world of beer dies. A tradition, an unbroken chain of brewers, stretching back literally to the Stone Age, is broken. The memories of the methods and flavors fade beyond any hope of recall and die. I would not hesitate to call it a cultural tragedy.

In most of the places in Europe where farmhouse ale is brewed today, the tradition seems likely to go extinct within one or two generations. Only in a few places, like Finland, Saaremaa in Estonia, and Stjørdal in Norway, does farmhouse brewing seem quite safely established. Voss in Norway has perhaps 50 active brewers, so brewing there may be safe for another generation or two. Hornindal, despite how famous it is as a brewing area, has perhaps 10 to 20 brewers at most, which will most likely keep the brewing alive in that area for at least one more generation.

In many places, however, brewing is down to just a couple of families still stubbornly holding out. In Ål in eastern Norway, two families still brew regularly and keep alive a yeast they call *gong*. Gong seems to be a separate type of yeast that only exists in this little village.

But two families is not much. One brewhouse that burns down, one child that does not like the old-fashioned beer is all it takes, and several thousands of years of tradition will be dead. And once it dies, it is lost forever.

Sverre Skrindo in Ål realized that, unless his only child, a daughter, liked the beer, then once he died Ål would be down to one family of brewers. At best. In desperation, Sverre gave his then 10-year-old daughter a pint of farmhouse ale and told her that if she drank it all he would give her 500 Norwegian kroner.* She drank it all, and now, 10 years later, she likes the beer and has learned to brew it. The tradition may be safe for another generation.

---

* The beer was very sweet and not very strong.

I started diving into the world of farmhouse brewing five years ago. Since then, several of my sources have passed away. Gone now are Olav Hegge, Per Dale, William Holden, Aarne Trei, Rasmus Kjøs Otterdal, and Andres Kurgpõld, each taking chunks of our common heritage with them. But the beer is still alive. Andrus Viil still brews Aarne's beer, just like the Raftevold brothers carry the torch for Rasmus. The brewers may be mortal, but the tradition lives eternal.

Figure 10.8. Per Dale about to serve his farmhouse ale to Martin Thibault, Francis Simard, and me. May 2014 in Flåm, Sogn, western Norway. Per Dale died unexpectedly just before Christmas 2014.

NOTES

Introduction

1. Per Kølster, *Alle tiders øl* (Copenhagen: Politikens forlag, 2007).
2. Martin Thibault, "In search of Norway's brewing traditions," *Beer Connoisseur*, issue 16 (2014).

Chapter 1

1. Eric Hobsbawm, *Age of Extremes: The Short Twentieth Century, 1914–1991* (London: Michael Joseph, 1994), 289.
2. Else-Marie Strese and Clas Tollin, *Humle: Det gröna guldet* (Stockholm: Nordiska Museets Förlag, 2015), 257.
3. Antanas Astrauskas, *Per barzda varvejo* (Vilnius: Baltos Lankos, 2008), 111. Content cited herein translated by Elma Caicedo.
4. NEG 7335.
5. Opedal, Halldor, *Makter og menneske*, Folkeminne i frå Hardanger VI (Oslo: Norsk Folkeminnelag, 1948), 60.
6. Jørund Geving (farmhouse brewer and maltster), Stjørdalen, Norway, personal communications to author, 2016–2019.
7. Hans Saakvitne, "Kor ein bryggjar Hardangerøl?" originally published in 1898, republished anonymously in *Hardanger Sogelag Årsbok* (Hardanger Historielag, 1984), 323–25.
8. Anders Salomonsson, *Gotlandsdricka: Traditionell kultur som regional identitetssymbol*, Skrifter utg. av Etnologiska sällskapet i Lund 10 (Karlstad: Press Förlag, 1979), 124.
9. Salomonsson, *Gotlandsdricka*, 125–126.
10. Magnus Olsen, *Egils lausavísur, Höfuðlausn og Sonatorrek*, Edda- og skaldekvad 4 (Oslo: Det Norske Videnskaps-Akademi, 1962), 78.
11. Jørund Geving (pers. comm.), 2016–2019; Pekka Kääriäinen (farmhouse brewer), Lammi, Finland, interview with author, August 7, 2018.
12. Halvor Bjåland (farmhouse brewer), Morgedal, Telemark, Norway, brewing session with author, May 31, 2015.
13. NEG 7398.

Chapter 2

1. Anna Blasco, Manel Edo, and M. Josefa Villalba, "Evidencias de procesado y consumo de cerveza en la cueva de Can Sadurní (Begues, Barcelona) durante la Prehistoria," in *IV Congreso de Neolítico Peninsular*, ed. Mauro S. Hernández Pérez, Jorge A. Soler Díaz, and Juan A. López Padilla, vol. 1 (Museo Arqueológico de Alicante, 2006), 429.
2. Patrick McGovern, "Retsina, mixed fermented beverages, and the cuisine of pre-classical Greece," in *Minoas and Myceneans: Flavors of Their Time*, ed. Yannis Tzedakis and Holly Martlewf (Athens: Kapon Editions, 1999), 206.

3. Max Nelson, *The Barbarian's Beverage: A History of Beer in Ancient Europe* (New York: Routledge, 2008), 45.

4. Patrick McGovern, Gretchen R. Hall, and Armen Mirzoian, "A biomolecular archaeological approach to 'Nordic grog'," *Danish Journal of Archaeology* 2, no. 2 (2013): 112–31.

5. Laurent Bouby, Philippe Boissinot, and Philippe Marinval,"Never Mind the Bottle. Archaeobotanical Evidence of Beer-brewing in Mediterranean France and the Consumption of Alcoholic Beverages During the 5th Century BC," *Human Ecology* 39, issue 3 (2011): 351–60, https://dx.doi.org/10.1007/s10745-011-9395-x; Hans-Peter Stika, "Early Iron Age and Late Mediaeval malt finds from Germany—attempts at reconstruction of early Celtic brewing and the taste of Celtic beer," *Archaeological and Anthropological Sciences* 3, issue 1 (2011): 44–46, https://dx.doi.org/10.1007/s12520-010-0049-5.

6. Soultana Maria Valamoti, "Brewing beer in wine country? First archaeobotanical indications for beer making in Early and Middle Bronze Age Greece," *Vegetation History and Archaeobotany* 27, issue 4 (July 2017): 615–19, https://doi.org/10.1007/s00334-017-0661-8.

7. Geir Grønnesby, "Bryggestein og kulturlag - spor etter gårdens opprinnelse," *SPOR* (NTNU University Museum), nr 1 (2014), 35.

8. P. Lagerås, "Aristokratin i landskapet. Paleoekologiska studier i Järrestads järnålder," in *Järrestad - huvudgård i centralbygd*, ed. B. Söderberg, Arkeologiska undersökningar, Skrifter 51 (Stockholm: Riksantikvarieämbetet, 2003), 243–270; Manfred Rösch, "Starkbier mit Honig," in *Mit Leier und Schwert: Das frühmittelalterliche "Sängergrab" von Trossingen*, Barbara Theune-Großkopf (Friedberg: Likias, 2010), 90–91.

9. Phil Rahn and Chuck Skypeck, "Traditional German Steinbier," special issue, *Zymurgy* 17, no. 4, 1994; Benedikt Rausch [nacron, pseud.], "Historical Gose Recipe Part 4," *Wilder-Wald* (blog), April 26, 2017, http://wilder-wald.com/2017/04/26/historical-gose-recipe-part-4/.

10. Rausch [nacron, pseud.], "Historical Gose Recipe Part 4."

11. 1Richard W. Unger, *A History of Brewing in Holland 900-1900: Economy, Technology and the State*, (Leiden: Brill, 2001), 20.

12. Kristof Glamann and Kirsten Glamann, *Nordens Pasteur: fortællingen om naturforskeren Emil Chr. Hansen*, (Copenhagen: Gyldendal, 2004), 135.

13. Antanas Astrauskas, *Per barzda varvejo*, (Vilnius: Baltos Lankos, 2008), 106. Content cited herein translated by Elma Caicedo.

14. Elfyn Scourfield, "Farmhouse Brewing," *Amgueddfa: Bulletin of the National Museum of Wales* 17 (Cardiff, 1974), 4–5; VOKO 313, 4110.

15. NEG 7559.

16. NEU 29999.

17. Ole-Bjørn Ese, Balestrand, Norway, interview with author, August 10, 2016.

18. Per Dale (farmhouse brewer), Flåm, Norway, interview with author, May 27, 2014; Halvor Nordal (farmhouse brewer), Høydalsmo, Norway, interview with author, June 1, 2015.

19. EU 7725.

Chapter 3

1. Sigvald Hasund, "Bygget som 'ølkorn' i det vestlandske havreområdet," in *Or Norges Bondesoge, Glytt og granskningar*, ed. S Hasund, vol. 1 (Oslo: Noregs Boklag 1942), 211.

2. Ove Arbo Høeg, *Planter og tradisjon: Floraen i levende tale og tradisjon i Norge*, (Oslo: Universitetsforlaget, 1974), 29.

3. Matti Wiking Leino, *Spannmål: svenska lantsorter*, Nordiska museets handlingar 142 (Stockholm: Nordiska Museets Förlag, 2017), 125.

4. EU 11098.

5. Åsmund Bjørnstad, *Vårt daglege brød: Kornets kulturhistorie*, (Oslo: Vidarforlaget, 2012), 130–31.

6. E. N. Naumov, "Istoriya pivovareniya i kultura potrebleniya piva v chuvashiy," *Journal of the Chuvash National Museum* (2000), 2, http://www.chnmuseum.ru/files/almanac2000/almanac2000_103.pdf.

7. Linda Dumpe, *Alus tradicijas Latvija*, (Riga: Latvijas Vestures Instituta Apgads, 2001), 190.

8. Juozas Petrulis, "Alus," *Kraštotyra* (1975), 238.

9. EU 8281.

10. Rae Phillips (farmhouse brewer and maltster), Birsay, Orkney, UK, personal communications to author, 2016.

11. Hans Olav Bråta and Merethe Lerfald, *Maten og matressursene i Gudbrandsdalen: historiske hovedtrekk siden steinalderen*, ØF-rapport 03/2012 (Østlandsforskning, Lillehammer, June 2012), 69.

12. Matti Wiking Leino, *Spannmål: svenska lantsorter*, Nordiska museets handlingar 142 (Stockholm: Nordiska Museets Förlag, 2017), 100, 211.

13. Hannu Ahokas and Marja-Leena Manninen, "Thermostabilities of Grain β-Amylase and β-Glucanase in Finnish Landrace Barleys and their Putative Past Adaptedness," *Hereditas* 132, no. 2 (April 2000): 116, https://doi.org/10.1111/j.1601-5223.2000.00111.x.

14. Jørund Geving (farmhouse brewer and maltster), Stjørdalen, Norway, personal communications to author, 2016–2019; Halland, Jogeir (farmhouse brewer and maltster), Stjørdalen, Norway, personal communications to author, 2017–2018.

15. Ilmar Talve, *Finnish Folk Culture*, Studia Fennica: Ethnologica, vol. 4 (Helsinki: Finnish Literature Society, 1997), 58.

16. Kristofer Visted and Hilmar Stigum, *Vår gamle bondekultur*. vol. 1 (Oslo: Cappelen, 1971), 196.

17. Asmund Sudbø, "Ølbrygging i gamle dagar," in *Årbok for Telemark* (Edland: Stiftinga Årbok for Telemark, 1971), 113.

18. Leino, *Spannmål*, 11.

19. Roar Sandodden (farmhouse brewer and maltster), Stjørdalen, Norway, personal communications to author, 2014–17; Morten Granas (farmhouse brewer and maltster), Stjørdalen, Norway, personal communications to author, 2014–2019.

20. NEG 7398.

21. Halvor Zangenberg, "Den danske Bondegaards Maltkølle," unpublished manuscript (Nationalmuseets Etnologiske Undersøgelser, Copenhagen, 1932), 17.

22. Tormis Jakovlev, "Unustatust ja uuemast Saaremaa koduõllenduses," in *Saaremaa Museum kaheaastaraamat 1995–1996* (1997), 123. Content cited herein translated by Virgo Vjugin; ERM KK-X, KV 52 230, 241 and KV 55 323, 327.

23. Antanas Astrauskas, *Per barzda varvejo* (Vilnius: Baltos Lankos, 2008), 137. Content cited herein translated by Elma Caicedo.

24. Kristofer Visted and Hilmar Stigum, *Vår gamle bondekultur*, vol. 2 (Oslo: Cappelen, 1971), 30.

25. Jakovlev, *Saaremaa Museum kaheaastaraamat 1995–1996*, 123; ERM KK-X, KV 52 230, 241 and KV 55 323, 327.

26. Sjur Herman Rørlien (farmhouse brewer), Dyrvedalen, Voss, Norway, personal communications to author, 2014–2019.

27. Jan G. T. Petersen, *Gamle gårdsanlegg i Rogaland 1: Fra forhistorisk tid og middelalder*, Instituttet for sammenlignende kultufjorskning, ser. B, Skrifter 23 (Oslo: Aschehoug & Co., 1933), 7–8.

28. Zangenberg, "Den danske Bondegaards Maltkølle," 2.

29. Maria Ivanovna (farmhouse brewer), Kudymkar, Komi Republic, Russia, interview and brewing session with author, July 18, 2017.

30. KU 2364.

31. EU 7725.

32. Bengt-Arne Røine, *Fortell Såmund – fortell mer: sagn, folkelivs- og bjørneskildringer fra Utkant-Norge*, (Oslo: Grøndahl, 1979), 117–19.

33. NEG 7622.

34. Aksel Helmen, *Frå det daglige liv på Hadeland i gamle dager* ([Gran?]: self-published, 1952), 44; EU 7833, Dalarna.

35. LUF 2954.

36. LUF 7979.

37. Ilmar Talve, *Den nordost-europeiska rian: en etnologisk undersökning*, Folklivsstudier, vol. 6 (Helsinki: Svenska litteratursällskapet i Finland, 1961), 12.

38. Talve (1961), 200.

39. EU 7725.

40. Geving, pers. comm.

41. Sandodden, pers. comm.

42. Odd Nordland, *Brewing and Beer Traditions in Norway*, (Oslo: Universitetsforlaget, 1969), 25.

43. Kjell Magnar Auran (farmhouse brewer and maltster), Innavætte såinnhuslag, Stjørdal, Norway, interview with author, June 1, 2018.

44. John Firth, *Reminiscences of an Orkney Parish: Together with Old Orkney Words, Riddles and Proverbs* (Stromness: printed by W.R. Rendall, 1920), 18; Michael Jackson, "Estonian, Finnish . . . and Orcadian," *All About Beer*, September 1, 2000, republished by Beer Hunter [online], September 6, 2001, http://www.beerhunter.com/documents/19133-001585.html.

45. Ilmar Talve, *Bastu och torkhus i Nordeuropa*, Nordiska Museets handlingar, vol. 53 (Stockholm: Nordiska Museets, 1960), 255–56.

46. Christen Jenssøn, *Den Norske Dictionarium Eller Glosebog* (Copenhagen, 1646; reprinted by J. W. Eides Forlag: Bergen, 1946), 18–19. Citations refer to the 1946 edition.

47. EU 11098.

48. NEG 13833, 1958.

Chapter 4

1. "Ein gamal tradisjon på Voss: Ølbrygging," conversation between associate professor Andreas Leiro and farmer Samuel Apeltun, recorded October 30, 1938, broadcast on NRK Radio, February 10, 1939, https://urn.nb.no/URN:NBN:no-nb_dra_1994-07326P.

2. Jackson Peter et al., "Genome evolution across 1,011 Saccharomyces cerevisiae isolates," *Nature* 556 (April 19, 2018): 339–44, https://doi.org/10.1038/s41586-018-0030-5.

3. Joaquin F. Christiaens et al., "The Fungal Aroma Gene *ATF1* Promotes Dispersal of Yeast Cells through Insect Vectors." *Cell Reports* 9, issue 2 (October 23, 2014): 425–32, https://doi.org/10.1016/j.celrep.2014.09.009.

4. Brigida Gallone et al., "Domestication and divergence of *Saccharomyces cerevisiae* beer yeasts." *Cell* 166 (September 8, 2016): 1404, http://dx.doi.org/10.1016/j.cell.2016.08.020.

5. Information for Labatt is from Graham G. Stewart, "Seduced by yeast," *Journal of the American Society of Brewing Chemists* 73, issue 1 (2015): 4; for Belgium from Jan Steensels microbiologist, University of Leuven (pers. comm. 2017–2019); for Harvey's from Ron Pattinson, "London Goose day two (part three)," *Shut up about Barclay Perkins* (blog), October 14, 2016, http://barclayperkins .blogspot.no/2016/10/london-goose-day-two-part-three.html.

6. EU 7799.

7. "Zum bäuerlichen Bierbrauen in Mecklenburg, Karl Baumgarten, 1966." Unpublished summary of archive data that Baumgarten typed up and sent in a letter to Matti Räsänen. Author's scanned copy.

8. Lars Levander, *Övre Dalarnes bondekultur under 1800- talets förra hälft. 3. Hem och hemarbete*, Skrifter utgivna av Kungl. Gustav Adolfs Akademien för folklivsforskning, 11, vol. 3 (Lund: Carl Bloms Boktryckeri, 1947), 447–48.

9. Loránt Ferkai, *Remekel a bicska*, (Budapest: Móra Ferenc Könyvkiadó, 1958), 51.

10. Eldar Nadiradze, *Georgian Beer* [bilingual: in Georgian and English] (Tbilisi: Meridiani, 2010), 78.

11. Sjur Herman Rørlien (farmhouse brewer), Dyrvedalen, Voss, Norway, personal communications to author, 2014–2019.

12. John Nerén, *Boka um Mälsa: Boken om Stora Mellösa*, Part 1 (Stockholm: Norstedts, 1944), 294.

13. Odd Nordland, *Brewing and Beer Traditions in Norway*, (Oslo: Universitetsforlaget, 1969), 255.

14. Ásdís Egilsdóttir, *Biskupa sögur*, Íslenzk fornrit XVI, vol. 2 (Reykjavík: Hið íslenzka fornritafélag, 2002), 155. Content cited herein translated from the original Norse by Eirik Storesund.

15. Zoran Gojkovic, Director of Research Strategy, Carlsberg Research Laboratory. April 19, 2018.

16. Richard Preiss, Microbiologist, Escarpment Labs, Guelph, Canada, personal communications to author, 2016–2019.

17. NEG 16921; Ugis Pucens, Ethnographer, Aizpute, Latvia, interview and brewing session with author, July 2015.

18. Preiss, pers. communications 2016–2019.

19. Brigida Gallone et al., "Interspecific hybridization facilitates niche adaptation in beer yeast," *Nature Ecology and Evolution* 3 (October 21, 2019): 1562–75, http://doi.dx.org/10.1038/s41559-019-0997-9.

20. Brigida Gallone et al., "Domestication and divergence of *Saccharomyces cerevisiae* beer yeasts," *Cell* 166 (September 8, 2016): 1397–410, http://dx.doi.org/10.1016/j.cell.2016.08.020.

21. Pliny, *Natural History*, B. xviii c. 12.

22. Max Nelson, "Beer in Greco-Roman Antiquity" (PhD thesis, University of British Columbia, 2001), 150–3.

23. Martin Thibault, personal communications to author, 2013–2019.

24. Martin Thibault, "Chicha: Bolivia's Tart Beer," *Beer Connoisseur*, September 14, 2015, https://beerconnoisseur.com/articles/chicha-bolivias-tart-beer.

25. National Collection of Yeast Cultures (NCYC), Norwich, UK, multiple unpublished analysis reports, and personal communications between author and collections manager Chris Bond.

26. Richard Preiss, Caroline Tyrawa, and George van der Merwe, "Traditional Norwegian Kveik Yeasts: Underexplored Domesticated *Saccharomyces cerevisiae* Yeasts," unpublished preprint, submitted September 27, 2017 [cited April 5, 2019], https://doi.org/10.1101/194969; National Collection of Yeast Cultures.

27. Freek Spitaels et al., "The Microbial Diversity of Traditional Spontaneously Fermented Lambic Beer," *PLoS ONE* 9, issue 4 (April 18, 2014): e95384, https://doi.org/10.1371/journal.pone.0095384.

28. V. Fabrizio et al. "Heat inactivation of wine spoilage yeast *Dekkera bruxellensis* by hot water treatment," *Letters in Applied Microbiology* 61, issue 2 (August 2015): 186–91, https://doi.org/10.1111/lam.12444; Zachary M. Cartwright et al., "Reduction of *Brettanomyces bruxellensis* Populations from Oak Barrel Staves Using Steam," *American Journal of Enology and Viticulture* 69 (October 2018): 400–409, https://dx.doi.org/10.5344/ajev.2018.18024.

29. Richard Preiss et al., "Traditional Norwegian Kveik are a Genetically Distinct Group of Domesticated *Saccharomyces cerevisiae* Brewing Yeasts," *Frontiers in Microbiology* 9 (September 12, 2018): 2137, https://doi.org/10.3389/fmicb.2018.02137.

30. Preiss et al., *Frontiers in Microbiology* 9: p. 10.

31. Martyn Cornell, "Fjord fiesta: The Norwegian farmhouse ales festival 2017," *Zythophile* (blog), October 6, 2017, http://zythophile.co.uk/2017/10/06/fjord-fiesta-the-norwegian-farmhouse-ales-festival-2017/.

32. Sigurd Johan Saure (farmhouse brewer), Sykkylven, Norway, personal communications to author, 2016–2019.

33. Richard Preiss and Iz Netto, "How low can you go: Impact of inoculation rate on Norwegian kveik yeast fermentation," Escarpment Laboratories (poster 76, Master Brewers Conference, Calgary, Alberta, October 31–November 2, 2019), https://www.mbaa.com/meetings/archive/Pages/default.aspx.

34. NEG 7518, LindÅs, Hordaland.

35. Preiss et al., *Frontiers in Microbiology* 9: p. 14.

36. Bjarne Muri (homebrewer), Oslo, Norway, personal communications to author, 2015–2017.

37. Kristoffer Krogerus et al., "A unique *Saccharomyces cerevisiae* × *Saccharomyces uvarum* hybrid isolated from Norwegian farmhouse beer: Characterization and reconstruction," *Frontiers in Microbiology* 9 (September 24, 2018): 2253, https://doi.org/10.3389/fmicb.2018.02253.

38. Kristoffer Krogerus, "Solving the Muri mystery," *Suregork Loves Beer* (blog), September 12, 2019, http://beer.suregork.com/?p=4094.

39. Preiss et al., *Frontiers in Microbiology* 9: p. 14.

40. Gallone et al., *Cell* 166: 1397–410.

41. Preiss, pers. comm. 2016–2019.

42. Per Kølster, *Alle tiders øl* (Copenhagen: Politikens forlag, 2007), 198; Simonas Gutautas (commercial brewer and historian), Vilnius, Lithuania, personal communications to author, 2015–2019.

43. NEG 7335.

44. Francisco A. Cubillos et al., "Bioprospecting for brewers: exploiting natural diversity for naturally diverse beers," *Yeast* 36, issue 6 (June 2019): 383–98, https://doi.org/10.1002/yea.3380.

45. Kristoffer Krogerus, "Physiology of Finnish Baker's Yeast (Suomen Hiiva)," *Suregork Loves Beer* (blog), August 28, 2014, http://beer.suregork.com/?p=3514.

46. Justin C. Fay et al., "A polyploid admixed origin of beer yeasts derived from European and Asian wine populations," *PLoS Biology* 17, no. 3 (March 5, 2019): e3000147, https://doi.org/10.1371/journal.pbio.3000147; Gallone et al., *Cell* 166: 1397.

47. Kristof Glamann, *Beer And Brewing In Pre-Industrial Denmark*, (Odense: University Press of Southern Denmark, 2005), 40.

48. Jakob Eitrheim (farmhouse brewer), Aga, Norway, interview and brewing session with author, December 2016.

49. Saure, pers. comm., 2016–2019.

50. Ragnar Hove (farmhouse brewer),Vik, Sogn, Norway, telephone interview with author, February 19, 2015.

51. Matti Räsänen, *Vom Halm zum Fass*, German edition (Helsinki: Suomen muinaismuistoyhdistys, 1975), *Kansatieteellinen arkisto* 25:157.

52. Anders Salomonsson, *Gotlandsdricka: Traditionell kultur som regional identitetssymbol*, Skrifter utg. av Etnologiska sällskapet i Lund 10 (Karlstad: Press Förlag, 1979), 79.

53. NEU 2897.

54. Jon Leirfall, "Liv og lagnad i Stjørdalsbygdene," Stjørdalsboka bind 1, del III, utgitt av Stjørdal og Meråker kommuner (1972), 180.

55. Räsänen, *Vom Halm zum Fass*, 156.

56. Räsänen, 163.

57. Mika Laitinen, *Viking Age Brew: The Craft of Brewing Sahti Farmhouse Ale*, (Chicago Review Press, 2019), 127.

58. Thomas Horne, *Norges 100 beste øl 2018*, (Oslo: Handverk forlag, 2017), 38.

59. Ivar Aasen, *Norsk ordbog: med dansk forklaring* (Christiania [Oslo]: P.T. Mallings boghandel, 1873), s.v. "kveik."

Chapter 5

1. Mika Laitinen, author, Jyväskylä, Finland, personal communications to author 2015-2020.

2. Ivar Aasen, *Norsk ordbog: med dansk forklaring* (Christiania [Oslo]: P.T. Mallings boghandel, 1873), s.v. "Mari-auga."

3. Eilert Sundt, "Lidt fra Oldtiden. I. Brygge-sten," in *Folkevennen*, vol. 14 (Kristiania [Oslo]: 1865), 322.

4. Sigurd Grieg, *Skiftet efter Eirik Bukk på Finnen*, (Oslo: Dybwad, 1934), 18.

5. Carl Niclas Hellenius, *Anmärkningar öfver finska allmogens bryggningssätt* (Åbo [Turku]: Åbo Kungliga Akademi, 1780), 18.

6. Geir Grønnesby, "Hot rocks! Beer brewing on viking and medieval age farms in Trøndelag," in *The Agrarian Life: Studies in Rural Settlement and Farming in Norway*, ed. Frode Iversen and Håkan Pettersson (Oslo: Portal forlag, 2016), 145.

7. Geir Grønnesby, "Bryggestein og kulturlag - spor etter gårdens opprinnelse," *SPOR* (NTNU University Museum), nr 1 (2014), 34.

8. Gronnesby, Archaeologist, Institutt for arkeologi og kulturhistorie NTNU Vitenskapsmuseet. pers. comm. 2017.

9. Karl Alfred Gustawsson, "Kokstenshögar," *Fornvännen*, 1949, 152–65; Merryn Dineley, "Experiment or Demonstration? Making fermentable malt sugars from the grain and a discussion of some of the evidence for this activity in the British Neolithic," in *Experimentation and Interpretation: The Use of Experimental Archaeology in the Study of the Past*, ed. Dana C.E. Millson (Oxford: Oxbow Books, 2010), 96–108.

10. Erin Mullally, "Letters from Ireland: Mystery of the Fulacht Fiadh," *Archaeology* 65, no. 1 (January/February 2012).

11. ERM KK-X, KV52: 251, as translated by Margo Samorokov.

12. Matti Räsänen, *Vom Halm zum Fass*, German edition (Helsinki: Suomen muinaismuistoyhdistys, 1975), *Kansatieteellinen arkisto* 25: 22–23.

13. Per Söderbäck, *Rågöborna*, Nordiska Museets handlingar, vol. 13 (Stockholm: Nordiska Museets Förlag, 1940), 99–100.

14. Nikolay Aleksandrovich Ivanitskiy, "Solvychegodskiy krestyanin yego obstanovka, zhizn i deyatelnost," *Zhinaya starina*, volume 1, Year eight (1898), 38.

15. NEU 2712.

16. Richard W. Unger, *A History of Brewing in Holland 900-1900: Economy, Technology and the State* (Leiden: Brill, 2001), 25.

17. Sigurd Johan Saure (farmhouse brewer), Sykkylven, Norway, personal communications to author, 2016–2019.

18. Malcolm Frazer, "Boil vs. No-Boil Berliner Weisse | exBEERiment Results!" *Brülosophy* (blog), November 14, 2016, http://brulosophy.com/2016/11/14/boil-vs-no-boil-berliner-weisse-exbeeriment-results/.

19. Fyodorov family (farmhouse brewers), Kshaushi, Chuvash Autonomous Republic, Russia, interview with author, July 22, 2017. Translator Aleksandr Gromov.

20. Åsmund Sudbø, "Ølbrygging i gamle dagar," in *Årbok for Telemark* (Edland: Stiftinga Årbok for Telemark, 1971), 118.

21. Halvor Bjåland (farmhouse brewer), Morgedal, Telemark, Norway, brewing session with author, May 31, 2015; Sverre Skrindo (farmhouse brewer), Ål, Norway, brewing session with author, December 2017.

22. Juozas Petrulis, "Alus," *Kraštotyra* (1975): 237–48.

23. "Keptinis alus" [in Lithuanian], uploaded by Lietuvos nacionalinis kulturos centras, November 4, 2015, YouTube video, 02:24, film of residents in Rokiškio rajono infusion mashing with baked wet grist, https://www.youtube.com/watch?v=K4CdMlUpZUI.

24. Martin Warren, "A Great Way to Lose a Day," *Poppyland Brewer* (blog), April 26, 2015, http://poppylandbrewer.blogspot.com/2015/04/a-great-way-to-lose-day.html.

25. Simonas Gutautas (commercial brewer and historian), Vilnius, Lithuania, personal communications to author, 2015–2019.

26. Vykintas Motuza (farmhouse brewer), Anykščiai, Lithuania, personal communications to author, 2016–2018.

27. ERM KK-X, KV51: 148.

28. "Keptinis alus," YouTube video, November 4, 2015.

29. Petrulis, "Alus," 238.

30. Antti Pahalahti (farmhouse brewer), Hartola, Finland, interview with author, August 11, 2018.

31. Ilmar Talve, *Bastu och torkhus i Nordeuropa*, Nordiska Museets handlingar, vol. 53 (Stockholm: Nordiska Museets Förlag, 1960), 422.

32. Gutautas, pers. comm., 2015–2019.
33. Räsänen, *Vom Halm zum Fass*, 43–44.
34. Alfred Lucas, *Ancient Egyptian Materials and Industries*, 4th ed. (London: Edward Arnold, 1962), 16–18.
35. NEG 7329.
36. NEU 29948.
37. EU 7830, 8463, 18429, and 29349.
38. EU 8463.
39. SLS Granborg, Groop, Ohman; KM 4, Ketola.
40. Jury Pleskačeŭski, "Asaviec village," unpublished manuscript, dated 2018. Archived as a PDF March 17, 2018.
41. Michael Jackson, Pocket Guide to Beer, (Putnam, 1982), 9.
42. From Jouni Kuurne, *Louhisaaren linnan talousreseptit (n. 1770–1850)* (Helsinki: Suomalaisen Kirjallisuuden Seuran Toimituksia, 2008) 60–62, as quoted by metukkalihis [Ilkka Miettinen], "Sahti of Louhisaari in 1780" [online], August 25, 2015, https://smetanafi.wordpress .com/2015/08/25/sahti-of-louhisaari-in1780/.
43. Grønnesby, "Bryggestein og kulturlag," 34.
44. Merryn Dineley, "Hearth mashing," *Ancient Malt and Ale* (blog), February 17, 2019, http://merryn.dineley.com/2019/02 /hearth-mashing.html.
45. Dineley, "Hearth mashing."
46. EU 30584.
47. Dagfinn Hovden (brewer), Ørsta, Sunnmøre, Norway, interview with author, March 10, 2019.
48. Sissel Tiril Rem, "Oppkok eller ikkje – det er spørsmålet," *Storfjordnytt*, March 12, 2008, http://www.storfjordnytt.no /nyhende08/11_olbrygging.html.

Chapter 6

1. Kristofer Visted and Hilmar Stigum, *Vår gamle bondekultur*, vol. 1 (Oslo: Cappelen, 1971), 320–23.
2. Matti Wiking Leino, *Spannmål: svenska lantsorter*, Nordiska museets handlingar 142 (Stockholm: Nordiska Museets Förlag, 2017), 11.
3. Stein Erik Skoug, *Kongeveien over Fillefjell: Vindhella og Galdane* (Oslo: Grøndahl, 1975), 27.
4. Gösta Berg and Sigfrid Svensson, *Svensk bondekultur*, (Stockholm: Albert Bonniers Förlag, 1934), 143.
5. NEU 4083.
6. Hans Olav Bråtå and Merethe Lerfald, *Maten og matressursene i Gudbrandsdalen: historiske hovedtrekk siden steinalderen*, ØF-rapport 03/2012 (Østlandsforskning, Lillehammer, June 2012), 109.
7. NEG 8833.
8. KU 2364.
9. Per Stundal (farmer), Aurland, Norway, telephone interview with author, October 5, 2017; see also Ole Højrup, Landbokvinden: rok og kærne, grovbrød og vadmel (Copenhagen: Nationalmuseet, 1966), 61.
10. EU 20853, Kulltorp.
11. Elfyn Scourfield, "Farmhouse Brewing," *Amgueddfa: Bulletin of the National Museum of Wales* 17 (Cardiff, 1974), 4–5.
12. NEG 9187.
13. NEG 7531.
14. Ian P. Peaty, *You Brew Good Ale: A History of Small-Scale Brewing* (Stroud, Glos.: Sutton Publishing, 1997), 187.
15. EU 8617.
16. Scourfield, *Amgueddfa*, 4–5; Hinrich Siuts and Fritz Bartelt, *Bäuerliche und handwerkliche Arbeitsgeräte in Westfalen: die alten Geräte der Landwirtschaft und des Landhandwerks 1890-1930* (Münster: Aschendorff, 1982), 212.
17. Kristofer Visted and Hilmar Stigum, *Vår gamle bondekultur*. vol. 2 (Oslo: Cappelen, 1971), 73.
18. EU 8469.
19. James George Frazer, "The Corn-Mother and the Corn-Maiden in Northern Europe," in *Spirits of the Corn and of the Wild*, part 5, vol. 1 of *The Golden Bough: A Study in Magic and Religion*, 3rd ed. (London: Macmillan and Co., 1912), 131–70; Åsmund Bjørnstad, *Vårt daglege brød: Kornets kulturhistorie* (Oslo: Vidarforlaget, 2012), 118.
20. Sverre Skrindo (farmhouse brewer), Ål, Hallingdal, Norway, personal communications to author, 2017–2018.
21. Visted and Stigum, *Vår gamle bondekultur*. 1:154.
22. Per Gjærder, *Norske drikkekar av tre* (Oslo: Universitetsforlaget, 1975), 42–43.
23. Odd Nordland, *Brewing and Beer Traditions in Norway* (Oslo: Universitetsforlaget, 1969), 10.
24. Helena Kjepso, Mølstertunet museum, Voss, Norway, conversation with author, September 29, 2018; Hannu Nurminen (farmhouse brewer), Sysmä, Finland, interview with author, August 9, 2018.
25. Astri Riddervold, *Drikkeskikker: Nordmenns drikkevaner gjennom 1000 år* (Oslo: Cappelen Damm, 2009), 50.
26. Tor Bruun, *Alkoholens historie: fra rennestein til kongens bord* (Porsgrunn: Norgesforlaget, 2009), 157; Gjærder, *Norske drikkekar av tre*, 42–47.

27. Nils Hertzberg, *Fra min barndoms og ungdoms tid 1827–1856* (Christiania [Oslo]: Aschehoug, 1909), 43.

28. Nils Linder, *Nordisk familjebok*, 2nd ed., vol. 15 (Stockholm: Gernandts boktryckeri., 1911), s.v. "kopskal".

29. Antanas Astrauskas, *Per barzda varvejo* (Vilnius: Baltos Lankos, 2008), 114. Content cited herein translated by Elma Caicedo.

30. B. Ann Tlusty, *Bacchus and Civic Order: The Culture of Drink in Early Modern Germany*, (Charlottesville: University Press of Virginia, 2001), 103–14.

31. Ragnar Hauge, *Lover om alkohol i Norge: fra landskapslovene til 1814* (Oslo: Rusmiddeldirektoratet, 1998), 24.

32. Gjærder, *Norske drikkekar av tre*, 66.

33. Andreas Leiro, *Skikkar og truer ved ølbryggjing* (Voss: Voss Folkminnenemnd, 1965), 90.

34. Ugis Pucens, ethnographer, Aizpute, Latvia, interview and brewing session with author, July 2015.

35. E. N. Naumov, "Istoriya pivovareniya i kultura potrebleniya piva v chuvashiy." *Journal of the Chuvash National Museum* (2000), 1–4, http://www.chnmuseum.ru/files/almanac2000/almanac2000_103.pdf.

36. Jon K. Rysstad, "Oppskrift på maltøl bryggjing," beer recipe handed out to participants at a 1996 brewing course.

37. EU 7794.

38. NEU 29948; NEG 7335.

39. Kjell Bondevik, "Bygg og brygg," *Norsk Folkekultur: folkeminne-tidsskrift* [journal] (Skein, Norway, 1928). Edited by Rikard Berge.

40. Gjærder, *Norske drikkekar av tre*, 41–42.

41. Halvor Nordal (farmhouse brewer), Høydalsmo, Norway, interview with author, June 1, 2015.

42. Eirik Storesund, "Sacred White Stones: Echoes of an Ancient Scandinavian Fertility Cult," *Brute Norse* (blog), June 24, 2018, https://www.brutenorse.com/blog/2018/3/5/sacred-white-stones-objects-of-an-ancient-scandinavian-fertility-cult.

43. LUF 11264, Ivetofta, Skåne, Sweden.

44. Nordal, interview, June 1, 2015.

45. NEG, questionnaire 35, s.v. "Brewing."

46. Torleiv Hannaas, "Ordsamling fra Robyggjelaget fraa slutten av 1600-tallet," Den norske historiske kildeskriftkommission (Kristiania [Oslo], 1911), 47.

47. Eirik Storesund, Philologist, New York, United States. Pers comm 2018.

48. Eldar Nadiradze, *Georgian Beer* [bilingual: in Georgian and English] (Tbilisi: Meridiani, 2010), 69.

49. ERM KK-X KV52: 251. Translated by Margo Samorokov.

50. ERM KK-X KV55: 277.

51. Ilmar Talve, *Finnish Folk Culture*, Studia Fennica: Ethnologica, vol. 4. (Helsinki: Finnish Literature Society, 1997), 174.

52. Anders Salomonsson, *Gotlandsdricka: Traditionell kultur som regional identitetssymbol*, Skrifter utg. av Etnologiska sällskapet i Lund 10 (Karlstad: Press Förlag, 1979), 25.

53. Linda Dumpe, *Alus tradicijas Latvija* (Riga: Latvijas Vestures Instituta Apgads, 2001), 73.

54. EU 8823.

55. NEG 7399.

56. Leif Vatle, *Kornet* (Osterøy museum, 1980), 37.

57. Atle Ove Magnussen, Vest-norsk Kulturakademi, Voss, Norway, personal communications to author, 2018.

58. Maria Ivanovna (farmhouse brewer), Kudymkar, Komi Republic, Russia, interview and brewing session with author; Beer Museum in Cheboksary, July 18, 2017.

59. EU 13337.

60. EU 8367, Fränninge, Skåne, Sweden.

61. NEU 28980.

62. Naumov, "Istoriya pivovareniya i kultura potrebleniya piva v chuvashiy," 1–4.

63. Simonas Gutautas (commercial brewer and historian), Vilnius, Lithuania, personal communications to author, 2015–2019.

64. Gutautas, pers. comm., 2015–2019.

65. Roar Sandodden (farmhouse brewer and maltster), Stjørdalen, Norway, personal communications to author, 2014–19.

66. Aarne Trei (farmhouse brewer), Pihtla, Saaremaa, Estonia, interview with author, August 10, 2016.

67. Sjur Herman Rørlien (farmhouse brewer), Dyrvedalen, Voss, Norway, personal communications to author, 2014–2019.

68. Reidar Eitrheim (farmhouse brewer), Aga, Norway, interview and brewing session with author, December 2016.

69. Tormis Jakovlev, "Unustatust ja uuemast Saaremaa koduõllenduses," in *Saaremaa Museum kaheastaraamat 1995–1996* (1997), 132, content cited herein translated by Virgo Vjugin; Paavo Pruul (farmhouse brewer), Sõru, Estonia, brewing session with author, August 11, 2016.

70. ERM KK-X KV52: 203, 213, 220.

71. Jakob Eitrheim (farmhouse brewer), Aga, Norway, interview and brewing session with author, December 2016.

72. Gjærder, *Norske drikkekar av tre*, 50.

73. Merete Moe Henriksen, "Stille vann har dyp bunn: Offerteoriens rolle i forståelsen av depotfunn belyst gjennom våtmarksdepoter fra Midt-Norge ca. 2350-500 f.Kr," PhD thesis, NTNU, Trondheim, November 2014.

74. For many examples, see throughout Tiina Võti, *Õllekannud* (Tallinn: Kirjastus "Kunst", 1986); see also Dumpe, *Alus tradicijas Latvija*, 122–23.

75. Gutautas, pers. comm., 2015–2019.

76. Võti, *Õllekannud*, photo number 72.

77. Peaty, *You Brew Good Ale*, 10.

78. NEU 2712.

79. NEU 28980.

80. EU 7725.

81. NEG 7512.

82. NEG 12457.

83. Nils Nersten, *Minner fra Setesdal*, (Arendal: P. M. Danielsens forlag, 1950), 82.

84. NEU 28980.

85. AFD R. Jessen-Schmidt.

Chapter 7

1. Frederik Thaarup, *Haandbog for Fabrikanter, Haandværkere og Laugs Interessenter for Aaret 1832* (Copenhagen); Jacob Nicolai Wilse, *Physisk, oeconomisk og statistisk Beskrivelse over Spydeberg Præstegield og Egn i Aggershuus-Stift udi Norge* (Christiania [Oslo], 1779), 377.

2. Manfred Rösch, "Starkbier mit Honig," in *Mit Leier und Schwert: Das frühmittelalterliche "Sängergrab" von Trossingen*, Barbara Theune-Großkopf (Friedberg: Likias, 2010), 91.

3. Karl-Ernst Behre, "The history of beer additives in Europe — a review," *Vegetation History and Archaeobotany* 8, no. 1/2 (June 1999): 35–48.

4. Eldar Nadiradze, *Georgian Beer* [bilingual: in Georgian and English] (Tbilisi: Meridiani, 2010), 75.

5. Martyn Cornell, "The long battle between ale and beer," *Zythophile* (blog), December 14, 2009, http://zythophile.co.uk/2009/12/14/the-long-battle-between-ale-and-beer/.

6. Else-Marie Strese and Clas Tollin, *Humle: Det gröna guldet* (Stockholm: Nordiska Museets Förlag, 2015), 122; Matti Räsänen, *Vom Halm zum Fass*, German edition (Helsinki: Suomen muinaismuistoyhdistys, 1975), *Kansatieteellinen arkisto* 25:130; NEG 8148.

7. Strese and Tollin, *Humle: Det gröna guldet*, 122.

8. Strese and Tollin, *Humle: Det gröna guldet*, 255–69.

9. Strese and Tollin, 270–71.

10. EU 7725.

11. Strese and Tollin, 59.

12. NEU 10769, Bårse; NEU 30568, Brøns.

13. NEU 3136.

14. NEU 1767.

15. Christine Reimer, "Humleavl paa Fyn," in *Danske Studier*, by Marius Kristensen and Axel Olrik, 174–84. (Copenhagen: Gyldendalske boghandel Nordisk forlag, 1915), 184.

16. Else-Marie Karlsson Strese et al., "Genetic Diversity in Remnant Swedish Hop (*Humulus lupulus* L.) Yards from the 15th to 18th Century," *Economic Botany* 68, issue 3 (September 2014): 231–45, https://dx.doi.org/10.1007/s12231-014-9273-8.

17. Svein Øivind Solberg et al., "Genetic variation in Danish and Norwegian germplasm collections of hops," *Biochemical Systematics and Ecology* 52 (February 2014): 53–59, https://doi.org/10.1016/j.bse.2013.12.014.

18. O. Kornyšova et al., "Capillary zone electrophoresis method for determination of bitter (α- and β-) acids in hop (*Humulus lupulus* L.) cone extracts," *Advances in Medical Sciences* 54, no. 1 (2009): 41–46.

19. Strese and Tollin, *Humle: Det gröna guldet*, 249.

20. Fyodorov family (farmhouse brewers), Kshaushi, Chuvash Autonomous Republic, Russia, interview with author, July 22, 2017. Translator Aleksandr Gromov.

21. NEU 8823, 23256.

22. Per Kølster, *Alle tiders øl* (Copenhagen: Politikens forlag, 2007), 198.

23. Ove Arbo Høeg, Eineren i norsk natur og tradisjon, Norsk skogbruksmuseums særpublikasjon no. 11 (Elverum: Norsk skogbruks-museum, 1996), 17.

24. Høeg, *Eineren i norsk natur*, 138–41.

25. Liv Borgen, "Einer - den nyttigste planten i norsk natur?" Skog og Landskap (archived website), available at Wayback Machine, accessed October 8, 2019, https://web.archive.org/web/20170707181518/http://www.skogoglandskap.no/Artsbeskrivelser/einer.

26. Høeg, *Eineren i norsk natur*, 24–78.

27. Høeg, 79–127.

28. EU 7686, Mjöbäck, western Sweden.

29. Ove Arbo Høeg, *Planter og tradisjon: Floraen i levende tale og tradisjon i Norge* (Oslo: Universitetsforlaget, 1974), 103.

30. Sverre Skrindo (farmhouse brewer), Ål, Hallingdal, Norway, personal communications to the author, 2017–2018.

31. Odd Nordland, *Brewing and Beer Traditions in Norway* (Oslo: Universitetsforlaget, 1969); Anders Salomonsson, *Gotlandsdricka: Traditionell kultur som regional identitetssymbol*, Skrifter utg. av Etnologiska sällskapet i Lund 10 (Karlstad: Press Förlag, 1979).

32. Reinerus Broocman, *En fullständig swensk hushållsbok* (Norrköping, 1736), §13; Engelbret Mandt, *Historisk beskrivelse over Øvre Tellemarken*, reprint edition with comments (Lokalhistorisk forlag, [1777] 1989), 107; Johan Molbech, *Afhandling om Ølbrygningen i sin fulde Udstrækning.* (Copenhagen: Gyldendal, 1796), 65; Anna Maria Rückerschöld, *En Liten Hushålls-Bok*, third pressing (Stockholm: J. C. Holmberg, 1790), 12.

33. Raimund Dürnwirth, "Vom Steinbier," *Carinthia I* (Klagenfurt, 1905) 95:10–19; Philipp Ritter von Holger, *Die Staatswirthschafts-chemie, als Leitfaden zum Behufe der öffentlichen Vorlesungen über diesen* (Vienna, 1843), 243.

34. Høeg, *Eineren i norsk natur*, 23.

35. Patrick McGovern et al., "A biomolecular archaeological approach to 'Nordic grog,'" *Danish Journal of Archaeology* 2, no. 2 (2013): 112–31.

36. Pekka Kääriäinen (farmhouse brewer), Lammi, Finland, interview with author, August 7, 2018.

37. Olav Sopp, "Lidt av øllets historie," in *Schous bryggeri: mindeskrift til hundredaarsjubilæet 1921*, ed. Nils Vogt (Kristiania [Oslo], 1921), 118.

38. Høeg, *Eineren i norsk natur*, 86.

39. Jan Karlsen, Professor of chemistry, University of Oslo, personal communications to author 2016.

40. Aave Nystein (farmhouse brewer), Bø, Telemark, Norway, personal communications to author, 2016–2017.

41. NEG 9448.

42. Seppo Lisma (farmhouse brewer), Ruovesi, Finland, brewing session with author, August 7, 2018.

43. Nordland, *Brewing and Beer Traditions*, 128.

44. Behre, *Vegetation History and Archaeobotany* 8, 39.

45. Roel Mulder, "Gruit: nothing mysterious about it," *Lost Beers* (blog), July 13, 2017, http://lostbeers.com/gruit-nothing-mysterious-about-it/; Susan Verberg, "The Rise and Fall of Gruit," *Brewery History* 174 (2018): 46–79.

46. K.E. Malterud and A. Faegri, "Bacteriostatic and fungistatic activity of C-methylated dihydrochalcones from the fruits of *Myrica gale* L," *Acta pharmaceutica Suecica* 19, no. 1 (1982): 43–46.

47. NEU 28927, 29948; EU 7701.

48. NEU 28927.

49. NEU 29948.

50. ERM KK-X, KV55: 323.

51. Mika Laitinen, *Viking Age Brew: The Craft of Brewing Sahti Farmhouse Ale* (Chicago Review Press, 2019), 127.

52. NEG 7319.

53. Høeg, *Planter og tradisjon*, 139.

54. NEU 28977.

55. Ola Grefstad, *Drikkestell for øl i Trøndelag* (Trondheim: Museumsforlaget, 2014), 17.

56. NEG 14060.

57. Laura Grubb, *Oumbärlig Rådgifvare för hvarje hem* reprint (Lidingö, Stockholm: Görling förlag, [1888] 2008).

58. Hans Jacob Wille, *Beskrivelse over Sillejords præstegield i øvre Tellemarken i Norge* (Copenhagen: Gyldendal, 1786), 128.

59. SLS: Eino Ketola, Portom, Anna Langgard, Narpes, and Borje Sidback, Portom; KM: R. Bergman, Jomala, and E. Ketola, Portom.

60. Gordon Virgo, "Antimicrobial properties of traditional brewing herbs," diss. submitted for Project work in Ethnobiology, Evolutionary Biology Centre, Uppsala University, 2010.

61. EU 7833.

62. Simonas Gutautas (commercial brewer and historian), Vilnius, Lithuania, personal communications to author, 2015–2019.

63. Anna Dampc and Maria Luczkiewicz, "*Rhododendron tomentosum* (*Ledum palustre*). A review of traditional use based on current research," *Fitoterapia* 85 (March 2013): 130–43, https://dx.doi.org/10.1016/j.fitote.2013.01.013.

64. Martyn Cornell, "Heather ale: Scots or Irish?" *Zythophile* (blog), July 23, 2008, http://zythophile.co.uk/2008/07/23/heather-ale-scots-or-irish/.

65. John Firth, *Reminiscences of an Orkney Parish: Together with Old Orkney Words, Riddles and Proverbs* (Stromness: printed by W.R. Rendall, 1920), 103.

66. Cornell, "Heather ale: Scots or Irish?"

67. Elfyn Scourfield, "Farmhouse Brewing," *Amgueddfa: Bulletin of the National Museum of Wales* 17 (Cardiff, 1974), 4–5.

68. NEG 7583.

69. NEG 7839.

70. EU 7790.

71. Juozas Petrulis, "Alus," *Kraštotyra* (1975): 237–48.

72. Fredric Joachim Ekman, *Beskrifning om Runö i Liffland* (Tavastehus, 1847), 95.

73. KU 2364.

74. Olav Klonteig, *Fjellbygder i attersyn: frå det gamle Tinn i Telemark* (Forlaget Grenland, 2000), 29–33.

75. J. Jizba et al., "The structure of osladin - The sweet principle of the rhizomes of Polypodium vulgare L," *Tetrahedron Letters* 12, issue 18 (1971): 1329–32, https://doi.org/10.1016/S0040-4039(01)96701-2.
76. Paavo Pruul (farmhouse brewer), Sõru, Estonia, brewing session with author, August 11, 2016.
77. ERM KK-X, KV52, 229.
78. Margo Samorokov, Historian, Pärnu, Estonia, personal communications with author, 2019.
79. NEG 11059.
80. ERM KK-X, KV52: 241.
81. NEG 7771, 7399, 7467.
82. EU 7840, 7956, 8168, and many others.
83. AFD Karoline Hansen.
84. EU 7755, 7779, 9002.
85. Antanas Astrauskas, *Per barzda varvejo* (Vilnius: Baltos Lankos, 2008), 135. Content cited herein translated by Elma Caicedo.
86. Michael Jackson, "From Leeds to Lithuania for mushy pea beer," *What's Brewing*, October 1, 1995, republished by Beer Hunter [online], June 7, 2000.
87. Justas Kaupas, marketing director at Biržu Alus, Biržai, Lithuania, interview with author, July 31, 2013.
88. Justas Kaupas, interview.
89. SM Pakruojo vl; SM Meskučiu vl.
90. SM Pakruojo vl, SM Meskučiu vl; Simonas Gutautas, pers. comm., based on Juozas Petrulis's unpublished notes in the Lithuanian National Library.
91. SM Pakruojo vl; SM Meskučiu vl.
92. Nordland, *Brewing and Beer Traditions*, 91.
93. NEU 12018.
94. NEG 9448.
95. NEG 7406.
96. NEG 7561.
97. Sopp, "Lidt av øllets historie," 118; Ivar Skare (farmhouse brewer and maltster), Ørsta, Norway, interview with author, March 2019.
98. Sopp, 118–19.
99. Ugis Pucens, ethnographer, Aizpute, Latvia, interview and brewing session with author, July 2015.
100. Petrulis, "Alus," 237–48.

Chapter 8

1. Sigurd Johan Saure (farmhouse brewer), Sykkylven, Norway, personal communications to author, 2016–2019.
2. Martyn Cornell, "Was water really regarded as dangerous to drink in the Middle Ages?" *Zythophile* (blog), March 4, 2014, http://zythophile.co.uk/2014/03/04/was-water-really-regarded-as-dangerous-to-drink-in-the-middle-ages/.
3. Astri Riddervold, *Drikkeskikker: Nordmenns drikkevaner gjennom 1000 år*, (Oslo: Cappelen Damm, 2009), 21.
4. NEU 2912.
5. NEU 8823.
6. NEU 8823.
7. NEU 20776, Jetsmark, northern Denmark.
8. George Ewart Evans, *Ask the Fellows who Cut the Hay*," (London: Faber and Faber, 1956), 60.
9. Anders Salomonsson, *Gotlandsdricka: Traditionell kultur som regional identitetssymbol*, Skrifter utg. av Etnologiska sällskapet i Lund 10 (Karlstad: Press Förlag, 1979), 24-25.
10. EU 8851.
11. Matti Räsänen, *Vom Halm zum Fass*, German edition (Helsinki: Suomen muinaismuistoyhdistys, 1975), *Kansatieteellinen arkisto* 25.
12. Muhammet Arici and Orhan Daglioglu, "Boza: A lactic acid fermented cereal beverage as a traditional Turkish food," *Food Reviews International* 18, issue 1 (2002): 39-48, https://doi.org/10.1081/FRI-120003416.
13. Riddervold, *Drikkeskikker*, 24–31.
14. Gösta Berg and Sigfrid Svensson, *Svensk bondekultur* (Stockholm: Albert Bonniers Forlag, 1934), 150; Salomonsson, *Gotlandsdricka*, 26.
15. James R. Nicolson, *Traditional Life in Shetland* (London: Robert Hale, 1978), 80.
16. Ivar Skare (Farmhouse brewer and maltster) Ørsta, Norway, interview with author, March 10, 2019; NEG 7518.
17. Terje Raftevold (farmhouse brewer), Innvik, Norway, interview and brewing session with author, July 2015, personal communications 2015–2017; Paavo Pruul (farmhouse brewer), Sõru, Estonia, brewing session with author, August 11, 2016.
18. Sjur Herman Rørlien (farmhouse brewer), Dyrvedalen, Voss, Norway, personal communications with author, 2014–2019.
19. Harald Opshaug (farmhouse brewer), Stranda, Norway, interview with author, May 28, 2014; Hannu Nurminen (farmhouse brewer), Sysmä, Finland, interview with author, August 9, 2018.

20. Antanas Astrauskas, *Per barzda varvejo* (Vilnius: Baltos Lankos, 2008), 143, content cited herein translated by Elma Caicedo; Vidmantas Laurinavičius, beer writer, Vilnius, Lithuania, personal communications to author, 2013–2018.

21. NEG 7538, Skjak, Oppland; Linda Dumpe, *Alus tradicijas Latvija* (Riga: Latvijas Vestures Instituta Apgads, 2001), 193.

22. Aarne Trei (farmhouse brewer), Pihtla, Saaremaa, Estonia, interview with author, August 10, 2016; Paavo Pruul, brewing session with author, August 11, 2016; Andres Kurgpõld (farmhouse brewer), Saaremaa, Estonia, interview with author, August 10, 2016.

23. C. Schöning and M. Igsi, *Hobøl herred 1814–1914: Bidrag til en bygdebeskrivelse* (Fredrikshald: E. Sem., 1914), 78.

24. ERM KK-X, KV54: 254. Translation by Margo Samorokov.

25. Schöning and Igsi, *Hobøl herred 1814–1914*, 77–78.

26. L. N. Simonova, *Kvasovarenie i domashneye pivovarenie* (St. Petersburg, 1898). Content cited herein translated by Aleksandr Gromov.

27. Simonova, *Kvasovarenie i domashneye pivovarenie*.

28. SM Rietavo vl.

29. ERM KK-X, KV51: 159.

30. Aleksandr Gromov, commercial brewer, Tver, Russia, personal communications with author, 2017–2018.

31. "Pivovary - myedovary, kvasniky," (St. Petersburg, 1865), content cited herein translated by Ivan Kamarinskiy; Olav Sopp, *Hjemmelagning av øl og vin* (Kristiania [Oslo]: Norli, 1917), 84.

32. N. I. Polevitskiy, *Domashneye prigotovlenie fruktovykh prokhladitelnykh napitkov* (Leningrad [St Petersburg]: Nachatki znaniy, 1927). Content cited herein translated by Ivan Kamarinskiy.

33. Räsänen, *Vom Halm zum Fass*, 99.

34. EU 8617.

35. NEG 16921, 18905, 21180.

36. August Bielenstein, *Die Holzbauten und Holzgeräte der Letten: Ein Beitrag zur Ethnographie, Culturgeschichte und Archaeologie der Völker Russlands im Westgebiet*, vol. 2 (Buchdruckerei der Kaiserlichen Akad. der Wissenschaften, 1918), 2:307.

37. Ingvar Svanberg et al., "Uses of tree saps in northern and eastern parts of Europe," *Acta Societatis Botanicorum Poloniae* 81, no. 4 (2012): 349, https://doi.org/10.5586/asbp.2012.036.

38. Svanberg et al., "Uses of tree saps," 347.

39. EU 7725.

40. Bielenstein, *Die Holzbauten und Holzgeräte der Letten*, 2:308.

41. Lars Levander, *Övre Dalarnes bondekultur under 1800- talets förra hälft. 3. Hem och hemarbete*, Skrifter utgivna av Kungl. Gustav Adolfs Akademien för folklivsforskning, 11, vol. 3 (Lund: Carl Bloms Boktryckeri, 1947), 501; EU 8469, Bjuråker, central Sweden.

42. Svanberg et al., "Uses of tree saps," 350.

43. Ove Arbo Høeg, *Planter og tradisjon: Floraen i levende tale og tradisjon i Norge* (Oslo: Universitetsforlaget, 1974), 245.

44. Carl Christian Grøndahl, "HelVed – Øl av bjørkesevje," Ølportalen, May 15, 2014, http://olportalen.no/2014/05/15/helved-ol-av-bjorkesevje/; Svanberg et al., "Uses of tree saps," 344.

45. Arthur Bredli, commercial brewer, Espedalen, Norway, email to author, January 4, 2018.

46. Bielenstein, *Die Holzbauten und Holzgeräte der Letten*, 308.

47. Bielenstein, 307; Hulda Garborg, *Heimestell: uppskrifter og rettleidingar for smaae hushald, helst paa lande* (Kristiania [Oslo]: Den 17de Mai, 1899), 136.

48. EU 7725.

49. Hans Jacob Wille, *Beskrivelse over Sillejords præstegiæld i øvre Tellemarken i Norge* (Copenhagen: Gyldendal, 1786), 96.

50. Levander, *Övre Dalarnes bondekultur under 1800*, 515; EU 8469.

51. Arthur Bredli, email, January 4, 2018.

52. Grøndahl, "HelVed – Øl av bjørkesevje.".

53. Arthur Bredli, email.

54. Riddervold, *Drikkeskikker*, 31; Nils Keyland, *Svensk allmogekost*, (Stockholm:Carlsson i samarbete med Institutet för folklivsforskning och Nordiska museet, 1989), Svenska vi, 240:79.; Vagn Brøndegaard, *Folk og flora*, vol. 1 (Copenhagen: Rosenkilde og Bagger, 1978), 72; Ilmar Talve, *Finnish Folk Culture*, Studia Fennica: Ethnologica, vol. 4 (Helsinki: Finnish Literature Society, 1997), 129; ERM KK-X, KV52: 245; Tomasz Madej et al., "Juniper Beer in Poland: The Story of the Revival of a Traditional Beverage," *Journal of Ethnobiology* 34, issue 1 (February 1, 2014): 84–103, https://doi.org/10.2993/0278-0771-34.1.84.

55. EU 7725.

56. Tomasz Madej et al., "Juniper Beer in Poland," 100; Ove Arbo Høeg, *Eineren i norsk natur og tradisjon*, Norsk skogbruksmuseums særpublikasjon 11 (Elverum: Norsk skogbruksmuseum, 1996), 100.

57. EU 8442.

58. EU 8549, 8623, 8761 (stick); EU 7779, 7790, 7804, 8313, 8458 (mittens).

59. NEG 7538; EU 7779, 7790, 8458.

60. NEG 7538.

61. EU 7725, 7790, 8963.

62. EU 8313.

63. EU 7804, 8420.

64. EU 8313.

65. NEG 11792; EU 7833, 8801; "Wikibooks kokbok," anonymous collaboratively authored cookbook on Wikibooks.org, version cited herein dated October 13, 2013, https://sv.wikibooks.org/wiki/Kokboken/Recept/Enb%C3%A4rsdricka.

66. Eva Crane, *The World History of Bee Keeping and Honey Hunting* (New York: Routledge, 1999).

67. For more detail see Lars Marius Garshol, "Mead: a Norwegian tradition?" *Larsblog*, April 3, 2018, http://www.garshol.priv.no/blog/387.html.

68. Ole Højrup, *Landbokvinden: rok og kærne, grovbrød og vadmel.* (Copenhagen: Nationalmuseet, 1966), 62; NEU 7685.

69. EU 8617.

70. Roger Pinon, "Recettes de bières de ménage en Wallonie et subsidiarement en Picardie," in *Studium et Museum*, ed. Édouard Remouchamps, 103-121 (Liège: Musée de la Vie Wallone, 1996).

Chapter 9

1. Jørund Geving (farmhouse brewer and maltster), Stjørdalen, Norway, personal communications to author, 2016–2019.

2. Halvor Bjåland (farmhouse brewer), Morgedal, Telemark, Norway, brewing session with author, May 31, 2015.

3. Bjørn Roth, microbiologist, Stavanger, Norway, personal communications with author, 2018–2019; Matt Del Fiacco, "Fermentation Temperature: Imperial Yeast A43 Loki (Kveik) | exBEERiment Results," *Brülosophy* (blog), April 8, 2019, http://brulosophy.com/2019/04/08/fermentation-temperature-imperial-yeast-a43-loki-kviek-exbeeriment-results/.

4. Sigurd Johan Saure (farmhouse brewer), Sykkylven, Norway, personal communications to author, 2016–2019.

5. Lars Marius Garshol and Richard Preiss, "How to Brew with Kveik," *Master Brewers Association of the Americas Technical Quarterly* 55, no. 4: 79.

6. Garshol and Preiss, How to Brew with Kveik," 78.

7. Richard Preiss, microbiologist, Escarpment Labs, Guelph, Canada, personal communications to author, 2016–2019.

8. Sigurd Johan Saure, pers. comm., 2016–2019.

9. Aave Nystein (farmhouse brewer), Bø, Telemark, Norway, personal communications to author, 2016–2017.

10. Jarle Nupen (farmhouse brewer), Ørsta, Norway, personal communications to author, 2016–2018.

11. Pekka Kääriäinen (farmhouse brewer), Lammi, Finland, interview with author, August 7, 2018.

12. Mika Laitinen, *Viking Age Brew: The Craft of Brewing Sahti Farmhouse Ale* (Chicago Review Press, 2019), 172.

13. DeWayne Schaaf, reply to Lars Garshol (Larsblog on beer), "I'm finishing up my English book (to be published next year), and I'm having a problem with the recipes. What should I tell Americans about juniper?" Facebook, April 8, 2019.

14. Lars Garshol, "I'm finishing up my English book," Facebook.

15. EU 7725; Kjell Magnar Auran (farmhouse brewer and maltster), Innavætte sånnhuslag, Stjørdal, Norway, interview with author, June 1, 2018.

16. Jørund Geving, pers. comm., 2016–2019.

17. Mika Laitinen, author, Jyväskylä, Finland, personal communications to author 2015-2020.

18. Mika Laitinen, pers. comm.

19. Jukka Ekberg et al., "Physicochemical characterization of sahti, an 'ancient' beer style indigenous to Finland," *Journal of the Institute of Brewing* 121, issue 4 (September 11): 5.

20. Mika Laitinen, *Viking Age Brew: The Craft of Brewing Sahti Farmhouse Ale* (Chicago Review Press, 2019).

21. Matti Räsänen, *Vom Halm zum Fass* German edition (Helsinki: Suomen muinaismuistoyhdistys, 1975) *Kansatieteellinen arkisto* 25.

22. Laitinen, *Viking Age Brew*, 68.

23. Laitinen, 69.

24. Per Kølster, *Alle tiders øl* (Copenhagen: Politikens forlag, 2007), 190.

25. O. Kornyšova et al., "Capillary zone electrophoresis method for determination of bitter (α- and β-) acids in hop (*Humulus lupulus* L.) cone extracts," *Advances in Medical Sciences* 54, no. 1 (2009): 43.

26. Simonas Gutautas, commercial brewer and historian, Vilnius, Lithuania, personal communications to author, 2015–2019.

27. Reda Kavaliauskaitė and Tomas Sutkaitis, "Naminio alaus gamyba ir vartojimas Šimoniu apylinkeje," *Liaudies Kultūra*, 2006/1 (106): 23–34, https://hdl.handle.net/20.500.12259/42371. Content cited herein translated by Remigijus Tranas.

28. Simonas Gutautas, pers. comm., 2015–2019.

29. Sigvald Ellkier-Pedersen, "Brygning af Gammeløl, 1975," [in Danish], uploaded by Stig Ellkier-Pedersen, December 29, 2015, YouTube video, 17:22, footage showing how farmhouse beer was brewed, recorded in 1975 in Jensgaard, Tiufkjær, south of Vejle, https://www.youtube.com/watch?v=NWq2CgsYjLg; Stig Ellkier-Pedersen, "Brygning af Gammeløl i 1975" [in Danish], uploaded by Stig Ellkier-Pedersen, December 29, 2015, YouTube video, 09:57, narrated slide series illustrating the old tradition of brewing farmhouse beer using Sigvald Ellkier-Pedersen's 1975 footage, https://www.youtube.com/watch?v=6daxIzVP-Z4. For *Vejle Amts Folkeblad* article, see slide series video at 09:30.

30. Jørund Geving, pers. comm., 2016–2019.

31. Jon Leirfall, "Liv og lagnad i Stjørdalsbygdene," Stjørdalsboka bind 1, del III, Stjørdal og Meråker kommuner (1972), 180.

32. Anders Mattson, "Så här går det til . . ." Recipe and explanation handed out at brewing courses (n.d.).

33. KU 2364.

34. EU 7779; KU 2364; Örjan Lindgren (Farmhouse brewer), Stånga, Gotland, Sweden. Phone interview conducted by Morgan Ingemarsson February 3, 2018; Anders Salomonsson, *Den gotländske kölnan.* Gotländskt Arkiv, 1977), 34.

35. Anders Mattson, "Så här går det til . . ." Recipe and explanation handed out at brewing courses (n.d.); KU 2364.

36. Anders Salomonsson, *Gotlandsdricka: Traditionell kultur som regional identitetssymbol.* Skrifter utg. av Etnologiska sällskapet i Lund 10. (Karlstad: Press Förlag, 1979), 79.

37. Örjan Lindgren (farmhouse brewer), Stånga, Gotland, Sweden, telephone interview conducted by Morgan Ingemarsson, February 3, 2018; Mattson, "Så här går det til . . ." handout.

38. Sjur Herman Rørlien (farmhouse brewer), Dyrvedalen, Voss, Norway, personal communications to author, 2014-2019.

39. Odd Nordland, *Brewing and Beer Traditions in Norway* (Oslo: Universitetsforlaget, 1969), 35.

40. Sjur Herman Rørlien, pers. comm., 2014-2019.

41. Nordland, *Brewing and Beer Traditions,* 35.

42. Aare Horn (farmhouse brewer), Obinitsa, Estonia, interview August 7, 2016 and email interview, November 2017.

43. E. N. Naumov,. "Istoriya pivovareniya i kultura potrebleniya piva v chuvashiy," *Journal of the Chuvash National Museum* (2000), 1-4, http://www.chnmuseum.ru/files/almanac2000/almanac2000_103.pdf.

44. Gutautas, pers. comm., 2015-2019.

45. Viktoras Dagys, "Miežiu salyklo alus," in *Žiobiškis 2000,* ed. Venantas Mačiekus et al. (Vilnius: Versmès leidykla, 2000), 817-21. Content cited herein translated by Remigijus Tranas.

46. ERM KK-X, KV52: 220.

47. EU 8702.

48. EU 8702, 42103.

49. Per Söderbäck, *Rågöborna,* Nordiska Museets handlingar, vol. 13 (Stockholm: Nordiska Museets, 1940), 99.

50. Ian Tait, Shetland Museum, email to author, June 3, 2016; Rae Phillips (farmhouse brewer and maltster), Birsay, Orkney, UK, personal communications to author, 2016.

51. George Ewart Evans, *Ask the Fellows who Cut the Hay* (London: Faber and Faber, 1956), 60.

52. Elfyn Scourfield, "Farmhouse Brewing," *Amgueddfa: Bulletin of the National Museum of Wales* 17 (Cardiff, 1974), 4-5.

53. Brian Glover, *Prince of Ales: The History of Brewing in Wales* (Stroud: Sutton Publishing, 1993); J. Geraint Jenkins, *Life and Tradition in Rural Wales* (Stroud: Amberley Publishing, 2009), 162.

54. Hinrich Siuts and Fritz Bartelt, *Bäuerliche und handwerkliche Arbeitsgeräte in Westfalen: die alten Geräte der Landwirtschaft und des Landhandwerks 1890-1930.* (Münster: Aschendorff, 1982), 208.

55. VOKO 121.

56. VOKO 423.

57. VOKO 4110.

58. VOKO 423.

59. VOKO 313. This archive document also contains accounts of a recipe, the use of top-fermented yeast, and brewing on a farm in Welbergen village.

60. Siuts and Bartelt, *Bäuerliche und handwerkliche Arbeitsgeräte in Westfalen,* 208.

61. Eldar Nadiradze, *Georgian Beer* [bilingual: in Georgian and English] (Tbilisi: Meridiani, 2010), 69.

62. Nadiradze, *Georgian Beer,* 117.

63. NEG 7398.

Chapter 10

1. Josh Oakes, "Oakes Weekly - November 24th, 2005: Deconstructing Beer Style, part II," Oakes Weekly, RateBeer.com, https://www.ratebeer.com/Beer-News/Article-560.htm.

2. Tuomas Pere, farmhouse and commercial brewer, Tampere, Finland, interview with author, August 3, 2018.

BIBLIOGRAPHY

Archival Sources

Much of this book is based on first-hand research in archives. These sources cannot be cited in the normal way, since they have never been published. Instead, they are referenced using archive keys, such as NEG 7771, where the prefix tells you what collection the document can be found in. Table 1 explains what each prefix means.

Table 1 Prefixes for Archival Sources

Prefix	Institution	Comment
AFD	Afdeling for Dialektforskning, Copenhagen University	Questionnaire C7
ERM	Estonian National Museum	Mainly questionnaire X
EU	Etnologiska Undersökningen, Nordic Museum	Questionnaire 58
KU	Kulturhistoriska Undersökningen, Nordic Museum	Renamed from EU in 1960s
KM	Finnish National Museum	Cited by last name.
LUF	Lunds Universitet, Folkminnesarkiv	–
NEG	Norsk Etnologisk Granskning	Questionnaire 35
NEU	Nationalmuseets Etnologiske Undersøgelser	Questionnaire 34
SLS	Svenska Litteratursällskapet	Series 820; cited by last name
SM	Šiauliai Aušros Museum, Lithuania	Questionnaire 8; cited by region
VOKO	Volkskundliche Kommission für Westfalen	No specific series

The Database

Throughout this book there are a number of statistical tables, visualizations, and maps that are given without any indication of what the source is. This section explains how they were produced.

I have taken all the archival sources described in the previous sectiob and tagged them in a database. For each response, I coded the source, the location, and the main information from the response, such as type of grain malted, pitch temperature, herbs used, adjuncts used, and so on.

In addition, I added to the database all the interviews and brewer visits I had done, plus recipes and other descriptions that I had collected from books, journals, newspapers, and other sources. Only descriptions that are first-hand accounts of brewing in a specific geographic area (generally no larger than county size) are included.

The statistics are produced by querying the database. My assumption is that the accounts are mostly reliable, since they are descriptions of brewing as it was in one specific place, written by someone familiar with that area. I also assume that, while there will be errors in the individual accounts, statistics built on a large number of accounts will give a picture that is at least roughly correct, because the accounts are independent of each other.

The total size of the database is 1,392 individual accounts, many of them with information on just a few aspects of brewing. In total, the database yields 22,468 data points.

Published References

Aasen, Ivar. 1873. *Norsk ordbog: med dansk forklaring.* Christiania [Oslo]: P.T. Mallings boghandel.

Ahokas, Hannu, and Marja-Leena Manninen. 2000. "Thermostabilities of Grain β-Amylase and β-Glucanase in Finnish Landrace Barleys and their Putative Past Adaptedness." *Hereditas* 132, no. 2 (April): 111–18. https://doi.org/10.1111/j.1601-5223.2000.00111.x.

Arici, Muhammet and Orhan Daglioglu. 2002. "Boza: A lactic acid fermented cereal beverage as a traditional Turkish food." *Food Reviews International* 18, issue 1: 39–48. https://doi.org/10.1081/FRI-120003416.

Astrauskas, Antanas. 2008. *Per barzda varvejo.* Vilnius: Baltos Lankos, 2008. Content cited herein translated by Elma Caicedo.

Behre, Karl-Ernst. 1999. "The history of beer additives in Europe — a review." *Vegetation History and Archaeobotany* 8, no. 1/2 (June 1999): 35–48.

Berg, Gösta and Sigfrid Svensson. 1934. *Svensk bondekultur.* Stockholm: Albert Bonniers Forlag.

Bielenstein, August. 1918. *Die Holzbauten und Holzgeräte der Letten: Ein Beitrag zur Ethnographie, Culturgeschichte und Archaeologie der Völker Russlands im Westgebiet.* 2 vols. Buchdruckerei der Kaiserlichen Akad. der Wissenschaften.

Bjørnstad, Åsmund. 2012. *Vårt daglege brød: Kornets kulturhistorie.* Oslo: Vidarforlaget.

Blasco, Anna, Manel Edo, and M. Josefa Villalba. 2006. "Evidencias de procesado y consumo de cerveza en la cueva de Can Sadurní (Begues, Barcelona) durante la Prehistoria." In *IV Congreso de Neolítico Peninsular*, ed. Mauro S. Hernández Pérez, Jorge A. Soler Díaz, and Juan A. López Padilla, 428–431. Vol. 1. Museo Arqueológico de Alicante.

Bondevik, Kjell. 1928. "Bygg og brygg." *Norsk Folkekultur: folkeminne-tidsskrift* [journal] (Skein, Norway), edited by Rikard Berge.

Bouby, Laurent, Philippe Boissinot, and Philippe Marinval. 2011. "Never Mind the Bottle. Archaeobotanical Evidence of Beer-brewing in Mediterranean France and the Consumption of Alcoholic Beverages During the 5th Century BC." *Human Ecology* 39, issue 3: 351–60. https://dx.doi.org/10.1007/s10745-011-9395-x.

Bråtå, Hans Olav, and Merethe Lerfald. 2012. "Maten og matressursene i Gudbrandsdalen: historiske hovedtrekk siden steinalderen." ØF-rapport 03/2012, Østlandsforskning, Lillehammer.

Brøndegaard, Vagn. 1978. *Folk og flora.* Vol. 1. Copenhagen: Rosenkilde og Bagger.

Broocman, Reinerus. 1736. *En fullständig swensk hushållsbok.* Norrköping.

Bruun, Tor. 2009. *Alkoholens historie: fra rennestein til kongens bord.* Porsgrunn: Norgesforlaget.

Cartwright, Zachary M., Dean A. Glawe, and Charles G. Edwards. 2018. "Reduction of Brettanomyces bruxellensis Populations from Oak Barrel Staves Using Steam." *American Journal of Enology and Viticulture* 69 (October 2018): 400–409. https://dx.doi.org/10.5344/ajev.2018.18024.

Christiaens, Joaquin F., Luis M. Franco, Tanne L. Cools, Luc De Meester, Jan Michiels, Tom Wenseleers, et al. 2014. "The Fungal Aroma Gene *ATF1* Promotes Dispersal of Yeast Cells through Insect Vectors." *Cell Reports* 9, issue 2 (October 23, 2014): 425–32. https://doi.org/10.1016/j.celrep.2014.09.009.

Cornell, Martyn. 2007 -. *Zythophile* (blog). http://zythophile.co.uk/.

Crane, Eva. 1999. *The World History of Bee Keeping and Honey Hunting.* New York: Routledge.

Cubillos, Francisco A., Brian Gibson, Nubia Grijalva-Vallejos, Kristoffer Krogerus, and Jarkko Nikulin. 2019. "Bioprospecting for brewers: exploiting natural diversity for naturally diverse beers." *Yeast* 36, issue 6 (June): 383–98. https://doi.org/10.1002/yea.3380.

Dagys, Viktoras. 2000. "Miežiu salyklo alus." In *Žiobiškis 2000*, edited by Venantas Mačiekus, Stanislovas Buchaveckas, Živilė Driskiuvienė, Petras Jonušas, Povilas Krikščiūnas, Rita Mačiekienė, et al., 817–21. Vilnius: Versmės leidykla. Content cited herein translated by Remigijus Tranas.

Dampc, Anna, and Maria Luczkiewicz. 2013. "*Rhododendron tomentosum* (*Ledum palustre*). A review of traditional use based on current research." *Fitoterapia* 85 (March): 130-43. https://dx.doi.org/10.1016/j.fitote.2013.01.013.

Del Fiacco, Matt. 2019. "Fermentation Temperature: Imperial Yeast A43 Loki (Kveik) | exBEERiment Results." Brülosophy (blog), April 8, 2019.

Dineley, Merryn. 2019. "Hearth mashing." *Ancient Malt and Ale* (blog), February 17, 2019. http://merryn.dineley.com/2019/02/hearth-mashing.html.

Dineley, Merryn. 2010. "Experiment or Demonstration? Making fermentable malt sugars from the grain and a discussion of some of the evidence for this activity in the British Neolithic." In *Experimentation and Interpretation: The Use of Experimental Archaeology in the Study of the Past*, edited by Dana C.E. Millson, 96–108. Oxford: Oxbow Books.

Dumpe, Linda. 2001. *Alus tradicijas Latvija*. Riga: Latvijas Vestures Instituta Apgads.

Dürnwirth, Raimund. 1905. "Vom Steinbier." *Carinthia I* (Klagenfurt) 95: 10–19.

Egilsdóttir, Ásdís. 2002. *Biskupa sögur*. Íslenzk fornrit XVI, vol. 2. Reykjavík: Hið íslenzka fornritafélag. Content cited herein translated from the original Norse by Eirik Storesund.

Ekberg, Jukka, Brian Gibson, Jussi J. Joensuu, Kristoffer Krogerus, Frederico Magalhães, Atte Mikkelson, et al. 2015. "Physicochemical characterization of sahti, an 'ancient' beer style indigenous to Finland." *Journal of the Institute of Brewing* 121, issue 4 (September 11): 464–73.

Ekman, Fredric Joachim. 1847. *Beskrifning om Runö i Liffland*. Tavastehus.

Erken, Henriette Schønberg. 1925. *Stor kokebok for større og mindre husholdninger*. Oslo: Kristiania Forlag.

Evans, George Ewart. 1956. *Ask the Fellows who Cut the Hay*." London: Faber and Faber.

Fabrizio, V., I. Vigentini, N. Parisi, C. Picozzi, C. Compagno, and R. Foschino. 2015. "Heat inactivation of wine spoilage yeast *Dekkera bruxellensis* by hot water treatment." *Letters in Applied Microbiology* 61, issue 2 (August): 186–91. https://doi.org/10.1111/lam.12444.

Fay, Justin C., Ping Liu, Giang T. Ong, Maitreya J. Dunham, Gareth A. Cromie, Eric W. Jeffery, et al. 2019. "A polyploid admixed origin of beer yeasts derived from European and Asian wine populations." *PLoS Biology* 17, no. 3 (March 5): e3000147. https://doi.org/10.1371/journal.pbio.3000147.

Ferkai, Loránt. 1958. *Remekel a bicska*. Budapest: Móra Ferenc Könyvkiadó. Content cited herein translated by Barnabas Davoti.

Firth, John. 1920. *Reminiscences of an Orkney Parish: Together with Old Orkney Words, Riddles and Proverbs*. Stromness: Printed by W.R. Rendall.

Frazer, James George. 1912. "The Corn-Mother and the Corn-Maiden in Northern Europe." In *Spirits of the Corn and of the Wild*, 131–70. Part 5, vol. 1 of *The Golden Bough: A Study in Magic and Religion*. 3rd ed. London: Macmillan and Co.

Gallone, Brigida, Jan Steensels, Stijn Mertens, Maria C. Dzialo, Jonathan L. Gordon, Ruben Wauters, et al. "Interspecific hybridization facilitates niche adaptation in beer yeast." *Nature Ecology and Evolution* 3 (October 21, 2019): 1562–75. doi:10.1038/s41559-019-0997-9.

Gallone, Brigida, Jan Steensels, Troels Prahl, Leah Soriaga, Veerle Saels, Beatriz Herrera-Malaver, et al. 2016. "Domestication and divergence of *Saccharomyces cerevisiae* beer yeasts." *Cell* 166 (September 8, 2016): 1397–410. http://dx.doi.org/10.1016/j.cell.2016.08.020.

Galteland, Olav. 1920. *Gamle segner frå Evje*. Kristiansand: Agder historielag.

Garborg, Hulda. 1899. *Heimestell: uppskrifter og rettleidingar for smaae hushald, helst paa lande*. Kristiania [Oslo]: Den 17de Mai.

Garshol, Lars Marius. 2005 -. *Larsblog*, http://www.garshol.priv.no/blog/.

Garshol, Lars Marius and Richard Preiss. 2018. "How to Brew with Kveik." *Master Brewers Association of the Americas Technical Quarterly* 55, no. 4: 76–83.

Gilliland, R.B. 1961. "*Brettanomyces*. I. Occurrence, characteristics, and effects on beer flavor." *Journal of the Institute of Brewing* 67, issue 3 (May–June): 257–61.

Gjærder, Per. 1975. *Norske drikkekar av tre*. Oslo: Universitetsforlaget.

Glamann, Kristof, and Kirsten Glamann. 2004. *Nordens Pasteur: fortællingen om naturforskeren Emil Chr. Hansen*. Copenhagen: Gyldendal.

Glamann, Kristof. 2005. *Beer And Brewing In Pre-Industrial Denmark*. Odense: University Press of Southern Denmark.

Glover, Brian. 1993. *Prince of Ales: The History of Brewing in Wales*. Stroud: Sutton Publishing.

Grefstad, Ola. 2014. *Drikkestell for øl i Trøndelag*. Trondheim: Museumsforlaget.

Grieg, Sigurd. 1934. *Skiftet etter Eirik Bukk på Finnen*. Oslo: Dybwad.

Grubb, Laura. (1888) 2008. *Oumbärlig Rådgifvare för hvarje hem*. Reprint, Lidingö, Stockholm: Görling förlag.

Grundtvig, Fredrik Lange. 1908. *Livet i Klokkergaarden*. Copenhagen: Det Schubotheske forlag.

Grønnesby, Geir. 2016. "Hot rocks! Beer brewing on viking and medieval age farms in Trøndelag." In *The Agrarian Life: Studies in Rural Settlement and Farming in Norway*, edited by Frode Iversen and Håkan Pettersson, 133–49. Oslo: Portal forlag.

Grønnesby, Geir. 2014. "Bryggestein og kulturlag - spor etter gårdens opprinnelse." *SPOR* (NTNU University Museum), nr 1., 32–35.

Gustawsson, Karl Alfred. 1949. "Kokstenshögar." *Fornvännen*: 152–65.

Hannaas, Torleiv. 1911. "Ordsamling fra Robyggjelaget fraa slutten av 1600-tallet." Den norske historiske kildeskriftkommission, Kristiania.

Hansen, Emil Christian. 1888. "Undersøgelser over Alkoholgjærsvampenes Fysiologi og Morfologi: 2. Om Askosporedannelsen hos Slægten Saccharomyces." In *Meddelelser fra Carlsberg Laboratoriet*. Copenhagen: Carlsberg Laboratories.

Hasund, Sigvald. 1942. "Bygget som 'ølkorn' i det vestlandske havreområdet." In *Or Norges Bondesoge, Glytt og granskningar*, ed. S Haslund, vol. 1, 208 26. Oslo: Noregs Boklag.

Hauge, Ragnar. 1998. *Lover om alkohol i Norge: fra landskapslovene til 1814*. Oslo: Rusmiddeldirektoratet.

Hellenius, Carl Niclas. 1780. *Anmärkningar öfver finska allmogens bryggningssätt*. Åbo [Turku]: Åbo Kungliga Akademi.

Helmen, Aksel. 1952. *Frå det daglige liv på Hadeland i gamle dager*. [Gran?]: self-published, 1952.

Henriksen, Merete Moe. 2014. "Stille vann har dyp bunn: Offerteoriens rolle i forståelsen av depotfunn belyst gjennom våtmarksdepoter fra Midt-Norge ca. 2350-500 f.Kr." PhD thesis, NTNU, Trondheim, November 2014.

Hertzberg, Nils. 1909. *Fra min barndoms og ungdoms tid 1827–1856*. Christiania [Oslo]: Aschehoug.

Hobsbawm, Eric. 1994. *Age of Extremes: The Short Twentieth Century, 1914–1991*. London: Michael Joseph.

Høeg, Ove Arbo. 1996. *Eineren i norsk natur og tradisjon*. Norsk skogbruksmuseums særpublikasjon 11. Elverum: Norsk skogbruksmuseum.

Høeg, Ove Arbo. 1974. *Planter og tradisjon: Floraen i levende tale og tradisjon i Norge*. Oslo: Universitetsforlaget.

Højrup, Ole. 1966. *Landbokvinden: rok og kærne, grovbrød og vadmel*. Copenhagen: Nationalmuseet.

Holger, Philipp Ritter von. 1843. *Die Staatswirthschafts-chemie, als Leitfaden zum Behufe der öffentlichen Vorlesungen über diesen*. Vienna.

Horne, Thomas. 2017. *Norges 100 beste øl 2018*. Oslo: Handverk forlag.

Ivanitskiy, Nikolay Aleksandrovich. 1898. "Solvychegodskiy krestyanin yego obstanovka, zhizn i deyatelnost." *Zhinaya starina*, volume 1. Year eight. 1898.

Jackson, Michael. 1982. *Pocket Guide to Beer*. Putnam.

Jakovlev, Tormis. 1997. "Unustatust ja uuemast Saaremaa koduõllenduses." In *Saaremaa Museum kaheaastaraamat 1995 – 1996*, 116–37. Content cited herein translated by Virgo Vjugin.

Jenkins, J. Geraint, 2009. *Life and Tradition in Rural Wales*. Stroud: Amberley Publishing.

Jenssøn, Christen. (1646) 1946. *Den Norske Dictionarium Eller Glosebog*. Copenhagen. Reprinted by J. W. Eides Forlag, Bergen. Page references are to the 1946 edition.

Jizba, J., L. Dolejš, V. Herout, and F. Šorm. 1971. "The structure of osladin - The sweet principle of the rhizomes of Polypodium vulgare L." *Tetrahedron Letters* 12, issue 18: 1329–32. https://doi.org/10.1016/S0040-4039(01)96701-2.

Kavaliauskaitė, Reda and Tomas Sutkaitis. 2006. "Naminio alaus gamyba ir vartojimas Šimoniu apylinkeje." *Liaudies Kultūra*. 2006/1 (106): 23–34. Content cited herein translated by Remigijus Tranas. https://hdl.handle.net/20.500.12259/42371.

Klonteig, Olav. 2000. *Fjellbygder i attersyn: frå det gamle Tinn i Telemark*. Forlaget Grenland, S.29-33.

Kølster, Per. 2007. *Alle tiders øl*. Copenhagen: Politikens forlag.

Kornyšova, O., Z. Stanius, K. Obelevicius, O. Ragazinskiene, E. Skrzydlewska, and A. Maruska. 2009. "Capillary zone electrophoresis method for determination of bitter (α- and β-) acids in hop (*Humulus lupulus* L.) cone extracts." *Advances in Medical Sciences* 54, no. 1: 41–46.

Krogerus, Kristoffer [suregork]. 2011 -. *Suregork Loves Beer* (blog). http://beer.suregork.com/.

Krossen, Dagfinn. 1978. *Bygdebok for Årdal. II: Kulturbandet*. Årdal kommune.

Lagerås, P. 2003. "Aristokratin i landskapet. Paleoekologiska studier i Järrestads järnålder." In *Järrestad – huvudgård i centralbygd*, edited by B. Söderberg, 243–270. Stockholm: Riksantikvarieämbetet, Arkeologiska undersökningar, Skrifter 51.

Laitinen, Mika. 2019. *Viking Age Brew: The Craft of Brewing Sahti Farmhouse Ale*. Chicago Review Press.

Leino, Matti Wiking. 2017. *Spannmål: svenska lantsorter*. Nordiska museets handlingar 142. Stockholm: Nordiska Museets Förlag.

Leirfall, Jon. 1972. "Liv og lagnad i Stjørdalsbygdene, bind 1, del 3." Stjørdal og Meråker kommuner.

Leiro, Andreas. 1965. *Skikkar og truer ved ølbryggjing*. Voss: Voss Folkminnenemnd.

Levander, Lars. 1947. *Övre Dalarnes bondekultur under 1800- talets förra hälft. 3. Hem och hemarbete*. Skrifter utgivna av Kungl. Gustav Adolfs Akademien för folklivsforskning, 11, vol. 3. Lund: Carl Bloms Boktryckeri.

Linder, Nils. 1911. *Nordisk familjebok*. 2nd ed. Vol. 15. Stockholm: Gernandts boktryckeri.

Lucas, Alfred. 1962. *Ancient Egyptian Materials and Industries*. 4th ed. London: Edward Arnold.

Madej, Tomasz, Ewa Pirożnikow, Jarosław Dumanowski, and Łukasz Łuczaj. 2014. "Juniper Beer in Poland: The Story of the Revival of a Traditional Beverage." *Journal of Ethnobiology* 34, issue 1 February 1): 84–103. https://doi.org/10.2993/0278-0771-34.1.84.

Malterud K.E. and A. Faegri. 1982. "Bacteriostatic and fungistatic activity of C-methylated dihydrochalcones from the fruits of *Myrica gale* L." *Acta pharmaceutica Suecica* 19, no. 1: 43-6.

Mandt, Engelbret. (1777) 1989. *Historisk beskrivelse over Øvre Tellemarken*. Reprint edition with comments. Lokalhistorisk forlag.

McGovern, Patrick. 1999. "Retsina, mixed fermented beverages, and the cuisine of pre-classical Greece." In *Minoas and Myceneans: Flavors of Their Time*, ed. Yannis Tzedakis and Holly Martlew, 206–8. Athens: Kapon Editions.

McGovern, Patrick, Gretchen R. Hall, and Armen Mirzoian. 2013. "A biomolecular archaeological approach to 'Nordic grog'." *Danish Journal of Archaeology* 2, no. 2: 112–31.

Molbech, Johan. 1796. *Afhandling om Ølbrygningen i sin fulde Udstrækning*. Copenhagen: Gyldendal.

Mulder, Roel. 2016 -. *Lost Beers* (blog) [English version]. http://lostbeers.com/category/blog/.

Mullally, Erin. 2012. "Letters from Ireland: Mystery of the Fulacht Fiadh." *Archaeology* 65, no. 1 (January/February 2012).

Nadiradze, Eldar. 2010. *Georgian Beer*. [Bilingual: in Georgian and English.] Tbilisi: Meridiani.

Naumov, E. N. 2000. "Istoriya pivovareniya i kultura potrebleniya piva v chuvashiy." *Journal of the Chuvash National Museum*. Online PDF. http://www.chnmuseum.ru/files/almanac2000/almanac2000_103.pdf. Partially translated by Yevgeniy Tolstoff.

Nelson, Max. 2001. "Beer in Greco-Roman Antiquity." PhD thesis, University of British Columbia.

Nelson, Max. 2008. *The Barbarian's Beverage: A History of Beer in Ancient Europe*. New York: Routledge. Kindle.

Nerén, John. 1944. *Boka um Mälsa: Boken om Stora Mellösa*. Part 1. Stockholm: Norstedts.

Nersten, Nils. 1950. *Minner fra Setesdal*. Arendal: P. M. Danielsens forlag.

Nicolson, James R. 1978. *Traditional Life in Shetland*. London: Robert Hale.

Nordland, Odd. 1969. *Brewing and Beer Traditions in Norway*. Oslo: Universitetsforlaget.

Nordland, Odd. 1967. "Drykk og drikkeskikk." In *Gilde og gjestebod*, edited by Halvor Landsverk, 130–46. Oslo: Samlaget.

Olsen, Magnus. 1962. *Egils lausavísur, Höfuðlausn og Sonatorrek*. Edda- og skaldekvad 4. Oslo: Det Norske Videnskaps-Akademi.

Opedal, Halldor. *Makter og menneske*. Folkeminne i frå Hardanger VI. Oslo: Norsk Folkeminnelag, 1948.

Pattinson, Ron. 2007 -. *Shut Up About Barclay Perkins* (blog). https://barclayperkins.blogspot.com/.

Peaty, Ian P. 1997. *You Brew Good Ale: A History of Small-scale Brewing*. Stroud, Glos.: Sutton Publishing.

Peter, Jackson, Matteo De Chiara, Anne Friedrich, Jia-Xing Yue, David Pflieger, Anders Bergström, et al. 2018. "Genome evolution across 1,011 Saccharomyces cerevisiae isolates." *Nature* 556 (April 19, 2018): 339–44. https://doi.org/10.1038/s41586-018-0030-5.

Petrulis, Juozas. 1975. "Alus." *Kraštotyra*: 237–48. Translated by Remigijus Tranas.

Petersen, Jan G. T. 1933. *Gamle gårdsanlegg i Rogaland 1: Fra forhistorisk tid og middelalder*. Instituttet for sammenlignende kulturforskning ser. B: Skrifter. 23. Oslo: Aschehoug & Co.

Pinon, Roger. 1996. "Recettes de bières de ménage en Wallonie et subsidiarement en Picardie." In *Studium et Museum*, edited by Édouard Remouchamps, 103-121. Liège: Musée de la Vie Wallone.

Polevitskiy, N. I. 1927. *Domashneye prigotovlenie fruktovykh prokhladitelnykh napitkov*. Leningrad [St Petersburg]: Nachatki znaniy. Content cited herein translated by Ivan Kamarinskiy.

Preiss, Richard, Caroline Tyrawa, and George van der Merwe. 2017. "Traditional Norwegian Kveik Yeasts: Underexplored Domesticated *Saccharomyces cerevisiae* Yeasts." Unpublished preprint, submitted September 27, 2017 [cited April 5, 2019]. https://doi.org/10.1101/194969.

Preiss, Richard, Caroline Tyrawa, Kristoffer Krogerus, Lars Marius Garshol, and George van der Merwe. 2018. "Traditional Norwegian Kveik are a Genetically Distinct Group of Domesticated *Saccharomyces cerevisiae* Brewing Yeasts." *Frontiers in Microbiology* 9 (September 12, 2018): 2137. https://doi.org/10.3389/fmicb.2018.02137.

Rahn, Phil, and Chuck Skypeck. 1994 "Traditional German Steinbier." Special issue, *Zymurgy* 17, no. 4 (1994).

Räsänen, Matti. 1975. *Vom Halm zum Fass: die volkstümlichen alkoholarmen Getreidegetränke in Finnland*. German edition. Kansatieteellinen arkisto 25. Helsinki: Suomen muinaismuistoyhdistys.

Råsberg, Atle. 2015. "Ei reise gjennom Sogn i 1812." *Jol i Sogn* (Sogn og Fjordane Ungdomslag).

Rausch, Benedikt [macron, pseud.]. 2016–2018. Wilder Wald - German Beer History. https://wilder -wald.com/.

Reimer, Christine. 1915. "Humleavl paa Fyn." In *Danske Studier*, by Marius Kristensen and Axel Olrik, 174–84. Copenhagen: Gyldendalske boghandel Nordisk forlag.

Rem, Sissel Tiril. 2008. "Oppkok eller ikkje – det er spørsmålet." *Storfjordnytt*, March 12, 2008. http://www.storfjordnytt.no/nyhende08/11_olbrygging.html.

Riddervold, Astri. 2009. *Drikkeskikker: Nordmenns drikkevaner gjennom 1000 år*. Oslo: Cappelen Damm.

Røine, Bengt-Arne. 1979. *Fortell Såmund – fortell mer: sagn, folkelivs- og bjørneskildringer fra Utkant-Norge*. Oslo: Grøndahl.

Rösch, Manfred. 2010. "Starkbier mit Honig." In *Mit Leier und Schwert: Das frühmittelalterliche "Sängergrab" von Trossingen*, Barbara Theune-Großkopf, 90–91. Friedberg: Likias.

Rückerschöld, Anna Maria. 1790. *En Liten Hushålls-Bok*. Third pressing. Stockholm: J. C. Holmberg.

Saakvitne, Hans. 1898. "Kor ein bryggjar Hardangerøl?" Originally from 1898, but republished anonymously in *Hardanger Sogelag Årsbok*, 1984, 323–25.

Salomonsson, Anders. 1979. *Gotlandsdricka: Traditionell kultur som regional identitetssymbol.* Skrifter utg. av Etnologiska sällskapet i Lund 10. Karlstad: Press Förlag.

Salomonsson, Anders. 1977. *Den gotländske kölnan.* Gotländskt Arkiv.

Schöning, C. and Igsi, M. 1914. *Hobøl herred 1814–1914: Bidrag til en bygdebeskrivelse.* Fredrikshald: E. Sem.

Scourfield, Elfyn. 1974. "Farmhouse Brewing." *Amgueddfa: Bulletin of the National Museum of Wales* 17 (Cardiff).

Simonova, L. N. 1898. *Kvasovarenie i domashneye pivovarenie.* St. Petersburg. Content cited herein translated by Aleksandr Gromov.

Siuts, Hinrich and Fritz Bartelt. 1982. *Bäuerliche und handwerkliche Arbeitsgeräte in Westfalen: die alten Geräte der Landwirtschaft und des Landhandwerks 1890-1930.* Münster: Aschendorff.

Skoug, Stein Erik. 1975. *Kongeveien over Fillefjell: Vindhella og Galdane.* Oslo: Grøndahl.

Solberg, Svein Øivind, Agnese Kolodinska Brantestam, Madeleine Kylin, Gitte Kjeldsen Bjørn, and Mette Goul Thomsen J. 2014. "Genetic variation in Danish and Norwegian germplasm collections of hops." *Biochemical Systematics and Ecology* 52 (February 2014): 53–59. https://doi.org/10.1016/j.bse.2013.12.014.

Söderbäck, Per. 1940. *Rågöborna.* Nordiska Museets handlingar, vol. 13. Stockholm: Nordiska Museets Förlag.

Sopp, Olav. 1917. *Hjemmelagning av øl og vin.* Kristiania [Oslo]: Norli.

Sopp, Olav. 1921. "Lidt av øllets historie." In *Schous bryggeri: mindeskrift til hundredaarsjubilæet 1921*, edited by Nils Vogt, 104–125. Kristiania [Oslo].

Spitaels, Freek, Anneleen D. Wieme, Maarten Janssens, Maarten Aerts, Heide-Marie Daniel, Anita Van Landschoot, et al. 2014. "The Microbial Diversity of Traditional Spontaneously Fermented Lambic Beer." *PLoS ONE* 9, issue 4 (April 18): e95384. https://doi.org/10.1371/journal.pone.0095384.

Stewart, Graham G. 2015. "Seduced by yeast." *Journal of the American Society of Brewing Chemists* 73, issue 1 (February 5, 2018):1–21.

Stika, Hans-Peter. 2011. "Early Iron Age and Late Mediaeval malt finds from Germany—attempts at reconstruction of early Celtic brewing and the taste of Celtic beer." *Archaeological and Anthropological Sciences* 3, issue 1: 41–48. https://dx.doi.org/10.1007/s12520-010-0049-5.

Strese, Else-Marie and Clas Tollin. 2015. *Humle: Det gröna guldet*. Stockholm: Nordiska Museets Förlag.

Strese, Else-Marie Karlsson, Maria Lundström, Jenny Hagenblad, and Matti W Leino. 2014. "Genetic Diversity in Remnant Swedish Hop (*Humulus lupulus* L.) Yards from the 15th to 18th Century." *Economic Botany* 68, issue 3 (September 2014): 231–45. https://dx.doi.org/10.1007/s12231-014-9273-8.

Sudbø, Åsmund. 1971. "Ølbrygging i gamle dagar." In *Årbok for Telemark*, 111–20. Edland: Stiftinga Årbok for Telemark.

Sundt, Eilert. 1865. "Lidt fra Oldtiden. I. Brygge-sten." In *Folkevennen*, 322–36. Vol. 14. Kristiania [Oslo].

Svanberg, Ingvar, Renata Sõukand, Łukasz Łuczaj, Raivo Kalle, Olga Zyryanova, Andrea Dénes, et al. 2012. "Uses of tree saps in northern and eastern parts of Europe." *Acta Societatis Botanicorum Poloniae* 81, no. 4: 343–57. https://doi.org/10.5586/asbp.2012.036.

Talve, Ilmar. 1960. *Bastu och torkhus i Nordeuropa*. Nordiska Museets handlingar, vol. 53. Stockholm: Nordiska Museets Förlag.

Talve, Ilmar. 1961. *Den nordost-europeiska rian: en etnologisk undersökning*. Folklivsstudier, vol. 6. Helsinki: Svenska litteratursällskapet i Finland.

Talve, Ilmar. 1997. *Finnish Folk Culture*. Studia Fennica: Ethnologica, vol. 4. Helsinki: Finnish Literature Society.

Thaarup, Frederik. 1832. *Haandbog for Fabrikanter, Haandværkere og Laugs Interessenter for Aaret 1832* (Copenhagen).

Thibault, Martin. 2014. "In search of Norway's brewing traditions." *Beer Connoisseur*, issue 16.

———. 2015. "Chicha: Bolivia's Tart Beer." *Beer Connoisseur*, September 14, 2015. https://beerconnoisseur.com/articles/chicha-bolivias-tart-beer.

Tlusty, B. Ann. 2001. *Bacchus and Civic Order: The Culture of Drink in Early Modern Germany*. Charlottesville: University Press of Virginia.

Tveit, Norvald. 1986. *Heimebrygg: ølet som gud elskar*. Oslo: Det Norske Samlaget.

Tyndall, John. 1877. *Fermentation and Its Bearings on the Phenomena of Disease*. Glasgow: William Collins, Sons, and Company.

Unger, Richard W. 2001. *A History of Brewing in Holland 900-1900: Economy, Technology and the State*. Leiden: Brill.

Valamoti, Soultana Maria. 2017. "Brewing beer in wine country? First archaeobotanical indications for beer making in Early and Middle Bronze Age Greece." *Vegetation History and Archaeobotany* 27, issue 4 (July): 611–25. https://doi.org/10.1007/s00334-017-0661-8.

Vatle, Leif. 1980. *Kornet*. Osterøy museum.

Verberg, Susan. 2018. "The Rise and Fall of Gruit." *Brewery History*, 174: 46–79.

Visted, Kristofer, and Hilmar Stigum. 1971. *Vår gamle bondekultur*. 2 vols. Oslo: Cappelen, .

Võti, Tiina. 1986. *Õllekannud*. Tallinn: Kunst.

Weiser Aall, Lily. 1953. *Vassbæring i Norge*. Småskrifter fra Norsk Etnologisk Granskning. Oslo: Norsk Folkemuseum.

Wille, Hans Jacob. 1881. Utrykte Optegnelser om Thelemarken. Edited by Ludvig Daae. Kristiania [Oslo]: A.W. Brøgger.

Wille, Hans Jacob. 1786. *Beskrivelse over Sillejords præstegiæld i øvre Tellemarken i Norge*. Copenhagen: Gyldendal.

Wilse, Jacob Nicolai. 1779. *Physisk, oeconomisk og statistisk Beskrivelse over Spydeberg Præstegield og Egn i Aggershuus-Stift udi Norge*. Christiania [Oslo].

Zelenin, Dmitrij. 1927. "Russische <Ostslavische> Volkskunde." De Ruyter, Leipzig.

Interviews and Personal Communications

This section only contains the subset of interviews actually cited in this book. Exact dates for interviews and brewing session have been given according to ISO 8601, that is, YYYY-MM-DD.

Aall, Carlo. Farmhouse brewer, Kaupanger, Norway. Brewing session 2013-11-26.

Auran, Kjell Magnar. Farmhouse brewer and maltster, Innavætte såinnhuslag, Stjørdal, Norway. Interview 2018-01-06.

Bjåland, Halvor. Farmhouse brewer, Morgedal, Telemark, Norway. Brewing session 2015-05-31.

Bredli, Arthur. Commercial brewer, Espedalen, Norway. Email 2018-01-04.

Dale, Per. Farmhouse brewer, Flåm, Norway. Interview 2014-05-27.

Eitrheim, Jakob. Farmhouse brewer, Aga, Norway. Interview and brewing session, December 2016.

Eitrheim, Reidar. Farmhouse brewer, Aga, Norway. Interview and brewing session, December 2016.

Ese, Ole-Bjørn. Balestrand, Norway. Interview 2016-10-08.

Fyodorov family. Farmhouse brewers, Kshaushi, Chuvash Autonomous Republic, Russia. Interview 2017-07-22. Translator Aleksandr Gromov.

Geving, Jørund. Farmhouse brewer and maltster, Stjørdalen, Norway. Personal communications 2016–2019.

Gjernes, Sigmund. Farmhouse brewer, Dyrvedalen, Norway. Brewing session 2014-05-24/25.

Gojkovic, Zoran. Carlsberg Research Laboratory.

Granås, Morten. Farmhouse brewer and maltster, Stjørdalen, Norway. Personal communications 2014–18.

Gromov, Aleksandr. Commercial brewer, Tver, Russia. Personal communications 2017–2018.

Gutautas, Simonas. Commercial brewer and historian, Vilnius, Lithuania. Personal communications 2015–2019.

Halland, Jogeir. Farmhouse brewer and maltster, Stjørdalen, Norway. Personal communications 2017–2018.

Halvorsgard, Bjarne. Farmhouse brewer, Ål, Norway. Phone interview, 2016-11-21. Interview in person December 2017.

Horn, Aare. Farmhouse brewer, Obinitsa, Estonia. Interview 2016-08-07, plus email interview November 2017.

Hovden, Dagfinn. Brewer, Ørsta, Sunnmøre, Norway. Interview 2019-03-10.

Hove, Ragnar. Farmhouse brewer, Vik, Sogn, Norway. Phone interview 2015-02-19.

Ivanovna, Maria. Farmhouse brewer, Kudymkar, Komi Republic, Russia. Interview and brewing session, 2017-07-18.

Käär, Lili. Farmhouse brewer, Kärdla, Hiiumaa, Estonia. Interview 2016-08-12.

Kääriäinen, Pekka. Farmhouse brewer, Lammi, Finland. Interview 2018-08-07.

Kambestad, Ove. Farmhouse brewer, Odda, Norway. Conversation in Voss, May 2014.

Kaupas, Justas. Marketing director at Biržu Alus, Biržai, Lithuania. Interview 2013-07-31.

Kjepso, Helena. Mølstertunet museum, Voss, Norway. Conversation 2018-09-29.

Kjøs, Rasmus. Farmhouse brewer, Hornindal, Norway. Interview 2015-07-05.

Kurgpõld, Andres. Farmhouse brewer, Saaremaa, Estonia. Interview 2016-08-10.

Laurinavičius, Vidmantas. Beer writer, Vilnius, Lithuania. Personal communications 2013–2018.

Lindgren, Örjan. Farmhouse brewer, Stånga, Gotland, Sweden. Phone interview conducted by Morgan Ingemarsson 2018-02-03.

Lisma, Seppo. Farmhouse brewer, Ruovesi, Finland. Brewing session 2018-08-07.

Lõppe, Kaido. Farmhouse brewer, Partsi, Hiiumaa, Estonia. Interview 2016-08-12.

Magnussen, Atle Ove. Vest-norsk Kulturakademi, Voss. Personal communications 2018.

Mattsson, Anders. Farmhouse brewer, Hablingbo, Gotland, Sweden. Interview 2015-07-31.

Motuza, Vykintas. Farmhouse brewer, Anykščiai, Lithuania. Personal communications 2016–2018.

Muri, Bjarne. Homebrewer, Oslo, Norway. Personal communications 2015–2017.

Nordal, Halvor. Farmhouse brewer, Høydalsmo, Norway. Interview 2015-06-01.

Nupen, Jarle. Farmhouse brewer, Ørsta, Norway. Personal communications 2016–2018.

Nurminen, Hannu. Farmhouse brewer, Sysmä, Finland. Interview 2018-08-09.

Nystein, Aave. Farmhouse brewer, Bø, Telemark, Norway. Personal communications 2016–2017.

Opshaug, Harald. Farmhouse brewer, Stranda, Norway. Interview 2014-05-28.

Pahalahti, Antti. Farmhouse brewer, Hartola, Finland. Interview 2018-08-11.

Pere, Tuomas. Farmhouse and commercial brewer, Tampere, Finland. Interview 2018-08-03.

Phillips, Rae. Farmhouse brewer and maltster, Birsay, Orkney, UK. Personal communications 2016.

Preiss, Richard. Microbiologist, Escarpment Labs. Guelph, Canada. Personal communications 2016–2019.

Pruul, Paavo. Farmhouse brewer, Sõru, Estonia. Brewing session 2016-08-11.

Pucens, Ugis. Ethnographer, Aizpute, Latvia. Interview and brewing session, July 2015.

Raftevold, Terje. Farmhouse brewer, Innvik, Norway. Interview and brewing session, July 2015. Personal communications 2015–2017.

Rivenes, Svein. Farmhouse brewer, Dyrvedalen, Voss, Norway. Interview 2018-09-02.

Rørlien, Sjur Herman. Farmhouse brewer, Dyrvedalen, Voss, Norway. Personal communications 2014–2019.

Roth, Bjørn. Microbiologist, Stavanger, Norway. Personal communications 2018–2019.

Røthe, Bjørne. Farmhouse brewer, Dyrvedalen, Voss, Norway. Brewing session 2018-09-02.

Sandodden, Roar. Farmhouse brewer and maltster, Stjørdalen, Norway. Personal communications 2014–19.

Saure, Sigurd Johan. Farmhouse brewer, Sykkylven, Norway. Personal communications 2016–2019.

Schiefloe, Ole Sivert. Farmhouse brewer and maltster, Stjørdal, Norway. Interview 2019-01-12.

Skare, Ivar. Farmhouse brewer and maltster, Ørsta, Norway. Interview 2019-03-10.

Skrindo, Ågot. Ål, Hallingdal, Norway. Interview 2017-02-18.

Skrindo, Sverre. Farmhouse brewer, Ål, Hallingdal, Norway. Personal communications 2017–2019.

Steensels, Jan. Microbiologist, University of Leuven. Personal communications 2017–2019.

Stundal, Per. Farmer, Aurland, Norway. Phone interview, 2017-10-05.

Syrjä, Raija. Farmhouse brewer, Hämeenkoski, Finland. Interview 2018-08-08.

Tait, Ian. Shetland museum. Personal communication by email 2016-06-03.

Thibault, Martin. Personal communication 2013–2019.

Trei, Aarne. Farmhouse brewer, Pihtla, Saaremaa, Estonia. Interview 2016-08-10.

Tuominen, Eila. Farmhouse brewer, Pertunmaa, Finland. Brewing session 2018-08-10.

Udriene, Aldona. Farmhouse brewer, Jovarai, Lithuania. Interview 2015-07-14.

Viheroja, Olavi. Farmhouse brewer, Hämeenkyrö, Finland. Brewing session 2018-08-06.

Vinge, Lotte. Farmhouse brewer, Busemarke, Møn, Denmark. Interview 2018-07-15.

Zhezlov, Dmitriy. Farmhouse brewer, Kirov, Kirov oblast, Russia. Brewing session, July 2017.

INDEX

A. Grigonio, 293

Aall, Carlo, 18, 20, 23, 24, 26, 35, 44, 84, 87, 142, 153, 231; photo of, 21; wort beer and, 25, 251

ABV, 25, 112, 205, 252, 254, 269, 270

Acer platanoides, 258

Acer pseudoplatanus, 259

Acetobacter, 233

adjuncts, adding, 241-43, 253

agriculture, 7, 263, 346; mechanization of, 35, 177; spread of, 29

Ål, 58, 116, 143, 150, 177, 194

alcohol, 30, 103, 252, 256; producing, 111

alder, 43, 65, 149, 244 276

alpha acids, 140, 225, 226, 291; content analysis, 225 (fig.)

alpine juniper (spp. *alpina*), 227

aludi, 340-41

Amble farm, 18; photo of, 19

American National Homebrew Competition, 123

ancestor worship, beer for, 186

Anders Mattson's Gotlandsdricke, recipe for, 305

Andrioniškis, stone brewing of, 137

Anheuser-Busch, 92

antimicrobial effects, 230, 231, 238

Apynys brewery, 293, 349

Arnøy, Johan, 99

aroma, 105, 114, 128, 231, 236, 239, 269, 270, 291; caramel, 282; herbal, 237; hop, 115, 155, 224, 226, 227; malt, 276; menthol-like, 235; orange-peel, 83, 87; phenolic, 92; smoke, 60, 65, 67, 69, 70; spice, 87

Astrup, Nikolai: painting by, 341 (fig.)

Babkova, Lidzija, 165

bacteria, 82, 90, 117, 128, 223, 248; lactic acid, 98, 122, 230, 253, 286

badstu, 67, 68, 69, 77, 282, 318; drawing of, 67 (fig.); photo of, 64, 66

Baltic states, 228, 349; time capsule for, 346-47

bappir, 164, 168

barley, 10, 31, 42, 45, 45 (fig.), 47, 175, 256, 282, 286, 304, 309, 318, 320, 323, 337, 340;

barley *(continued)*
adaptability of, 46; black, 51; Chevalier, 51; commercial, 54; Domen, 54; drying, 139; four-row, 49, 49 (fig.); Harrington, 54; Klages, 54; low-quality, 46; malting, 54; preferred times of, 50 (table); six-row, 49, 49 (fig.), 50; two-row, 49, 49 (fig.), 50; varieties of, 49-51, 53-54
barley ale, 285
Barsnes fjord, photo of, 18
Bartelt, Fritz, 340
bay laurel (*Larus nobilis*), 238
beech wood, 64-65
beer: ancient/historical, 32, 127; archaeological, 100; Belgian-style, 343, 354; boiled, 141; finished, 25 (photo); kettle-heated, 167; modern, 8, 24; oven-heated, 167; roaring of, 214 (photo); serving, 213-14; strong, 214, 252, 253; weak, 231, 254
beer bowls, 207-8; photo of, 206
beer flaws, 214-15, 217
Beitland, Håvard, 45
Belgian blonde, 114
Belgian-style beer, 353, 354
bere, 50, 337
Berliner weisse, 142, 143
berm, 116, 123, 124
berries, 31, 100, 219, 231, 254
Betula pendula, 258
Betula pubescens, 258
Bickerdyke, John, 239
Bielenstein, August, 258
bière de garde, 37, 276
biochemistry, 3, 20, 231
birch, 65, 70, 174, 186 (fig.), 258, 286
birch sap, 276; tapping, 258, 258 (fig.), 259
birch sap beer, 258-59
Biržai, 34, 293, 350
Biržu Alus Širvenos, 243; photo of, 243
Biržu Duona, 157
bitter orange peel (*Citrus x aurantiuim*), 237
bitterness, 25, 26, 141, 226, 235, 238, 273, 286; hop, 227, 309; juniper and, 231, 232, 233

Bjåland, Halvor, 268
Bjerg, Niels, 215
Bjørneby farm, 53
blackberry leaves, photo of, 240
blackcurrant, 240, 259
blande, 251, 253; photo of, 251
Blaxhall, 249, 337
Blom farm, 183
bogbean (*Menyanthes trifoliata*), 239, 337
boiled ale, 142-43
Bond, Chris, 90, 91
Bornholm, 235, 252
bouza, 164
braga, 256-57
bran, 217, 242
Brand, Marcus, 242
bread: beer, 163; malt, 320; pans, 328; rye, 48, 101, 254, 256; wheat, 48, 224
bread putty, 195; photo of, 195
breeding, 48, 50, 51, 53; photo of, 52, 53
Brettanomyces, 81, 89, 90, 98, 104, 111, 116, 117, 293
brewhouses, 74; painting of, 33 (fig.); photo of, 19, 129, 132, 152
brewing: craft, 4, 8, 127, 241, 354; early, 30, 31; life cycle and, 34; modern, 2, 3, 15; preparations for, 194-96; supplies, 120, 171; traditional, 121, 355; women and, 187, 188, 189, 189 (map)
brewing equipment, 12, 135, 190-92, 194; cleaning, 214; drawing of, 13 (fig.)
brewing process, 10, 12, 127, 132 (fig.), 164, 260; evolution of, 165, 166 (fig.), 167-71; stone, 134 (fig.); stone/kettle, 167; traditional, 14, 349; variety of, 8
brewsters, brewers and, 187-90
briskebaka, 195
bröddricka, 257
brome (*L. bromus*), 49
Brouwerij De Ranke, 227
brown ale, 214
brown boiled beers, 308-9
Brulosophy blog site, 143, 183

buckets, 12, 190, 191, 194, 195, 199

buckwheat, 49, 256

burial mounds, 179, 186

Buttercup Night (Astrup), 341 (fig.)

butyric acid, 165, 332

Cafe Permyak, 325; photo of, 325

Can Sadurní cave, 30

Cantillon Lou Pepe, 128

caramel, 75-76, 128, 157

caramelization, 137, 154, 157, 162, 327, 328

caraway (*Carum carvi*), 236

carbonation, 25, 133, 214, 227, 243, 268, 270-71, 282, 290, 353; fermentation and, 201-2; level of, 202; low, 155

cardamom, 264

Carlsberg, 92, 93

Carlsberg Research Laboratory, 102, 104

carrots, 242

cask ales, 201, 268, 282

casks, 177, 191, 195, 202, 225, 227, 241

cauldrons, 341; photo of, 30, 32

cellaring, 99, 205, 214

chamomile (*Matricaria chamomilla*), 239

chicha, 106, 107

chimneys, 74, 74 (fig.)

Christianity, 10, 186, 211

Christmas beer, 15, 186

Chuvashia, 75, 96, 102, 184, 192, 196, 200, 225, 226, 322, 350

Chuvashians, 49, 76, 200, 323; photo of, 322

cinnamon, 264

Čižas, Ramūnas, 2

Clarke, Arthur C., 3

Clarke, Lucy, 242

cloves, 259, 264

commercial breweries, 7, 8, 33, 92, 94, 122, 268, 270; development of, 32; farmhouse brewing and, 279; hops and, 224

common polypody (*Polypodium vulgare*), 240

common yew (*Taxus baccata*), 275

coriander, 236, 264

corn ale, 337

craft beer, 38, 227, 352, 354; hops and, 224

craft brewing, 4, 8; farmhouse brewing and, 354; modern, 127, 241, 354

Crane, Eva, 262

Dahl, Johan Christian: painting by, 186 (fig.)

Dahlerup, Hans Birch, 14

Dale, Per, 356; photo of, 356

Debaryomyces hansenii, 104, 123

decoction, 12, 151, 165

derevenskoye pivo, 321

diacetyl, 44, 270

dimethyl sulphide (DMS), 142

Dineley, Merryn, 169; hearth mashing and, 168, 168 (photo)

Dmitriy Zhezlov's Farmhouse Ale, recipe for, 321-22

Drageset, Oddvin, 133; photo of, 203

dricka, 276, 303

drinks: alcoholic/acidic, 250 (table); choosing, 247; common names/by local language, 250 (table); fermented, 250 (table); ritual, 182

Dundulis, 157

dunkel, 154

duonkepis, 158, 328; examples of, 158 (photo)

Dyrvedal-Style Vossaøl, recipe for, 313

Dyrvedalen valley, 96, 99, 121, 202, 270, 308, 310, 345; photo of, 82

Eila Tuominen's Sahti, recipe for, 289

Eitrheim, Jakob, 120, 205; photo of, 190

Eitrheim, Jarand: photo of, 190, 308

Eitrheim, Reidar: photo of, 308

Eitrheim family, 120, 194, 309

enzymes, 53, 57, 60, 143, 151, 162, 167, 241, 256, 281; malt, 68, 141, 275, 276

ergot, 216 (fig.)

Escarpment Labs, 114

esters, 270

Evans, George Ewart, 249

farmhouse ales, 18, 37, 177, 257, 278-80; adjuncts in, 242-44; bowl of, 277 (photo); brewing, 7, 175, 240, 268, 285, 351; carbonation of, 201-2; Chuvashian, 322, 323; classification of, 278 (fig.); Danish, 296; English, 337; fermentation of, 201, 202; festival for, 41, 233, 280; Finnish, 276, 285; German, 296; hopping rates for, 226 (fig.), 227; juniper and, 229, 233; Lithuanian, 104, 347, 349; modern, 352-55; Norwegian, 20, 81, 332; Russian, 159, 321; styles of, 278, 278 (table), 279; sugar beer and, 264; Swedish, 303, 318; traditional, 25, 213, 279; Welsh, 339; Westphalian, 340

farmhouse beer, 2, 37, 219, 337; problems with, 214-15, 217

farmhouse brewing, 4, 26, 32, 122, 170, 279, 291, 308; Chuvashian, 350; commercial, 8, 33, 37, 279, 353; craft brewing and, 354; decline of, 95, 188-89, 345; development of, 10, 33, 35, 199, 355; Estonian, 350; European, 352 (map); Finnish, 351; history of, 1-2, 7-8, 10, 12; Latvian, 350; learning about, 20, 37; modern, 34, 352-55; modern brewing and, 8, 15, 268; Norwegian, 20, 46, 351, 351 (map); processes of, 166 (map), 170 (map); Russian, 350; styles in, 276, 278; survival of, 18, 107, 190; traditional, 2, 3, 354, 355; Ukrainian, 350; women and, 190

Fårö, 46, 47, 303, 304

Fay, Justin C., 119

fermentation, 12, 24, 99, 101, 102, 108, 112, 117, 118, 133, 140, 141, 143, 167, 185, 200, 202, 207, 225, 235, 251, 253, 269, 270, 272; carbonation and, 201; end of, 271; lactic, 256; lambic, 111; mash, 164-65; photo of, 88, 119, 201; primary, 98, 104; rapid, 120; secondary, 201; short, 98; spontaneous, 106; yeast and, 165

Fermentation and Its Bearing on the Phenomena of Disease (Tyndall), 7

fermentors, 83, 104, 106, 185, 253, 270, 349

ferulic acid, 92

festarøl, 181

filter materials, 243-44

final gravity (FG), 3, 143, 270

Finlandia, 351

Finlandia Sahti, 122, 287; photo of, 287

Finnen, 134

Firth, John, 239

flavors, 38, 128, 202, 204, 226, 227, 239-41, 247, 261, 286, 329; adding, 243; caramel, 138-39, 326, 327; classification by, 279; final, 127; hop-like, 235; juniper, 231, 232, 233, 273; kveik, 112, 270; off, 92, 98, 104, 111, 114, 116, 119, 242, 269, 353; orange-peel, 87, 90; peat-smoke, 337; phenolic, 92, 111, 114, 116, 119, 269; producing, 231; raw ale, 141, 171, 280; rye, 101, 162; smoke, 45, 64-65; straw/grain, 282; woody, 45, 244; yeast, 120

flocculation, 119, 270

flour, 256; barley, 217; rye, 101, 102, 103, 139, 139 (photo), 167, 217

Fraoch, 239

Frøyne farm, 13

fruit, 100, 128, 254

fuddling cup, 213

Funen, 151, 226, 242, 296, 351; hops from, 224

funeral beer, 180, 190

Fyodorov family, 226, 323

Fyodorovna, Marina, 75, 76, 96, 102, 138, 184, 200, 323; photo of, 117, 323

gammeltøl, 200, 296

germination, 58, 58 (fig.), 215, 275

Geving, Jørund, 26, 43, 123, 183, 267, 275-76, 280; malt and, 42; photo of, 43

Gharsen, Ghar Smith, 268

giardiasis, 248

Gibson, Brian, 286

gildesøl, 200

ginger, 264

Gjerde, Johannes: photo of, 16

Gjernes, Brynjulv, 83

Gjernes, Gunliev, 89, 309

Gjernes, Sigmund, 92, 118, 120, 123, 142, 143, 157, 182; brewing by, 82, 83, 84, 86, 87, 89, 90, 309; kveik of, 90, 91; photo of, 83, 84; yeast of, 90, 95

Gjertveit, Ola H.: photo of, 36

gjest/gjester, 123

glycerol, 273

Gojkovic, Zoran, 102

gong, 116, 355; photo of, 116

Gotland, 46, 64, 74, 75, 119, 121, 175, 223, 228, 230, 231, 237, 239, 299, 303; agriculture in, 304; photo of, 303

gotlandsdricke, 70, 230, 276, 303-6, 351, 354

Gotlandsdricke from Fide, recipe for, 306

grain, 7, 31, 34, 46, 58, 59, 179, 276, 309; breeding, 48, 50, 51, 52 (photo), 53; drying, 69; growing, 35, 47, 51, 54-55, 57; harvesting, 176, 176 (photo); landrace, 51, 51 (photo), 53, 225; malting, 46 (table), 47, 54, 57, 346; regret, 47; seed, 50, 51, 57; sprouting, 175; types of, 45-49, 45 (fig.), 50

Granås, Morten, 59

grapes, 30

grist, 151, 165, 340; photo of, 150

Groll, Josef, 92

Gromov, Aleksandr, 143, 254

Grønnesby, Geir, 137

Grubbs, Laura, 237

gruit, 233

Grundtvig, Fredrik, 247

Gutautas, Simonas, 153, 200, 211, 239, 350; on keptinis, 328-29

Gwaun Valley, 339, 352

Hallingdal, 116, 177, 229, 351; recipe for, 317-18

Halvorsgard, Bjarne, 99, 120

Hansa Borg Brewery, 181

Hansen, Emil Christian, 33, 98, 106, 272; yeast propagation apparatus of, 93 (fig.)

Hardanger, 13, 121, 124, 143, 183, 194, 204, 205, 226; beer from, 276; kveik in, 120

Hardanger Sagelag Årsbok (Saakvitne), 267

Hardangerøl, 276; recipe for, 310

harvest ale, 176-77

harvesting, 175, 176, 177, 185; mechanization of, 54; photo of, 176

Harvey's brewery, 93, 104, 123

Haugen, Terje, 268; photo of, 316

Haugse, Hans, 99

headache, removing, 88 (photo)

heather (*Calluna vulgaris*), 239

hefeweizen, 114, 128, 282

Hegge, Olav, 356

Hegge farm, 71; photo of, 42

heimabrygg, 308-9

Helland, Tor Ølver, 99

Hellenius, Carl Niclas, 137, 253

herbs, 32, 219, 221, 223-41, 259, 264; for farmhouse brewing, 220 (table)

Hertzberg, Nils, 181

Hiiumaa, 63, 184, 202, 234, 240, 253, 290; brewing on, 350

Hitler, Adolf, 340

Hobsbawm, Eric, 173

Høeg, Ove Arbo, 228, 229

Hognesaunet Såinnhuslag, 299

Højrup, Ole, 249

Holden, William, 356

Hollolan Hirvi, 351

Hollolan Hirvi Sahti, 139, 287

Holmboe, Thorolf: painting by, 169 (fig.)

homebrewing: future of, 355; modern, 20, 123, 143, 351; supplies for, 120

honey, 31, 256; adding, 100, 243, 262, 263-64; collecting, 263, 263 (fig.)

honeyguide (*Indicator indicator*), 262, 262 (fig.)

hop cones, 223, 224

hop pollen, 221

hop tea, 140, 141, 155, 170, 239, 291, 293; boiling, 225; cookers, 349; photo of, 226, 234

hopping rates, 226, 226 (fig.), 227

hops, 7, 32, 35, 84, 131, 148, 165, 174, 205, 219, 230, 239, 264, 268, 300, 340; analysis of, 225, 225 (fig.); aroma, 89, 115, 155, 224, 226, 227, 269; Bavarian, 224; boiling, 23

hops *(continued)*
  (photo), 140, 151, 170, 238; Cascade, 224, 322; Continental, 224; Danish, 224; dry, 171, 225, 227; filtering, 24 (photo); gathering, 224, 227, 279; growing, 12, 223, 224, 225, 322; juniper and, 231, 233; lautering and, 225; low-alpha, 223; malt and, 164; noble, 224, 225, 227; photo of, 144, 222; rope/cloth and, 223; Saaz, 26, 226; Serebryanska, 322; Swedish, 225; using, 24, 170, 221, 223-27, 286, 341
Hornindal, 57, 63, 94, 121, 140, 201, 351, 355; festival in, 41, 45; kveik in, 128-31, 133
horns, photo of, 211
horseradish, 257
Hovden, Dagfinn, 170-71
Hovland, Martin O.: photo of, 36
humlebeit, 141, 151, 170, 225, 282
Husdal, Ivar, 165, 332
Hveem, Håken, 90
hydrometers, 13, 141
Hyllestad, 196
hyssop (*Hyssopus officinalis*), 217

IBUs, 25, 26, 223
Igsi, M., 254
infusion, 142, 149, 151, 169, 170, 219, 231, 232, 261, 293, 304
Institute of Forestry Research, 228
IPAs, 227, 269, 276, 279
Island Koduõlu, 290-91
Ivanovna, Marina, 102, 192, 219, 325

Jackson, Michael, 165, 276, 351
Jacobsen, J. C., 93
Jamanen, Poavila: photo of, 100
Jamanen, Triihvo: photo of, 100
Jančys, Ignas, 153, 154, 155; photo of, 152, 155
Jančys, Vytautas, 153, 154, 155, 193; brewing process of, 162, 162 (fig.); keptinis and, 244; photo of, 152, 153, 155
Jančys family: beer of, 156 (photo); brewing process of, 157 (fig.), 162

Jarl, Sigvalde: drawing of, 180 (fig.)
Jensgård i Tiufkjær, recipe for, 297
Jørund Geving's Stjørdalsøl, recipe for, 300-301
Jovaru Alus Brewery, 141, 293, 349; photo of, 293, 347
Julius Simonaitis's Kaimiškas, recipe for, 294
juniper, 12, 32, 33, 65, 84, 89, 128, 149, 192, 192 (fig.), 208, 211, 221, 226, 227-33, 236, 261; baking, 195; brewing with, 231, 243, 244, 273, 275; collecting, 183, 231, 275, 279; hops and, 231, 233; photo of, 228, 230
juniper berries, 229, 259, 260, 262, 276, 282, 340; harvesting, 261, 261 (photo); photo of, 260
juniper berry beer, 259-62
juniper branches, 20, 22, 23, 26, 84, 131, 135, 141, 148, 195, 223, 229, 231, 232, 233
juniper infusion, 23, 83, 84, 111, 129, 140, 183, 195, 229, 231, 232, 279, 281, 286, 340; photo of, 20, 21, 84, 232, 274
juniper oil, 89, 182
juniper pollen, 229
juniper syrup, 262; photo of, 262
Juniperus californica, 275
Juniperus communis, 227, 231, 273
Juniperus oxycedrus, 275
Juniperus sabina, 275
Juniperus scopulorum, 275
Juniperus virginiana, 275
Jutland, 35, 64, 75, 76, 200, 226, 233, 299

Kääriäinen, Pekka, 26, 273, 279, 287
kaimiškas, 142, 280, 293
kaimiškas alus, 293
Kambestad, Ove, 122
Karelians, 162; photo of, 14
Karlsen, Jan, 230
Kaupanger, 19, 37, 82, 83; brewing in, 15, 17-18, 20, 23-26
Kaupanger road, illustration of, 174 (fig.)
keptinis, 2, 49, 151, 157, 165, 167, 244, 257, 291, 349; brewing, 153-55, 157 (fig.), 162, 163, 326, 327, 328-29
kettles, 83, 143, 147, 168, 191, 251; copper, 12,

31, 33 (fig.), 84, 87, 89, 129, 134, 340, 341; metal, 134, 137, 138, 140, 164, 169, 170; photo of, 316

kilns, 63, 286; badstu-type, 64 (photo), 66 (photo), 67 (fig.), 282, 318; drawing of, 75 (fig.); drying in, 73; fireplaces and, 75; Gotland-type, 74 (fig.); malt, 42, 43 (photo), 60, 64 (photo), 70, 74 (fig.), 77, 224

Kittelsen, Theodor: drawing by, 183 (fig.)

kjenge, 208; photo of, 209

kjerringa, 71; photo of, 72

kjone, 73, 74; drawing of, 73 (fig.)

kjøpskål, 181; drinking, 181 (fig.)

Kjos, Rasmus, 57, 63

koduõlu, 119, 142, 149, 202, 230, 236, 290-91, 354; photo of, 291

kolmikkann, 213; photo of, 213

Kølster, Per, 1, 227

Komi peoples, 192, 325

Kõpp, E., 180

korchaga, 161, 192, 256; photo of, 160

kornøl, 142, 214, 236, 280, 281-82, 290, 308, 354

kotikalja, 257, 257 (fig.)

Kråksmåla, 101, 215, 258, 259

Krogerus, Kristoffer, 119

Kshaushi, 75, 143, 193, 322, 323

Kudymkar, 102, 103, 192, 219, 325

Kurgpõld, Andres, 356

kuurna, 148, 149, 169, 192, 286, 353; photo of, 193

kvass, 163; GOST standard for, 254; making, 256, 257; mass-produced, 254, 255 (photo); oven beers and, 163; vendor selling, 255 (photo)

kveik, 94, 110-12, 114, 115, 116, 120, 121-22, 282, 286, 300, 318; commercial, 270, 271; discovering, 81-84, 86-87, 89-90; fermentation with, 270; genomes of, 115 (fig.); Hornindal, 112; laboratory analysis of, 90-91; photo of, 86, 272; strains of, 112, 114, 117, 268, 271; term, 123-24; using, 120, 128-31, 131 (photo), 133, 269, 271; vintages of, 121 (photo); working with, 268-72. See also yeast

Labatt, 93

Labietis brewery, 238

Labrador tea (*Rhododendron groenlandicum; Ledum groenlandicum*), 239

lactic acid, 98, 122, 230, 253, 256, 286

Lactobacillus, 233

Lähdeniemi, Petteri: photo of, 122

Laitinen, Mika, 143, 235, 273, 286, 287; sahti and, 145-46

lambic, 45, 111

Lammin Sahti, 287

landøl, 142, 296

Landøl from North Jutland, recipe for, 298

Landøl from South Funen, recipe for, 307

landraces, 50, 51, 53, 54, 55, 224, 225, 309, 337

Langlo, Stein, 90, 124, 207

Latham, Geoff, 328

Laukinių Aviečių, 349; photo of, 348

Laurinavičius, Vidmantas, 347

lauter tuns, 23, 131, 141, 146, 149, 151, 155, 161, 168, 175, 196, 205, 236, 243; B-type, 191, 191 (fig.), 192, 194, 194 (photo); juniper in, 231; photo of, 22, 130, 155, 348; preparing, 194-95; S-type, 190 (photo), 191, 192, 192 (fig.), 194; steel, 194, 194 (photo)

lautering, 87, 140, 142, 143, 149, 155, 162, 164, 165, 235, 244, 251, 281, 286; hops and, 225; photo of, 160, 193

Leirfall, Jon, 122

lemon juice, 257

lemon peel, 259

lice, 224, 238

licorice, 240

lingonberry, 45

Lisma, Seppo, 146, 147, 148; photo of, 193

Livet i Klokkergaarden (Grundtvig), 247

loaves, malt, 162, 163, 163 (photo)

Lødemel, Olav, 94

Louhisaari Estate, brewing process of, 167, 167 (fig.)

Lucas, Alfred, 164

Luumaki-Style, recipe for, 332

Maillard reactions, 137, 143, 154, 327

Mainland Estonian Oven-Based Beer, recipe for, 331

Malaga, 15

malt, 10, 14, 31, 34, 35, 41, 49, 100, 130, 135, 141, 143, 163, 241, 253, 256; badstu-kilned, 309; barley, 149, 215, 293; basta burned, 68; beech-smoked, 43; "bread," 326; buying, 33; caramel, 76, 291; Chuvashian, 276; cleaning, 73, 322 (photo); color of, 60; commercial, 279, 286; crushed, 167, 168; drying, 43 (photo), 59-61, 60 (table), 61 (photo), 62 (photo), 63-65, 67-71, 73-77, 77 (map), 286, 299, 309; green, 43, 67, 69, 340, 341; ground, 196; hops and, 164; kilned, 282; loose, 341; making, 32, 42-45, 190, 243, 275-76, 279, 309; milling, 196, 197; Munich, 286; pale, 63, 154, 275, 276, 282, 293; Pilsner, 63, 83, 87, 89, 282, 286, 290; roasting, 154; rye, 64, 256; Saana, 299; sahti, 286; smoked, 64-65, 67-71, 73-75, 275, 304, 318; taxation of, 337; *tuoppi*, 286; undried, 78, 78 (photo), 162; unsmoked, 61, 63; wort and, 213

malt drying shelf, photo of, 62

malthouses, 63; photo of, 62

malting, 12, 41-42, 46, 47, 49, 51, 77, 187, 251, 280, 299, 346; farmhouse, 46 (table); grain for, 46 (table); life cycle and, 34; methods, 42, 45, 60; turf, 341

maltotriose, 92, 111

maltsters, 45, 59, 64, 68, 73, 276, 299, 304

maple, 258

Marina Fyodrovna's Farmhouse Ale, recipe for, 324

Marina Ivanovna's Sur, recipe for, 326

Markeset farm, photo of, 248

marsh tea (*Rhododendron tomentosum; Ledum palustre*), 238, 290

Märzen, 296

mash, 31, 84, 86, 131, 153, 155, 157, 159, 163, 168, 232, 235, 251, 253, 268; baked, 154 (photo), 155 (photo), 328-29; boiling, 137, 137 (photo), 138, 143, 145-49, 145 (photo), 147 (photo), 151, 165, 225; carmelization of, 162; complex, 149, 151; fermented, 164-65, 167, 332; heating, 134, 281; infusion, 142, 149, 151, 169, 170, 219, 234, 293, 304; kettle, 151, 162, 169, 286; pasteurization of, 141; rest, 147; souring of, 149; step, 143, 149; stirring, 146 (photo), 147, 184; stuck, 205; temperatures of, 328 (fig.)

mash boxes, photo of, 153

mash tuns, 83, 84, 87, 135, 137, 161, 164, 349; photo of, 348

mashing, 84, 129, 149, 165, 237, 280, 291, 332; changes in, 167; cold, 149; decoction, 151, 165; hearth, 168, 168 (photo), 169; heat sources for, 167; long step, 286; oven, 162, 169; photo of, 152

Maskin, 53-54, 299

McGovern, Patrick, 229

mead, 262-64

Mesila, Jüri, 63

microbiology, 2, 91, 92, 332

microorganisms, 37, 98, 102, 104, 108, 141, 182, 215, 253

Middle Ages, 32, 33, 34, 67, 140, 164, 197, 221, 233, 248

Middle East, 164; agriculture in, 29; beer brewing in, 30

milk, 247, 248, 249

millet, 49, 323

Mølster farm, 181

Morgedal, 99, 143, 268

Motuza, Vykintas, 137, 139, 154

mouthfeel, 141, 214, 243, 269, 282, 290

mugs: ceramic, 212; drinking, 208, 210 (photo), 211

Muren, Lars Olav, 99

Muri, Bjarne, 112, 114

Myrica gale, 233

Nakazawaea, 103

Nakazawaea holstii, 2, 104, 116, 293

National Collection of Yeast Cultures (NCYC), 90, 105, 110, 128

Naumov, E. N., 200, 323

NEIPA, 269

Nelson, Max, 106

Nestern horn, photo of, 211

Nestor, 254

nisse, drawing of, 183 (fig.)

Nøddebjerggaard farm, photo of, 296

Nordal, Halvor, 186, 188, 195

Nordbo, Gregar O.: photo of, 64

Nordfjord, 142, 281

Nordic Museum, 10, 184

Nordic Pärm, 290

Nordic region, 17 (map)

Nordland, Odd, 71, 142, 231, 244, 309

Norwegian Ethnographic Survey, 248

Norwegian Ethnological Research, 3

Nossemark Stone Beer, recipe for, 334

Nupen, Jarle, 272

Nystein, Aave, 231, 272

oak coffin, photo of, 31

Oakes, Josh, 347

Oat Beer, 341-42; recipe for, 342

oats, 45, 45 (fig.), 46, 47, 175, 256, 341

OG. *See* original gravity

Olavi Viheroja's Sahti, recipe for, 288

Ole of Kjørro, 174

ôllekann, 208, 213; photo of, 210

Ølnes, Sven: photo of, 24

Ølnes farm, 18

ølstaup, photo of, 209

Olut Pryki Raum, 287, 351

oppskåke, 133, 202, 204-5; photo of, 132, 203

orange-peel, 87, 90, 98, 259

original gravity (OG), 3, 14, 25, 143, 269, 270, 286, 287

Orkney Islands, 50, 64, 75, 211, 239, 337, 352

Ørsta, 69, 170, 214, 282, 351

Otter, Maris, 50

Otterdal, Rasmus Kjøs, 356

oven beers, 162-64, 320; kvass and, 163

ovens, 74, 75, 158, 159, 163; photo of, 75, 158; sauna, 69 (photo); stone, 66 (photo)

Öxabäck Ale, 318; recipe for, 319

Paavo Pruul's Koduõlu, recipe for, 292

Pagarid, Louna: malt loaves by, 163 (photo)

Pahalahti, Antti, 73

Panevežys, 2, 212, 326, 347

parasites, 216 (fig.), 238

Pärm Euroferm, 290

Pasteur, Louis, 33, 92-93

pasteurization, 141

pea beer, photo of, 243

peas, adding, 243

peat, 64-65, 67

Pediococcus, 215, 233

pegs, drinking to, 213

Pere, Tuomas, 352

Perevičius, Vidmantas, 244, 349

pesticides, 53

Petrulis, Juozas, 155, 244

Philips, Rae, 239

Pichia, 104, 110-11

Pichia holstii, 104

Picts, 239

Pihamaan Sahti, 287

Pihanmaa, 351

Pihtla brewery, 291, 349; photo of, 290

Pihtla Õlleköök, 291

Pihtla Õlu, 291

Pihtla Pruulikoda, 291

Pilsner, 35, 92, 276

Piniavos brewery, 244, 293, 347, 349; brew kit at, 348 (photo)

pitching, 25, 97, 97 (fig.), 98, 98 (fig.), 99, 106, 133, 139, 140, 142, 155, 165, 167, 183, 184, 188

plant galls, photo of, 91

Plavinš, Reinis, 238, 239

Pleskačeŭski, Jury, 165

Pliny the Elder, 106

plowing, 54-55; carving of, 29 (fig.)

Pope's Yard Brewery, 328

Poppyland Brewery, 151

porter, 15, 154, 157, 269, 276; color of, 155; concentrate, 25; emergence of, 33

potatoes, adding, 241-42, 241 (photo)
Preiss, Richard, 112, 114, 117
Prie Uosio, 212
Primary Chronicle (Nestor), 254
Pruul, Paavo, 184, 202, 223, 229, 234-35, 240
Pucens, Signe, 134-35
Pucens, Ugis, 134-35, 184, 195; brewing process of, 134 (fig.), 137; photo of, 135, 136
Punakallio, Matti, 194; photo of, 353
Pyynikin brewery, 287, 351

Quechua Indians, 106
querns, 78, 196, 197, 260; drawing of, 196 (fig.); photo of, 197, 199

Raftevold, Ståle, 214, 356
Raftevold, Terje, 121, 122, 140, 141, 142, 182, 201, 202, 356; beer by, 128 (photo); brewhouse of, 129 (photo); brewing by, 129, 130, 131, 131 (fig.), 133; farmhouse ale of, 201; photo of, 97, 130, 131
Rågö Stone Beer, recipe for, 335
raisins, 243, 259
Ramunas Čižas, 349
rapataari, 253
Räsänen, Matti, 121, 251, 287
raspberry beer, 349
raspberry canes, 244, 349
RateBeer.com, 141, 347
rauchbier, 43, 44
raw ale, 165, 171, 280-82, 349; brewing, 133, 140-42, 163, 190, 280-81; photo of, 128
Reidar Hovelsen's Kornøl, recipe for, 284
Resaland farm, photo of, 15
rhubarb, 320
ria, 69, 70, 139, 286; diagram of, 70 (fig.)
ritual beer, 177, 179-82
rituals, 180, 207, 213; toasting, 179; work, 176-77
Rivenes, Svein, 96, 99, 188, 213; kveik of, 90, 91; photo of, 203
Roar Sandodden's Christmas Beer, recipe for, 302

roaring, 214; demonstrating, 214 (photo)
rope, making, 173-74, 182
Rørlien, Sjur, 15, 196, 213, 252, 309, 345
rostdrikke, 253-54, 256
Røthe, Bjørne, 227
Russian Ethnographic Museum, 158
rye, 45, 45 (fig.), 48, 96, 149, 256, 320, 323; growing, 47; harvesting, 52 (photo); roasting, 286

S-methylmethionine (SMM), 142
Saakvitne, Hans, 15, 267
Saaremaa, 61, 63, 121, 180, 204, 208, 238, 253, 290, 291, 349, 350, 354, 355
saccharometers, 33
Saccharomyces cerevisiae, 90, 91, 98, 102, 104, 105, 110, 111, 114, 116, 117, 293
Saccharomyces pastorianus, 104
Saccharomyces uvarum, 114, 116
Saccharomycetales, 103, 104; yeast species of, 103 (fig.)
sage, 264
sahti, 119, 145-46, 149, 194, 230, 276, 290, 351, 352, 354; analyzing, 286; brewing, 127, 146, 194, 280, 285, 285 (map), 286; commercial, 233; fermenting, 122 (photo); photo of, 285; stone, 139
Sahtikrouvin brewpub, 194, 351
såinn, 42, 69, 70, 304; diagram of, 71 (fig.); photo of, 43, 72; Stjørdal-style, 275
såinnhus, 42; photo of, 301
såinnhuslag, 299
St. Eldbjørg, 179
St. John's wort (*Hypericum maculatum; Hypericum perforatum),* 236
saison, 37, 117, 118, 269, 276, 280
Salamiestis, 239, 244
Salomonsson, Anders, 18, 121, 190, 304
Salutaguse, 290
Samuelsson, Per, 347
Sando, Kolbjørn: photo of, 318
Sandodden, Roar, 44-45, 184, 201, 300; såinn of, 73; såinnhus of, 301 (photo)

Sauna Session, 259

saunas, 67, 69, 73, 159, 161; photo of, 69, 158; smoke, 251, 286

Saure, Sigurd Johan, 120, 248, 269, 272

Schaaf, DeWayne, 275

Schiefloe, Ole Sivert, 280

schnapps, 224

Schöning, C., 254

schwarzbier, 154

Sepp, Meelis, 290; malthouse of, 62 (photo), 63

Seto Koduõlu, 163, 280, 320

Seto Koduõlu "Bread," recipe for, 320

Shitovo, 78; photo of, 159

Short Twentieth Century, 1914-1991, The (Hobsbawm), 173

Sigmund Gjernes's Vossaøl, recipe for, 311

Simard, Francis: photo of, 356

Simonaitis, Julius, 117, 200, 225, 227; photo of, 118

Simonova, L. N., 254

Simonys-Style Kaimiškas, recipe for, 295

Siuts, Hinrich, 340

Skaden, Orjan B.: farm of, 129 (photo)

Skare, Gunnar, 65, 69-70, 233, 282

Skare, Ivar, 69, 214

skokubolle, 205

Skrindo, Ågot, 58

Skrindo, Sverre, 151, 177, 194, 231, 355; gong of, 116, 116 (photo); photo of, 150

small beer, 182, 248, 251-53, 254, 276, 285, 300, 351

Sogn, 14, 15, 124, 142, 196, 198, 204, 226, 231, 248, 308, 309; landscape of, 17

Sogndal, 17, 185, 186; photo of, 16, 18

Sognefjord, 15

Sogneøl, recipe for, 314

Solberg, Svein Øivind, 230

Solvychegodsk Stone Beer, recipe for, 336

Sopp, Olav, 230, 244

sour beer, 122, 214, 215

sowing, 51, 55; photo of, 178

sparge water, 149, 231, 281

spices, 35, 83, 87, 219, 221, 223-41, 259, 264

Steen-Olsen, Eirik, 82, 83

steeping, 57-59

Stjørdal, 59, 69, 70, 71, 72, 119, 121, 122, 123, 171, 183, 196, 221, 276, 280, 299, 304, 351, 355; malt making in, 42-45; Maskin and, 54; photo of, 42

Stjørdalen, 71, 183, 267; kilns in, 73

stjørdalsøl, 43, 44, 45, 299-300; photo of, 44

Stone Age, 31, 32, 50, 355

stone beer, 154, 168, 278, 334; brewing, 14 (photo), 134-35, 137-39, 169 (fig.)

stone brewing, 139, 167, 168, 169; mashing methods and, 170; photo of, 139; remnants of, 137-38

stones, 135, 143, 187, 195, 196, 229, 328; adding, 136 (photo), 137, 137 (photo), 139; brewing, 31, 32, 134, 137, 167; cracked, 138 (photo); fire-shattered, 31; fractured, 138; heating, 136 (photo), 167, 168; hot, 76, 77, 139, 162; used, 140 (photo)

stout, 154

stoves, great, 157-59, 161-64, 169

Stranda, 90, 123, 128, 207

straw, 149, 236, 244, 337

Strese, Else-Marie: hops and, 223

strike water, 140, 169, 231

Sturluson, Snorri, 179

Su Puta, 293, 349

Suffolk Farmhouse Ale, recipe for, 338

sugar, 35, 57, 106, 119, 151, 153, 175, 201, 213, 252, 253, 259, 260, 261, 264, 276, 300, 323, 328; adding, 241; caramelization of, 154, 155, 163; fermentable, 100; natural sources of, 91; simple, 111

sugar beer, 264

sugar beets, 256

Suiti people, 350

Sundt, Eilert, 134, 137

Sunnfjord, 281, 341

Sunnmøre, 123, 204, 281, 351

Suomen Hiiva, 119, 122, 286, 290

superstitions, 182-87, 188, 289

Sure, Sigurd Johan, 248

Svalöf research station, 53; photo of, 52
Sve farm, 123
sweet gale (bog myrtle), 32, 221, 233-35, 238, 259, 290; photo of, 234
Syrjä, Raija, 197
syrup, 35, 241, 259, 282
syrup beer, 264

Taako ÖÜ, photo of, 290
Taako Pihtla Õlu, 291
taar, 253, 254
taari, 127, 128, 285
Tanker Brewery, 259
tansy (*Tanacetum vulgare*), 237-38; photo of, 237
taste, 128, 281, 353, 354; aroma and, 239
taxation, 34, 233, 337
Telemark, 66, 68, 99, 116, 175, 179, 188, 195, 196, 234, 236, 240, 351
Telemark (beer), recipe for, 315
temperance movement, 35, 177, 339
temperature, 23, 91, 118, 327; caramelization, 327 (table); drying, 59, 61, 64, 68; fermentation, 96, 98, 112, 269; mash, 145, 149, 151, 153, 154, 158, 159, 167, 316, 328 (fig.); pitching, 97, 97 (fig.), 269, 309
Terje Raftevold's Kornøl, recipe for, 283
terroir, 353
thermometers, 13, 33, 34, 60, 130, 145, 146, 153
Thibault, Martin, 106, 141; photo of, 356
Thorhallson, Thorlak, 99
Thörnblad, J. W., 177
thujone, 236, 238
toasts, 180, 213; ancestor, 186; purchase, 181; ritual, 182
tobacco, 59, 241
toffee, 44, 67, 155, 157
Tollin, Clas: hops and, 223
toxins, 235, 236, 238, 239, 275
Traditional Specialty Guaranteed (TSG), 287
treak, 229
treble X, 15
Trei, Aarne, 208, 238, 356
trick cups, 212, 213; photo of, 212

troughs, 195; malt-drying, 76, 76 (photo)
Tuftene, Marta: photo of, 16
Tune Stone, 190
Tuominen, Eila, 146, 147-48; photo of, 146, 148
turkehelle, photo of, 62
Tyndall, John, 7

Udriene, Aldona, 48, 59
United Gypsies, 287, 351
Untappd, 141

Vaitekunas, Vincas, 205
Vanylven, 164, 165; brewing process from, 164 (fig.)
Vanylven-Style, recipe for, 333
vessels, 58, 194, 195; brewing, 235; cleaning, 199, 231; drinking, 207-8, 211-13; wooden, 196
Vestrheim, Einar, 99
Viheroja, Olavi, 145, 146, 148; barn of, 144 (photo); photo of, 144
Vik, Tor, 14, 196
Viking Sahti Malt, 286
Vikonys, 153, 154, 157, 194
Vinge, Lotte, 249, 296
vodka, 18, 212
vorlauf, 26
Voss, 15, 63, 82, 84, 89, 90, 91, 92, 96, 99, 120, 121, 124, 134; brewhouse in, 33 (fig.); photo of, 82
Voss Museum, 309
vossaøl, 90, 157, 213, 327, 354
Vossaøl à la Vossestrand, recipe for, 312
Vsekhsvyatskoye, 159, 161-62
Vytautas Jančys's Keptinis, recipe for, 329

walnut leaves, 239
Warren, Martin, 151
water, 143, 199-200, 247-48, 249
water mill, photo of, 198
Welsh Farmhouse Ale, recipe for, 339
Westphalia Folklore Commission, 340
wheat, 45, 45 (fig.), 47, 48, 103, 217, 224, 256, 323; bread-quality, 48; emmer, 51 (photo), 103

whisky, 18, 67

White Labs, 114

Wiking, Carl, 259

wild radish (*Raphanus raphanistrum*), 239

Wille, Hans Jacob, 179, 237

Williams Brothers Brewery, 239

wine, 353; making, 30, 31, 57

Winstrup, Peder, 223

witbier, 237

witch's broom, 135, 191 (fig.); photo of, 135

World History of Beekeeping and Honey Hunting (Crane), 262

wormwood (*Artemesia absinthium*), 165, 235-36

wort, 25, 26, 33, 89, 101, 131, 135, 139, 153, 170, 185, 191, 239, 251, 256; black, 155; boiling, 133, 138, 141, 142, 170, 171, 182, 183, 281, 327; cooling, 25, 98, 318 (photo); hops and, 225; lautered, 87, 155 (photo), 160 (photo), 252; malt and, 213; photo of, 88, 161; run off, 151; sahti, 146; sieving, 187 (photo); sugars in, 327 (table); tasting, 24

yarrow (*Achillea millefolium*), 237

yeast, 14, 100, 101, 201, 240, 280, 291, 337, 355; #3 Stranda, 112; #4 Muri, 112, 113 (photo), 114; #14 Eitrheim, 113 (photo); #16 Simonaitis, 117, 227; #20 Espe, 112; #40 Rima, 323; ale, 104, 269; aromatic, 89, 91; baker's, 104, 119, 279, 286, 287, 290; Belgian, 89, 105, 272; borrowing, 94-95; bottom-fermenting, 104, 271; bread, 95, 118-20, 119 (photo), 122, 256, 299; brewer's, 92, 103, 105, 105 (fig.), 107, 114, 114 (fig.), 119, 271, 273, 287; collecting, 96, 97 (photo), 105, 133, 185, 271, 287; dialect words for, 124 (map); diastatic, 105, 281; domesticated, 91-92, 105; dried, 85 (photo), 106, 272; family, 83, 293; family tree, 105-7, 105 (fig.), 110, 115 (fig.); farmhouse, 81, 98, 103, 107-12, 114-24, 269, 272-73, 318; fermenting, 12, 112, 165; growing, 91, 114; hefeweizen, 89, 92, 114,

115; homegrown, 94, 121, 286, 304; Idun Blå, 299; kveik and, 124, 282; laboratory, 90, 94; lager, 45; midsummer, 100, 101-2; non-kveik, 272-73; non-*Saccharomyces*, 103, 232; phenolic, 92; photo of, 91; *Pichia*, 104, 110-11; pitching, 25, 98, 98 (fig.), 99, 106, 133, 139, 140, 155, 165, 167, 183, 184, 188, 261, 272; properties of, 111 (table), 120; repitching, 92, 93, 99, 105, 106, 107; revolution in, 92-94; *Saccharomyces*, 323; Safale, 25, 155; saison, 92, 117-18, 269, 279; sake, 105; species of, 103-5, 103 (fig.,), 111, 118, 299; Sunnuntai bread, 286; top-fermenting, 91, 93, 104, 123, 269; traditional, 122, 123, 300; wild, 82, 91-92, 98, 99, 105, 107; wine, 105; yeast cultures and, 109, 110 (fig.), 270. *See also* kveik

yeast cakes, 96, 102, 106; replicas of, 96 (photo)

yeast cultures, 33, 34, 81, 99, 102, 103, 106, 116, 256, 323; farmhouse, 107 (map), 108-9 (table); identifying, 107; infected, 98, 272; maintaining, 94-95; mixed, 270, 271; Norwegian, 110; Russian, 117; single-strain, 93, 271; uncontrolled, 111; yeast strains and, 109, 110 (fig.), 270

yeast log, photo of, 95

yeast rings, 87, 95
    photo of, 85, 88

yeast starter, 175
    photo of, 117, 131, 240

Ylijoki, Jouko, 127, 165

Zhezlov, Dmitriy, 78, 159, 162, 167, 192, 323; brewing kit of, 161; dacha of, 159 (photo); photo of, 78, 160, 161

Žiobiškis-Style Keptinis, recipe for, 330

Zosimus of Panopolis, 106

Zythophile blog, 239